Developing quality systems in education

DATE DUE

International standards for the assessment of quality have been around for many years, and have proved an important influence in the drive to make British manufacturing and service industries more competitive. Educational institutions have not escaped the influence of the quality movement, and the FE sector in particular is now being actively encouraged to introduce the BSI's quality assurance standard BS 5750. Universities and schools are also attracted by a standard which will improve, if not quality itself, then the management of quality. This book presents an overview of the pitfalls, problems and vicissitudes of implementing quality standards in education. It explores theoretical issues, such as the relationship between the customer and academic culture, but has a strongly practical theme, looking at the advantages and disadvantages of quality systems, case studies of attempts at implementation and proposals for future developments across the education sector as a whole.

Geoffrey D. Doherty is Professor and Dean of the Faculty of Education at the University of Wolverhampton.

D0162239

Developing quality systems in education

Edited by Geoffrey D. Doherty

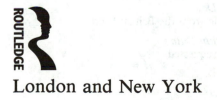

London and New York

First published 1994
by Routledge
11 New Fetter Lane, London EC4P 4EE

Simultaneously published in the USA and Canada
by Routledge
29 West 35th Street, New York, NY 10001

Barnett, R. (1992) 'The idea of quality – voicing the educational', *Higher Education Quarterly* 46(1), 3–19.
Rhodes, L.A. (1992) 'On the road to quality', *Educational Leadership* 49,6:76–80. Reprinted with permission of the Association for Supervision and Curriculum Development. © 1992 by the Association for Supervision and Curriculum Development. All rights reserved.
Hansen, L. (1993) 'Bringing total quality improvement into the college classroom', *Higher Education* 25,3, April 1993. Reprinted with permission of Kluwer Academic Publishers.
Hubbard, D. (May 1994) 'Can Higher Education learn from factories?', *Quality Progress*, 93–97. © 1994 American Society of Quality Control. Reprinted with permission.

Typeset in Times by
Pat and Anne Murphy, Highcliffe-on-Sea, Dorset
Printed and bound in Great Britain by
Biddles Ltd, Guildford and King's Lynn

British Library Cataloguing in Publication Data
A catalogue record for this book is available from the British Library

Library of Congress Cataloging in Publication Data
A catalogue record for this book has been requested

ISBN 0–415–09829–7

GOODNESS . . . QUALITY . . . EXCELLENCE?

Goodness is not the same as being, but even
beyond being, surpassing it in dignity and power.

(Plato)

Any kind of excellence renders that of what it is
the excellence *good*, and makes it perform its function *well*.

(Aristotle)

Obviously some things are better than others . . . but what is
betterness?

(Pirsig)

Quality is the loss to society the moment the goods are shipped.

(Taguchi)

My definition of quality is: 'I know it when I see it!'
You better believe that I do . . . (it) makes me – and lots of others –
'glow' and 'tingle'.

(Peters)

Contents

Part III Further and vocational education

Part IV Schools

Illustrations

TABLES

Contributors

RONALD BARNETT is Reader in Higher Education in the Centre for Higher Education Studies at the Institute of Education, University of London. He is one of the most-published, best-known and authoritative writers on higher education in the United Kingdom.

IAN CLELAND. For many years Chief Inspector for the Dudley Metropolitan Borough Education Services, he has been dedicated to quality improvement for some time. Under his leadership the Dudley Inspectorate and the schools for which they have been responsible have achieved a high national reputation for quality in the United Kingdom.

GEOFF HAMPTON was Deputy Headmaster of Buckpool, a large comprehensive school in the Dudley Metropolitan Borough which is part of Ian Cleland's 'quality network'. He has recently been appointed to a Headship in Wolverhampton.

W. LEE HANSEN is Professor of Economics at the University of Wisonsin – Madison. He has become deeply interested in attempting to develop a total quality approach involving the students, themselves, in improving the classroom learning experience.

MICK HARRISON is Vice-Chancellor of the University of Wolverhampton – sometime sociologist and prime mover of the University's BS 5750 and TQM initiatives. BS 5750, in particular, is a high-risk strategy for any educational organization – particularly a university.

JACKY HOLLOWAY is a researcher in the Business School of the Open University. Jacky is concerned with researching total quality systems and their suitability to higher education rather than how TQM actually operates in the learning situation.

DEAN L. HUBBARD is the President of the Northwest Missouri State University. Northwest is a small university (by American standards), which has, under Dean Hubbard's leadership, become completely involved in the development of TQM.

JEFF JONES and JOHN MATHIAS are, respectively, Inspector in the Hereford and Worcester LEA and Principal Lecturer in the School of Education of the University of Wolverhampton. They have become a well-known duo in the evaluation of staff appraisal and its contribution to quality in schools in the United Kingdom.

IAIN MACROBERT is Director of the Quality Assurance Unit at Sandwell College of Further and Higher Education which was the first further education or higher education institution in the United Kingdom to gain BS 5750 accreditation. This successful initiative was led by him.

JOHN MARSH, now an independent consultant, was formerly the Quality Manager of the Avon Training and Enterprise Council, where he was responsible for not only developing a TQM system in the Avon TEC but also for providing quality advice and quality workshops for local industry, commerce and public-sector institutions.

LEWIS A. RHODES is prominent in the United States as a protagonist for TQM and Associate Executive Director of the American Association of School Administrators.

SUE RICHARDS is Director of the recently-formed Public Management Foundation. This Foundation, and the Office for Public Management from which it developed, are private consultancies committed to improving competence, expertise and quality in the public sector.

EDWARD SALLIS, Associate Principal of Brunel College of Arts and Technology, Bristol, is a very well-known practitioner and writer about both BS 5750 and TQM in further education and schools.

SAM SCHAUERMAN, DONNA MANNO and BURT PEACHY are, respectively, President, Staff Co-ordinator and Associate Dean of Organizational Planning at El Camino College, California, an institution well-known in the United States for its commitment to quality and community development.

SUSAN STOREY, Head of Quality Assurance Unit at the University of Wolverhampton, is the university's BS 5750 Management Representative. She is working at the 'sharp end' of systems development and quality assurance. A contributor to Ellis (1993), she has become a well-known 'product champion' of quality systems in UK universities.

HELEN STOTT is a member of the Centre for Educational Development at the University of Wolverhampton. She is a successful BSI Lead Auditor and consultant for BS 5750 and TQM systems both in the United Kingdom and overseas. She is the University of Wolverhampton's internal quality consultant.

MYRON TRIBUS is one of the best-known exponents of total quality in education. A follower of W. Edwards Deming, he has extensive experience of the
application of TQM in American schools, colleges and community developments. He is currently helping the British Deming Association to have a
similar impact on education in the United Kingdom.

Editor's foreword

I should like to make some comments about this book before the reader starts dipping into it. First, it is *not* a textbook or a do-it-yourself quality handbook, nor does it provide facile answers to difficult questions about such controversial issues as: the nature of quality; whether to embrace Total Quality Management or the British Standard 5750 – or both; the management of change and leadership quality . . . and so on. What, however, it does provide is a set of protocols from a wide cross-section of educationists and educational organizations in both the United Kingdom and the United States, which will allow the reader to share practitioner reflections on the problems, successes and failures of doing quality in education.

It may seem that the University of Wolverhampton is over-represented. This is because, although I know of commitment from other UK universities (for example, Aston and South Bank), Wolverhampton is alone in its efforts to achieve BS 5750 as a basis from which to develop a total quality culture.

I have written a rather lengthy introduction in the form of (to use current Strategic Management jargon) an 'environmental scan' of the quality scene. The deliberately heavy referencing is intended to provide the interested reader and potential practitioner with easy access to helpful resource material. Although I have attempted to be as objective as possible, reporting negative reactions based on practical experiences as well as ideological reservations, it will be apparent that, personally, I have no doubt that the methodologies provided by one form or another of a structured quality system could be applied to advantage in any school, college or university.

There will always be, of course, the typical British 'yes – but' responses to all this: 'Yes – but it's only old wine in new bottles!', 'Yes – but it's only the flavour of the month!', 'Yes – but it will cost too much!'. . . . These are (understandably?) defensive reactions to the threat of change. However, two pressures – the drive to close the enormous quality gap between western industry and Japan and the billions of pounds of GNP being poured into education – make it very unlikely that 'quality matters' are merely the flavour of the month: of the decade, perhaps. If we do not take steps as academics and teachers to demonstrate that we, ourselves, can regulate the quality of our provision, the government will do it for us and, perhaps, in a more radical manner than is being currently suggested.

I hope that reading this book will both reinforce and provide practical help to the converted, convince the undecided that it can be done and is worth while to do and, at least, give the rest cause for thought. For those who are looking for a vision, the concept of quality driven by education into the general community as explored by Rhodes and Tribus might have some inspirational potential.

G.D. Doherty
University of Wolverhampton
1993

Acknowledgements

First and foremost I should like to thank Mick Harrison – Vice-Chancellor of the University of Wolverhampton and a man of greater vision than he will readily admit – for thrusting me into a position from which it is possible to make something happen. Second, I should like to thank my colleagues who have become involved in the 'quality debate' – and off whom I have bounced ideas for the last three years or so, especially the quality 'product champions' in the Quality Assurance Unit. Last, but certainly not least, I should like to thank two people without whose efforts and support this book would never have seen the light of day: Margaret Andrews, my long-suffering secretary, and Ann Lewis, our total quality Walsall Campus Librarian.

Abbreviations

BSI	British Standards Institution
BTEC	Business and Technical Education Council
C & G	City and Guilds
CAR	Corrective Action Request
CATE	Council for Accreditation of Teacher Education
CHES	Centre for Higher Education Studies
CNAA	Council for National Academic Awards
CVCP	Committee of Vice-Chancellors and Principals
EFQM	European Foundation for Quality Management
FEFC	Further Education Funding Council
FEU	Further Education Unit
HEFCE	Higher Education Funding Council, England
HECW	Higher Education Funding Council, Wales
HEQC	Higher Education Quality Council
HMI	Her Majesty's Inspectorate
IIP	Investors in People
ILP	Individual Learning Plan
LEA	Local Education Authority
MBA	Master of Business Administration
MBO	Management by Objectives
MIS	Management Information System
MRT	Management Review Team
NACCB	National Accreditation Council for Certification Bodies
NCVQ	National Council for Vocational Qualifications
OFSTED	Office for Standards in Education
PI	Performance indicator
PIT	Process Improvement Team
PRP	Performance Related Pay
QC	Quality Circle
QFD	Quality Function Deployment
QHE	*Quality in Higher Education*
QIT	Quality Improvement Team
ROA	Record of Achievement

RSA	Royal Society of Arts
SCOTVEC	Scottish Vocational Education Council
SEAC	Schools Examination Advisory Council
SPC	Statistical Process Control
SQM	Strategic Quality Management
TEC	Training and Enterprise Council
TEED	Training, Education and Enterprise Directorate
TQI	Total Quality Improvement
UGC	University Grants Committee
VIT	Voluntary Improvement Team

Part I

Some general and theoretical issues

1 Introduction
The concern for quality

Geoffrey D. Doherty

THE QUALITY JUNGLE

There is nothing unusual about educationists having concerns for quality. This has been going on for a long time – certainly since Plato's training programme for the Guardians in *The Republic* (vii). However, since the White Paper, *Education and Training for the Twenty-first Century* of 1991 there has been a massive burgeoning of interest in what some cynics these days refer to as the 'quality business'. We now have a plethora of custodians of quality, all of whom are at least to some extent legitimated by the Education Reform Act of 1988, the Further and Higher Education Act of 1992 as well as the White Paper with its concerns for quality and accountability. The latter, particularly, not only referred to levels of quality assurance: quality control, validation and examination, and external assessment, but also specifically mentioned quality systems – BS 5750 and Total Quality Management (TQM), of which more later.

Merely to list some of the quality custodians in the United Kingdom makes daunting reading:

Higher Education Funding Council, England (HEFCE)
Higher Education Funding Council, Wales (HEFCW)
National Council for Vocational Qualifications (NCVQ)
Scottish Vocational Education Council (SCOTVEC)
Higher Education Quality Council (HEQC)
Further Education Funding Council (FEFC)
Council for Accreditation of Teacher Education (CATE)
Her Majesty's Inspectorate (HMI)
Local Education Authority Advisers
Royal Society for the encouragement of Arts, Manufacturers and
    Commerce (RSA)
Business and Technician Education Council (BTEC)
Schools Examination Advisory Council (SEAC)
City and Guilds (C & G)

This is not to mention professional bodies, such as the English Nursing Board (ENB) or the Law Society, which exert considerable influence over the validation and accreditation of qualifications providing exemptions from professional examinations. These bodies are representative of a wide range of external stakeholders in the quality of various forms of educational provision. The United Kingdom is by no means exceptional in this respect, as a glance at the contents of the report of the 1991 Hong Kong Conference on Quality Assurance will confirm (Craft 1992). This has led to some exasperation amongst academics: 'the quality vocabulary is the one that must be learned by any aspiring academic who wishes to escape from the increasingly arduous daily chore of actually teaching more and more students' (Editorial, *Higher Education Quarterly* 1992) and to *The Higher* setting up a fairly regularly recurring item entitled 'Quality Debate'. The contributions range from short letters to full-scale articles and allow acerbic academics either to let off steam or make serious contributions, or both. One of the early articles (Brennan and Silver 1992) raised a whole series of questions about the future of quality assurance 'posed by the CNAA's demise'. These included: peer review; approval of external examiners; external subject experts; regular course review; sectoral development services; training programmes; and student feedback. They also raised, but did not pursue in depth, several other issues, including quality management, which are addressed in a variety of ways in the subsequent chapters of this book:

> will it become more important to know *where* someone has studied rather than *what* they have studied or what class of degree they have obtained? How will questions of access and opportunity relate to the overall pattern of provision, and not just to that of individual institutions? Will honours classifications survive a significant increase in student numbers? Is a transcript system on the cards? Can the British system of external examiners safeguard comparability and resist hierarchies becoming more pronounced? . . . Questions of quality are at the heart of the concerns. The ghosts of the CNAA may well not be confined to a building in Gray's Inn Road.

The implications of some of these statements – Records of Achievement; open access; changing concepts and measures of quality – resonate for further education and schools as well as for higher education. Subsequent letters argue the pros and cons of HEFCE versus HEQC methodologies, ownership of quality teaching as a *business* transaction, and so on (Armitage 1993; Jack 1993; Hibbert 1993; Sparkes 1993) but perhaps the most despairing statement emanates from Fred Inglis (1993): 'There are no books on my desk, only quality papers. These are the dry thoughts of their dry season. Let virtues be forced upon us by their impudent crimes.' Indeed, it is interesting to speculate how Eliot (1948) and Leavis (1943) might have contributed to this debate.

It is also tempting to look for straightforward, simplistic reasons for the development of this veritable forest of quality assurance trees. Elton (1992) provides a succinct and attractive theory based on the breakdown of mutual trust between the government and higher education in particular, but the argument holds good for the education system in general. He interprets the old British University Grants Committee (UGC) as a buffer which stood between the government and the universities for sixty years. However, in 1969 Shirley Williams, the Secretary of State for Education, put forward thirteen discussion points with the intention of introducing some economy into the university system. They were rejected out of hand by the Committee of Vice-Chancellors and Principals (CVCP). This was the beginning of the 'erosion of mutual trust', and readers will be aware that somewhat later the Prime Minister, James Callaghan – in his famous Ruskin College speech of 1976 – initiated the 'Great Debate' about education in schools. The root concerns were: educational standards; education for work; 'value for money'; and these were just as much matters of concerns for the Labour Party as they were, subsequently, for the so-called Thatcherite Tories. This general decline in trust is well documented in Maclure (1988). In the university system relationships deteriorated further until the UGC 'was replaced in 1987 by the Universities Funding Council . . . an arm of government. By now trust had disappeared completely and been replaced by imposed rules' (Elton 1992: 25).

He considers these rules which lead to quality audit, quality assessment and the use of performance indicators and concludes by drawing comparisons between the United Kingdom and other countries: 'in Britain, the Secretary of State for Education and Science has given it as his view that "the best means of steering the system is using money; institutions are more likely to do things they will get money for" (MacGregor 1991)' (Elton 1992: 26). This is a policy which is still pursued by the current Minister (John Patten) in respect of Fee Band 1 students in 1993: the drop in fees to £1,300 represents a 31 per cent cut for humanities and social science students. Elton also makes the point that this methodology is not used in either Germany or the United States. However, there is some evidence that, in the United States at least, the situation may change. In another 'Quality Debate' article, Lucy Hodges quotes the president of an American university on the subject of future freedom from federal government control of the accreditation system: 'I cannot make predictions, because of the cost of higher education, the pressure that is coming from the public and certainly from government officials to give assurance that universities and colleges are spending their time effectively serving students' (25 February, 1993).

More recently, in an editorial (April 1993) 'Right questions or quality', it is pointed out that, 'Despite endless talk of teaching quality, the fundamental issue "Is this a good teacher?" has been disregarded'. The editorial was a response to the results of a Centre for Higher Education Studies

(CHES) (Loder 1992, 1993) report on quality in higher education research project. It concludes:

> The CHES policy paper has made a timely intervention into the quality debate, by pointing out that quality may be a buzz-word in higher education, but it is in danger of becoming just a background noise. Universities and individual staff need to face up to the pressing issue of training before the Government decides to do it for them.
>
> (*Higher Education Quarterly*, April 1993)

The continuing issue of trust applies equally to the rest of the education system in the United Kingdom and has made considerable impact on quality assurance and self-management in schools (Johnston 1992):

> It is specifically in relation to the issue of trust and respect that the roots of the quality assurance problems in Britain originate. Trust begets trust in a web of circularised interrelationships. Teachers and schools see central government as having lost trust in their ability to meet society's needs and to be responsive to the continually renewing demands this makes in terms of educational provision.
>
> (1992: 173)

This issue of trust is taken up by Peters (1992) in an interesting analysis of the application of managerialist ideology, strategic management and performance indicators to the public sector as a whole, not merely education: 'it has provided a major rationale for restructuring the whole public sector, for privatisation strategies and the introduction of managerialist techniques and practices' (p. 127).

Such practices are seen as totally antithetical to the interests, methodologies and goals of groups of persons broadly concerned with enhancing the social good. Nevertheless, the activities and attitudes of the government and, indeed, some of the other stakeholders mentioned earlier in this section can be seen to have hardened over the last decade: just as the academics are now becoming increasingly exasperated with the policy makers, so the policy makers became exasperated with the educationists' endless capacity for talk without action, for rationalization without, as they saw it, results. Plenty more examples could be quoted: Gorbutt *et al.* (1991) are entertaining on the 'myth of rational management'; Becher (1992) provides a plausible rationale for the 'non-corporate' university; and Gammage (1992) is interesting on the complexities of education and teacher education which cannot be constrained by 'simplistic input–output models of education'. Interesting, plausible and convincing as these and other such analyses may be to other academics, they are likely to fall on deaf ears in a system where the stakeholders have lost trust in and therefore sympathy with the providers. Perhaps it is appropriate to conclude this section with an extreme example of the academic knee-jerk reaction to criticism. This is from an editorial in the *Higher Education Review* in response to the *Executive*

Summary of the Quality in Higher Education Project conducted by the University of Central England (1992). After rubbishing the report and its methodology, the writer concludes: 'Higher education scarcely needs more definition of quality, criteria, questionnaires and three-year projects. What is required is that academics should know what they are doing, understand the nature of it and do it as well as maybe – together with apt institutional means for making this overt.'

This section has attempted to demonstrate beyond reasonable doubt that the 'stakeholders' simply do not believe that the old 'institutional means' were apt. It seems we have a problem here.

WHAT IS QUALITY?

Conventional wisdom and common sense demand some discussion of what is meant by 'quality' before considering quality systems. One problem, of course, as noted in the first section, is that, given the chance, this is as far as the academic or the educationist will go. The meaning of quality can be discussed *ad infinitum* since there is no consensus view, thus avoiding the need to do anything: 'Quality . . . you know what it is, yet you don't know what it is. . . . If no one knows what it is, then for all practical purposes it doesn't exist at all. But for all practical purposes, it does exist' (Pirsig 1976).

This is the 'you can't-define-it-but-you-know-it-when-you-see-it' argument and a favourite quotation for writers on quality, particularly those who wish to pursue this 'I-know-it-when-I-see-it' argument which in certain circumstances leads to those exclusive, if not elitist, attitudes which produce confrontations when quality judgements are being made. Pirsig actually spends the next couple of hundred pages or so exploring its metaphysical, romantic and classical connotations but, whilst the journey may be fascinating, he does not produce much that will help the educational programme designer (there is plenty that might help the programme deliverer), and perhaps his best advice is: 'Hold quality undefined. That's the secret' (1976: 213). Can the academics do better? There is certainly a mounting volume of literature on the subject, some of which follows Pirsig's advice: for example Cryer (1993) manages to produce a very useful primer for helping universities to prepare for a visit from an HEQC audit team without attempting to define quality at all, though in the foreword Malcolm Frazer writes: 'Quality in higher education is not the same as satisfying a customer with, for example, the latest model of motor car. Quality in higher education embraces, but is not synonymous with, effectiveness, efficiency and accountability.'

Ellis (1993), in his introduction to *Quality Assurance for University Teaching*, states, with somewhat more precision: 'Quality itself is a somewhat more ambiguous term since it has connotations of both *standards* and *excellence*' (p. 3). This is a theme which has been explored at some length in the *The Higher*'s 'Quality Debate', where the word 'quality' is, for the most part, used synonymously with 'excellence': 'A clear distinction is needed between "Standards" and "Quality". These are slippery words with many meanings which bedevil this whole debate' (editorial, 11 December 1992). The words are problematic because 'The difficulty in talking about standards is that the concept is, like "truth", or "goodness", or "beauty", both logically indispensable and yet impossible to define without consider-able philosophical elaboration' (Pring 1992: 21). For an extensive elabora-tion of the concepts of quality, quality control and peer review in education, see the whole edition of the *British Journal of Educational Studies* 1992, from which this is quoted. See also Buxton (1993) and Brookman (1993a) who are concerned that the post-CNAA quality system may become even more bureaucratic and unwieldy. Brookman perceives a pragmatic solution to the Quality versus Standards debate as: 'The professional bodies would set the standards, while an institution's quality would depend on how well their students succeeded in meeting them' (1 January 1993). This is echoed in a recent editorial (6 August 1993) which sets out a vision for higher education in the twenty-first century. The editorial is complimentary about the sector's performance in maintaining quality whilst expanding rapidly. It sees expansion as a 'good thing' which should continue, underpinned by a national common curriculum for school years culminating in a 'single system of examinations at 16'. Amongst the requirements for the HE system it includes: 'a national accreditation system to broker the standards attached to the wide range of qualifications on offer'. It envisages a joint body formed out of the Higher Education Quality Council and the National Council for Vocational Qualifications with powers to demand self-assessments to inspect and to recommend 'withdrawal of accreditation and loss of public funding'.

This does not sound very different from the 'Purpose, Aims and Object-ives' of OFSTED (1993): 'The purpose of OFSTED is to improve standards of achievement and quality of education through regular independent inspection', or from the FEFC (1993) intention, in order to meet the White Paper's *Education and Training for the Twenty-first Century* requirement for external assessment: 'To . . . rely on two approaches: the use of per-formance indicators, assessment based on inspection'.

The Higher's vision for higher education postulates an accreditation system 'independent of political interference and therefore ministerial appointment' (editorial, 6 August 1993), hence its preference for HEQC (currently 'owned' by the Council of Vice-Chancellors and Principals) rather than HEFCE's Quality Assessment Division. This preference does not take into account that 'failure of mutual trust' described in the first section, so perhaps *The Higher* is backing the wrong horse.

Whichever way, this analysis shows the three sectors of the education system adopting, being required to adopt by 'political interference', a common model of quality derived from the old HMI approach based on Delphic knowledge tempered by the wisdom of wide experience. This is normative and paternalistic − at the best − and in no way empirical or relative to the aims and purposes of the institution under inspection, be it school, college or university. Of course, the inspectors are to be external, independent agents, contracted by OFSTED, FEFC or HEFCE. 'The inspector is dead! Long live the inspector!'

In fairness it has to be said that all three groups share the rhetoric of 'institutional mission'. The White Paper encourages a pluralistic approach. The needs of modern society, its citizens, its business and manufacturing enterprises are multi-faceted, so there is room for diversity, particularly amongst further and higher education institutions. The FEFC Circular 93/11 is as explicit about college aims as is the HEFCE (1993) 'template' used to analyse self-assessment and claims for excellence in respect of 'the particular institution, its mission and the subject-specific aims and object-ives'. Of course, the university sector is also already subject to visitation by HEQC's Division of Quality Audit which is concerned not so much with assessing quality (whatever that means) as with auditing processes, procedures and their operation. It is concerned with assuring that an institu-tion has an effective and efficient system for managing quality rather than with the 'quality' of its outcomes. It is this dual HEFCE/HEQC system which is regarded as cumbersome and bureaucratic both in Europe (Brookman 1993b) and by the Commonwealth Vice-Chancellors as reported in *The Higher* (6 August 1993).

There is no shortage of literature on the subject. One of the most prolific contemporary writers on the subject of higher education is Barnett (1990, 1992a, 1992b). He is concerned with the concept of higher education and that there is no theory of higher education, worth mentioning, in the United Kingdom (1990: 3−29); no theory of higher education, no theory of quality in higher education. He tackles both problems (1990 − see pp. 201−6 and the whole of 1992a) establishing criteria for higher education and postu-lating that without a single, overarching concept of higher education there will be various models of quality, depending on what particular concept of higher education is favoured (1992a: 1−43). In the end he accepts a minimalist definition of quality in higher education where:

> it has been demonstrated that, through the process, the students' educa-tional development has been enhanced: not only have they achieved the particular objectives set for the course but in doing so, they have also fulfilled the general educational aims of autonomy, of the ability to participate in reasoned discourse, of critical self-evaluation, and of coming to a proper awareness of the ultimate contingency of all thought and action.
>
> (1992a: 61)

These read as necessary but not sufficient quality characteristics, and they would not do as quality characteristics for the education system as a whole, though, with some modification (such as 'greater autonomy' and so on) they might do very well as a preliminary set of characteristics on which to build a theory of value-added. As we have seen, quality (except in the usage of quality as any attribute – this stone has the 'quality' of hardness) and excellence are synonymous, so a 'quality' educational experience should deliver some good value, or value of goodness, which is susceptible to measurement. Generally speaking, Barnett has much to offer but is difficult to apply outside the confines of higher education.

Pollitt (1992) provides a succinct and very readable overview of 'what is quality' in public services. He is helpful in defining parameters and raising the key issues, for example,

> If one asks who determines what is a high quality service? at least two very different answers are possible. On the one hand it could be those experienced in providing the service, especially if they are professionals such as doctors, lawyers, teachers and so on. But equally one might argue that in the end it is those who use the service who can tell whether it is of high quality or not. If it meets their wants and needs, it is a quality service, if it does not, it is not.
>
> (1992: 3)

He outlines a number of different definitions and approaches to quality but concludes: 'For all these reasons a single, generic definition of public service quality is hard to establish' (p. 3).

This pluralistic view is supported by Harvey and Green (1993a, 1993b). They discuss the apodictic view (I instinctively know it) which they declare useless for '*assessing* quality' and the standards approach (HMI) which they categorize as 'traditional' (1993a: 9–13), pointing out that the problem with standards is that (1) they cannot be objective and (2) they are subject to negotiation and change. They then discuss 'quality as perfection or consistency' (pp. 15–21), identifying two modes: (1) zero defects or right first time, conforming to specifications and (2) fitness for purpose which might mean either meeting customer specifications or mission goals and objectives, which means an institution meeting its own stated objectives. These definitions of quality are susceptible to systemization, as will be discussed in the next section. However, this is not to say that they are not problematic. When customers are students, there are well-known problems related to feedback, especially in relation to how it is gained, who owns it and what is done with it (Silver 1992). In Harvey and Green (1993b) they comment on their three-year project on *Quality in Higher Education* (1992). It was in the context of the difficulties of either defining quality in education or being able to distinguish precisely between customers and interested groups that they made a pragmatic decision to adopt a 'stakeholder' approach: 'Various stakeholder groups have been identified ranging from students and staff through accreditors and assessors to employers and the government. The aim is to find out the views on quality of each of these groups' (1993b: 144).

Their report (it was this that triggered the curmudgeonly antagonistic editorial response in the *Higher Education Review* quoted in the first section) should be read in conjunction with the CHES report, quoted earlier. Together they provide a huge amount of valuable 'customer feedback' for anyone interested in quality in education and in higher education particularly.

This short survey of the confusing debate on 'what is quality' helps to explain why it is difficult to convince the various stakeholders – including the government – that institutions do, indeed, have apt methods of making their quality processes explicit.

Once we move away from the problematics of definition to consider the practical methodologies of quality assurance and control, we set foot on much firmer ground. From the sources already cited, especially Ellis (1993) and Cryer (1993), we can readily define the following processes:

Quality assurance: a system based on 'feedforward' – i.e. a means of ensuring that errors, as far as possible, are designed out. In education, quality assurance examines the aims, content, resourcing, levels and projected outcomes of modules, programmes and courses.

Quality control: a system based on 'feedback' – i.e. a means of gaining information so that errors can be corrected, in manufacturing by inspection. In education, quality control (internally, at least) requires feedback from staff, students and, ideally, employers. It requires regular monitoring and review of modules, programmes and courses.

Quality management: the complete process set up to ensure that the quality processes actually happen – in education, market analysis, curriculum development (not so important in schools since the advent of the National Curriculum), strategic and course planning, resourcing, validation, monitoring and review of student learning experiences.

Quality audit: internal and/or external audit of the quality management system. Audit checks that the system does what it says it is going to do and has written, documented evidence to prove it. Any properly documented process can be audited, whether educational or manufacturing. Educationists generally find audit distasteful – shallow, undemanding – since either the evidence of conformance to processes and procedures is there or it is not. There is no argument about it.

Quality assessment: the judgement of performance against criteria – either internally or externally. A potential source of conflict, precisely because quality criteria for education are so difficult to agree. See Keefe (1992) on the HEFCE's consultation paper on quality assessment.

Quality enhancement: a system for consciously and consistently improving the quality performance of any process. This implies a sophisticated system for staff development and training as well as conscious methods of addressing and solving systemic problems: the same for any process, educational or otherwise.

These quality processes are to be found in all quality systems in some shape or form.

WHAT QUALITY SYSTEM?

Sallis and Hingley (1991) produced a very useful paper on college quality assurance systems which is still an essential read for any educational system thinking of embarking on systematic quality improvement. In it they say:

> There are essentially three systems of quality assurance for a college to choose between:
> • BS 5750 Quality Systems (BSI 1987 and 1990);
> • Total Quality Management (TQM);
> • a system of the college's own devising.
>
> (1991: 4)

In 1993 this is only partially true since to this list 'Investors in people' could certainly be added, as could systems derived from either the Baldridge Award (the American 'Quality Award') or the European Quality Award (1993), though these, perhaps, would fall into the category 'of the College's own devising'.

The British Standards Institution (BSI) produce a comprehensive guide – *Handbook Twenty Two: Quality Assurance* (1990) – which contains not only the British Standard for Quality Systems (BS 5750, 1987) but also a whole set of other standards which relate to it. Of these, BS 4778, Quality Vocabulary is the most useful. In it can be found BSI definitions of most of the terms already mentioned in this chapter, including Quality System: 'The organisational structure, responsibilities, procedures, processes and resources for implementing quality management' (p. 7), and, indeed, Quality itself: 'The totality of features and characteristics of a product or service that bear on its ability to satisfy stated or implied needs' (p. 4). It will be observed that this definition of quality is customer-driven, that is, it is based on stated or implied needs. In both BSI definitions and standards it is important to realize that every word is heavy with meaning. In devising a BS 5750 quality system, every word in these definitions (and in the eighteen to twenty points of the standard) *must* be taken into account. Thus 'totality' means everything that affects the quality of a product or service; similarly 'needs' means 'needs' *not* 'wants': needs analysis is allowed – customers do not always know what they need.

It can be argued that Total Quality Management is not a system in the BS 5750 sense (Harvey and Green 1993b). However, anyone who has implemented or tried to implement TQM will testify that the BSI definition certainly applies. 'Investors in people' just about qualifies as a 'quality system' in that it requires:

- top-down commitment;
- a strategic plan with goals and objectives, *all* understandable and possessed by *all* staff;
- identification of resources to deliver the plan;
- regular review of the training plan;
- training and development throughout the employee's entire career;
- evaluation and audit of the training programmes.

It is, however, limited in its focus to training and staff development (and, therefore, attractive to persons-orientated cultures, such as educational institutions (Handy 1985)) and, though worthy in very many respects, hardly capable of meeting the 'totality' criterion of the BSI definition. Therefore no further reference will be made to it in this introduction.

In addition to Sallis and Hingley, there is another excellent, general account of the two remaining systems – BS 5750 and TQM – produced with its usual efficiency by the Further Education Unit (FEU): *Quality Matters: Business and Industry Quality Models and Further Education* (1991). This describes the systems, their principles and practice, and compares them with the philosophy and practice of further education colleges. It is noted that a few colleges are attempting either to introduce TQM and BS 5750 simultaneously, or to use BS 5750 as the first stage of a TQM policy (1991: 12). In the conclusion it is emphasized that 'Any approach to quality improvement therefore should be designed or chosen with learners in mind, because all efforts should be directed at improving their chances of success' (p. 13).

The paper then sets out a number of criteria that a good quality system should meet and, wisely, leaves it to the college to decide what to opt for. In a discussion of the relevance and suitability of both systems, Middlehurst (1992) clearly favours TQM as more appropriate to the culture of educational and public sector organizations in general, though he identifies a number of barriers to 'quality' as 'an organising principle in higher education' – an issue which will be considered later in this introduction.

BS 5750; ISO 9000; EN 29000

These three standards – British, International and European – are identical and currently under general discussion with the intention of bringing them even more into line with modern TQM practices and the needs of service industries (Durand *et al.* 1993), and this should be borne in mind when considering the suitability of the standard to educational institutions. BSI Quality Assurance (1992) has already published a set of guidance notes for the application of the standard to education, and the National Accreditation Council for Certification Bodies (NACCB) has also circulated a proposed code of practice for the standard as applied to education. The point is that the Standard, although written with manufacturing in mind, is capable of interpretation for a wide range of services. The guidelines will help, but it is up to each individual organization to interpret the Standard and relate it to its own quality aspirations. The organization defines the level of quality (service quality, in respect of education) which will satisfy its customer needs – explicit or implicit – and then establishes a system which will demonstrate how it will deliver *and document its delivery* of the product or service. In other words, the Standard is about the management of a quality system which will deliver the institution's own specified quality standards which are sufficient to meet the needs of its customers.

There is no shortage of BS 5750 'textbook' material, and highly recommended are the following: Freeman (1993); Fox (1991); Walkin (1992); Green (1991); West-Burnham (1992); Sallis and Hingley (1991). However, it must be said that although the books will help, they give absolutely no concept of the real difficulties of attempting to get an educational organization to come to grips with an effective quality system of the kind required to achieve BS 5750 accreditation.

BS 5750 is not an easy option. Only the individual institution can decide whether it is worth the time, the effort, the cost and the not inconsiderable pain. 'No gain without pain' is certainly true of this process. The reasons why the University of Wolverhampton decided to opt for BS 5750 are described elsewhere (Doherty 1993). Given the chaotic 'quality assessment' environment described in the first and second sections of this chapter there may be therapeutic advantages in designing and implementing a quality system which will stand up to the same scrutiny as any other BS 5750-accredited firm or enterprise receives. There may also be market advantages – particularly for further education colleges which have a very close interface with industry and commerce and for those sections of a university in a similar position. There are very considerable internal advantages – like clarifying one's own system – which accrue from the discipline required to set up BS 5750, whether accreditation is achieved or not.

There are contra-indications, as it were, which organizations should be aware of. The *Observer* and the *Sunday Times* ran a series of articles (Halliday 1993a, 1993b) drawing attention to the undisputed fact that BS 5750 does not of itself guarantee excellence – only that the organization has a quality system which can be relied on consistently to deliver its own defined and documented quality standards: much better than nothing, some would observe. Tony Tysome in *The Times Higher Education Supplement* (somewhat gleefully?) reported 'Ministers warned off "kite-mark" for Colleges' (July 1991) – rather strange considering how hard the government (in the shape of the Department for Employment through its various 'training' initiatives over the last decade) has been pushing and funding further education colleges to take the BS 5750 route to quality. The real problems for small firms, especially of over 'over-consultation', of over-bureaucratization, of misunderstanding and of disillusionment are well documented in Rock (1992), though the article also makes clear that for many firms the increased internal efficiency and improved competitiveness brought as a result of the 'rigours of gaining the standard' were not in dispute.

Similarly, it is not in dispute amongst those colleges which have become involved with BS 5750 that the discipline, whatever its limitations, does have positive advantages. This is well put by Henry (1991):

> First, I do not see BS 5750 and TQM as alternatives. An organisation can be aiming for TQM and using BS 5750 as a vehicle for achieving it – it can be a useful milestone rather than the millstone as it is usually portrayed.
>
> Second, I have heard representatives of organisations saying: 'Oh, we're not interested in BS 5750 – we're TQM'. When questioned further they have a naïve view of TQM which is based on smiling at everyone and copping out on much of the hard ground work to systems which has to be taken.
>
> (1991: 15)

The links between BS 5750 and TQM and the problems both systems pose for further and higher education are also discussed by McElwee (1991) in a generally supportive article which concludes: 'Quality then has to be defined at a number of levels. BS 5750 is a short term strategy. For quality to be a serious issue it needs to be embraced as a complete package. Imposing BS 5750 will not change the culture. TQM will' (p. 21).

Finally, that educational institutions can successfully achieve BS 5750 is now proved. Several further education colleges have done this; Sandwell, the first to succeed, is represented elsewhere in this volume and there are many more in the 'pipeline'. Also two schools have been accredited; one is Hesley Hall School in Tichhill, Doncaster. This school intends to move on from BS 5750 to meet the Investors in People standard (Education Equipment 1993). The other is Kates Hill Primary school in Dudley (Merrick 1993), which is currently projecting, like Sandwell, a very positive image of the value of BS 5750: 'The result, they say, is a more effectively managed school, where roles and responsibilities are clearly defined and teachers can feel more confident about delivering the curriculum.'

However, it is clear, even from these success stories, that many educational institutions do perceive that gaining BS 5750 accreditation may be no more than a staging post on a longer journey.

TOTAL QUALITY MANAGEMENT AND THE IDEAL OF CONTINUOUS IMPROVEMENT

As indicated in the last section there are many obvious links between BS 5750 and TQM, and some educational institutions – of which the University of Wolverhampton is an example – regard gaining the Standard as a basis from which to achieve a TQM culture.

From the outset, it must be emphasized that most educational institutions and even some firms are not happy with the word 'management', with its connotations of control, hierarchy, Taylorism and, generally, impersonal and *uncaring management attitudes*. This has led to a variety of alternatives, such as

Total Quality Culture,
Total Quality Enhancement,
Total Quality Care,
Total Quality Learning,

all of which are attempts to mitigate these negative reactions. However, they derive from a misunderstanding of the term. The whole basis of TQM is that every member of an organization at whatever level is *personally* responsible for the quality management of her or his own part of the processes which contribute to the delivery of a product or a service. BS 5750 requires the individual to conform to the agreed processes and procedures; TQM requires the individual to be committed to their continual improvement. The successful implementation of a TQM strategy is very much more concerned with the transformation of 'hearts and minds' than is a BS 5750 Quality System: it requires a missionary zeal which, whilst inspiring from the top down, must generate commitment from the bottom up.

Being missionary, TQM has generated a large number of gurus, each of whom has emphasized some particular facet of 'quality'. The best known of these are Deming (1988), Juran (1988), Ishikawa (1985), Crosby (1984), Peters and Waterman (1982) and Peters (1988). Juran and Ishikawa emphasize quality control (by the individual, not through inspection); Crosby, zero defects and reduced costs; Peters, responsiveness to customer demand; and Deming, delighting the customer and good, old-fashioned pride in one's work. All have slightly different philosophical emphases, but common to all is the clear perception that 'quality' is concerned with providing maximum customer satisfaction whilst keeping costs down. There are other writers who might qualify as 'gurus' but they are so heavily focused on manufacturing industry that they are not altogether relevant in this context. An excellent and comprehensive account of the gurus can be found in Bendell (1991), and there are any number of competent introductions and commentaries, such as Oakland (1989), Neave (1990), Bank (1992) and Sallis (1993b). The following quotation from Bank (1992) gives a flavour of the 'missionary zeal' referred to above:

> Total quality management is part of a holistic approach to progress. It is in ascendancy as the year 2000 approaches. . . . The image that comes to mind is the Chinese tangram – millions of these ancient puzzles with individuals locked into tight boxes. Total quality has the potential power to transform the tangrams into running figures, liberating people at work to become more truly themselves and more creative.
>
> (1992: 195)

Part of the vision is thus 'persons-orientated' and concerned with 'empowering' the individual to become freely able to contribute to and communicate with her or his organization – a concept explored at length in Peters (1992). All this is exciting, stimulating, challenging and not, at first sight, antithetical to the attitudes and involvement of educationists. It is hardly surprising, therefore, that TQM gets a better press than BS 5750.

Sallis *et al.* (1992) once again provide a relatively short but very helpful guide to the introduction of TQM to educational institutions. They also provide a useful comparison, with case studies, of the differences between TQM and BS 5750. A number of generic TQM characteristics, differently emphasized by various experts, can be identified:

- The customers' expectations and requirements are most important.
- Quality is what meets the customers' needs, not what the producer specifies.
- Quality to the customer depends on the effectiveness of internal client chains – a *sine qua non*.
- Teamwork is essential.
- Hierarchies should be cut down to no more than four levels between the bottom and top management.
- Continuous quality improvement is based on small-scale incremental activity – *Kaizen*.
- Total commitment from management – *leadership* from the top is essential.
- Long-term commitment is essential – success is never complete, as the constantly changing external environment requires constant re-adjustment of the enterprise.
- The key aim is organizational transformation to a 'quality culture'.
- Staff appraisal for development is essential.
- Staff participation and commitment based on education and training are essential.
- Recognition of good performance by individuals or teams is needed.
- Benchmarking and the measurement of change are needed to underpin the system.
- Getting out and getting involved is essential – management 'walk the talk'.

Furthermore, there are some crucial questions to be answered before TQM can profitably commence, for example:

- What is the nature of the business?
- What are the critical success factors?
- What is the corporate mission?
- How does quality fit into the corporate business plan?
- What are the quality costs?
- How can progress be measured?

Answering these questions must lead to management decisions, which may require quite extensive consultations. When taken, the decisions need to be fully communicated throughout the organization. Some of these processes are now familiar to universities and further education colleges which have been involved for several years in strategic planning, and also to schools which have been required to produce development plans since the Education Reform Act of 1988. Between 1990 and 1992 Consultants at Work (Miller and Inniss 1990, 1992) produced a series of booklets for the Training, Education and Enterprise Directorate (TEED) of the Department of Employment. These were all concerned with quality improvement, and *Strategic Quality Management* is generally useful for its overview of a TQM approach to college management, and the series particularly so for its methodology for establishing *Quality characteristics, Quality standards* and *Quality measures*. These can be applied at any level in an organization and are a particularly effective way of getting small teams to address specific quality issues.

The TQM philosophy is thus perceived as being more in accord with traditional educational values than the, perhaps more brutal, manufacturing-orientated BS 5750. This aspect of TQM has been persuasively argued by Horwitz (1990), who states:

> A total process is one which recognizes that everyone in the organisation contributes in some form or another to the end product or service to the customer. Everyone means that every function and every level in the organisation is involved in the process.
>
> (1990: 56)

She concludes: 'This philosophy is already highly visible in education. We do not have a heavy bureaucracy unaware of their effect on the customer' (p. 58). There is plenty of support for this point of view from the practitioners, such as Muller and Funnell (1991, 1992a, 1992b), who argue that at the 'heart' of quality is the 'role played by the learner': 'This view which offers a substantial challenge to aspects of traditional practice in vocational education and training, accords with the tenets of TQM and supports the liberal educational notions underpinning student autonomy' (1992b: 260). Or Sommerville (1993): 'it has been most rewarding to see people grow and develop and hopefully, all in the interests of providing a good service to our customers' (p. 5). Indeed, Stephenson and Weil (1992) are quite unequivocal in their definition of 'quality' in higher education as the provision of learning experiences which go beyond traditional knowledge and skills to develop competence, autonomy and effectiveness in the organization and application of knowledge and skills. They thus identify the *student* as the prime customer.

Most of these supportive statements relate to developments in further and vocational education which, as already noted, is deeper into 'quality systems' (both in Britain and in the United States) than either schools or higher education. Nevertheless, having said this, there is a growing volume of supportive statements from those sectors too, for instance, Arat Arkin (1993) gives an interesting report of how, with help, support and training provided by IBM, the William Howard School, Cumbria, has been developing TQM based on the Baldridge Award model. Two headteachers, Mooney (1993) and Samuel (1993), comment (though with differing degrees of enthusiasm) on TQM as a perhaps inevitable future development:

> If we can deliver to parents and pupils with consistency on education to meet their requirements, if genuine empowerment leads staff to a greater sense of ownership, if – above all else – there is evidence of continuous improvement, then the whole exercise will have been worthwhile.
>
> (Samuel 1993: 391)

Mooney, however, is more sceptical, because of government policy, about the capacity of schools in the United Kingdom to apply TQM as it is being applied in some schools in America. He is referring to W. Edwards Deming's bitter opposition to grading, which he considers antithetical to the TQM philosophy. Sallis (1993a) describes how TQM can be developed in the school environment, reiterating some of the warnings he has given elsewhere (1992 and 1993b) in respect of further education: 'TQM requires a long-term commitment. It is not just another project. It is a journey and not a destination. For this reason, TQM is not "achieved", but is always something to be striven for' (p. 33). Other interesting accounts of the problems, pitfalls and rewards of embarking on a TQM journey are reported by Coates (1993), Deputy Head of Somervale School in Avon, and Dupey (1993), Headteacher, Ecclesbourne School, Derby – the latter in a paper presented at the 1993 Sixth Annual Conference of the British Deming Association. This association is particularly interested in the development of TQM in educational organizations, as is its counterpart in the United States, and is in the process of setting up a consortium of interested schools in the West Midlands. Elsewhere in this volume it will be seen that the Deming approach is considered most appropriate to education in many American schools, colleges and universities.

Much less has been written about real encounters with TQM in the UK higher education system for the obvious reason that this is where the penetration is weakest. However, in respect of the USA, Coates (1991) is informative about Oregon State University, and the whole of *New Directions for Institution Research*, 71, Fall 1991, is devoted to TQM in American universities. Similarly, the whole of *Higher Education*, 25, 1993, is devoted to case studies from British as well as American universities. The British universities represented are Aston, South Bank, Ulster and Wolverhampton, all of which report varied and, generally speaking, positive experiences. Elsewhere, there are also some fairly general discussions of how TQM methodology might be applied in higher education, such as Prabhu and Lee (1990), Hill and Taylor (1991) and Sutcliffe and

Pollock (1992). Hill and Taylor are particularly clear about methodology, problems of implementation and benefits, concluding:

> Universities are likely to reap significant benefits from an appropriate implementation of total quality management. However, implementation would require considerable planning and management commitment to cultural change. Part of this cultural change would involve the formation of a team ethos and a cross-functional approach to improvement. Universities would need to have a much clearer focus on what quality means in this context, and, more importantly, what it means to their customers.
>
> (1991: 9)

A much more sceptical analysis of 'total quality' in the context of the Conservative government's implementation of market-based methods of resource allocation is to be found in Oliver (1993). He discusses at length the implications of consumer, output-based systems of control (of which TQM is an example) for the structures and cultures of universities. They are likely to be radical and, because it is very difficult for a university, being a complex set of frequently divergent sub-units, to agree on corporate object-ives, unpalatable to many people. Nevertheless, he concludes of 'total quality' that

> Being customer focused, this has developed explicitly within a com-mercial, market driven tradition. This model carries clear prescriptions, most of which would fundamentally challenge existing structures (and cultures) of many universities. At the institutional level, a much greater driving down of accountability is implied, with sub-units – for example departments – being given greater discretion in how they use resources, and being subject to intensive performance measurement. The imposi-tion of quasi-market mechanisms external to the universities will create a pressure for such mechanisms to be replicated internally.
>
> (1993: 57)

Oliver is looking at the down side of quasi-markets and customer orienta-tion, putting, incidentally, a different complexion on the TQM 'quality characteristic' of employee empowerment. Nevertheless there is a reluctant and grudging acknowledgement that 'total quality' may have much to offer universities which are struggling to adapt to their changed economic circum-stances. There is plenty of other more positive support for TQM in the public services generally. A good example, giving very practical advice about successful implementation, is Smith (1993), who explores system improvement for service industries and considers processes and roles at all levels in the organization. Similarly, English (1990) offers some very practical advice, and makes the point that service and manufacturing industries are more alike than different, since most quality problems derive from people, concluding:

Public service organisations start with a significant advantage over their opposite numbers in the private sector. Employers, such as doctors, nurses, teachers, housing officers, social workers, have a far stronger desire to service their customers than those who join industrial companies. The challenge is to turn this enthusiasm into effective satisfaction of customer requirements.

(1990: 148)

It seems, then, that TQM, despite its pluralistic, customer-driven definition of quality, is generally recognized as having much to offer to educational organizations committed to developing some form of quality improvement system. According to Hill and Taylor (1991: 7), the benefits include: sustained improvement; increased external customer satisfaction; cost savings of up to 10 per cent of operating costs; the development of cross-functional teams, improvement in morale, commitment and motivation; new ways of management which promote corporate goals, accountability and involvement; and to their list might be added improved internal client chains and greater potential for innovative development.

The key TQM goal of changing the culture of an organization has already been identified. This is a fundamental tenet of TQM theory: Bank (1992), Sallis (1993b) and frequently reiterated in management and quality journals. For instance, P.E. Atkinson (1990) gets quite excited about the commonly repeated excuse that there is something special about the Japanese and their culture which makes TQM an 'easy' option: 'Nonsense. Take a trip around any Mitsubishi, National Panasonic, Hitachi or Nissan plant in the West and you will find a culture propagated by Westerners' (p. 8). Notwithstanding, these westerners have equalled and sometimes surpassed Japanese productivity rates. Later he admonishes western managers thus:

To promote the right value system which is sensitive to total quality, managers have to learn to do one thing. Learn to love people as they do their own family and themselves. Learning to love people, looking at them as people, is a major step. Looking at your people from the neck up, not from the neck down, is a good start.

(1990: 9)

All the quality gurus are agreed that most problems, inefficiencies and system weaknesses can be laid at the door of management − 80 per cent at least, since the only people with the power to improve processes and so improve quality are the managers themselves. Their chief problem is that they do not listen to what their people tell them − even when they ask the questions; Ishikawa (1985), for instance, is adamant that the poor performance of British industry in particular can be attributed to incompetent management. In a further article Atkinson (1991) expands this theme, pointing out: 'Years of neglecting to provide managers and supervisors with the necessary skills cannot be wiped out by sending them on a series of TQM workshops' (p. 17). He makes the point that there is plenty of evidence of managers 'managing' – *seeing things are done right* but not much evidence of managers 'leading' – *seeing that right things are done*: 'Managers who adopt a "corporate change drive" through leadership behaviour will succeed while others are still listing reasons why they cannot change!' (p. 19).

There seems to be considerable consensus, certainly amongst exponents of TQM, as to what 'quality leadership' means. Frequently repeated qualities are: *willingness to make things happen – taking risks; developing trust; clarity of mission, roles and communication; changing the culture by good example; 'walking the talk'* (Seddon 1991). These characteristics are explored at some length in a very persuasive article by Darling (1992). He comments:

> In reality, it turns out that neither superior care of customers nor constant innovation – two of the three cutting and sustaining edges of quality in an organisation – are built upon managerial genius, unusual operational techniques, or mystical strategic moves or countermoves in the market-place. Both are built, instead, on the existence of committed people which emanates from a solid foundation of listening, trust and respect for the dignity and creative potential of each person in the organisation. This foundation facilitates the establishment of a 'winning team' of people committed to the achievement of the firm's goals and objectives for quality.
>
> (1992: 4)

Writing about the leadership culture at Virginia Tech, Leffel *et al.* (1991) list and then discuss in very similar terms a very similar set of leadership characteristics concluding:

> TQM must begin with the development of the leadership team working toward a shared vision, shared values, and a repertoire of leadership skills. Change will not occur immediately either in personnel or in the institutional culture. Leadership development must be a value and a process that evolves within the institution over a period of five to ten years.
>
> (1991: 71)

Finally, Mortimore (1993), commenting on the factors which are demonstrably contributing to improved school effectiveness, names: 'flexible, though positive leadership by the headteacher, the involvement of staff in joint decision-making, the use of appropriate rewards and incentives, and (in the case of primary schools) parental involvement' (p. 11). These voices from industry, commerce, education – colleges and schools alike – are all echoing the same theme: strong leadership leads to a strong culture leads to an environment conducive to the development of TQM.

None of these writers is suggesting that the management of cultural change is easy, though it is fairly easy to identify typical 'academic' responses. The very fact that educationists come from a 'quality-orientated' culture can be a barrier. Evaluation is part of good professional practice – including self-evaluation. That is drummed into every beginning teacher in the United Kingdom and United States. So is the methodology: contextualize; plan; implement; evaluate. This is not very different from the Deming Quality Loop: plan; do; check; act. Furthermore, university and college lecturers take striving for excellence in scholarship, teaching and research as a given (Hill and Taylor 1991). This is well put by Coates (1993):

> What problems have we faced in our work with TQM? Well, perhaps the biggest has been convincing people that 'quality' matters. So much baggage is attached to any educational change that has its origin in industry and commerce. The language of 'quality' puts up a kind of cultural barrier which is difficult to overcome.
>
> (1993: 37)

The philosophy of TQM, being customer-driven, does in fact, challenge some of those previously comfortable assumptions that 'our' (the producers' perception) of 'quality' is all that matters. Academics do not like this:

> the recent move to School-based apprenticeship models of training may be characterised as being market-led (production quality) and linked to appraisal of performance. It is the latter model which seems to match the spirit of the eighties, owing more to Marks and Spencer than Marx and Weber.
>
> (Gorbutt *et al.* 1991: 39)

Altogether more interesting are those writers who see TQM as a Machiavellian plot to seduce the workers into a form of subservience which appears to be freedom – for example, Alan Johnson, Assistant Secretary of the Post Office Union, reported in the *IPM Journal* (1991), or Watkin (1993) who sees 'Japanization' as a fiendish Taylorist plot:

> it is wise to recall Cole's argument that 'Japanese managers have achieved a more thorough going implementation of scientific management to an extent that its founder Frederick Taylor, could not even have imagined'.
>
> (1993: 28)

Such is the potency of the drive towards total quality that even the Trades Union Congress has been constrained to make some serious comment. *The Quality Challenge* (1992) is a very interesting document – full of equivocations, reservations and coy responses to initiatives such as the 'Citizens' Charter', which are indicative of potential culture conflicts which are themselves important barriers to implementation, but the conclusion is eventually reached that

> Whilst it would be ultimately self-defeating for unions to oppose schemes which genuinely offer participation and a degree of worker satisfaction, it is essential that union input is acknowledged and credited by staff and management. The question is often not whether to oppose such schemes but how to integrate them effectively into local union structures.
>
> (1992: 19)

The unions, it appears then, are reluctant but realistic. It goes without saying that to overcome these barriers and problems is one of the key leadership tasks in the management of quality change.

What, the reader may well ask, is different from all this and the standard MBA diet of leadership and change theory? It is certainly true that many of the writers on quality already cited themselves refer to standard management texts – such as on leadership and change: Bennis and Nanus (1985); Bennis (1989); Burn (1978); Drucker (1985); Baldridge (1975); Fullan (1991); and on strategic management: David (1991). Other relevant texts – particularly in respect of the links between strategic management and quality – are: Ohmae (1983, 1990); Bowman (1991); and Kanter (1985, 1990). For the theorist these texts are essential reading. The difference is that TQM is about action, not theory. Some of the gurus – Crosby, Peters, Deming – draw from standard management theory, sociology, psychology, economics, what they need in order to craft implementation strategies. Deming and his followers are a particularly good example of how, having started out with the famous 'fourteen points' (which read like 'tips for TQM'), they found it necessary to get to grips with some deeper theory in order to underpin his wisdom. Deming is full of 'wise' insights, such as 'Look after the process as the product will look after itself'; 'Survival is not compulsory.' This theory is described as the System of Profound Knowledge and comprises four elements: understanding a system and theory of optimization; some knowledge of statistical theory; some theory of knowledge; some knowledge of psychology, of which a very clear account will be found in Neave (1990) and also Cornesky *et al.* (1990). The theory enlightens, it does not obscure, and it is eminently and instantly applicable in any work-place in either manufacturing or service industry. There is a problem – which is another key difference between TQM and 'standard' management practice. Success depends on an educated workforce. What is needed is 'education, education and more education' (Ishikawa 1985) – *not* mere training. The implementation of TQM requires a multi-skilled workforce with cross-functional capabilities and a capacity to work together in teams.

As TQM has spread since 1950 (the year Deming went to Japan to talk to Japanese executives about improving the quality of their products) from eastern to western companies, so a set of sophisticated tools has been developed for its implementation. There is no space here for a full description of what they are and how they can be used, though some of them can be seen 'at work' later in this volume. They are all concerned with methodologies for improving teamwork or problem analysis.

These techniques are intended to be used by quality teams. Again, these are variously named, but are most commonly referred to as:

- Quality circles (QCs);
- Quality improvement teams (QITs).

They are *not* committees, they do *not* have chairpersons and secretaries, they do *not* produce minutes, but they *do* produce solutions – which, in a TQM system, get embedded in the processes very quickly. To succeed, they must have training; access to data; support from senior management; meet in company time; and receive recognition for success (Collard 1985). Given support, there is ample evidence that QCs and QITs will succeed: 'Quality Circles are not a panacea, but they can have dramatic results in terms of staff involvement, morale, and identification with the aims of the organisation' (T. Atkinson 1990: 89). Without support they will fail (Hill 1991).

Finally, in order to help to embed the team methodology, the typical TQM firm will have as a key element in its training programme a course or module on Facilitator Training – Foster and Dewhurst (1991), Walley and Kowalski (1992). Facilitators will be trained in the use of the TQM tools. They will start with basic group work and team building as described in Scholtes (1988), and then move on to master the more specific tools – those requiring some statistical capability. These techniques have been in use in the great Japanese firms such as, for instance, Nissan, Toyota, Hitachi and Mitsubishi for more than a generation. Their QCs and QITs have been taking small steps forward – *Kaizen* – which have resulted in great improvements. Similar developments are now taking place in western companies such as Federal Express, IBM, Rank-Xerox, Philips, Parcel-Force and BT, many of whom, particularly IBM, Rank-Xerox, Philips and BT, are more than ready to share their expertise with educational organizations. The process of education and training in such organizations goes deep – frequently right down to the lower supervisory level for facilitator training and to the shop floor for 'basic tools'. This has implications for educational organizations. What is the 'shop floor'? If, as most would argue, the process and the product are inseparable in a learning experience, then the student must be involved. Facilitator training for students? The basic tools in the primary school? This is not a wild vision, as some of the articles in this volume will demonstrate. There is nothing in TQM training which is not wholly compatible with the RSA Capability Approach in Higher Education, the Enterprise in Higher Education Initiative, the aims of the Comino Foundation in schools, or the aims of the National Council for Vocational Qualifications. Laurie Taylor gave an impassioned plea for getting rid of degree classifications at the Deming Conference (1993) and, indeed, TQM philosophy is well in line with the recommendations of the *Assessment Issues in Higher Education Report* (Atkins *et al.* 1993), produced for the Department of Employment.

By now it will be obvious why Tony Henry remarked that TQM was more than 'going round smiling at everyone'. Neither TQM nor BS 5750 is to be embarked upon lightly. They are not for negative thinkers or for satisficers – of whom there are plenty in education – that version of reality (Ackoff 1970) will not do for survival in the twenty-first century. In the final analysis the organization itself must decide whether the pain of exercising lateral thinking in order to adapt these systems, both of which originated in the manufacturing sector, not only to education but to *its own position* in the education environment, is worth the effort.

ABOUT THE REST OF THIS BOOK

The following eighteen chapters contain a mixture of articles or conference papers already published elsewhere and material specifically written for this publication from both Britain and the United States. They have one common element. They are all reflections on recent or fairly recent practice or thoughts about the practice of quality delivery in educational organizations. Each one, in its own way, attempts to tease out some of the problems inherent in the quest for quality in theoretical, systemic and institutional contexts.

The chapters are divided into four parts. *Part I* is concerned with theoretical and general issues. Richards and Harrison are analysing the paradigm shift from producer-defined to customer-defined quality from the somewhat different perspectives of politics, on the one hand, and sociology on the other. Richards sees the shift as a continuum, moving from the 'administrative' to the 'efficiency' to the 'customer' and finally the 'consumer' paradigm. In this process the 'professional' ends up with significantly less influence on the definition of the 'public good', the existence of which is not challenged. Harrison, however, develops a post-modern theory of quality based on the disintegration of 'authority' where the paradigm shifts are from elitist to mass higher education, normative to relative values and producer to customer-designed quality. Post-modern society has only one method of social control: the market. Thus, since education (like other public sector services) has no true market because individuals cannot pay for mega services of this kind, a quasi-market has to be constructed. The quality assessment systems – HEFCE(QA) and HEQC(QA) – thus use the language and metaphors of business: 'mission-based', 'quality audit', 'quality system' and so on, with a consequent loss of producer (that is, 'professional') authority. From different starting points they reach the same conclusion. Barnett also explores customer-driven points of view. His analysis of quality being dependent on having a 'model' of higher education implies different customers, the government, the student and so on, each with a different set of expectations and thus a different set of criteria for quality. He opts for a model of higher education which is based on the more traditional educational values of development of mind, but even he, who most certainly speaks up for the 'professional' corner, explicitly admits that there are several different stakeholders whose voices, nowadays, must be listened to.

Tribus, an American TQM expert, guru even, in the world of education and deeply committed to the Deming approach, gives some practical ideas about how to get to grips with doing TQM in educational institutions. However, he is clear about the purposes of education, and he is very much in accord with Barnett's developmental view of quality. He is also clear that the TQM philosophy of ownership, empowerment and participation, together with many of the TQM tools, can and should be applied in schools, even at the primary level. He is against grading (de-motivating) and in favour of Records of Achievement (ROAs). His is a strong, but practical, vision of the importance of TQM in education at all levels. Similarly practical are Jones and Mathias on the importance of developmental staff-appraisal as part of a TQM system. They see this as a powerful way to change the culture of the organization – provided that it is linked with positive attitudes to the development of quality. They are just as dismissive as Deming and Tribus of grading and its commitment to performance-related pay. If Tribus is about 'how to do TQM with the students', Jones and Mathias is about 'how to do TQM with the staff'.

Holloway's contribution is an interesting example of the researcher's problem: there are never enough data to be quite sure! She asks all the right questions, but because of her perceived lack of either a definitive theory of quality or a coherent organizational paradigm it is impossible to come to a conclusion. Nevertheless, she has very interesting and useful observations on clashes of culture, comparisons of TQM with standard management-of-change theory and so on. She perceives that TQM might be the appropriate response to the current obsession with external assessment and verification – but, then, it might not.

Part II deals with developments in higher education. Storey gives a vivid account of the trials and tribulations, successes and failures of the University of Wolverhampton's current BS 5750 and TQM initiatives. Storey should be read in conjunction with Stott – a University of Wolverhampton consultant, who is working both in the university itself and in industrial companies to set up BS 5750 and TQM systems. Despite the different cultures, many of the organizational problems are the same. Both provide fascinating, real-life examples of the barriers to implementation described in the introduction.

The contributions from the United States indicate, to use an old CNAA compliment, a much more 'mature' approach to TQM than will be found in any UK examples – except, possibly Clayton in *Higher Education* (1993). Dean Hubbard's contribution describes a university (Northwest Missouri State) – albeit of manageable size – a long way down the TQM road and having used many of the TQM methodologies described in the introduction, including measurement of key success factors. It is interesting to observe that Hubbard, unlike most of the American universities cited in the introduction and reported in *Higher Education* (1993), started with the academic rather than the service functions of the institution. Hansen (Wisconsin—Madison) is particularly interesting in that he describes, in detail, how a TQM approach in which students were active participants was evaluated. Readers will be interested to observe the differences and similarities between this and traditional student 'feedback'.

Part III, Further/Vocational Education Institutions in Britain and the United States, clearly demonstrates how much further advanced in both TQM and BS 5750 is this sector of education than the rest on both sides of the Atlantic. These chapters speak for themselves. Sallis links TQM, BS 5750, Strategic Management and Investors in People in a comprehensive and authoritative account of developments in further education. He is especially interesting on the importance of leadership qualities. MacRoberts gives a particular example of the experiences of Sandwell College in gaining BS 5750 accreditation which provides a lively case study of the realities from which Sallis's more general account is derived.

Schauerman and his colleagues provide an account of the application of TQM in the American community college system. Schauerman is particularly interesting on customer orientation and on the use of QFD, a method (TQM tool) for translating the 'voice of the customer' into college language.

At the end of this section, Marsh provides a fascinating account of the introduction and implementation of TQM in a Training and Enterprise Council (TEC). He describes how the theory was applied and how all the 'classic' reactions, culture clashes and cynicisms were managed, but perhaps most interesting is his account of the methodology in action: QCs (which they christened *Voluntary* Improvement Teams), QITs, rewards and recognition, the development of a training workshop and toolkit pack and the importance of involving the strategic managers. Having made a successful start in the TEC, the next stage was to take it out into the community, offering a TQM resource to colleges, the local authority and schools.

Part IV is devoted to schools. Here, the contrasts between the American and British experiences and approaches are more marked than in the university and further education sectors. Hampton draws parallels between the quality problems of survival faced by an urban comprehensive school in the new 'quasi-market' ethos and the problems of the Japanese in the 1950s. He describes how the school looked at TQM as a means of self-improvement. Actually, the methodology used, and the school's development of a 'Quality Handbook' approach shows that the influence of BS 5750 (encouraged by the LEA) was also strong. Hampton provides a clear and comprehensive account of the benefits the school has gained at all levels, including its 'philosophy of management' and general 'ownership' of quality from its TQM/BS 5750 initiative. This chapter should be read in conjunction with Cleland's on 'Quality networks'. Buckpool School is a particular example of Dudley Metropolitan Borough LEA's general quality policy in action. It is obvious from Cleland's account that it is not by chance that Kates Hill

Primary School, which has achieved BS 5750 accreditation, is a Dudley school. This LEA has developed an impressive and well-resourced infrastructure (now under threat from current government educational policies) which amounts to a 'quality network' through which best practice can be transmitted and which can provide a constant source of encouragement and support. Cleland's is a local and regional, large-scale vision.

This is paralleled in the American contributions by Rhodes's account of the application of the Deming method in schools. He regards Deming's version of TQM as holistic and potentially acceptable to teachers, and is quite clear about the paradigm shift, the change in mindset, needed to refocus the school's activities on the customer. Tribus gives a fairly detailed report of the application of Deming's method in one American high school. The results are impressive, but the school is atypical – a small residential regional school in Alaska. Nevertheless, it is currently the only account of TQM applied wholeheartedly and consistently to the improvement of learning experiences in a whole institution for long enough to observe the results of TQM in action. Some interesting quantitative evaluation is given of impressive improvements to critical success factors. These chapters clearly demonstrate that the Deming methodology can be used to effectively reinforce educational values that most teachers share, giving both the teacher/facilitator and the learner greater empowerment over the learning process itself and greater freedom for personal development.

The four parts of the book show how a wide cross-section of educational institutions from both sides of the Atlantic are attempting to introduce TQM in some form or other. The generic characteristics identified earlier in this chapter are thematic to all these accounts, case studies and analyses, as are the barriers to implementation and the problems they present, about which the contributors have been remarkably frank. It was stated at the outset that this was not intended to be any kind of textbook. Nevertheless, should the reader be interested in developing a quality system, he or she might learn a great deal from these experiences of reflective practitioners.

Finally, the documents do not provide any complete answers to the research questions asked by Holloway in *Part I*. They certainly raise a number of questions to which research projects might provide answers – for instance, in respect of culture change, cost-effectiveness, job-satisfaction, improved communication, and general 'quality' improvement, though the fact that there is no agreed theory of quality presents methodological problems in respect of measuring improvement. There remains the issue of social control. Read Harrison, Tribus and Rhodes in juxtaposition. Does this American experience of Deming in school represent a subtle extension of Taylorism into the classroom and beyond into the community? Or does it show how creative thinkers can take out the positive elements of a manufacturing technique and use them to enable educationists to achieve their visions, goals and objectives more effectively? If the quality of the learning experience is improved, does it matter?

REFERENCES

Ackoff, R.L. (1970) *A Concept for Corporate Planning*, New York: Wiley.

Arkin, A. (1993) 'Quality strained through jargon', *School Management* (May).

Armitage, A.M.D. (1993) 'Paramount role of management', *The Times Higher Education Supplement* (5th Feb.).

Atkins, M.J. *et al.* (1993) *Assessment Issues in Higher Education*, London: HMSO, Department of Employment.

Atkinson, P.E. (1990) 'Creating cultural change', *Management Services* (Nov.).

—— (1991) 'Leadership, total quality and cultural change', *Management Services* (June).

Atkinson, T. (1990) *Evaluating Quality Circles in a College of Further Education*, University of Manchester: Manchester Monographs.

Baldridge, J.V. (1975) *Managing Change in Educational Organizations*, Berkeley, CA: McCritchen.

Bank, J. (1992) *The Essence of Total Quality Management*, Hemel Hempstead: Prentice-Hall International (UK).

Barnett, R. (1990) *The Idea of Higher Education*, Buckingham: Open University Press.

—— (1992a) *Improving Higher Education: Total Quality Care*, Buckingham: Open University Press.

—— (1992b) *Learning to Effect*, Buckingham: Open University Press.

Becher, T. (1992) 'Making audit acceptable: a collegial approach to quality assurance', *Higher Education Quarterly* 46(1).

Bendell, T. (1991) *The Quality Gurus*, London: Department of Trade and Industry.

Bennis, W. (1989) *On Becoming a Leader*, M.A.: Addison-Wesley.

Bennis, W. and Nanus, B. (1985) *Leaders*, New York: Harper & Row.

Bowman, C. (1991) *The Essence of Strategic Management*, Hemel Hempstead: Prentice-Hall International (UK).

Brennan, J. and Silver, H. (1992) 'Who will lead the charge or sound the retreat?', *Times Higher Education Supplement* (25 Dec.).

British Journal of Educational Studies 40(1) (Feb. 1992).

British Standards Institute (QA) (1992) *Guidance Notes for the Application of ISO9000/EN29000/BS5750 to Education and Training*, Milton Keynes: BSI, QA Document No. QGN/9310/395, Issue 2.

Brookman, J. (1993a) 'Flying standard for quality', *Times Higher Education Supplement* (1 Jan.).

—— (1993b) 'Bordered by red tape', *Times Higher Education Supplement* (5 March).

Burn, J. (1978) *Leadership*, New York: Harper & Row.

Buxton, N.J. (1993) 'At least two dragons emerge in place of CNAA', *Times Higher Education Supplement* (1 Jan.).

Coate, E.C. (1991) 'Implementing total quality management in a university setting', *New Directions for Institutional Research* 71 (Fall).

Coates, P. (1993) 'Embracing quality', *Managing Schools Today* 2(7).

Collard, R. (1985) 'Quality Circles: why they break down and why they hold up', *Personnel Management* (Feb.).

Cornesky, R.A. *et al.* (1990) *W. Edwards Deming: Improving Quality in Colleges and Universitites*, New York: Magna Publications.

Craft, A. (ed.) (1992) *Quality Assurance in Higher Education: Proceedings of an International Conference, Hong Kong 1991*, London: Falmer Press.

Crosby, P.B. (1984) *Quality Without Tears*, New York: McGraw-Hill.

Cryer, P. (1993) *Preparing for Quality Assessment and Audit*, Sheffield: Committee of Vice-Chancellors and Principals.

Darling, J.R. (1992) 'Total quality management: the key role of leadership strategies', *Leadership and Organisational Development* 13(4).

David, F.R. (1991) *Concepts of Strategic Management*, 3rd edn, New York: Merrill.

Deming, W.E. (1988) *Out of the Crisis*, Cambridge: Cambridge University Press.

Department of Education and Science (1988) *Education Reform Act*, London: HMSO.

—— (1992) *Further and Higher Education Act*, London: HMSO.

Department of Education and Science/Employment/and the Welsh Office (1991) *Education and Training for the Twenty-first Century*, vols 1 and 2, London; HMSO.

Doherty, G.D. (1993) 'Towards Total Quality Management in higher education: a case study of the University of Wolverhampton', *Higher Education* 25(3).

Dupey, R. (1993) 'Deming goes to school: quality in Ecclesbourne School', Occasional Paper, Salisbury: British Deming Association.

Durand, G. *et al.* (1993) 'Updating the ISO 9000 Quality Standards: responding to market-place needs', *Quality Progress* (July).

Eliot, T.S. (1948) *Notes Towards a Definition of Culture*, London: Faber & Faber.

Ellis, R. (ed.) (1993) *Quality Assurance for University Teaching*, Buckingham: Open University Press.

Elton, W. (1992) 'Quality assurance in higher education: with or without a buffer?', *Higher Education Policy* 5(3).

European Foundation for Quality Management (1993) *The European Quality Award*, Brussels: EFQM.

Foster, M. and Dewhirst, R. (1991) 'Facilitator skills', *Managing Service Quality* (Sept.).

Fox, M.J. (1991) *Ensuring Your Business Achieves Profits from BS 5750: a Practical Guide*, Letchworth: Tech. Communications (Pub.) Ltd.

Freeman, R. (1993) *Quality Assurance in Training and Education*, London: Kogan Page.

Fullan, M. (1991) *The New Meaning of Educational Change*, New York: Teachers College, Columbia University.

Further Education Funding Council (1993) 'Circular 93/11: assessing achievement' (16 April), Coventry: FEFC.

Further Education Unit (1991) *Quality Matters: Business and Industry Quality Models in Further Education*, London: FEU.

Gammage, P. (1992) 'Quality: the tension between quality and process', Occasional Paper no. 1, Standing Conference on Education and Training of Teachers.

Gorbutt, D. *et al.* (1991) 'Quality support: measurement and myth', *Assessment and Evaluation in Higher Education* 16(1).

Green, G.D. (1991) *Guide to the British Standard 5750 Quality System*, Slough: Langcet Ltd.

Halliday, S. (1993a) 'BS5750 – never mind the quality', *Sunday Times* (14 Mar.).

—— (1993b) 'More on the BS5750 fiasco', *Sunday Observer* (18 April).

Handy, C.B. (1985) *Understanding Organizations*, 3rd edn, Harmondsworth: Penguin.

Harvey, L. *et al.* (1992) *Criteria of Quality*, Quality in Higher Education Project, Birmingham: University of Central England in Birmingham.

Harvey, L. and Green, D. (1993a) 'Defining quality', *Assessment and Evaluation in Higher Education* 18(1).

—— (1993b) 'Assessing quality in higher education: a transbinary research project', *Assessment and Evaluation in Higher Education* 18(2).

Hesley Hall School. *Education Equipment* 34(2) Feb. 1993.

Higher Education Funding Council, England (1993) *Assessment of the Quality of Education: Self-Assessment*, Annex, Para 1 (2 July).

Henry, T. (1991) 'Quality counts', *Perspective* (16 April).

Hewings, D.J. (1992) 'Quality management systems for training organisations', *Transaction* (May).

Hibbert, F.A. (1993) 'Ownership', *Times Higher Education Supplement* (5 Feb.).

Hill, F.M. and Taylor, W.A. (1991) 'Total Quality Management in higher education', *International Journal of Educational Management* 5(5).

Hill, S. (1991) 'Why Quality Circles failed but Total Quality Management might succeed', *British Journal of Industrial Relations* 29(4).

Hodges, L. (1993) 'Buddy, spare some time', *Times Higher Education Supplement* (25 Feb.).

Horwitz, C. (1990) 'Total Quality Management: an approach for education', *Educational Management and Administration* 18(2).

Inglis, F. (1993) 'Paper mountains not up my street', *Times Higher Education Supplement* (5 Feb.).

Ishikawa, K. (1985) *What is Total Quality Control? The Japanese Way*, New York: Prentice-Hall.

Jack, M. (1993) 'Untying red tape', *Times Higher Education Supplement* (5 Feb.).

Johnston, J. (1992) 'Quality assurance, school self-management and the contradictions of control', *European Journal of Education* 17(1/2).

Juran, J.M. (1988) *Juran on Planning for Quality*, New York: Free Press.

Kanter, R.M. *The Change Masters*, London: Unwin-Hyman.

—— (1990) *When Giants Learn to Dance*, London: Unwin-Hyman.

Keefe, T. (1992) 'The quality is strained', *Times Higher Education Supplement* (11 Dec.).

Leavis, F.E. (1943) *Education and the University*, London: Chatto & Windus.

Leffel, G. *et al.* (1991) 'Assessing leadership culture at Virginia Tech', *New Directions for Institutional Research* 71 (Fall).

Loder, C. (1992) 'Identifying and developing a quality ethos for teaching in higher education', Newsletter 2, Centre for Higher Education Studies (CHES), University of London: Institute of Higher Education.

—— (1993) 'Identifying and developing a quality ethos for teaching in higher education. Newsletter 3, Centre for Higher Education Studies (CHES), University of London: Institute of Higher Education.

McElwee, G. (1991) 'Is flying a quality kitemark enough?' *General Educator* 13 (Nov.–Dec.);

MacGregor, K. (1991) 'Quality controller puts faith in money lever', *Times Higher Education Supplement* (13 Dec.).

MacLure, S. (1988) *Education Re-formed*, Sevenoaks: Hodder & Stoughton.

McRobb, M. (1990) *Writing Quality Manuals for ISO 9000 Series*, Kempston: IFS Publication.

Merrick, N. (1993) 'Prototype for progress', *School Management* (May).

Middlehurst, R. (1992) 'Quality: an organising principle for higher education?' *Higher Education Quarterly* 46(1).

Miller, J. and Inniss, S. (1990a) *Improving Quality – a Guide for Course Teams*, Ware: Consultants at Work.

—— (1990b) *Managing Quality Improvement – a Guide for Middle Managers*, Ware: Consultants at Work.

—— (1992) *Strategic Quality Management – a Guide for Senior Managers*, Ware: Consultants at Work.

Mooney, T. (1993) 'Quality across the board', *Education* (26 Feb.).

Mortimore, P. (1993) 'Searching for quality', *Managing Schools Today* 2(5).

Muller, D. and Funnell, F. (1991) 'Promoting quality in further and higher education', *Learning Resources Journal* 7(2).

—— (1992a) 'An exploration of the concept of quality in vocational education and training', *Education and Training Technology International* 29(3) (Aug.).

—— (1992b) 'Initiating change in further and vocational education: the quality approach', *Journal of Further and Higher Education* 16(1) (Spring).

Neave, H.R. (1990) *The Deming Dimension*, Knoxville, TN: SPC Press Inc.

Oakland, J.S. (1989) *Total Quality Management*, Oxford: Butterworth-Heinemann.

OFSTED (1993) *Corporate Plan 1993–1994 to 1995–1996* London: OFSTED.

Ohmae, K. (1983) *The Mind of the Strategist*, Harmondsworth: Penguin Books.

—— (1990) *The Borderless World*, New York: HarperCollins.

Oliver, N. (1993) 'Quality, costs and changing strategies of control in universities in the UK', *Journal of Educational Administration* 31(1).

Peters, M. (1992) 'Performance and accountability in post-industrial society: the crisis of British universities', *Studies in Higher Education* 17(2).

Peters, T.J. (1988) *Thriving on Chaos*, London: Macmillan.

—— (1992) *Liberation Management*, London: Macmillan.

Peters, T.J. and Waterman, R.H. Jr. (1982) *In Search of Excellence*, New York: Harper & Row.

Pirsig, R.M. (1976) *Zen and the Art of Motor Cycle Maintenance*, London: Corgi Books.

Plato (trans.) F.M. Cornfield (1944) *The Republic*, London: Oxford University Press.

Pollitt, C. (ed.) (1992) *Considering Quality: an Analytic Guide to the Literature on Quality and Standards in the Public Services*, London: Centre for the Evaluation of Public Policy and Practice, Brunel University.

Prabhu, V. and Lee, P. (1990) 'Implementing Total Quality Management (TQM)', *Teaching and Learning Bulletin*, Newcastle Polytechnic, Issue 3 (March).

Pring, R. (1992) 'Standards and quality in education', *British Journal of Education* 40(1) (Feb.).

Rock, M. (1992) 'Twists and turns on Quality Street', *The Director* (Dec.).

Sallis, E. (1993a) 'Pursuing excellence', *Managing Schools Today* 2(6).

—— (1993b) *Total Quality Management in Education*, London: Kogan Page.

Sallis, E. and Hingley, P. (1991) 'College quality assurance systems', Mendip Papers, Blagdon: Coombe Lodge.

Sallis, E. *et al.* (1992) 'Total quality management', *Coombe Lodge Report* 23(1).

Samuel, G. (1993) 'Customised approach', *Education* (21 May).

Scholtes, P.R. (1988) *The Team Handbook: How to Use Teams to Improve Quality*, Madison, WI: Joiner Associates.

Silver, H. (1992) *Student Feedback: Issues and Experiences*, London: Council for National Academic Awards.

Smith, A.K. (1993) 'Total Quality Management in the public sector', *Quality Progress* (July).

Sommerville, A. (1993) 'TQM in practice', *Newscheck with Careers Service Bulletin* 3(7) (May).

Sparkes, J. (1993) 'First define your goal, then set about achieving it', *The Higher* (5 Feb.).

Stephenson, J. and Weil, S. (eds) (1992) *Quality in Learning*, London: Kogan Page.

Sutcliffe, W. and Pollock, J. (1992) 'Can the Total Quality Management approach used in industry be transferred to institutions of higher education?', *The Vocational Aspect of Education* 44(1).

Taylor, L. (1993) Address, no papers, to the 1993 British Deming Association.

Times Higher Education Supplement (1993) 'A vision for the 21st century', Editorial (6 Aug.).

—— (1993) 'Charting the way to quality', Editorial (11 Dec.).

Trades Union Congress (1992) *The Quality Challenge: a TUC Report on the Trade Union Response to Quality in Public Services*, London: Congress House, TUC.
Tysome, T. (1991) 'Ministers warned off "kite-mark" for colleges', *Times Higher Education Supplement* (12 July).
Walkin, L. (1992) *Putting Quality into Practice*, Cheltenham: Stanley Thornes.
Walley, P. and Kowalski, E. (1992) 'The role of training in total quality implementation', *Journal of European Industrial Training* 16(3).
Watkin, P. (1993) 'Japanization and the management of education in Australia', *International Journal of Educational Management* 7(2).
West-Burnham, J. (1992) *Managing Quality in Schools*, London: Longman UK.

2 The consumer paradigm in public management

Sue Richards

Who defines the public good? Who decides who gets what, when, where and how? Who makes the crucial decisions that turn an infinite number of demands for service into a manageable number of legitimate needs to be met? These have always been difficult questions to answer, since they are concerned with concepts which are, in their nature, elusive. But they are especially important questions for public managers, since the evidence seems to point to significant changes taking place in the 'rules of the game' governing public service management.

Who has the legitimate right to exercise power over the key issues about the priorities which are set for resource use? We might have known the answer to that question in the past. There was some agreement about what those rules were for a long period in the post-war state when each of the key participants understood the boundaries around their own domain and the limitations of their scope to affect the world outside that domain. Experience tells us that the 'pattern' has changed and continues to change. We see politicians urging managers to break into existing patterns of professional practice in order to reduce costs. We see consumers being used by managers to assist them in breaking into the professional domain. We see professionals and other producer interests courting consumers in order indirectly to influence the decisions about resource allocation which politicians make.

It is a confusing picture of changing patterns of behaviour, of informal and emergent rules, and of shifting power plays. I shall try to clarify that confusion, and to explore the changes so that managers and other practitioners of public management may be assisted in their understanding, and so that a wider public may have better access to these changes. I shall do that initially through the development of our conceptual model, and then by testing the model by linking it to the world of practice.

The next sections of this chapter crystallize the key features of these changes in three related paradigms. This is not intended as an historical account of the changes, although we can illustrate the meaning by historical examples that occur in different public services. Three paradigms are outlined: a public administration paradigm, an efficiency paradigm, and an emergent consumer paradigm, the last of these being a tentative formulation based on what seems not to be emergent practice.

THE PUBLIC ADMINISTRATION PARADIGM

The public administration paradigm developed during a period of steady growth and incremental change in public service. After the foundations of the welfare state had been laid in the post-war period, there followed a time of steady growth in public expenditure and a broad consensus about how welfare expenditure should be allocated. Both the formal rules of engagement between the participants in the governance of public service and the behaviour patterns which developed illustrated a gradual incrementalist, negotiated order. No battle was so crucial that it had to be fought to the death, since the changes were that if you lost out this year you might win next year. By current standards spending levels were not high, but the expectations of public service were also lower, and there were usually enough new resources so that the money for new projects could be found without having to cut back on other spending.

Figure 2.1 Key domains within the public administration paradigm and the sources of legitimacy on which they draw for support

Figure 2.1 illustrates the key domains within the public administration paradigm and the sources of legitimacy on which they draw for support. Elected politicians, and those officials who work as their immediate assistants, draw on the electoral mandate given to them by citizens. Although the actual democratic process may be imperfect, election conveys the right to make decisions on behalf of the community of citizens.

In this paradigm, no distinction is made between consumer, elector and citizen. The roles are not differentiated. Accountability flows upwards from public service producers to political leaders and through them to the electorate. Accountability for a particular public service therefore becomes entangled in the wider processes of political accountability and then almost inevitably gets lost. If a ministerial resignation is the only penalty for a service failure, the chances are that the penalty will not be paid, the lessons will not be learned and the failure will be repeated.

The second key domain is the producer domain. Legitimacy in this domain comes from the possession of expert knowledge which is essential to the service production process. Turning broad policy objectives into specific instructions which guide the actual behaviour of staff in relation to the service at the point of delivery, and going through all the stages in between, is a highly complex process. This complexity enables service staff to influence what will be done, and almost invariably shifts intended outcomes. This is particularly the case where professional staff are involved.

Many public service producers are professionals – self-regulating, endorsed by society, with a delegated right to control entry and to set standards of conduct and, through custom and practice in the public administration paradigm, to influence public service policy. They do this both at the policy formulation stage and through the implementation cycle. Public service professionals usually do not see themselves as mere technicians, willing to supply their skills within whatever service purposes are defined by politicians. They promote professional values and subscribe to their own definition of public purpose.

The occupants of the producer domain, particularly those with professional status, promote the values associated with their knowledge and expertise. The occupants of the political domain promote the values of their political programme. They are brought together through the integrative role of the administrator; hence the label applied to this paradigm.

The administrator has the role of negotiating the common ground of disputed value territory. Administrators keep the show on the road, settle disputes and make things happen. Although not necessarily neutral in value terms, there is an essential disengagement from the battle to define purpose. The administrator role exists to deliver the best workable compromise between two powerful domains. Administrators in the public administration paradigm are driven by process values rather than purpose.

Illustrations

The public administration paradigm is not historically bounded. It is the essence of a mode of operation which, in some services, still exists today but whose full flowering was in the period of steady welfare expenditure growth of the 1950s and 1960s.

- In the NHS, the hospital or district administrator worked through consensus management to achieve agreement on direction for the service in question.
- The administrative class in the higher Civil Service possessed high skill levels as fixers of agreements between the participants in public services, handling the ambiguities which ease the making of agreements (although the ambiguity may get in the way of clarity at the implementation stage).
- The town clerk role in local government was conceptualized as a mediator of the forces that play from the political and producer domains. Even when the title was changes to 'chief executive', the role content in practice often stayed the same.

• In higher education, leading professionals succeeded in dominating the definition of purpose, constrained on cost grounds by politicians, and assisted by an administrative structure which had essentially a support role.

THE EFFICIENCY PARADIGM

The political and economic base on which the public administration paradigm rested began to shift, and these factors explain the development of a new set of game rules, the efficiency paradigm. In the 1970s, the UK economy was rapidly being exposed as internationally uncompetitive, but the public administration paradigm was predicated on the availability of public expenditure growth. Increased spending was what facilitated the gentlemen's agreement that is at the core of the paradigm. But projections of expenditure growth to meet perceived need were based on unrealistic assumptions about the capacity of the economy. Public expenditure growth therefore came to be seen as a major problem.

Although it took a number of years for the impact to percolate through the whole public sector, the watershed date was the IMF crisis of 1976. Anthony Crosland's comment on the implications for public spending of those events – 'the party is over' – perhaps best encapsulates the notion of a turning point for public services Assumptions of steady growth and fair shares for all were put under pressure. Faced with this situation, cuts in public spending were almost inevitable, whatever the ideology of the government in power. The government in question, however, brought in a package of policies aimed not only at reducing public spending but also at extracting much greater efficiency from the public spending which did occur.

In these economic and political circumstances, the public administration paradigm was dislodged by the new efficiency paradigm. The driving force was the need to reduce public expenditure and to get better value for money for the expenditure which remained. Instead of being content to accept the negotiated outcomes of existing resource decision processes, one set of actors, central government politicians, sought to shift the previous balance of powers within the public domain so that their requirements for reduced spending would be more clearly met. A key assumption was the proposition that public sector organizations tend to be inefficient because, lacking the discipline of competition, they succumb to the producer interest. Where possible, therefore, the remedy was to apply market disciplines to provide a counter-pressure. Where market disciplines were difficult to mobilize, direct pressure from the top of the organization was used to establish a new order. Instead of the administrator negotiating common ground between two powerful domains, the administrator role was transformed into a managerial role to exert pressure on the producer domain to yield greater efficiency.

Figure 2.2 illustrates the nature of the efficiency paradigm. The paradigm focuses on the creation and development of an integrative role that is managerial rather than administrative, a role which those in the political domain would find an effective instrument for delivering higher efficiency.

Figure 2.2 The nature of the efficiency paradigm

The administrator's adeptness at negotiating workable compromises for incremental change became a less valuable quality. What was needed in these new circumstances was an integrator who would create a new order by shifting the balance of power between politicians and the producers of public service, the professionals and the other staff. If production was to be carried out more cheaply, managerial capabilities – the capacity to achieve purpose, deliver objectives and hit targets – were required to break into and change the standard operating procedures of production staff. Sometimes this would mean changing the pattern of labour use, sometimes a lowering of standards of service, but the purpose of the manager in the efficiency paradigm was to deliver politicians' objectives of lower spending and increased efficiency.

Illustrations

The period since 1979 yields many examples in practice of pressure to extract greater efficiency. Sometimes this pressure was exerted through the mechanisms of direct control, sometimes through market mechanisms, and sometimes through a combination of both. Market mechanisms often took time to put in place, so they were the chosen instruments of intervention only where central government did not directly control the public service in question. Where sectors of the public service were under the direct control of central government – the Civil Service and the NHS – ministerial directives were a more immediate means of initiating paradigm change.

- The creation and development of a managerial cadre within the Civil Service was a principal goal in Derek Rayner's work to change the culture of Whitehall. This was followed by the introduction of management planning and control systems in the Financial Management Initiative and by a management development initiative in the Top Management Programme which aimed at exposing top Civil Servants to the world of the private sector.
- In the NHS, the Griffiths general management initiative was the source of equally radical change. Organizations were restructured and roles were

redefined. Management development and training schemes accompanied these changes. The Resource Management Initiative and clinical budgeting which followed were similarly designed to transform the loose integrator role of the administrator into the corporate general manager, whose job was to define corporate purpose and achieve corporate results.

- In the case of local government, the pressure to reduce expenditure and deliver more efficiency was exerted partly through ministerial directive, in the various squeezes on central funding and requirements to cap local spending and reduce local taxation. However, although these may be effective weapons to pursue spending reductions, they are impossibly blunt instruments with which to generate efficiency gains. To the government of the day, market forces seemed to supply the necessary disciplines to promote productivity increases. They required services progressively to be put out to competitive tender – the application of the market mechanism. In some situations, where local political control came from the same part of the ideological spectrum as in central government, local political forces were driving in that direction anyway. In other situations, local government managers found themselves cross-pressured between central and local politicians, each with their own capacity to define purpose. The statutory and financial framework of local government, however, makes it nearly impossible to resist pressure from the centre, and local government, too, has been driven inexorably into the efficiency paradigm.

  The previous paragraph should be read in the light of local government's own cultural inheritance, and particularly in the light of earlier rounds of public service modernization not discussed in this chapter. The corporate management movement, the creation of the role of chief executive, the development of strategic policy units – the echoes could still be heard of earlier reforms aiming at a managerial rather than administrative paradigm, but much of it had run into the sand in the face of producer, particularly professional, resistance and political suspicion. The difference in the 1980s was the change in political economy. In government, too, the party was over. Becoming more managerial was no longer just the right thing to do: central government pressure made it a necessity.

- Higher education presents a different picture again. While politicians have been concerned about levels of funding, they have not in the past sought to direct activity. Higher education's administrative traditions are of weakness in the political domain and strength in the producer domain. The Jarratt Report of 1985 signalled a change, and the Education Reform Act 1988 provided levers for change in the then polytechnic and further education sector. Changing patterns of financial control, corporate status for polytechnics and the consequent creation of the chief executive role and, above all, the market forces that are unleashed by funding following students, all pushed higher education over the brink of the managerial efficiency paradigm, at a pace much faster than happened in the other cases discussed.

The story so far is of changed economic circumstances leading to the creation of a new efficiency paradigm for public services. This accounts for the major sea-changes observed in the public domain in the 1980s. However, we are currently observing phenomena which indicate that something else is happening. We may be witnessing the emergence of a new paradigm. It is these new phenomena, difficult to explain within the terms of the efficiency paradigm, that have provided the starting point and the inspiration for this project.

NEW PATTERNS, NEW PARADIGM?

Those who manage public services, and anyone observing that process, cannot help but be impressed by the rhetorical power of the 'customer' concept. It came to signify a positive shift in culture, and provided a justification for managers and producers to work together for a common purpose of improved quality of service. A concern for the customer seemed to appeal to older consumerist values in public service which were an inheritance from the public administration paradigm. At the same time, being customer-orientated was consistent with learning from the private sector, the best performing parts of which were market-driven rather than cost-driven.

The rhetorical significance of the customer was recognized in the launch of the Citizen's Charter. Central government sought a position for itself as defender of the 'little' customer against the big battalions of monopoly public service producers. Since the customer may not have the power to take his business elsewhere, a framework of charter regulation for minimum standards reinforces his voice by creating disciplines for performance. The Charter initiative came after much useful work to empower customers had already been begun in public services. None the less, the Citizen's Charter gives added weight to the recognition that performance should involve a focus on service outputs. The Charter is therefore further evidence in support of the argument that a customer-orientated management has been a development of some significance.

The purpose of this research project is to examine whether this development constitutes a paradigm shift as significant as that from public administration to efficiency. The map of this paradigm would look something like Figure 2.3, with managers holding three rather than two sets of relationships.

How do we explain the emergence of the customer? Does it signify shifting patterns from which a new paradigm is emerging to transform the efficiency paradigm? What does the practice we observe tell us about all of this? We suggest four factors which help to explain the presence of the customer on the legitimacy map as a player in a potential new paradigm.

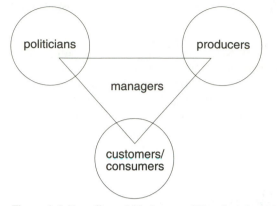

Figure 2.3 Paradigm shift from public administration to efficiency

1 *The unintended consequences of managerial efficiency*   'Do it like the private sector' became a watchword for many public service managers, propounded by central government ministers and others who were seeking efficiency. Much has been written elsewhere about how different the public domain is from the private sector. Although those arguments are intellectually powerful, we should not overlook the actual impact on managers of contacts with their private sector counterparts.

   Central government politicians may have intended that public service managers learn how to carry out the wishes of their political masters more efficiently, skilfully and entrepreneurially. But those who came into contact with the private sector observed an exhilarating world where hierarchy is (or should be, in an effective firm) tempered by markets as a legitimating principle, where actions are justified according to whether they deliver what customers want and are prepared to pay for, and thus lead to a healthy bottom line. The unintended consequences of greater contact may have been to import the private sector's market legitimation into the public domain, even though the economic foundations are different. This results in the customer becoming a legitimate contender to define the public good.

2 *Managing through markets*   In the efficiency paradigm, 'direct drive' through the organizational hierarchy and 'managing through markets' were twin approaches to pushing for increased efficiency. Where direct drive was possible, in the case of the Civil Service and the NHS, that was the approach initially taken. Local government, and later higher and further education, were primarily the target of market-orientated strategies, used in the absence of direct managerial control by central government. Over time, the balance between the two strategies has shifted, and market approaches have been extended. Both the NHS, through the White Paper agenda, and the Civil Service, through market testing, are now subject to the 'managing through markets' approach.

Much has been done – in the pursuit of efficiency – to allocate resources through markets, thereby mimicking the forces to which the private sector is subject. In perfect markets, firms which do not adequately serve customers cease to exist, and it is therefore clearly in the interests of those who direct such firms to ensure that customer interests are met. The perfect market is an abstract concept rather than an actuality, distorted in practice for a whole range of reasons, but the closer we approach it the more we are likely to find market-led behaviour. Markets in the public service are unlikely to approach perfection. Much more common is the 'quasi-market', where market-like mechanisms are in place, but within a highly regulated context.

In the quasi-market, resource allocation is through market-like processes, but the possibility of business failure, of the provider organization ceasing to exist – with the incentives for a customer-orientation which this imposes – is modified through politically authorized planning and regulating mechanisms. Locally managed schools, and the internal markets in the NHS and in higher education are examples of quasi-markets. Customer interest may be expressed either collectively through a purchasing authority or individually, but their choices make some direct impact on resource allocation amongst providers. In these circumstances, as in free markets, the customer plays as significant a role on the map as does manager, producer or politician.

3 *Leadership and cultural change*   In the 1980s, managers in both public and private sectors rediscovered leadership. The 'excellence' literature evoked the need to transcend the mechanistic models of management which had previously prevailed. Japanese success in delivering productivity and quality improvement in manufacturing provoked a diagnosis of western failings. The diagnosis focused on western tradition which neglects the organizational culture. Some gains in public sector efficiency could be made through cost-cutting exercises, but the big productivity opportunities were available only through developing an organizational culture which drove for performance improvement and where the values behind performance were embedded in the heart and minds of the members of the organization. Cultural change requires that old patterns of behaviour be challenged, and that a vision of the new culture be developed to seize the imagination and inspire staff to better things. In order to be really productive, organizations must serve values which go beyond productivity. Cost-cutting does not inspire, but service to the customer does.

Lessons from failed cultural change initiatives tell us that top managers must live the new values and vision if they are to stand any chance of convincing their staff to change. Appeals to customer service values which are made in a cynical fashion do not work to unlock the processes of cultural change. Staff see through them. The most they do is produce cynical compliance, lip-service to the new values which thinly disguises the failure to generate fundamental change. To be most effective, organizational leaders must believe in the vision and really live the values. In order to be effective at delivering real productivity improvements, and thus succeed in the efficiency paradigm, cultural change in public service needs to call on a genuine customer orientation; this, in turn, undermines the basis of the efficiency paradigm by empowering interests which may challenge the purposes defined by central government politicians.

4 *Consumerism*   The terminology in this chapter so far refers to 'customers'. Customers in the market have the power of the purse, and our argument suggests that the consumer in public services is newly empowered partly because of the power of the purse. This development converges with older public service traditions of consumerism, pre-dating the changes which underpin the efficiency paradigm. The new customer orientation was nourished by this older inheritance.

The practice of public services in the public administration paradigm was heavily influenced in its early phase by public service professionals. Their domain was unchallenged as standard operating procedures were developed in the early years of the welfare state. Consumers of those services were encouraged to believe that the professional knew best. But challenges to that orthodoxy were numerous, as it became clear that professionals sometimes do make mistakes – the dissatisfaction of local communities and their political representatives at the impact of professional planners and architects on urban renewal in cities, the disabling professionalism of some social work practice, campaigns against the medicalization of maternity, the rise of the welfare rights movement.

The aims of the welfare rights and community development movements were to assist the consumers of public services to take a more active role in the planning and delivery of those services. In seeking to empower consumers, they posed challenges to both the existing political and professional domains. Some community development was publicly funded and much of it was swept away during the 1970s, but the ideological legacy lingered on, part of the belief system of many public officials, but put on one side during unfavourable political times.

Perhaps the 'customer' of the efficiency paradigm offers a cloak of political respectability for consumer values which have a different set of political connotations. The existence of this older tradition helps to explain the alacrity with which the customer has been adopted. Managers who adhere to the older values of consumerism seek to incorporate them into current thinking. From this point in the chapter, we shall use the term 'consumer' rather than 'customer', to denote this complex 'merged' meaning.

Illustrations

The four factors described above suggest why the consumer has new significance, but more important is the behaviour we observe which indicates that a new paradigm is emerging. We see public service managers balancing local housing politicians against local housing tenants, who have been empowered in the 1980s as customers by significant changes in the statutory framework for social housing. We see general managers in health forcing professionals to ascribe a value to the time of consumers by introducing appointments systems. We see headteachers responding to the demands of parents and the market for school education, as funding begins to follow pupils – sometimes to the detriment of vulnerable children who took up more than their 'fair' share of resources in the past.

In the traditional public machine bureaucracy such as social security or employment services, where legitimacy comes top-down from the minister via top officials, the old producer culture delivered notoriously poor service, and is fundamentally challenged by a consumer-orientated approach. Managers seeking to deliver better service may use the (notional or actual) consumer as a means of empowering themselves to challenge the producer domain. They also challenge the political domain within which these producer practices have flourished. Ministerial agreement in principle may have been given for these changes, but ministers and their core department Civil Servants are in practice equally challenged by customer empowerment. Even in central government, managers espousing a consumer orientation may in effect be establishing *de facto* new rules for behaviour which differ from the old rules – public service managers through their practice creating a new paradigm?

The model in Figure 2.3, the 'triangle' model, focuses on a new dynamic in the pattern of relationships, through enabling us to conceptualize shifting patterns of alliance between the various actors. The eternal triangle of childhood friendships, which seem to weave endless variations on the idea of two against one, is a helpful metaphor. Figure 2.3 shows a pattern of three domains, or spheres of influence, with the triangle in the middle constituting the common ground on which purposive action is located. Our key questions in this project concern how public managers act to meet the challenges, pressures and opportunities that present themselves from what seem now clearly to be three – rather than two – sets of interests. The separate relationships which the public manager establishes with groups of politicians, producers/professionals and consumers (each of which, in themselves, will contain competing and conflicting interests) is the focus of study. How does the public manager balance all of these interests to produce effective and efficient social results?

This focus on the public manager does not imply that the other actors are less significant, only that the Public Management Foundation's agenda involves exploring the nature of public management. We will want to examine the kinds of managerial processes that are put in place and the kind of actions that are undertaken in order to engage and respond to the three sets of actors, particularly when faced with conflicts between the interests. Where the interests overlap, the direction of management action is relatively straightforward. What does the manager do when that is not the case, when consumers demand services different from those that the politicians they elect are prepared to fund, when consumers demand services that producers are not prepared to provide, or when professionals demand working conditions that are not in the interests of the consumers being served? How does the public manager go about creating common ground when none exists? What are the allegiances evoked and the alliances created in this situation? How, through compromise or negotiated settlement, does the manager create a triangle big enough to enable definitive actions to be taken to resolve conflict and to limit the further contesting of purpose?

The Citizen's Charter itself is an example of setting standards for the consumer which are straightforward enough to be comprehensible, thus enabling the consumer to exert pressure on producers and politicians to improve quality of service. Many managers would quarrel with the actual standards that are set, and particularly with the often inadequate means of redress available if standards are not met. None the less, power relationships are changed, consumers are empowered, and that has unpredictable consequences which need to be understood.

We see old behaviour patterns adapting to the empowered consumer's presence on the map, but the picture is not yet clear and needs further study and analysis. One particular element of this analysis is developed here. It is important in this analysis to disentangle the various elements of the consumer role, drawing in particular a distinction between the consumer as an actual or potential receiver of services, and the consumer as citizen, member of a community which seeks to govern itself. The next section of this chapter discusses these issues.

CONSUMERS AND CITIZENS

The emergence of the consumer creates ambiguities in role and challenges to old rules in the efficiency paradigm, and that ambiguity is an important facilitator of change. The ambiguity is further enhanced by the powerful rhetoric surrounding the notion of the consumer. There is a suspicion that the rhetoric may disguise actual reductions in service dressed up in the language of consumer empowerment. What seems to have happened is that apparent consumer empowerment to make individual choices that influence the service received, at the micro level, appear to have gone hand in hand with a reduction in the scope for influence at the macro level of public policy and management.

Public policy and the strategic management of public services, and the operational management of service provision, are increasingly separated.

In other paradigms, participants in the political and producer domains sought to influence both the formulation and the implementation of public service policy, albeit to differing degrees. A significant current development is the separation of that formerly unified territory into macro-level service policy activity, where the framework for public policy and management is set, and micro-level service provision activity, where service practice is set. Figure 2.4a illustrates how a matrix may be constructed with boxes for high and low involvement in macro- and micro-level issues.

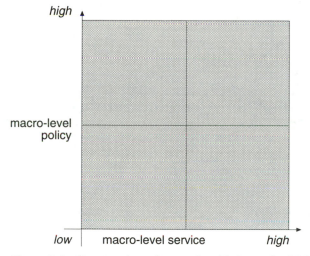

Figure 2.4a Construction of a matrix with boxes for high and low involvement in macro- and micro-level issues

Figure 2.4b (the same as Figure 2.4a, but with the actors from Figure 2.3 superimposed) shows a map with fewer occupants of the macro-policy space. We now see the consumer with high involvement in service practice issues, having moved from the bottom left to the bottom right, but necessarily still in the bottom half of the matrix. Consumers are empowered to be concerned with their own individual service experience. How housing estates are managed, how schools are run, whether individual out-patients appointments are made – in this emerging paradigm these are all available for consumers to influence. Consumers contend with service producers and operational managers about how the service will be provided.

Consumers are not empowered, however, to define the public good on whether assets received from council house sales shall be re-used for social housing, on what is taught in the National Curriculum, on the level of social security benefits or on the level of resources available for extra-contractual referrals in the NHS. Their emergence as a player on the legitimation map is confined to micro-level issues.

Producers, especially professionals, have in the past occupied the top right-hand box – high involvement in both macro- and micro-level issues.

Their involvement in the production of services led, especially in the case of professional producers, to considerable success in influencing macro issues. Professionals in education and health, for instance, have exercised much macro-level influence. The separation into purchaser and provider organizations makes it much less feasible to extend legitimacy from one box to another. Producers, including professionals, now find themselves increasingly relegated to micro territory. They also have to share their micro-level box with newly empowered consumers.

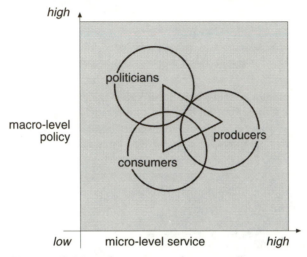

Figure 2.4b Map of occupants of macro-policy space

Producers have disappeared from the high macro level. Consumers do not enter this part of the map. Moreover, much has also happened under the efficiency paradigm to exclude some occupants of the political domain, politicians whose claim to legitimacy rests on the local electorate. In order to maintain central government control over public spending, more and more resources which would have been channelled through local authorities are now delivered through special purpose bodies which have no electoral legitimacy independent of central government. Urban development corporations and training and enterprise councils are two cases in point. The funding council for grant-maintained schools is another, which may replace the local education authority as the focus for the local co-ordination of school education.

Further changes have occurred whereby local authority representation on governing bodies has been removed. Corporate status in the higher and further education sector removes the (somewhat indirect) influence of local politicians on macro-level issues in that sector. With the abolition of the old District Health Authority, which included elected representatives, the direct influence of local politicians over macro-level issues concerning the health of local citizens was removed.

In practice, few of the cases quoted above were shining examples of democracy. Imperfect as the processes were, however, they left a gap. Consumer empowerment to enter only the micro level, the apparent expulsion of producers from the macro level, and the exclusion of sources of political legitimacy which compete with central government – all of these factors suggest that the involvement of citizens in the making of policy for managing public services has been reduced.

What does the public manager have to say about that? Some public managers may be relatively little affected by the reduction in scope for citizen involvement in macro-level issues. As strategic policy-making and operational delivery have been separated, so a delivery of orientation has opened up within public management. Public managers who are focused upon delivering public services to specified contract will concentrate on serving the needs of service consumers as set out in the terms of the contract, although they will also have an interest in how the next contract comes to be specified. But public managers working at the level of strategic service policy are vitally interested in involvement at the macro level, and we will be examining new ways of enhancing such involvement. We will call involvement at the macro level citizen 'empowerment', and distinguish it from consumer empowerment at the micro level. Just as we observe innovative practice to involve consumers at the micro level, similarly there appear to be interesting initiatives to empower citizen involvement at the macro level. Despite the formal reduction in their linkages to local political structures, some purchasing managers in health are seeking to consult citizens about the nature of their health-purchasing strategies. In local government, there are several examples of citizen involvement strategies which aim to involve people directly or indirectly in macro-level planning, thereby seeking to enhance local government's claim to govern on behalf of communities.

In this chapter, I started with the term 'customer', but found it necessary to change the word to 'consumer', in order to incorporate values which were antithetical to the efficiency paradigm. I find at this stage in the argument that we need to enrich the concept of 'consumer' with that of 'citizen', to go beyond the individual focus into the field of collective action. Public management, by definition, concerns the way in which public, collective decisions are made. Public management systems need to arrive at decisions in such a way that the actors involved regard them as binding on the collectivity. The public manager has to find a way of creating enough common ground – of persuading enough competing interests to enter the triangle – to allow definitive, binding decisions to be made. When is a decision not a decision? When powerful actors bend their energies to changing it rather than working with it. Government without consent cannot last.

The powerful dynamic for change expressed in the efficiency paradigm displaced the emphasis in the public administration paradigm on the engineering of consent, and this was justified by an overriding national purpose of improving performance and getting more efficiency. This concern for the processes of consent is an inheritance from the old public administration paradigm which has been submerged just as the efficiency paradigm, with its emphasis on performance, has become dominant. But the process whereby decisions are made affecting a collectivity, as opposed to a consumer, matters if the outcomes are to be acceptable. As a citizen, I may accept decisions that go against my interests if I believe they have been fairly resolved.

A NEW CONSUMER PARADIGM?

I have argued in this chapter that the governance of public services has been transformed and is being transformed. The public administration paradigm was challenged by the political and economic circumstances which led to the emergence of the efficiency paradigm, with its emphasis on getting more for less. The efficiency paradigm in turn seems not to be challenged, for reasons which are discussed in the chapter, by a move to incorporate a consumer focus. The new practice of public management suggests that a consumer orientation is taking hold and is shifting the balance of powers which had previously prevailed.

However, this is a tentative and preliminary conclusion. All that is clear is that this development needs to be investigated. We know that many participants in public management now use the language of consumer in their discourse, but we do not really know what difference that makes to practice and outcomes. What are the social results that emerge from a consumer paradigm? What difference does it make?

'Consumer' is a term which many people use. How they define it in practice is likely to vary. The consumers of public services may simply be defined as the immediate recipients of the service, rather like customers in the private sector. This definition would lead us to see the delivery of the service as a private transaction between service deliveries and recipients. For example, the nature of the service delivered to children by schools, under this definition, would be of concern only to schools and pupils and their parents. Or, there may be much broader definitions of consumer, to include the concept of citizen, whereby the interests of a much wider group play a part in the transaction. To use the education example again, how far is a consumer orientation being interpreted in practice in a way that takes note of the demands of the wider society? If this reference to education indicates polarities in definitions of the consumer, how is the line steered in practice between these two polarities?

ACKNOWLEDGEMENT

This chapter is the product of much discussion in the Public Management Foundation and in the Office for Public Management. It also owes a debt to Robert Maitland, former Principal of the Foundation. The development of this project has benefited from all of these contributions. Responsibility for the chapter, however, remains with the author.

3 Quality issues in higher education
A post-modern phenomenon?

M.J. Harrison

The theme of this chapter is the changing, and increasingly paradoxical, nature of the relationship between the state and higher education. The 'quality debate' in higher education is best understood within these changing, contradictory relationships. Although the debate about quality in higher education is international, as is the changing nature of the relationship between the state and higher education, the precise relationship between government and higher education in the United Kingdom enjoys some peculiarly British charactistics – peculiar, because of a prior historical situation in which the universities, to a degree unique by European standards, enjoyed an almost total autonomy from the state. They were, in a sense, publicly funded private corporations. Comparative European measures of participation suggest that the move towards a mass system of higher education is bound to have a profoundly radical and traumatic impact on these uniquely British institutional arrangements for the delivery of higher education. This explains the frequency with which the term 'crisis' is used to describe the condition of British universities (Peters 1992: 123–5).

Neave describes these general movements thus:

> at times of change, when the dynamics of institutional development are being shifted to external society, whether that external society is defined in terms of the 'consumer ethic' or by the reinforced control, *direct or indirect* [emphasis mine], of government, the essential nature of the previous contract becomes revealed by dint of departing from it as well as by the introduction of new norms.
>
> (Neave 1990: 113)

In the United Kingdom both government and the major opposition parties are firmly committed to the attainment of a *mass* system of higher education. It is the profundity of the break with 'the previous contract' that engenders a marked crisis mentality (Peters 1992) within British higher educational institutions.

Again Neave (1985) highlights the radical departure from the past that this new vision of mass higher education engenders with his description of the post-Robbins expansion up to 1985:

The British move toward mass higher education extended elitist criteria to the non-elite sector of polytechnics and colleges of higher education, thus giving rise to a far greater degree of homogeneity in patterns of access between different sectors – university and non-university – than had ever existed. In short, mass higher education in Britain was elite higher education written a little larger.

(Neave 1985: 350)

The current vision of mass higher education is not only of a vast increase in the size and scale of provision but also contains an officially sanctioned call for institutional differences in provision – that is to say, a pluralism of mission and function. This is, indeed, a radical break with the past.

Martin Trow, commenting, from an American point of view, on the British degree and the romantic obsession with standards, wrote in 1987:

Underlying all these beliefs and sentiments, broadly held among British academics but also civil servants and politicians, to the effect that this degree, wherever offered and awarded, should be of high quality and roughly common value. In this respect the British degree is, so to speak, still on the gold standard.

(Trow 1987: 274)

and again: 'One thing that such a commitment precludes is *wide diversity in the system*' (Trow 1987: 276).

The theme of this chapter is the puzzle presented by a simultaneous political commitment to a mass access, pluralistic system of higher education together with a similar commitment towards the maintenance of quality in the image cast by traditional elitist concepts of standards. This is the peculiarly British angle on the changing relationship between the state and higher education.

The terms of reference, for example, of the original cross-binary pilot exercise in quality judgements required that its agents report upon *both absolute and relative* quality and standards. This reveals the current 'quality debate' to be both enigmatic and perplexing. I would claim that insights gleaned from post-modern theorizing allow us at least to situate this puzzle. They also contain some common themes which are of relevance to the general debate which surrounds the quality and delivery of the public services across the board.

Peter Scott (1991b) describes this quintessentially post-modern relationship between public institutions and the wider society thus:

As knowledge, and inevitably the institutions through which it is realised, become more *central* to the mechanism of post-industrial economy, of an 'information society', of a democratic culture, it is inevitable that the old demarcations between it, and them, and this economy, society and culture will be worn away.

(Scott 1991b: 12)

Indeed, in my view, it is the ambivalence of this ever-changing relationship, its paradoxical nature, in which the state increases its powers of accountability over public bodies yet divests itself (or attempts to) of the responsibility for funding their activities (for example, introduction of student loans) that needs to be explained. The state invents new agencies of control and then distances itself from them. It is this restless busyness, this ambivalent process of relinquishment and renewal that require explanation.

Neave describes these changes in either/or terms. He defines this changed state/higher education relationship as being either the 'consumer ethic' or 'reinforced direct or indirect control'. It is my view that all these types of control are advancing simultaneously. This restless process of retreat and advance, of creation of and distancing from new control agencies, is a direct consequence of the ambivalent impact of post-modern conditions upon the state/university relationship. Mass higher education is such a radical departure for Britain that the new relationships of state and higher education have their own unique characteristics.

Since this is basically an essay upon changing patterns of social control, I want to look at one of the key institutions for the maintenance of standards that has accompanied the expansion in higher education since the 1960s. This serves as a particular example of the resituating of the state/public service relationship in the context of movement from modern to post-modern social arrangements. It also serves to highlight the 'peculiarly' British assimilation of these broader societal forces.

Both Neave and Trow describe the post-Robbins expansion as one that remained fundamentally elitist. Their observations characterized the post-Robbins phase of expansion as a quantitative expansion of the elitist (gold standard) system. The recent celebration of a mass pluralistic system based upon diversified institutions marks a profound break with these 'gold standard' models of the past.

The example is that of the Council for National Academic Awards (CNAA). The CNAA had a charter that required that its awards be 'comparable to those of the Universities'. It has been the major agency for validating courses and accrediting institutions in the public (Local Authority, National Advisory Body/Polytechnics and Colleges Funding Council) sector up to the recent elimination of the binary line. It also provides an excellent example of the control machinery used to contain expansion within an essentially elitist, gold standard, framework described by both Trow and Neave.

I want to use some of the insights provided by the French historian of ideas, Michel Foucault. Foucault's massive works were an exploration of the big ideas that were created during the Enlightenment and have been extended, modified and expanded into typically modern cultural formations. As such they were concerned with the unique joining of the absolutist state and the political economy of early capitalism that formed the 'modern'. 'Foucault was always one for rendering the familiar strange. He was also one to engage in the relentless pursuit of understanding the strangeness that he discovered behind the mask of familiarity' (Hoskins 1990: 29). Hoskin claims to have unearthed a simple, but hidden, theme in Foucault's work: namely, that he was a closet historian of education – a crypto-educationist unmasked!

One of Foucault's recurrent themes was the social construction of *discipline*. Hoskin claims that throughout Foucault's diverse works, ranging from the creation of academic subjects to the formation of prisons, there lay a prolonged discourse on discipline. Interwoven with this was a hidden concern with the crucial role of education in shaping the contemporary world, the world we construe as distinctly *modern*.

Foucault's over-arching insight was the impossibility of uncoupling, historically or conceptually, power and knowledge. Hoskin (1990) argues that the very ambiguity of the notion of discipline – its double meaning – provides the key to Foucault's covert educational preoccupations. Discipline, on the one hand, is a distinct body of knowledge such as philosophy or physics. Discipline, on the other hand, is concerned with the sphere of power, military regulation, sexual restraint, classroom conformity. The very etymology of the term is, according to Hoskin, derived from a preoccupation with getting 'learning' into the child. The two sides of the knowledge/power coupling. 'Panopticon the "all-seeing eye" of surveillance which is also a judgment, does not even have to be looking to make one feel watched. The micro-technology of Panopticon combines the deployment of force and the establishment of truth' (Foucault 1977).[1]

CNAA was just a power/knowledge system, a custodian, a pacifier, a maker of docility through *examination*. The discipline of the CNAA system was one of packaging and legitimating knowledge by way of power.

The early days of Council were dominated by university members making their pupils docile through the *examination*, the written document, scrutinizing their performance by way of the oral interrogation and, as they became imbued with discipline, allowing them into their ranks as peers. Tested, examined and purged of ill-discipline, the examined became the inquisitor. External peer review gave way to accreditation. Internally managed peer review for mature institutions turned the gaze inward. The pupil had internalized the discipline and progressed to maturity.

The persistent image in CNAA reports was one of steady *progress* toward increased *maturity*. Accreditation, an important step for the now almost 'mature' corporate body, signified the progress away from infantile, ill-disciplined mind/body functions. The parent can 'die' once the children have internalized the standards of maturity and progress. The colonizer can return to the metropolis once the natives have been made docile, educated into the ways of civilization – disciplined, in the sense of organizing knowledge into acceptable, measured and, above all, examinable and *standardized* packages. Disciplined, here, means being able to perform self-controlled replications of the appropriate drills, eventually applying self-correction towards the appropriate contours of knowledge. Power and knowledge can now be self-administered, within the subjective space of the mature/adult institution. Panopticon, the all-seeing eye, the machinery of self-administered peer review, is now part of the corporate independent body. The examination is now passed, the sentence discharged, the child matured, the patient cured, the native made civilized. It could be said that the CNAA was one of the last great acts of colonial administration, one of the last truly modern triumphs of the belief in universal progress.[2]

If all is progress and maturity, why now this external pressure for scrutiny, accountability and quality control?

The early history of the CNAA was dominated by university academics, who themselves (apart from the ubiquitous British system of external examiners) lacked any clear system of validation, formalized peer review or quality control. They, in the minds of officialdom, had a monopoly over the means of conducting legitimate academic discourse. They had the credentials to conduct the examination, the maturity to administer the disciplines (both knowledge and power) that constituted the early CNAA. They and the CNAA officers virtually 'invented' a new academic panopticon. Let me make several comments here:

1 CNAA was a 'panopticon' for quality assurance in public sector higher education invented by full-time officers and university academics. 'In the past whilst polytechnics were under a quite rigorous regime the universities were almost free to *determine their own standards* (Kogan 1991: 85). It was in order to examine, test and provide discipline for expanding, local authority-administered mass higher education providers that university academics, used to a tradition of self-administered standards and collegiate government were employed. Their own types of collegiate government, in Foucault's terms, resembled pre-Enlightenment means of social control – control by interpersonal familiarity, observation by proximity, a form of social control appropriate to a village community or a monastic order. The very fear of mass higher education institutions and their lack of 'traditions' in controlling standards made this new form of panopticon necessary.[3]

2 Only recently has quality control become an issue for the 'traditional' universities:

> the universities were first impelled – reputed by the threat of the introduction of inspectors (HMI) – into the assessment of their teaching and to create an Academic Audit Unit which would evaluate universities' own procedures for the assessment of teaching.
>
> (Kogan 1991: 85)

3 It is precisely because most of the 'traditional' universities are now unambiguously required to be mass higher education providers that they are being forced into a common system of 'three-tiered quality control' and assessment. The three-tiered nature of the system is an essential

ingredient for a full-blown panopticon in higher education. Internal quality assurance systems, evaluated by external audit, are capped by a judgemental apparatus linked to the funding agency. The all-seeing external eye, buttressed and operationalized by the internal gaze, with examination and categorization by external 'peers' is the final outcome. It is not surprising, since this system resembles the audit practices of industry and commerce, the regulation of prisons, and the administration of social security by the state, that lay members of governing bodies and the funding council have a crucial role as mediators, as ombudsmen. They are the chosen means for regulating 'panopticon' within the academic system.

The necessity for panopticon is then two-fold:

(a) Mass institutions require panopticon because of their very *mass quality*. Administration of elitist institutions is best left to the elites themselves. Given the close interpenetration of the elite universities and the higher echelons of government and Civil Service, this self-government was achieved by way of resemblance. The management and control of mass institutions – the surveillance of the masses – requires an 'ordering', a scrutiny and examination by 'external' *authority*. Thus, whilst 'there has been a trend towards internal systems of quality assurance and control in which the institution has primary responsibility for the quality of the courses that it offers', this has been accompanied by a 'parallel pressure on higher education institutions to make their quality assurance systems more explicit and open in the interests of public accountability' (Burrows *et al*. 1992: 9).

The problem is that the source of such external authority under conditions of post-modernism is eroded and the administration of the post-modern university bedevilled by systematic pluralism. It is no coincidence that it is the 'resilience of pluralism' that is defined by theorists of post-modernism as *the* outstanding characteristic of contemporary society.

(b) Universities continue to be funded primarily from public sources. Hence 'pressure for improved accountability for the use of public funds has also led to increased emphasis on demonstrating that the outcomes of higher education are appropriate' (Burrows *et al*. 1992: 9.

Like the recipients of welfare in the consumer society, the public services, which cannot or will not be privatized, are not fully amenable to the blandishments of seduction. They therefore require a strong element of its twin – repression. Repression requires surveillance, categorization, measurement and examination. Like those in receipt of welfare, they – the publicly funded – cannot be trusted. They both share the common characteristic of not being totally integrated into the disciplines of the market. ' "Seduction's" twin "repression" is reserved for those unwilling or unable to conform to full market disciplines – the "diminished" consumer' (Bourdieu 1984). Douglas Hurd made the following observation: 'Under

Margaret Thatcher, two strategic decisions were rightly taken – not to privatise either health or education. So reform is within the framework of public services' (Hurd 1992: 6).

Post-modernist theories' most significant discovery about the nature of the past two decades has been the self-perpetuating and self-reproducing capacity of *consumer culture*: the discovery of the supreme resilience and superb ability of market-based, information-centred societies to reproduce themselves without recourse to policing and surveillance. It is the capacity of the consumer market to make the consumer dependent upon itself that is the ultimate source of this stability. It is those who are least incorporated within the market and least amenable to market seductions that require the examining eye – the public services and the recipients of welfare!

Consumer dependence develops along the following lines:

> first new commodities make the necessary chores that much easier, and then the chores become too difficult to do unaided. . . . The private car, together with the running down of public transport, carves up the town no less effectively than saturation bombing, and creates distances that can no longer be crossed without a car.
>
> (Haug 1986: 53–4)

Market dependence also arises with the progressive destruction of social skills – the 'other' serves as a tool for self-authenticity. Stability, intimacy and permanence are always *conditional* upon the individualized search for 'authenticity'.

> This is the social void easily filled by the market. Unable to cope with the challenges and problems arising from their mutual relations, men and women turn to marketable goods, services and expert counsel; they need factory-produced tools to imbue their bodies with socially meaningful 'personalities', medical or psychiatric advice to heal the wounds left by previous – and future defeats.
>
> (Bauman 1987: 164)

The market is then the major means of social integration, solidarity and legitimacy. This has a series of correlates, including a marked decline in the interest of the state in controlling ideologies of legitimation, even in requiring ideological conformity (beliefs in core values). Party politics become an attempt to convince the electorate, by means of the marketing apparatus, who is the best able to service the market efficiently and provide higher levels of consumer satisfaction.

Higher education, however, in an information-based/knowledge-relevant, post-industrial society is not just a consumer good but is part of the very *infrastructure* of production that services the market. It is simultaneously an object to be consumed (and part of the consumers right to have access to it), yet an inextricable part of the production process.

The goal for the university becomes its optimal contribution to the best performance of the social system. The goal demands the creation of two kinds of skill indispensable to the maintenance of the social system: those necessary to enhance competitiveness in the world market and those necessary for fulfilling the need for its internal cohesion.[4]

(Peters 1989: 103)

It was obviously one of the key decisions, according to Douglas Hurd, of the Thatcher years *not* to privatize – not to place responsibility for higher education provision onto the market. Added to this was a perceived need to see radical expansion (mass provision) as a necessary condition for the enhancement of national competitiveness.

It is inevitable that if the state remains the major paymaster for higher education it will require greater accountability from those in receipt of its largesse. It is also true that if elite institutions, based upon collegiate self-governance or, as Vught (1991) describes it, government by committee, become *mass* institutions, control will have to come increasingly from outside and extrinsic criteria will become the measure. Not only is there economic necessity behind accountability but social need to control a mass activity, a mass activity to some degree autonomous from the direct, seductive reach of the market. Higher education is a mass activity that is no longer amenable to elitist, collegiate self-government. If elite higher education is suited to self-governing elites (and implicit means of quality assurance) (Burrows 1992: 3), mass higher education is suited to its alternative – panopticon!

In 1984, Sir Keith Joseph declared that the principal objectives for higher education should be quality and value for money. He was then defining the long-term, contorted mission for mass higher education. In so doing he established an agenda for the public services as they were forced to become reconciled with post-modern conditions.

The post-modern economy and society is a market entity. Unlike *modern* socio-economic formations, the key principles of the *post-modern* era are:

1 the triumph of consumption over production;
2 the increased salience of consumer satisfaction over work discipline;
3 a reduction in the importance of economic organization compared with consumer orientations. This has consequences for the operations and scope of the state.

Since social cohesion, discipline and social legitimacy are largely provided by the market, the importance of engineering legitimacy and compliance diminishes as a key state function. Save for those who are 'bad' consumers – the recipients of welfare – and 'bad' producers – those whose activities are funded by public funds – social cohesion is provided by the market mechanisms of 'seduction'.

In present-day society, consumer-conduct (consumer freedom geared to the consumer market) moves steadily into the position of simultaneously, the cognitive and moral focus of life, the integrative bond of the society, and the focus of systematic management. In other words, it moves into the self same position which in the past – during the 'modern' phase of capitalist society – was occupied by work in the form of wage labour. *This means that in our time individuals are engaged (morally by society, functionally by the social system), first and foremost as consumers rather than as producers.*

(Bauman 1992: 49; emphasis mine)

and again:

With the skill of shopping paramount, the certainty which counts most and promises to compensate for all other (absent) certainties, is one related to buying choices. Fashion, supported by the *statistics of other people's choices*, offers such certainty. One buys 'Whiskas' with less fear of personal inadequacy once one knows that out of ten cats six prefer it to all others.

(Bauman 1987: 165–66; emphasis mine)

It is hardly surprising that the nature of quality control in higher education should increasingly resemble, reflect and internalize these key features of the post-modern era. If statistics suggest that six out of every ten students prefer Wrottersly Polyversity, then one can have confidence in one's own choice and in the integrity of that institution!

Mass higher education is an inherently democratic concept. But it is the democracy of the market place. The state, with the objective of providing for the enhanced labour requirements of post-industrial production, and the function of reproducing sufficiently discriminating (educated) consumers, must encourage increased participation in higher education. But it is to individuals as *consumers* that the appeal must be made. The supply of those willing to enter higher education, should it be made a fully private good or service, would never be equal to the demands of industry, commerce and the professions for 'players capable of acceptably fulfilling their roles at the pragmatic posts required by institutions' (Lyotard 1984: 48). Since it is clear that industry itself is not willing to pay the price for this increased participation the state must remain *the* main source of funding. The state, in a post-modern society, has, however, surrendered much of its past powers of direction and control which were *unmediated* by the *market*. As described previously, there is within the state apparatus a *reducing significance of legitimation*, which means a declining interest in providing political and ideological systems for its own and wider societies' reproduction. Hence the state will attempt to distance itself from being seen to exert direct control over the resources of provision or from direct responsibility for the nature of that provision. The strategy the state will adopt will inevitably involve:

1 the creation of a market-like appearance for all publicly provided and subsidized entities;
2 the invention of a market-like language to describe public service provision.

The consumers of higher education must make informed choices. Yet there are no market signals (prices) to allow them to do so. Hence the state creates a quasi-market, a substitute set of market signals via an apparatus of quality assessments, league tables and performance indicators.

In short, since Leviathan cannot privatize higher education, and like the poor, homeless and destitute, higher education remains a burden upon the provident taxpayer, it requires an 'internal' market, a simulated set of market signals, to determine its funding and to structure consumer preferences. Market testing is not just a fashionable political ideology but a vocalization of the only language-game the state is capable of playing.

Post-modernism's 'persistent pluralism', its inherent lack of moral authority or consensus concerning agreed standards as to the nature of superiority and inferiority, forces the state, in the absence of a real market, to create an apparatus of quality control and monitoring which simulates market-*like* conditions, signals and languages.

The state must also attempt to dissociate itself from the *direct* political and the ideological function of defining and, above all, administrating quality control and quality judgements. Ideally, the apparatus of quality judgement – the panopticon – will be self-administered surveillance and control. Hence those who argue that the state is increasing its direct powers over the academic community misunderstand the dilemmas of control facing the post-modern polity. Whilst it is true that the state is exerting greater control over the administration of higher education than has been the case in the past, the 'executive state thesis' fails to explain why the state uses intermediary, mediating bodies such as HEFC and Quality Audit to exert this control on the state's behalf.

If the 'All Seeing Eye of the Prince' (Neave 1986: 168) is making a take-over bid to control the universities and undermine academic freedom, why did the state not insist upon HMI, already a direct arm of the state apparatus, being the new panopticon for the administration and surveillance of quality? As the state apparatus seeks to dissociate itself from involvement in issues and terrains of actual or potential ideological conflict and control, it disbands HMI and encourages by threat and incentive (market seductions) the new amalgamated higher education sector to develop its own monitoring systems for quality audit and judgement. A parallel move is the desire to 'privatize' the Schools Inspectorate. This arms'-length approach is not a function of irresponsibility, liberal concern for academic freedom or, even, negligence. It is inherent in the post-modern condition. Ministers are required to have views, opinions and ideologies. However, direct involvement in the ideologies of educational control has the unhappy consequence of being blamed for outcomes! Therefore, experts should always be responsible for determining the content and evaluating the quality. When one group of experts fails to confirm the current, and ever-changing, prejudices of government, then get rid of them and get another, more ideologically sound grouping! 'Quangos' are inherent in the post-modern condition. The power of the purse is the ultimate sanction of the state, but the conduct of 'debate' should be enshrined in expertise. Since intellectual expertise – like all things – is available on the market, then fashion will always produce the legitimating expert. Furthermore, fashion itself is rife in pluralistic, educational circles, and the state can ill afford to become over-identified with these fleeting changes – changes which work at different tempos from those of government.

The 'traditional' ideology of university education was 'not to make financial control a vehicle for either administrative or academic control by central government' (Neave 1985: 347). This hands-off approach was appropriate to the management of elitist institutions by elites. The current use of quangos is not an extension of this traditionalism.

The complexity and post-modernity of the universities themselves militate against direct ministerial/political interference. A further reason for the removal of HMI from the higher education quality game lies, then, in the nature of the universities themselves as vanguards of post-modernism.

Before moving towards analysis of the condition of the university and its own processes of knowledge production, we need to look at the nature of ideology and ideological thought in the passing universe of the modern.

Bauman (1992) summarizes the predominantly modernist ideologies, which stress unitary systems, rationalist consensus, as *monophilic*:

> 'Monophilia' is marked by the belief in a simple and essentially atemporal world (or at least an essential reducibility of the world to simple factors and indivisible units), by the conviction that the 'proper world' can be constituted by a thorough *application of one dominant and decisive standard*, and that extraordinary rupture of continuity originated and managed by a condensed effort of will ('belief in miracles') may secure the passage from *one class of uniform phenomena to another*.
>
> (Bauman 1992: 84; emphasis mine)

Monophilia is only sustainable when meta-narratives have credibility.

The debate concerning quality in higher education can be usefully seen as just such an attempt to impose a 'monological' view over such an 'extraordinary rupture', the 'rupture' being the movement from a restricted elite system of higher education towards a more open 'mass system'.

Let me just take one example. The CNAA (audit of quality assurance systems: feasibility study report, February 1992) publication on audit and quality assurance systems makes little mention of *standards* as a key issue. My reading of the document resulted in finding the word 'standards' once. This was a quotation from a parallel document published by the CVCP

(Academic Audit Unit, Annual Report of the Director 1990/91, January 1992). This latter document takes 'standards' as its central theme and mentions the word many times. Indeed, this pilot body's own terms of reference were to review 'the universities' mechanisms for monitoring and promoting the academic standards that are necessary for the achievement of their stated aims and objectives'. I do not believe that this difference is merely semantic. It is a result of quite distinctive, but inchoate, fundamental assumptions concerning the whole issue of quality and quality monitoring.

An English university academic commentator on the British system of quality monitoring observed, prior to the abolition of HMI: 'HMI is an estimable body, mainly consisting of able former teachers, with no record of judging research based teaching, and quite often recruited for qualities quite different from those prized by the most esteemed universities' (Kogan 1991: 86).

This suggests an identification of 'real' quality with the apparatus of research. Consequently, teaching quality and research are viewed as a couple. Only knowledge imbued with research ethics, and, given the paradigm of science, identified with 'big science' and hence big money and expensive equipment, would make it in his power/knowledge stakes![5]

The very nature of the contemporary university is knowledge production and management. The post-modern condition describes, however, a universe in which absolute values and, therefore, absolute notions of truth, beauty and excellence are redundant. Lyotard succinctly describes this post-modern condition as 'incredulity towards meta-narratives'. In this universe of moral relativism both 'standards' and 'quality' are themselves made relative. There is, however, a premium upon socially relevant knowledge and its dissemination.

In this moral vacuum where experts have diminished recourse to absolute notions of worth and quality, it is not surprising that the state distances itself from this terrain of discord and withdraws its own identifiable agents (HMI) from the fray. By putting the process of evaluation in the hands of 'experts', 'peers' and 'professionals' it creates its distance from and diminishes its responsibility for the nature of discriminations that must be made in the cause of public accountability. Since the acclaimed experts, the intelligentsia of academics, the self-chosen, are inherently 'elitist', selective, categorizing and hierarchical, they will inevitably try to diminish the wealth and worth of pluralism amongst and between institutions. They will, equally inevitably, meet with opposition and need to be replaced by other mechanisms of panopticon, peopled by new experts and recycled converts from the old, discredited regimes. In attempting to establish categorical absolutes of value eschewing the realities of persistent pluralims and institutional diversity they will sow the seeds of their own destruction. As did the CNAA. Quality control is a process of constant replacements of new cadres with ever-original market simulations, languages and icons.

It should be remembered that the post-modernist discourse arose out of the fields of aesthetics and art criticism. The post-modern solution to the 'crisis' in culture – the collapse of absolute values, of absolute criteria for truth and beauty and, indeed, of the central modernizing project of *progress* in art and architecture is the market.

'Modern art' (with its rejection of past traditions), cubist geometry, technological visions of futurism, surrealist flirtations with Freudian dream sciences, abstract enactments of psychoanalytic processes, were all premised upon future, Utopian visions of scientific order – an absolute aesthetic of *progress*.

Replacing this absolute aesthetic of progress is the market. 'It is enough if it works' – reviews, art galleries, exhibitions enable the consuming public to redefine what *is* art dynamically, as an ongoing negotiated process, rather than by some elite appeal to universal transcendental standards, whether these standards be traditional forms of classicism or scientific forms as in modernism.[6]

With this image in mind, let us turn to the internal pluralism and lack of absolute values and standards within the contemporary academic community. Peter Scott's (1991a) seminal analysis of 'The idea of mass higher education' points out the following paradox:

> Just when the university has become a more powerful centripetal institution the knowledge which is its chief commodity has become diffuse, opaque, incoherent, centrifugal. The process of disintegration, so marked in aesthetics in the first half of the 20th century, at any rate in the West, has carried over into the intellectual life in the century's final years.
>
> (Scott 1991a: 12)

This disintegration has three basic causes:

1 Subdivision into specialist sub-disciplines which undermines any notion of a coherent, broader intellectual culture.
2 Wider definitions of knowledge have become accepted. This, in turn is a result of the erosion of older ideas as to what is academically respectable, together with the impact of new technologies.
3 Post-modernism itself – deliberately decentred diversity, incoherence.

Also the widening of access to intellectual life, its possible democratization, make it increasingly impossible to talk of the wholeness or commonness of an intellectual culture.

Given, then, the persistent pluralism of post-modern forms and the heterogeneity of its institutions, the pursuit of 'pure' academic standards or absolute notions of academic quality become as futile as the pursuit of 'pure' socialism!

Where the state ceases either to engineer public legitimacy directly or accept legitimacy production as its (exclusive) or even necessary function, it will inevitably seek to distance itself from issues, institutions and themes where legitimacy is a central issue or potential problem. Since the sources of legitimacy are increasingly located in the arena of *market−consumer* relationships it is inevitable that the state will attempt to divest itself of responsibility for regulating, adjudicating and judging these relationships − even where it is forced to continue with the responsibility for paying for these potential theatres for discord and relativism!

The new multi-tiered regime of quality control and assessment is best peopled by academics since discrimination, critique and judgement is what, after all, they are good at! But they in turn must be constantly restratified and rehierarchized, since there is no permanent or absolute standard of quality to determine their enduring worth. They obviously cannot be trusted to people the system entirely, since 'going native' is one of the key dangers inherent in regimes of relativism and pluralism. Hence performance indicators, performance by objectives and lay governors must be supplemented by appraisal systems in an attempt to give '*objectivity*' to this morass of subjectivity.

Matthew Arnold (1963) defined the great educational project of discipline through high culture. This elite view of education and culture was made possible because what people at the pinnacle of civilization *saw* as graceful and deserving *was* indeed graceful and deserving. George Steiner on post culture says that it was the privilege of Arnold's and Voltaire's vision not to know what we know today. Ignorance gave confidence (Steiner 1976).

NOTES

1 Students of the history of ideas will remember that the concept of *panopticon* was believed by Jeremy Bentham to have been his own 'new' invention. According to Bentham, it was his own 'Christopher Columbus's egg'. Bentham claimed that he had invented a new technology of power designed to solve the problem of surveillance. Classification, examination, observation and discipline confined within designed architectures of space, as a systematic means of control were, however, traced by Foucault to origins much earlier than those of Bentham. These origins were at the beginnings of the modern era, when knowledge and power were incorporated for the purpose of aiding and abetting the emerging absolute states with dealing with the twin problems of incorporating the masses and the destruction of local, peasant particularism. Bentham merely added the technologies of industrialism to the repertoire of panopticon.

2 It is no coincidence that one of the most articulate critiques of the attempt to apply performance indicators to higher education should come from an author who was at the time of writing a CNAA officer. Barnett (1988: 108) argues that any HEI worth its salt must adhere to 'four intrinsic purposes'. These are: (1) concern with the development of each student's autonomy, (2) taking corporate responsibility for standards and future development, (3) fostering of a 'culture of critical discourse', and (4) concern to make this form of higher education − essentially one of critical enquiry − available to all who can benefit from it and who wish to have access to it. For Barnett these conditions are 'fundamental' and 'essential', and incidentally are not able to be fully captured by performance indicators. The point of this extensive quotation from Barnett is not to devalue the merits of his contribution. Rather, to point to the essentialist language, the

reliance upon 'critical discourse' as the key exclusive descriptor of the HEI. This is the emancipatory mission of modernism writ large and, again no coincidence, the state-of-the-art CNAA position upon 'mature' institutions before it (CNAA) inevitably joined the great quality controller in the sky.

3 It should be remembered that the devices of panopticon (prisons, workhouses, asylums and schools in the forms we now understand them) were first invented as a means of control and surveillance over the masses when social control of a face-to-face nature disintegrated with the great waves of enclosure – when masses of rude and sturdy beggars threatened the established order of things!

4 Peters is here summarizing the views of Lyotard (1984) on the future of higher education. In this vision of higher education 'the transmission of knowledge as the training of an elite capable of guiding society towards its emancipation' (Peters 1989: 103) will cease to be legitimate, and what will be required simply to supply the system with 'players capable of acceptably fulfilling their roles at the pragmatic posts required by the institutions' (Lyotard 1984: 48).

5 Some commentary from a post-modern perspective upon science provides a useful counterweight to the Kogan equation of 'true' quality with the apparatus of science. Lyotard sees the increasing tendency for science to become dominated by technology; that is, to become increasingly reliant upon large-scale technology (such as computers) as necessary for the 'production of proof'. This technology is able to win agreement through the vastness of its data. Thus science becomes more subordinated to the development of the project of technology which is concerned with 'optimization' rather than 'truth' games. Obviously this has implications for funding. The point of these remarks is to take a less sanguine view of the identification of quality *per se* with the apparatus of 'big science' than that suggested by Kogan.

6 It is not the intention of this chapter to argue that there is a clear empirical distinction between post-modern and modern societies. Rather it is to indicate that ideal typical characteristics associated with high modernism are now on the wane, to be supplanted by distinctive tendencies and features which are no longer compatible with social typologies that have described modern society. Post-modernism is, by definition, not a completed or completable process. It is merely a useful device to ascertain the radical nature of the break with modernity.

REFERENCES

Arnold, M. (1963) *Culture and Anarchy*, Cambridge: Cambridge University Press.

Barnett, R.A. (1988) 'Institutions of higher education: purposes and "performance indicators" ', *Oxford Review of Education* 14(1): 97–112.

Bauman, Z. (1987) *Legislators and Interpreters*, Cambridge: Polity Press.

—— (1992) *Intimations of Post Modernity*, London: Routledge.

Bourdieu, P. (1984) *Distinction, a Social Critique of the Judgment of Taste*, London: Routledge.

Burrows, A., Harvey, L. and Green, D. (1992) in *Approaches to Quality and Assurance in Higher Education: A Review*, *Quality in Higher Education*, 1992.

Foucault, M. (1977) *Discipline and Punish*, London: Allen Lane.

Haug, W.F. (1986) *Critique of Commodity Aesthetics*, Cambridge: Polity Press.

Hurd, D. (1992) *Sunday Times*, 3 Aug.

Hoskin, K. (1990) 'Foucault under examination: the crypto-educationalist unmasked' in S.J. Ball (ed.) *Foucault and Education, Disciplines and Knowledge*, London: Routledge.

Kogan, M. (1991) *The Case of the United Kingdom*, CRE-action, Morges, No. 96.

Lyotard, J.F. (1984) *The Postmodern Condition: a Report on Knowledge* G. Bennington and B. Massumi (trans.), Minneapolis: University of Minnesota Press.

Neave, G. (1985) 'Elite and mass higher education in Britain: a regressive model?' *Comparative Education Review* 29(30): 347–61.

—— (1986) 'The all-seeing eye of the Prince in western Europe', in G.R.C. Moodie (ed.) *Standards and Criteria in Higher Education*, Society for Research into Higher Education/NFER, Windsor: Nelson.

—— (1990) 'On preparing for markets: trends in higher education in western Europe, 1988–1990', *European Journal of Education*, 25(2): 105–22.

Peters, M. (1989) 'Techno-science, rationality, and the university: Lyotard on the "postmodern condition" ', *Educational Theory* 39(2): 93–105.

—— (1992) 'Performance and accountability in "post-industrial society": the crisis of British universities', *Studies in Higher Education* 17(2): 123–39.

Scott, P. (1991a) 'Knowledge's outer shape, inner life: the idea of mass higher education 2', *Times Higher Education Supplement* (16 Aug.).

—— (1991b) 'Confusion as evidence of health: the idea of mass higher education 3', *The Higher*, 23 Aug., p. 12.

Steiner, G. (1976) *Extraterritorial*, New York: Atheneum.

Trow, M. (1987) 'Academic standards and mass higher education', *Higher Education Quaterly* 41(3): 268–92.

Vught, F.A. (1991) 'Higher education quality assessment in Europe: the next step: evaluation and quality', CRE-action, No. 96.

4 The idea of quality

Voicing the educational

Ronald Barnett

SUMMARY

What counts as quality is contested. The different views of quality generate different methods of assessing quality and, in particular, alternative sets of performance indicators (PIs). However, PIs are highly limited in their informational content, and have nothing directly to tell us about the quality of the educational processes. Given the contested character of 'quality', performance evaluation should be framed so as to permit the equal expression of legitimate voices, though founded on the teaching staff's critical self-reflections. The anarchy of viewpoints that this approach might seem to generate can be combated in part by focusing performance review on the educational processes and the educational development of the students. Doubts remain about the allegiance of the academic community to such an educational agenda.

VOICES OF QUALITY

In his book *The Higher Education System*, Burton Clark depicted in triangular form the dominant influences on the shape of the higher education system (Clark 1983). He distinguished between systems influenced primarily by the academic community, those in which the state plays the major part, and those which are open to the market to a significant degree. That typification is helpful in understanding higher education in the contemporary quality debate. We can hypothesize that the three forces picked out by Clark give rise to three methodological approaches to quality: that the state will tend to favour numerical PIs; that the academic community will favour peer review; and that the market-led system will respond to consumer preferences.

These three contrasting methodologies produced by the separate social forces are tantamount to rival definitions of quality (Yorke 1991). The state, in its determination to promote a more efficient system, will come to regard as of a high quality those institutions which on the PIs, show up as being able to propel increasing numbers of graduates into the labour market in the most cost-effective way. The peer review system, favoured by the academic community, will in its operation reflect the values around which the academic community is orientated; namely, the values of advancing knowledge and of assisting the development of the minds of those who present themselves to the academic community. Markets reflect a range of conflicting views and no a priori predictions can be made about their outcomes.

In the modern world, there are many social groups (including the parents of would-be applicants and the employers of their offspring as graduates) who are expressing their sentiments about quality, and the system responds – more or less – to those different voices. There is less a genuine debate about quality, therefore, than a babel of voices, their different messages reflecting alternative starting points and claims on higher education itself (cf. Rorty 1989).

'Quality' can be seen as a metaphor for rival views over the aims of higher education. Those contemporary perceptions include the following: technicist (the imposition of technical instruments); collegial (the collective voice of the academic community); epistemic (the territorial claims of a particular disciplinary community); consumerist (the claims of the participants or would-be participants); employers (the voice of the labour market accepting the products of the system); professional (the voices of the separate professional bodies); and inspectorial (the voices of the state and other external agencies with an authorized right to inspect higher education and pronounce on what they find).

These various voices contributing to the debate are groups of actors attempting to secure their claim either to continue to defend their traditional idea of higher education and their means of valuing it (the academic community), or to impose alternative views of higher education with new means of assessing it. The debate over quality in higher education should be seen for what it is: a power struggle where the use of terms reflects a jockeying for position in the attempt to impose own definitions of higher education.

In this chapter, I analyse the idea of quality by picking up on that sketch. I do three things. I offer an overview of views of higher education, by distinguishing between dominant and marginal perceptions of the purposes of higher education. Secondly, I examine the relationship between conceptions of higher education and approaches to performance review and, in particular, will focus on PIs. Finally, I indicate a possible unifying idea not obviously present in the current quality debate as a way of doing justice to that idea in performance assessment.

DOMINANT CONCEPTIONS OF HIGHER EDUCTION AND PIs

A general connection exists, I would claim, which can be expressed in the form of a principle. There is a logical and three-fold connection between different conceptions of higher education, different approaches to quality, and the identification of PIs.

This principle takes the following general form:

Concept of higher education → concept of quality → kinds of PIs

That is, behind our sense of what constitutes quality, there lies – whether explicitly formed or held tacitly – a view as to the ends that higher education should serve. In turn, those prior conceptions will generate different methodologies for evaluating quality, and in particular will sponsor alternative sets of PIs. In what follows, I explore that assertion, by tracing the connections between different conceptions of higher education and their associated PIs. In the first part of my analysis, I pick out four dominant contemporary conceptions of higher eduction:

1 *Higher education as the production of highly qualified manpower*   On this view, higher education is seen as a process of filling particular slots in the labour market with individuals who are going to be 'productive'. Graduates are seen as 'products', as outputs having a utility value in the economy. Here, quality is a measure of the ability of students to succeed in the world of work. Accordingly, the PIs adopted will be the percentage of graduates flowing into employment and, more especially, their career earnings (or 'rates of return', as economists call them).

2 *Higher education as a training for a research career*   Here, the definition of higher education is framed by those members of the academic community who are active in research. Quality, on this view, is measured less in terms of the achievement of students than in the research profiles of the staff. The PIs generated by this view of higher education are the related output and input measures of staffs research activity – e.g. (in the United Kingdom) the number of Fellows of the Royal Society, the amount of research income attracted by an institution and the staff's publications output.

    In so far as students' accomplishments come into play, it is in their qualifications on entry, as evident, in the United Kingdom, in A-level point scores. Here it is assumed that it is entrants with 'high' entry qualifications who alone have demonstrated their ability to survive in the hothouse research environment, and to acquire the accoutrements of academic discourse and interaction.

3 *Higher education as the efficient management of teaching provision*   Through the 1970s and 1980s, in UK institutions of higher education, the student–staff ratio has moved steadily upwards. Correspondingly, institutions' unit costs have declined. Part of the accompanying story is that numbers of students in the system have grown remarkably (in the United Kingdom, having doubled to 1 million) in that period. In the awkward language of today, we are in the midst of a shift from an elite to a mass system of higher education.

The result is that the student body has changed so that it contains a larger number and a larger proportion of mature students and a greater number of younger students admitted on the basis of unconventional qualifications and from diverse backgrounds of all kinds. Together, these factors place increased demands on institutions to harness their resources so as to achieve an ever-higher level of teaching efficiency.

On this view of higher education, institutions are understood to be performing well – are of high quality – if their throughput is high, given the resources at their disposal. Consequently, on this conception of quality, PIs are sought which can capture its heightened sensitivity towards efficiency. Non-completion rates and proportions of students obtaining 'good degrees' are drawn on. So too, unit costs, especially as reflected in student–staff ratios themselves, as well as other financial data, come into play as key means of assessing the performance of institutions.

4 *Higher education as a matter of extending life chances* This conception is that of the potential consumers of higher education. Here, higher education is prized as a means of social mobility. It becomes a civil good, valued for its ability to offer opportunities to all to participate in the dominant social institutions, and to enjoy the benefits of modern society. As a result, here, higher education becomes the outcome of unfettered social demand, whatever it turns out to be. And the attempt to switch round our institutions so that they are fully open to social demand is seen most obviously in 'flexible' admissions policies and practices, as moves are made towards open access.

On this view of higher education, the key PIs lie in the percentage growth of student numbers and in the range of institutions' entrants. Do the figures reveal a widening of the intake to include students from socio-economic backgrounds normally under-represented in higher education? (One UK University has set as targets, specified proportions of its intake from students of specific ethnic origins.) Do they include significant proportions of mature students, of part-time students, and perhaps of disabled students?

Those, then, are four different, if overlapping, conceptions of the purposes of higher education, each with its associated definition of quality, and with a distinctive set of PIs likely to emerge from those different approaches.

Yet these four conceptions are not totally dissimilar. In all four, higher education is seen as a total system, in which students enter as inputs, are processed, and emerge as outputs. Higher education is seen as a black box, opaque to those on the outside: none of these four views is focused on, or even indicates, an interest in the quality of the educational process, or the character of the learning accomplished by the student. Indeed, it does not really matter what goes on in the black box as long as the quality of desired inputs and outputs is achieved.

ALTERNATIVE CONCEPTIONS OF HIGHER EDUCATION AND PIs

If this chacterization of the dominant contemporary conceptions of higher education is accepted, what alternative conceptions are available which do take seriously the quality of the student experience? Again, in no attempt to be comprehensive, four conceptions can be identified.

The first of these is the exposure of students to, and their initiation into, academic forms of knowing and experience. This conception has been articulated separately by philosophers of education, notably Michael Oakeshott and R.S. Peters. It identified a process which Oakeshott has referred to as a conversation across the generations (Fuller 1989). The essence of this conception is that education is seen as a continuing – indeed, never-ending – process, not to be confused by performance at endpoints and outputs; and that it is self-consciously marked off from the issues and concerns of the world.

Such a conception of higher education will seem too remote, too ethereal and even self-indulgent to some. But other conceptions, still little voiced in the general debate, present themselves.

A second such alternative view, among the academic community in the western world at least, is that a key purpose of higher education lies in the development of the individual student's autonomy and integrity (Baird 1989). Higher education places demands on students to be able to stand on their own feet, framing and sustaining their own arguments. Students acquire, we might say, the ability to be their own person.

A third conception in this mould is that in which higher education is seen as the formation of general intellectual abilities and perspectives, with the student attaining a breadth of vision and grasp beyond the confines of a single discipline. This view has been articulated both in the United States and, through the work of the CNAA, in the United Kingdom (Bok 1986; CNAA 1990, principle A4.3.3).

A final alternative conception of higher education is that in which higher education is understood as the development of critical reason (cf. McPeck 1990). This aim has two sub-plots. First, there is a drive here to develop the individual student's powers of critical reason. And this includes the added drive to see that the student becomes self-critical, for critical thinking has to start with oneself. The other variation on the theme is that of higher education developing a general capacity to engage in a critical commentary on the host society, so sustaining an oppositional function for higher education (Scott 1984).

COMPARING CONCEPTIONS

The first four (dominant) conceptions set out above contain a sense of higher education as a system, whether at national or at institutional levels, and its assessment is a matter of judging the outputs against the inputs. The second four just picked out, in contrast, are educational in orientation and are concerned with the development of the minds of individual students and inevitably prompt a further concern with the educational processes which promote the desired states of mind. It is, I would contend, educational conceptions of higher education of this latter kind which are largely absent from our current debates over quality.

There is a related point. In identifying the first four conceptions (concerned with systems and institutions) we were able to notice PIs associated with each one, though different in each case. In contrast, the second set of conceptions do not easily lend themselves to evaluation by numerical PIs. The complexity and open-endedness of the human transactions involved are not captured by the fixity and simplicity of numbers. So, when we find ourselves in the realm of PIs, we should perhaps first ask: which conceptions of higher education are being ruled in and which conceptions are being ruled out?

PIs AND STATE POWER

It would be legitimate to respond to the analysis so far presented: so what? Why not let all the proponents of these different conceptions of quality, with their associated PIs, work things out amongst themselves? After all, we are in a market situation – increasingly across the whole world – so that sounds as if it might be a plausible suggestion.

However, the actors in the game are not on a level playing field. The debate is not one of equals. The weight of power lies with the state, which – through its funding bodies – is orchestrating the debate over performance indicators and is building in evaluations on quality into its resource allocation processes (Pollitt 1990).

There are a number of points to note here. The first is that the state is less in the business of improving the system and more in the business of controlling the system. 'Control' is meant here in two senses. First, the sheer costs of higher education: higher education is big business (at around ECU5 billion per annum in the United Kingdom) and is threatening to exceed the limits of the taxpayer's endurance. The costs have to be kept in check. In turn, PIs which reflect an institution's efficiency are favoured; student–staff ratios and student output, for example.

A second form of control by the state is the kind of education itself. Graduate destinations and their achievements on the labour market are felt to say something about institutional performance, and the PIs in turn encourage the provision of programmes of study, and of subject areas, which are directly linked to particular professions and forms of employment.

These forms of control reveal themselves in the fact that agencies of the state increasingly wish to compare institutions against one another. This in itself has a number of consequences.

First, in order to be seen to be making legitimate comparisons, state agencies require apparently 'objective' measures of performance. They also require measures of performance which are easy to handle. Agencies faced with budgetary decisions do not wish to have to make nice judgements about the relative worth of an institution. They want things to be much more straightforward. Numerical PIs meet the policy requirement (Pollitt 1987).

Secondly, for some commentators, PIs are attractive because, being numerical in character, they appear to be value-free. It is apparent, on the analysis just given, that numerical PIs are shot through with values. They bear the imprint of the state having an underlying interest in power and control over higher education (Barnett 1988). Numerical PIs are a form, to employ the terminology of critical theory, of technological reason operating in the modern society (Held 1980).

So a general lesson is that, of any evaluation method, we should be prepared to ask the question: what set of values and interests are being promoted here? We should not take as a valid answer the reply that there are none at stake.

DOES 'ADDED-VALUE' ADD VALUE?

One recognized problem with PIs is that they are insensitive to context, and to the particularities of individual institutions with their contrasting missions and student intakes. One way of getting round this problem, some believe, lies in the idea of value-added. The term is much used in contemporary debate but perhaps with insufficient precision of meaning. For our purposes, we may take the use of 'value-added' to signal an attempt to put an institution's output performance – as measured, for example, by its degree results – in a relationship with its input (as measured by some kind of measurement of entrants' entry qualifications). The implication – and it is a correct one – is that entry qualifications and degree performance by themselves tell us very little. As PIs, they are remarkably uninformative. Only through placing those two kinds of PIs together can we derive meaningful interpretations of the information they yield.

More specifically, the case for value-added is that it is unfair to make judgements about an institution's degree success rates, unless we know something about the qualifications of the intake it started with. It makes little sense to compare two institutions through the performance of their graduates if the students of one institution started at a relatively disadvantaged position (having 'poorer' qualifications on entry) in relation to those of the other institution. Instead of simply comparing degree results in themselves, it is far better to assess the extent to which students have made progress from their respective starting points while they have been at the institution.

Value-added, then, is an attempt to make objective assessments about an institution's performance but in a way which does justice to its mission.

The reasoning behind value-added is that, yes, PIs are largely uninformative in themselves, but if we put them into a relationship with one another, then we can reach surer ground.

However, we should proceed carefully before enthusiastically embracing value-added as a means of making PIs legitimate. If the idea of value-added is to make sense, we have to assume that there is a stable relationship between students' performance at the points of entry and exit. Here, there is the obvious rejoinder that the statistical correlations between entry and exit are weak, in some subjects at least. But there is a more fundamental point.

Higher education, if it is to justify the qualifier 'higher', has to allow for a form of educational development in which students are able to attain a particular level of insight. The term 'higher' is particularly appropriate because, in a genuine process of higher education, students attain a level of conceptual understanding which enables them to interrogate the experiences which they encounter. They reach, literally, a higher perspective on their own thoughts. In this sense, higher education is a form of meta-education.

Critical self-reflection, deep conceptual understanding, a sense that there are no resting points: these are the hallmarks of higher education. But if these are the special characteristics of higher education, then there is no necessary relationship between students' attainments on entry and those at the point of exit. For their higher education experience is intended precisely to offer them a new order of experience, to equip them with new frameworks of thought and action and to challenge their grasp on things (Barnett 1992).

But if that point is granted, then the idea of 'value-added' is in difficulty. The analysis I have just offered implies that it is improper to make simple comparisons of students' states of mind and intellectual achievement at the point of entry to higher education and at their exit; for the states of mind in question may be quite different kinds. We see this in practice, often enough. Not infrequently, students do say at the end of their course or some years subsequently that it has had a profound impact on the way in which they see things and on their general outlook.

It will be remembered that value-added is being offered to us because of the acknowledged shortcomings of entry qualifications and degree performance as PIs. It follows that if value-added is in trouble as a kind of super PI, in putting selected PIs into a relationship with one another, then PIs as a whole are in trouble.

THE PERFORMANCE OF PIs

The sureness, the stability, and even the objectivity that numerical PIs seem to offer is illusory. To believe that we can say something of real insight about the quality of an educational process by describing it in numerical terms is an illusion. Qualities and quantities are different kinds of entity. Running them together is, in philosophical jargon, a category mistake.

A couple of analogies may be helpful. Wine connoisseurs in judging the quality of wines do give wines a numerical score. But the numerical score 14 points out of 20, say, is never intended to be a substitute for the more qualitative evaluations. For that, the connoisseur resorts to a particular language – of tastes like raspberries or rhubarb, and other evocative terminology. The numerical evaluations – if, indeed they are used at all – are an aid to comparing one wine with others, but the quantities tell us virtually nothing about the qualities of the wines.

Another analogy comes from the world of competitive sport, where the comparative assessment of performance is integral to the character of the activity. Compare swimming and diving: judging the quality of higher education is more like judging the performance of a diver than a swimmer. With the swimmer, we can get out our stop-watch, and see how quickly a specified distance has been covered, and how far ahead of a rival a winner has finished. But in assessing the diver's performance, a more judgemental approach is necessary. Again, the judgement can be expressed in numerical terms, but the numbers are based on a prior judgement and reflect the judgement. They do not emerge into the world by themselves and are based only partly on an arithmetical measurement of the diver's performance. How many turns were accomplished before hitting the water, and whether the diver's entry was at 90 degrees are important considerations; and to that extent a numerical evaluation is part of the evaluation. But marks are also given for style, and that reflects a non-numerical aesthetic judgement by the assessors.

With PIs in higher education, the numbers come first, and then we are asked to make a judgement on the numbers. This is the accountant's or the bureaucrat's approach to evaluation. It is pernicious, because it discourages us from having to make difficult judgements about the character of higher education. It is too easy to rest with the superficial story offered by the numbers than delving into the deep structure of the educational process which produced them.

A further feature of the numerical PIs favoured by state agencies is that, logically, they can only tell us (at best) something about the past. In themselves, they cannot give us insight into the future or even suggest ways in which things ought to be modified or improved. For that, not only do we have to make judgements but we also have to exercise our imagination.

PLACING PIs

Even if it is granted that the informational content of PIs is limited, it does not follow that they are of no help to us whatever.

Perhaps the first principle in trying to assess a complex human activity like higher education is that we should use whatever evidence and whatever methodologies we can lay our hands on. The fault – if there is one – lies in making improper deductions from the information with which we are presented. If we find that interesting, numerical patterns are arising out of our PIs, it would be myopic not to take some account of it.

If, for instance, we find an especially high rate of students failing to complete their course, then enquiries should be made to see what is going on. It might turn out to be entirely justified if, for example, a high proportion of the students turn out to have transferred to another programme.

Investigations of this sort might have a happier intention. We might discover that a course had a pattern of degree results much higher than comparable courses. There, we might be interested in uncovering how the course team was achieving such good results, in order that we might in turn disseminate to other courses and institutions guidance on the teaching practices that were responsible. On the other hand, the enquiries might turn out to prompt some critical questions about the quality of the examining process.

So PIs are not to be dismissed entirely. They can prompt investigations which in turn can lead to insights into the quality of what is on offer. PIs have a place, even if they cannot give us a direct insight into quality.

It might be felt that what is being advanced here is what has come to a common view about PIs, that they have to be put into some kind of balance with other evidence before sound judgements can be made. But to say even that is to grant PIs a status higher than that which they deserve, for that viewpoint downplays the investigative and judgemental processes required to make any sense of PIs. By themselves, they are devoid of informational content. No non-controversial story can be read from PIs alone. Interpretations, linked to prior values over purposes, cannot be avoided in institutional or programme evaluation.

PIs have, we might say, the status of an appendix. That is to say, in an evaluation report on an institution, the data reflected through the application of a set of PIs should be included but tucked away at the back, in an appendix. It is the reports on the investigations of the educational processes and the intepretations of the findings – which would have been necessary anyway – that should form the body of the report.

RECONCEPTUALIZING PEER REVIEW

If PIs are an inadequate means of assessing institutions or courses of higher education, what principles might more appropriately inform these efforts? I go back to my examples of wine connoisseurship and diving. Higher education is, we might be willing to admit, somewhat more complex than either of those activities. And if they call for skilled judgements by recognized authorities, then perhaps that is a basis for assessing the quality of higher education.

This proposal sounds perhaps like a plea for retaining control of academic affairs in the hands of academics through a peer review process carrying limited accountability (accountability being confined to the closed circle of academic peers). It looks like an attempt to keep evaluation in the academic corner of the triangle we began with, rather than permitting it to move either in the direction of more state co-ordination or more market influence. That, however, is not being suggested. What I am positing is the possibility of a different kind of evaluation.

The objection confuses form of process with the parties engaged in it. Because I have been arguing that interpretations are inescapable, based on prior values, and that modern society contains many groupings with a legitimate interest in the quality of higher education, it follows that those legitimate voices should find a place among the interpretations. Certainly, questions arise over who has a legitimate voice, and what weight should be accorded to the voice. Nevertheless, those different voices have to find a forum, a means of dialogue, in which they can engage with one another; otherwise, no clear messages for action will emerge.

Consequently, a mode of evaluation founded on a critical dialogue suggests itself; but to describe this as a 'peer dialogue' would be to mislead over its fundamental character. 'Peer review' is an imprecise term, but it retains such connotations of closure and of working within given conceptual frameworks that it is better avoided here. The essence of the mode of evaluation I am proposing is precisely that it is not a dialogue among the academics involved in delivering the service but is a forum in which all legitimate parties can make themselves heard.

The first grouping with a legitimate voice remains, even so, those who are conducting the activities themselves; and for four reasons. First, those conducting the activities – the members of a course team running a course, for example – are supposedly competent authorities in their own right. Secondly, it is they who are nearest the educational process, and it is the quality of that which is in question. Thirdly, as professionals, there is an onus on them to be self-critical about their own activities.

All those reasons apply to any set of professional activities. My last reason is more specific to the academic world. Critical dialogue is supposed to mark out the academic world. It reflects the sense that claims to knowledge are only provisional. Academics, in their academic activities, have an eye on themselves, aware that there can always be a challenge to what they are saying and doing. If that is the case for research and scholarship, the value of critical and mutual peer dialogue suggests itself as an appropriate principle for evaluating teaching activities.

A course team, for instance, needs continually to have in mind that the curriculum, and its teaching and learning methods, could be quite other than it is. So, the course team should be charged with orchestrating – on a suitably periodic basis – a throughgoing review of the course for which it is responsible. Being professional in the delivery of a course calls for the enactment of a continuing programme of critical reflection which may approach the status of action research (Carr and Kemmis 1986).

We should also expect students to be involved in the critical review for they have a legitimate – though not the only – viewpoint to express in the matter. The principle of accountability alone suggests that the dialogue should be extended further. However, the other legitimate parties brought in – from other courses in the institution, from other institutions or from the wider society – are there to supplement and to buttress the self-critical efforts of the responsible professionals. Their commentaries will be ineffective if they are imposed on those who are immediately responsible. The comments of outsiders, if they are to bite, have to mesh to some extent with the perceptions that the course team has framed for itself.

On the other hand, a presumption of correctness should not lie with the course team. The critical dialogue should have point rather than be a mere ritual or a means of legitimizing decisions and actions already determined by the course team. That consideration provides a justification for admitting into the critical dialogue voices from domains outside the academic community. If the critical dialogue is to be a genuine debate, it follows that the communication processes must remain undistorted by unequal power among the participants. In the terminology of Jurgen Habermas's critical theory, the dialogue should approach the form of 'the ideal speech situation', characterized by an open but unconstrained discourse, where the only motive is a shared concern for a better way of doing things (cf. Rasmussen 1990, ch. 4).

Admittedly, what counts as a better way may be controversial. The base-line criteria may well vary between the interested parties. A balance has to be struck between (1) allowing all parties with an interest in the quality of the programme to have their say so that the different perceptions of quality are voiced, (2) ensuring that the discourse is not weighted unduly towards any one interest group, and (3) allowing the academics in immediate contact with the students appropriate professional space to form their own judgements.

Such a set of considerations for framing the character of performance review may seem to open the way to debate entirely open-ended in scope, so that the professionals are bombarded with contrasting messages as to both the character of a programme and the means of evaluating it. It may also appear to be devoid of criteria which will assist in choosing between the rival perceptions of higher education aims and definitions of quality. Indeed, a dearth of guiding principles is perhaps a logic of the contemporary post-modern age, which declines to embrace grand over-arching narratives or ideologies (Lyotard 1984). If higher education is contested (our starting point), then it is only proper that the contending forces work themselves out in a pragmatic spirit.

That is a position not to be lightly dismissed. But it is just possible that a general principle or perspective is available to enable us to steer a path through the quality thickets.

VOICING THE EDUCATIONAL IN PERFORMANCE REVIEW

Higher education is essentially an educative process. If we are seriously interested in assessing the quality of higher education, we have to find some way of getting at the character of the educational processes. Looking at staff's research records or at the employment rate of students is not going to do that. We have to find some way of getting a perceptive insight into the character of the course, as delivered by the course team and as experienced by the students. Quite simply, we have to gain an informed sense of the character of the educational activities in question (whether the review is being conducted at the level of a course, a department or an institution).

This is not, in itself, a plea that the students' perceptions are to count most. Student feedback is an essential element in an evaluation strategy since the students collectively constitute a key interest group and deserve a real but not a dominant voice. Clients of a professional service are not necessarily the best judges of the quality of the service they receive, even if they form a low evaluation of those services and choose to acquire them instead from rival professionals.

The point here is that educational judgements ought to be central to an educational review. That may seem banal; but it should not be assumed that academics (who may have other and justifiable research and scholarly interests) or the state agencies or employers or the students themselves are automatically going to be guided by educational considerations. The point applies to institutional as well as to course review. If we are assessing an institution as a whole, we have to find some way of judging the significance that the institution attaches to improving the quality of the teaching and learning that goes on inside it.

Secondly, the methods have to be appropriate to the forming of educational judgements. Assessments of educational processes cannot rest – we have seen – on PIs. PIs do not even indicate, though they may prompt interesting questions and investigations leading to further information. Rather, we have to devise evaluation strategies that will provide insight into the character of the student experience and so generate evidence which gives a basis on which to make complex judgement about what is going on in an institution, or in a course.

Processes of performance review aimed at illuminating the character of educational processes will have more impact if they are intended to improve the quality of what is on offer (that is, have a futures-orientation), rather than to make judgements on what has happened in the past. Making an assessment with an eye to the future will often require imaginative perceptions on the part of the assessors. A judgement that we should be going in that direction rather than this calls not just for a sense of a single future possibility but for the imaging of alternative futures.

ACADEMIC COMMUNITY BUT AN EDUCATIONAL COMMUNITY?

There remains a final consideration. On the analysis provided here, an important question has been begged. Is the academic community itself seriously interested in conducting by and for itself a searching educational evaluation of its own teaching activities? Does it really want to bring off the educational agenda just sketched out? We should not assume that it is and does. It is an open question whether the academic community, in its 'tribes and territories' (Becher 1989), is framed more by its research interests than its teaching interests. The extent to which the academic community is prepared to adopt the professionalism of self-critique and a scrupulous concern for a quality of delivery towards its teaching activities, buttressed by a rigorous peer review system (again, focusing on its teaching), is unclear.

Certainly, under the influence of the CNAA, such a system took root in the former UK polytechnics and colleges sector, in which institutions made significant attempts both to bring together different parties and to evolve evaluation practices which illuminate the character of the course in action (Barnett 1990). With the demise of the CNAA, with polytechnics retitled 'universities', and with the pressures on the use of resources facing all institutions, it remains to be seen whether that evaluation system (or something like it) will be developed by the universities or whether it too will wither away.

REFERENCES

Baird, J.R. (1989) 'Quality: what should make higher education "higher"?', *Higher Education Research and Development* 7(2): 141–52.
Barnett, R. (1988) 'Institutions of higher education: purposes and performance indicators', *Oxford Review of Education* 14(1): 97–112.
—— (1990) *Changing the Patterns of Course Review*, CNAA Project Report, London: CNAA.
—— (1992) *'Aiming Higher'*, ch. 2 in *Improving Higher Education: Total Quality Care*, Buckingham: Open University Press.
Becher, A. (1989) *Academic Tribes and Territories*, Buckingham: Open University Press.
Bok, D. (1986) *Higher Learning*, London and Cambridge, MA: Harvard University Press.
Carr, W. and Kemmis, S. (1986) *Becoming Critical: Education, Knowledge, and Action Research*, Lewes: Falmer.
Clark, B. (1983) *The Higher Education System: Academic Organization in Cross-national Perspective*, London: University of California Press.
Council for National Academic Awards (1990) *Handbook*, London: CNAA.
Fuller, T. (1989) *The Voice of Liberal Learning: Michael Oakeshott on Education*, New Haven, CT, and London: Yale University Press.
Held, D. (1980) *Introduction to Critical Theory: Horkheimer to Habermas*, London: Heinemann.
Lyotard, J.F. (1984) *The Postmodern Condition: a Report on Knowledge*, Manchester: University of Manchester Press.

McPeck, J.E. (1990) *Teaching Critical Thinking*, London: Routledge.
Pollitt, C. (1987) 'Measuring university performance: never mind the quality, never mind the width', *Higher Education Quarterly* 44(1): 60–81.
—— (1990) 'The politics of performance assessment: lessons for higher education', *Studies in Higher Education* 12(1): 87–98.
Rasmussen, D.M. (1990) *Reading Habermas*, Oxford: Blackwell.
Rorty, R. (1989) *Contingency, Irony and Solidarity*, Oxford: Oxford University Press.
Scott, P. (1984) *The Crisis of the University*, Beckenham: Croom Helm.
Yorke, M. (1991) *Performance Indicators: Observations on their Use in the Assurance of Course Quality*, CNAA project report, No. 30, London: CNAA.

5 Total Quality Management in education

The theory and how to put it to work

Myron Tribus

W. Edwards Deming has often said, 'Experience alone teaches nothing.' If you do not have a theory to provide a framework to understand your experience, you do not accumulate thirty years of experience; you merely repeat one year thirty times.

In discussing the application of Total Quality Management (TQM) in education, it is useful to distinguish between management and leadership. Both are needed. Dalton[1] has proposed the following definitions:

> Leadership is the ability to develop a vision that motivates others to move with a passion.

> Management is the ability to organize resources and co-ordinate the execution of tasks necessary to reach a goal in a timely and cost-effective manner.

Both leadership and management are required. Covey contrasts them, using the following example:[2]

> You can quickly grasp the important difference between the two if you envision a group of producers cutting their way through the jungle with machetes. They're the producers, the problem solvers. They're cutting through the undergrowth, clearing it out.
>
> The managers are behind them, sharpening their machetes, writing policy and procedure manuals, holding muscle development programs, bringing in improved technologies and setting up working schedules and compensation programs for machete wielders.
>
> The leader is the one who climbs the tallest tree, surveys the entire situation, and yells, 'Wrong jungle!'
>
> But how do the busy, efficient producers and managers often respond? 'Shut up! We're making progress.'

By 'theory', we mean a connected set of concepts, residing in our heads. The concepts represent our image of 'reality'. We use them to make predictions about how our future depends on our actions.

The purpose of this chapter is to describe how the theory of management developed by W. Edwards Deming may be applied to the educational process. The theory was originally developed to improve the management of manufacturing enterprises. Over time it has been extended to service industries, government and even not-for-profit enterprises. It is important to consider how best to apply the theory of education. *The school is not a factory*.

BY WHAT CRITERIA SHOULD WE JUDGE A THEORY OF MANAGEMENT IN EDUCATION?

There is no shortage of proposals for reform in education. Nor is there a shortage of good ideas and research results. The task is not just to pick one of them, but rather it is to develop a comprehensive approach within which to implement the many good works known to us. The theory of management developed by W. Edwards Deming provides an excellent framework within which to examine proposals for improvement.

Any theory of education reflects the philosophy, either explicitly or implicitly, of the philosopher. Education is the means whereby adults pass on to children their beliefs, values and desires for the future. Whatever is done in education represents a philosophy and a system of values: our beliefs regarding the good, the true and the beautiful.

The Deming theory of management is based on a humanistic philosophy. It begins with the belief that all people are educable, that they want to do a good job and that they deserve respect. They are not born mean, but can be made so. The philosophy behind the Deming approach values the self-esteem of those who learn and those who teach.

The Deming theory of management goes beyond the historical views of management in specifically recognizing the impact of the *system* on the behaviour of people. Deming often cites a rule he attributes to Juran: When there is a problem, 85 per cent of the time it is with the system; 15 per cent of the time it will be with the workers. Lately Dr Deming has suggested that the numbers should be 95 per cent and 5 per cent. To deal with a problem, therefore, Deming advises to begin with an examination of the system which, an overwhelming amount of the time, he argues, is the source of the problem.

Concern for how people respond to managerial actions is crucial to the success of quality management, which is why Deming emphasizes the need for managers to understand elementary principles of psychology and the scientific basis for these principles. Deming's view takes into account statistical variation. He calls for management by fact, which implies data taking and statistical analysis of the data before decisions are made.

Because Deming views systems as the means whereby human wealth and happiness may be obtained, he warns against managerial actions which lead to less than optimum *system performance*. He especially argues against managing each component as though it were separate from the others, an approach which occurs, for example, when accountants try to make each activity its own 'profit centre'. He warns against approaches which pit the person against the system or against other persons. Deming believes in personal responsibility, but goes beyond that concept to consider the special responsibilities of those who manage systems. Conventional approaches to management, that is, as discussed in *Fortune Magazine*, often dwell upon the *rewards* of management, for example, by publishing annual salary surveys. Deming dwells upon the *obligations* of management.

A satisfactory theory of education should address the teaching/learning processes as central to the mission of the institution, and it should bring to bear on these processes tools for improvement. The theory should also address the related issues of parental participation, school administration, teacher training and evaluation. A satisfactory theory, therefore, should be 'holistic'. The theory should take into account research in the field of education and social sciences. The theory should have a scientific basis, but it should also have a moralistic basis. It should be based on an understanding of what is fair and what is good for society, even if these determinations in specific situations are not always easy to make.

The fruits of education occur in the future. A good system for the management of education demands a long-range perspective. Long-range planning requires consistency of purpose, communicated to all through a vision of what the enterprise ought to be. A really good system of management will alter the goals and objectives of the educational system, recognizing trends and changes in the environment. In spite of change, the *basic philosophies of management and teaching* should remain constant. Moving from the one-room schoolhouse to the computer-based modern school should call for a change in *methods*, but not for a change in *objectives* and *philosophy*.

SOME SPECIFIC QUESTIONS TO ASK OF ANY THEORY OF EDUCATION

If presented with a theory of management in education, ask:

1 On what philosophy is it based? Is the philosophy explicit?
2 What is the implied set of values behind the theory?
3 What vision of the future motivates the theory?
4 Is the theory *holistic*, i.e. does it recognize education as a *system*? Does it deal with the teaching/learning processes? With the responsibilities of leadership and management?
5 Is the theory based upon, and does it make explicit use of:
   (a) psychology of people, taken individually and in groups?
   (b) systems theory?
   (c) statistical variation?
   (d) a theory of knowledge?

6 Does it identify a particular set of tools and techniques to make it practical to reduce the theory to practice? Do these tools and techniques span the activities from teaching, learning, leading, managing, as well as relations with people outside the system?

7 Is the theory capable of being:

   (a) *Descriptive*, i.e. provide language and concepts which help us understand what we see? Does it increase insight?

   (b) *Predictive*, i.e. enable us to predict, with a reasonable probability, what will happen in the future? Does it help us to decide what to observe? Does it identify *leading* indicators of improvement?

   (c) *Normative*, i.e. provide a guide to action without being proscriptive?

8 Has the theory ever been reduced to practice with good results?

9 Does the theory call for widespread participation and promote continuous learning on the part of everyone in the system, not just the students?

A holistic approach to management requires concern with the seven elements depicted in Figure 5.1 below.[3] The omission of any one link in the chain renders the theory inoperable.

	Vision	Strategy	Skills	Resources	Rewards	Organization	No followers
Philosophy		Strategy	Skills	Resources	Rewards	Organization	Confusion
Philosophy	Vision		Skills	Resources	Rewards	Organization	False starts
Philosophy	Vision	Strategy		Resources	Rewards	Organization	Anxiety
Philosophy	Vision	Strategy	Skills		Rewards	Organization	Frustration
Philosophy	Vision	Strategy	Skills	Resources		Organization	Bitterness
Philosophy	Vision	Strategy	Skills	Resources	Rewards		No co-ordination
Philosophy	Vision	Strategy	Skills	Resources	Rewards	Organization	Success!

Figure 5.1 Seven elements required for quality management. Each has a function which cannot be omitted.

Any approach to education should be examined to see if it deals with all of the above seven elements.

HOW DO WE KNOW IT WILL WORK?

When teaching about quality management, Professor Shoji Shiba usually puts the following diagram on the board (Figure 5.2):

Figure 5.2 PITM is forbidden! (PITM = Prove It To Me.)

By 'PITM' he refers to the expression 'Prove It To Me'. People often demand that we prove, ahead of time, that quality management will work in their enterprise. They say, 'Sure, it works in industry. But can you prove it works in education?' Dr Deming habitually responds to such questions with the remark, 'Survival is not mandatory'. He knows there are some things which one cannot 'prove'. To 'prove' is to demonstrate, by words and logic, that something is true. No one can *prove* a theory. We can *disprove* theories in many ways. For example, we can prove logical inconsistency, or supply counter-examples. But we cannot *prove* a theory. Even if we point to years and years of social research supporting our contentions, it does not provide proof.

We can often point to experiments, conducted in systems which were only partially organized for quality management, but these are capable of many interpretations and do not serve as proof. They do not persuade those who are doubtful. In many areas of life, 'proof' that a *normative* theory works can only be *experiential*. For example, unless you have experienced co-operative learning, or independent study, in competitive-free environments, there is no way anyone can 'prove' to you that co-operative education really works. The best we can say is, 'Try it. Give it a chance. You'll like it.'

MOVING THE THEORY FROM INDUSTRY TO EDUCATION

In adapting quality management, originally developed for business enterprises, it is important to keep in mind certain differences between education and business:

- The school is not a factory.
- The student is not a 'product'.
- The *education* of the student is the product.

- Successful completion of the product requires the student to participate as a worker, co-managing the learning process.
- Teaching and learning are two different processes.

  Teaching is more akin to management than to detailed supervision of activities.

  Learning is more akin to research and development (R&D) than it is to an assembly process. Attempts to organize R&D as though it were merely an assembly of ideas to be managed in the style of an assembly line have been disastrous. The same is true in education.
- In industry, quality management requires every manager of every process to identify a customer. If a process has no output for which there is a customer, why do it?

  Educators are not habituated to the concept of 'customer'. They are apt to believe that a process should continue because 'we've always done it that way'.

There are many 'customers' for the product, that is, for the student's education. In order of importance they are:

1 The students, themselves, for they must live with the product for the rest of their lives.
2 Their parents, for they, too, must live with the product and they are the ones who, in general, pay for it.
3 Future employers, who will have to pay to obtain the benefits of the student's education.
4 Society in general, as represented by governmental agencies, which pay a large fraction of the cost of the education, desires, therefore, that the student, as an adult, becomes a contributing member of society.

WHAT SHOULD A GOOD EDUCATION PROVIDE FOR LEARNERS?

The objective of every school, or university, should be to provide, for each student, opportunities to develop in four categories:

- *Knowledge*, which enables us to understand.
- *Know-how*, which enables us to do.
- *Wisdom*, which enables us to set priorities.
- *Character*, which enables us to co-operate, to persevere and to become respected and trusted members of society.

We refer to these four components as the *contents* of the education. A theory of management for education should consider not only the contents, but also the system, environment, style and processes required to deliver the contents. Because the contents will vary from school to school and community to community, the theory addresses *how* the contents are determined.

HOW DOES QUALITY MANAGEMENT DIFFER?

Existing approaches to management in education do pay attention to both the contents, which too often considers topics, such as mathematics, science, art, English and history, as independent topics, not part of a *system*. Likewise, existing approaches treat the method of delivery too often merely in terms of the physical environment, the schedule and the methods of testing. What distinguishes quality management from conventional management are these considerations:

1 Concern to define achievement by reference to the purpose of education, not standardized tests.
2 Concern for processes instead of organizations, to make form follow function.
3 Concern for improvement of processes instead of working only on outputs.
4 Concern to involve all players in the improvement process, not just the faculty.
5 Concern that every person in the system understands how the system works, what the system is supposed to do and how well it is doing it.
6 Concern to optimize the performance of the system as contrasted to optimizing components of the system, i.e. beyond raising scores in specially identified subjects.
7 Concern that every person is educated to participate in the improvement process, i.e., that everyone becomes response-able. Too often conventional approaches to management are concerned only to identify people who are responsible. Quality management is more concerned to fix the system than to fix the blame.

In industry we have learned to pay close attention to the processes which produce the goods and services. The important principle derived from industrial experience is:

If you want to improve a product or service,
pay close attention to the processes which produce the product or service.
Measurements on the product or service provide, at best,
lagging indicators. They are too late to provide more than regrets.
Measuring the characteristics of the process provides leading indicators
upon which actions may be taken to ensure a good result.

A keystone in the Deming philosophy is the continuous improvement of all processes. It is not important to identify, at any one moment, the best process someone else has developed. Rather, the enterprise and its managers should learn to develop the habit of continuous improvement. Any theory of management which seeks the best process for delivering a service, and then organizes itself to keep that process constant with time is suspect.[4] Although today there is much attention paid to 'bench-marking', that obsession should be understood as a crutch for managers who do not know how to make their organizations obsessive about improvement. The justification given by most managers, for their focus on 'bench-marking', is that it supplies a motivation for the workforce. 'See how well *they* are doing it? We ought to be able to do at least as well!' An obsession with bench-marking relieves the managers from having to *lead* the way in improvement and of having to inspire creativity in the workforce. If boards of directors understood their jobs, they would appoint as CEOs only those who have demonstrated their ability to *lead* people in the processes of improvement. School boards who understand quality would look first at candidates for superintendent by asking for strong evidence of leadership coupled with good managerial skills.

THE IMPORTANCE OF THE VISION

Each of the categories of the contents will be considered in turn, but before they can be discussed meaningfully, it is important to discuss why the vision of the future is so important (see Figure 5.1). A vision for education must look ahead, to the time when the education will be put to use, and consider the threats and opportunities those being educated will face. The choice of what to include, under the headings of *knowledge, know-how, wisdom* and *character*, will depend upon this vision of the future.

It is not enough to have a vision which relates to how the *contents* of education should change. It is also necessary to understand the changes required for the educational system itself. Under quality management there is much less of a focus on the curriculum. Rather, the question is, how should the *system* change to adapt to, and possibly influence, the future? The vision should not only anticipate the future, but should aim to meet the future in the best possible way.

Educational systems are complex. Teachers are professionals and should be so treated. Teaching and learning is what takes place when the teacher closes the door and starts to speak. The test of a vision for a school is the extent to which it influences what happens behind the closed doors.

TWO OFFICIAL VISIONS OF THE FUTURE – AMERICAN 2000 AND THE SCANS REPORT

The Federal administration in Washington has produced two rather different visions for education. The Secretary of Education has published 'America 2000', which emphasizes national testing, high standards for maths and science, and improved control over the physical environment in schools – specifically, reduced drugs, greater safety, and better preparation for schooling.

The second vision is from the Secretary of Labor, and is known as *A SCANS Report for America 2000.*[5]

Table 5.1 The SCANS Report

Workplace know-how

The know-how identified by SCANS is made up of five competencies and a three-part foundation of skills and personal qualities that are needed for solid job performance. These include:

COMPETENCIES – effective workers can productively use:

- *Resources*: allocating time, money, materials, space and staff;
- *Interpersonal skills*: working in teams, teaching others, serving customers, leading, negotiating, and working well with people from culturally diverse backgrounds;
- *Information*: acquiring and evaluating data, organizing and maintaining files, interpreting and communicating and using computers to process information;
- *Systems*: understanding social, organizational and technological systems, monitoring and correcting performance, and designing or improving systems;
- *Technology*: selecting equipment and tools, applying technology to specific tasks and maintaining and trouble-shooting technologies.

THE FOUNDATION – competence requires:

- *Basic skills*: reading, writing, arithmetic and mathematics, speaking and listening;
- *Thinking skills*: thinking creatively, making decisions, solving problems, seeing things in the mind's eye, knowing how to learn, and reasoning;
- *Personal qualities*: individual responsibility, self-esteem, sociability, self-management and integrity.

In an addendum to the original SCANS report,[6] the Department of Labor has identified the following changes as desirable for K-12 education:

- Teaching should be offered 'in context', that is, students should learn content while solving realistic problems. 'Learning in order to know' should not be separated from 'learning in order to do'.
- Improving the match between what work requires and what students are taught requires changing how instruction is delivered and how students learn;
- High performance requires a new system of school administration and assessment;
- The entire community must be involved.

The vision of the US Department of Education is basically a call for a return to older paradigms of education, with an emphasis on testing and competition. Within that framework, schools are encouraged to try something new, anything. The underlying premise of the America 2000 approach is that having schools compete with one another is 'good'. The free market approach to education is 'good'. Developing national testing programmes, which score and rank one school against another, is 'good'. America 2000 also calls for safe schools, elimination of drugs and other enhancements in the school environment. It is legitimate to ask: 'Why hasn't this been undertaken earlier? Why are these *new* goals for the *future*?' I conclude that America 2000 does not begin with a vision of the future. It seems to be aimed only at repairing what is obviously wrong today. It is certainly a step in the right direction, but it represents a limited, near-term vision, at best eight years out.

The SCANS report, Table 5.1, on the other hand, presents a table of competencies which industrial representatives identified as necessary to a flexible, competent workforce in the future. In my opinion it is a much better vision for the future of education and provides much better guidance to educators. *The proper test of a vision statement is not how high sounding it is but rather whether it helps those who are trying to fulfil the vision.*

One of the big advantages of the American system of education is that the US Secretary of Education does *not* have very much power! Educational policy is in the province of the individual states, and within the states, often is set by counties and school districts. It seems to me that, for the health of the nation, we should nurture diversity in educational approaches. We nurture 'seed banks' to assure that in the future, no matter what plant diseases may arise, there will be a multiplicity of seed types from which we may obtain new strains. Diversity in education should be reflected in the choices made with respect to the balance amongst knowledge, know-how, wisdom and character, as chosen by different school districts. I submit that it is healthy for the nation if different schools define these contents differently, but I also believe no school should omit any one of them.

My conclusion from studying the two reports is that it would be better for the country if the Department of Labor were combined with the US Department of Education. In any case, neither department, fortunately, has control over the contents of education. The main point I would make in this regard is that, while quality management uses techniques to assure that whatever is done is consistent with the aims and goals of the enterprise, it does not dictate these aims and goals. Thus, it seems to me incumbent on the local school boards and communities to decide for themselves what to include under the four headings: knowledge, know-how, wisdom and character.[7]

IMPORTANCE OF DEFINING LEVELS OF COMPETENCY TO THE SELECTION OF WHAT TO INCLUDE UNDER THE HEADINGS 'KNOWLEDGE' AND 'KNOW-HOW'

When discussing knowledge and know-how, it is important to define levels of competency associated with each. Thus, we may desire that children at the fourth grade become competent in using a computer, but the *level* of competency to which we aspire for them should be different than for a university student. The concept of *level of competency* is not new in education. We may use the following table to illustrate the idea.[8]

Table 5.2 Levels of competency

Level 1	Recall, remembering knowledge Acquire by: reading, viewing, listening Tell, name, list, define. Who? When? Where?
Level 2	Understanding, comprehension Develop by: explaining, developing vocabulary, reflecting what has been said. Demonstrate by: Giving main idea, predicting, evaluating cause and effect.
Level 3	Problem-solving, given this, find that Develop by: solving 'textbook type' problems. Demonstrate by: solving problems on tests, proving relationships, formal presentations of solutions.
Level 4	Creative application, identifying problems in fuzzy situations, creating new methods of solution for new classes of problems. Develop by: problem formulation in a variety of circumstances. Demonstrate by: original work, publishable in a journal or converted to product or service of use in the market or acclaimed by audiences.

When the school board, the superintendent, the principals, the parents and the teachers, with some student representation, develop a specification for the contents, it is essential that each competency be described with reference to a *level*, using an agreed scheme such as the one illustrated above.

Students should have a hand in the development of agreed descriptions of levels of competence. Only then can they become partners in improving the processes of teaching and learning. Of course, the degree of participation will depend upon the ages of the learners. For adults the participation should be as equals. My colleague, Theresa Hicks, has demonstrated that students can contribute even at the level of the second grade. At this level, they require considerable coaching, of course, but the implications for their future development as response-able co-managers of their education, by this kind of participation are enormous.

A useful tool for specifying knowledge and know-how is the 'Quality characteristics evolution diagram', or tree diagram, illustrated in Figure 5.3.

CHARACTER AND WISDOM

It is interesting to observe that the development of character is considered to be of paramount importance in kindergarten and the early grade-school levels. As students move higher and higher in the educational system, wisdom and character receive less and less attention, until, at the level of the university, only the football coach seems to care about the development of character.

By character, we mean the collection of traits, such as:

Honesty	Initiative	Curiosity
Truthfulness	Integrity	Co-operativeness
Initiative	Self-esteem	Humility
Ability to work alone	Ability to work in groups	Perseverance
Trustworthiness	Conviction	Principles

Each school district should generate its own list of character traits they wish to see in their students. The list should be developed with broad participation, including parents, representatives from industry, teachers, students and the administration.

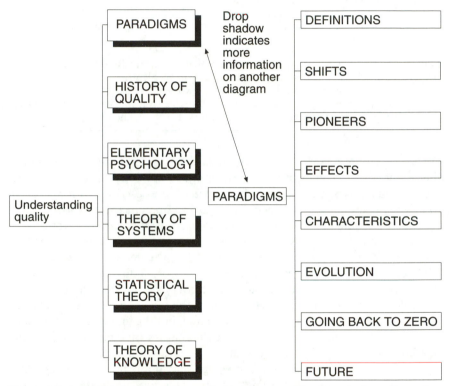

Figure 5.3 A quality characteristics evolution diagram. The drop shadow allows the diagram to deal with whatever level of detail is required without requiring a wall to display it. Thus the diagram to the right shows how the topic 'Paradigms' would be expanded in another detailed tree structure. Each of the drop-shadowed boxes is similarly expanded in another diagram.

The selection of desirable character traits will not always be easy. For example, there are questions in every community regarding religious and sex education. We are all aware that the question of prayer in schools has been discussed *ad nauseam*, but no matter how the courts may rule and no matter how the matter may be decided *legally*, proponents of various views will not be silenced easily. Quality management techniques, such as nominal group technique, affinity diagrams and other methods to organize thinking about complex problems,[9] provide methods for developing a consensus on difficult issues.

ENQUIRY AND PROJECT-CENTRED EDUCATION

The key to the development of wisdom and character is enquiry or project-centred learning. Students should undertake to do something which they recognize as important and rewarding to do. It should be fun and, at the same time, serious. The project should have an output, such as a service or a product. It could even be a proposal for legislation. The output could be an improvement in an activity within the school. Whatever is undertaken, there should always be a customer for the output.

We visualize the quality-managed school as developing its educational programme around a number of student projects. Projects lend themselves to co-operative learning. Teachers and students can observe barriers to co-operation and can identify non-cooperative behaviour.

Many educators have learned that when students engage in a project which serves others, it brings out the best in students. Even those who were previously seen to be 'problems' perform better.

The main difficulty for most teachers and administrators in project-orientated education is the changed relationship between teacher and learner. It is more difficult for the teacher to prepare a 'lesson plan'. In addition, methods to evaluate what has been learned are more subtle. In the old-fashioned approach, the students may be observed sitting, silently, as the teacher presents the information. Having presented a well-defined content, the teacher then uses a standardized test to see what the students have retained. The results of a standard test allow comparisons to be made amongst students or with other classes and with national norms. Unfortunately, though the conventional approach is easier on teachers, and provides 'objective numbers' which may make some people feel better or worse, it does not address the purposes of education.

National tests:

1 do not touch upon the development of wisdom and character;
2 do not deal with know-how;
3 are harmful to the students (half of them are in the lower 50 percentile);
4 for students and teachers alike, teaching to achieve test scores is *boring*!

The students at Mt Edgecumbe High School, after a few years' experience with quality management methods, developed the table below to illustrate the changed relationship between teacher and learner.

The development of wisdom and character require different methods of instruction. This fact has been recognized in the second SCANS report. The differences are summarized in Table 5.4.

Table 5.3 Roles of teachers and students

Teachers	DO TO	DO FOR	DO WITH	ENABLE
Students	No choice, captive, antagonist	Captive, passive, dependent	Dependent, accepting follower	Independent investigator, seeker of knowledge, joy in learning
	Let me out!	I'm OK	It's OK	joy in learning

→ Direction of increasing autonomy →

Table 5.4 The conventional classroom compared with the SCANS classroom

From the conventional classroom	*To the SCANS classroom*
Teacher knows answers:	More than one solution may be viable and the teacher may not have it in advance.
Students routinely work alone.	Students routinely work with teachers, peers and community members.
Teacher plans all activities.	Students and teachers plan and negotiate activities.
Teacher makes all assessments.	Students routinely assess themselves.
Information is organized, evaluated, interpreted and communicated to students by teacher.	Information is acquired, evaluated, organized, interpreted and communicated by students to appropriate audiences.
Organizing system of the classroom is simple: one teacher teaches 30 students.	Organizing systems are complex: teacher and students both reach out beyond school for additional information.
Reading, writing and maths are treated as separate disciplines; listening and speaking, are often missing from the curriculum.	Disciplines needed for problem-solving are integrated; listening and speaking are fundamental parts of learning.
Thinking is usually theoretical and 'academic'.	Thinking involves problem-solving, reasoning and decision-making.
Students are expected to conform to teacher's behavioural expectations; integrity and honesty are monitored by teacher; student self-esteem is often poor.	Students are expected to be responsible, sociable, self-managing, and resourceful; integrity and honesty are monitored within the social context of the classroom; students' self-esteem is high because they are in charge of their own learning.

Source: Fort Worth Public Schools

SPECIFIC SUGGESTIONS FOR PUTTING QUALITY MANAGEMENT TO WORK IN SCHOOLS

Getting started

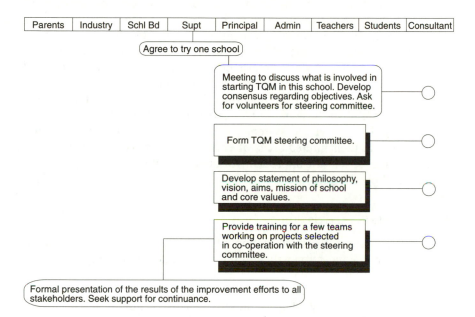

Figure 5.4 One way to get started, with leadership from the top (based on a suggestion from Larrae Rocheleau, Superintendent of Mt Edgecumbe High School, Sitka, Alaska). The arrows show who should provide leadership in the activities. In this example, the school principal is the leader. The small circle indicates assistance from the consultant. A box represents a task. An elongated box with rounded ends represents a meeting. A drop shadow on a box indicates that more detail is to be found in another diagram.

As indicated in Figure 5.1, success requires that a number of elements be in place. Therefore, if quality management is to be *successfully* applied in schools, it is essential that the transformation be led by an administrator; namely, superintendent, principal, headmaster or headmistress and so on. What does that person do? Figure 5.4 presents a process for getting started. It is not the *only* way to start, but it demonstrates some of the elements required for success. The chart in Figure 5.4 illustrates one of the more powerful tools in quality management. The chart is called a 'deployment flow chart' because it shows how the people are deployed in connection with a task. Deployment flow-charting displays the work and how the people interact with one another and the process. It is the only tool which displays these elements on one sheet of paper. The arrows leading into the boxes tell who should supply leadership. As with the quality characteristics evolution diagram, the drop shadow indicates that there is more detail to be found on another related diagram.

The objective is to bring about a state in which all elements of the school are working together in common purpose. This objective does not mean that it is impossible for an individual teacher to put some of the ideas to work in the classroom until everyone has agreed to the overall effort. If everyone waits for the leaders in education to start, we shall wait forever. Sometimes individual teachers have to begin anyway and do what they can. However, unless the entire system is changed, the work of an individual teacher will be frustrated. I would not advise teachers to wait until the entire system is improved before experimenting. Just be prepared for battles! We should be grateful to those hardy pioneers who went ahead anyhow, without waiting for the entire system to change before they tried quality management in their limited areas of control. They have provided us with tangible evidence that the approach works (in a limited way) and given us a glimpse of how things could be.

Getting started in the classroom

To a certain extent, the introduction of TQM in a school is more easily accomplished in connection with administration and maintenance, for these activities are similar to many activities already carried on in industry. In these kinds of applications, it will be possible to obtain considerable help from people in industry who are already practising quality management. Locate nearby companies which are already involved in TQM. Experience shows that they are more than willing to help. Examples of applications of TQM in the administrative tasks of a university are given in a recent publication.[10]

Introducing TQM in the classroom, however, is more of a challenge. There are fewer people around to help. Although the new paradigm for quality education is different from the approaches *mandated* by many people in authority in the school system, it is not that far removed from what many teachers want to do but cannot because the system will not allow them. The AASA has established a network of people interested in TQM in education and those who wish to pioneer can obtain considerable help from others of like mind who have signed up for the network. All that is required is a fax machine and the address list.

Here are some things which characterize TQM in the classroom:

1 The student as co-manager of the teaching/learning process

The teacher and learner should, at the beginning of every session, and especially at the beginning of the term, review and discuss their mutual objectives. The teacher should review and develop class consensus on the *knowledge, know-how, wisdom* and *character traits* expected to be developed. This is the most important step in the overall process, for without a consensus concerning what is to be done, it will not be possible to develop the co-operation so essential to co-management.

At the lowest levels, say in K-12 (British equivalent Key Stage 2), it is not usually necessary to argue with the children about what should be learned. Experience shows they are eager learners at the level, unless their home conditions have militated against it.[11] Experience with Head Start and similar programmes provides examples of what to do to overcome this handicap. As one moves higher and higher in the system, there will be a point at which students are not eager to learn a particular subject. 'Do I have to take algebra?' If the answer is 'Yes you must. It is required,' the teacher may be asserting authority but it is unlikely that the student will be ready to give that extra effort which leads to a quality result. One of the most important tasks of a teacher is to provide a basis for internal motivation towards a subject. This is why the SCANS report emphasizes the doing of work as a part of learning. Applications of algebra to everyday life are plentiful, and a good teacher can always show examples which will interest most students.

People learn best when they feel the need to know. Projects will inevitably deal with the need for algebraic manipulations, and these ought to be introduced *before* students are formally introduced to algebra. With such experiences behind them, students are more likely to accept that it is a rational requirement. In the end, of course, people often have to 'take' something they do not want and teachers cannot shun this responsibility. In a TQM-managed school, however, this forced feeding will be a rare event.

An essential part of the consensus-building is the definition of the levels of competence required. The teacher should have in mind some minimum level to be required of all students but should not inhibit those who wish to go beyond. Consensus should be established on how the competence is to be displayed, what the students have to do to demonstrate they have achieved the level of competence agreed upon, how they are expected to acquire it and what the teacher is expected to do to help. How the teacher and learner will know the competence has been attained should also be agreed upon.

Many teachers have had such poor experience with students that they do not believe that a consensus can be developed and that the students will then stick with it. Teachers have described their experiences in producing this consensus, even in inner-city schools and with students from homes where there are drugs and child abuse. These reports are becoming available now and are most heartening.[12]

According to Theresa Hicks, who has been experimenting with this approach in the second grade, the children are fascinated with the chance to help set the rules. They will often help the teacher to establish better discipline, self-discipline, than could be achieved before.[13] The teacher may have to intervene to prevent the children from becoming too harsh in dealing with those students who disturb the learning environment. The teacher may use these occasions as a way to introduce elementary considerations of psychology in a practical context.

2. The use of internal motivators rather than external motivators

One of the most difficult aspects to let go in the older paradigms in education is the use of external motivators to make the children do what is desired. 'Spare the rod and spoil the child' lives on in the minds of many teachers and parents, even when physical abuse is prohibited by law. Teachers who pioneer in quality management in the classroom, and rely on intrinsic motivation, will have to deal with criticism from well-meaning colleagues, parents, school boards and even some unenlightened employers.

For most teachers, the problem is not so much just to let go of the old ideas. Rather, it is knowing what to do instead. So many of us are habituated to using external motivators, we often feel we are not doing our jobs if we leave them out. Some examples of unhealthy external motivators are:

1 competitions for prizes;
2 grading students 'on the curve';
3 threats regarding poor performance;
4 special honours for good performance;
5 segregation of students into different classes by 'ability';
6 criticism without appreciation of accomplishment.

Internal motivators are called into play when a learner understands what it means to do something very well, has had a hand in setting the rules whereby an excellent job is to be recognized, knows that there is someone who shares the joy of knowing the job was well done and is taught to self-assess the work as it is ongoing. The key is not just to make students *responsible*, it is to make them *response-able*.

When we say that students should be made *response-able*, we mean that the teacher should make certain the learner has available the tools required for self-improvement and for improvement of processes. Older students can profit from the excellent book by Covey.[14]

There is pleasure in seeing self-improvement when it has been documented. This is the strength of the Boy Scout merit badge system. The badge shows that the student has been examined by someone who agrees that the work done was of good quality. It was not part of a contest. Anyone who can do the required tasks can earn one. The standards are (or should be) rigorous. The examiner helps the youngster if the job is not right and provides coaching to get it right. The badge does not signify that someone else has been beaten. It signifies conquest of self.

A powerful stimulant to internal motivation is to be part of a team in which each member of the team relies on the output of the other team members. This self-motivation, which is so evident in sporting events, also takes place in group projects. For example, a team of second-graders decided, with encouragement from their teacher, to develop an inexpensive egg incubator which might be used to help protect endangered species. With this objective in mind, the team needed to investigate such topics as at what temperature to maintain the eggs, how to protect the eggs, what to do when the eggs hatch, and so on. Each student investigated a different part of the project and reported back to the group. The internal motivation was intense. Reading, listening, presentation skills were developed almost as a by-product.

The co-operative spirit can be quickly destroyed if the students are set to competing for grades.

The teacher should discuss with the students

1 the objectives for the class, in the development of wisdom and character;
2 how the teacher and the students will know if they are progressing.

Of course this means the introduction of topics not normally introduced at the lowest grade levels, but the omission of this emphasis on the development of wisdom and character is a modern phenomenon. A review of the McGuffey readers used so widely at the turn of the century shows the deep concern for the development of character and wisdom our forefathers had. For a generation of youngsters growing up on farms, it probably worked, for a farmer cannot be of poor character and succeed. Nature is more unforgiving than an urban society. I do not propose to return to the McGuffey readers, for they are inappropriate to our times. The objectives remain; the means should change.

SOME PRINCIPLES CARRIED OVER, UNCHANGED, FROM INDUSTRIAL EXPERIENCE

Experience in industry with quality management may be distilled into a few simple principles. The first, and fundamental, is the Process Principle:

> The quality of the product
> is determined by the quality
> of the process which produces it.
> If you want to improve a product or service,
> concentrate on improving the process which produces it.

Assistant Principal Franklin P. Schargel of the George Westinghouse Vocational & Technical High School in Brooklyn gave me the following application of this principle. The administration was concerned over the number of students failing their subjects. Student failures are extremely expensive, for they create increased costs in money, time and effort in later years. At some critical value of failure rate, the entire system will come to a halt.

The process leading to success or failure involves the giving of assignments, the discussion with students, the homework, the testing and the general interaction of the teacher with the class. A flow chart may be made by students and teachers, depicting the processes which occur between the time the student receives an assignment and the time it is completed and evaluated. A study of students who were failing showed that the critical problem for these children was their failure to do the homework. There were other problems, revolving around language, reading ability, and so on, but a Pareto diagram of the causes of failure showed that this was by far the largest item. To reduce failures, therefore, the learning processes of the failing students had to be changed. The causes behind the failure to do homework were examined; namely, the process associated with just doing homework was studied in detail, and it was found that there were several reasons for failure to do homework, mostly beyond student control (that is, systems problems, Juran's principle). Therefore, special time was set aside during the school day and student tutors were assigned. In short order the failure rate declined by half. By concentrating on the *processes* and not just increasing the pressure on teachers or students for the desired result, the failure rates were reduced.

At Mt Edgecumbe High School, students were taught how to analyse their own study habits, after which the results on tests improved. But more important than that, they participated with their instructor in examining all aspects of the teaching/learning process. The teacher also changed what he or she was doing. By concentrating on the process, together they improved the product.

The role of tests and testing

Deming's point 3 is this: *cease dependence upon mass inspection*. This point translates directly into education. The change parallels what has been learned in industry. For years American managers hired inspectors to inspect the work of their employees. Quality did not really improve; rather, the poor quality work did not get out. Costs went up, and the customer saw mostly what was just good enough to pass inspection. Dr Deming told me that when he went to Western Electric in the 1920s there were 30,000 people making telephone sets and 10,000 people inspecting their work. The job of the workers was to get their product past the inspectors, and the job of the inspectors was to catch them if they did something wrong. This is no way to reduce cost. It is no way to achieve improved telephones. It is no way to work.

The only legitimate purpose of an examination in the classroom is to help the teacher and learner to decide what to do next.

Students and teachers should agree on what is to be accomplished, how it is to be judged, what level of competence is minimally acceptable and how it will be demonstrated. The phrase 'If it isn't perfect it isn't done' was coined by the students at Mt Edgecumbe High School. This does not mean that all work is equivalent. Some students may aim for a higher level of accomplishment. For example, one student developed a computer program giving an encylopaedic discussion of certain plants in Alaska. So did other students. Each student handed in perfect work, but some students made much more extensive contributions than others.

Some people worry that, without grades, potential employers will not be able to judge potential applicants for employment. But grades do not bear upon the competencies cited in the first SCANS report. Evidence of accomplishment should be developed by citing accomplishments. The second SCANS report referred to earlier, for example, proposes that each student develop a dossier, with accomplishments listed and signed by appropriate faculty and others, attesting the correctness of the descriptions. Students should aim to develop the best list of demonstrated competencies they can. The school should describe the minimum standards to which all students are held. This description should be in complete detail, in so far as the administration and faculty are prepared to authenticate it. The SCANS report gives a sample dossier. This approach is much superior to the giving of grades and the ranking of students or schools.

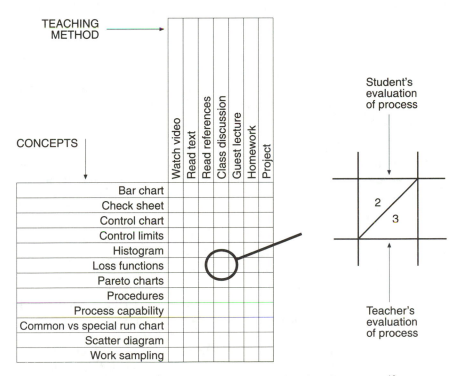

Figure 5.5 A QFD approach to improving the teaching/learning process[15]

A METHOD WHEREBY STUDENTS HELP THE TEACHER TO IMPROVE THE LEARNING PROCESS

Figure 5.5 shows an adaptation of a 'quality function deployment' chart.

In Figure 5.5 the rows represent the elements of knowledge and know-how that the teacher and students have agreed represent the learning objectives in the class. The columns represent the experiences the teacher has arranged for the students to have. The intersection of the row and column has room for two numbers. These numbers represent the student's and teacher's evaluations of how well the experience helped the student. The numbering system should be worked out (probably by a team of students) so that when numbers are assigned they have approximately the same meaning to everyone. The numbering system should be very crude, say 0 to 2 meaning 'no value', 'some value' to 'very valuable'. The numbers, in themselves, should not be given any significance, but the ratings can be the basis for discussion and improvement.

CONCLUSION

There are so many more aspects of quality in education that it requires a book to do justice to them. Remember that the main objective of the teacher is to put quality into education, which may well be defined as follows:

> *Quality* in education is what makes learning a pleasure and a joy. Some measures of student performance may be increased by threats, by competition for grades or by prizes, but the attachment to learning will be unhealthy. It requires a quality experience to create an independent learner.

> *Joy* in learning is ever-changing. What is thrilling at one age is infantile at another. Teachers must be ever-alert to engage the students in a discussion of what constitutes a quality experience. The negotiations and discussions are never done.

It takes constant engagement to wed a student to learning.

I must close with a warning. Once people have learned to walk, they will not return to crawling. Once students have tasted the joy of learning in an educational institution which runs according to quality management principles, they will not accept something inferior. Up to this point in time I have met only a few students who have moved from a quality learning experience to the conventional classroom. There are so few of them they have no option but to keep a low profile while they seethe in anger. They tell me so. As the quality revolution in the classroom catches on and more students are produced who understand what quality in education can be, it is inevitable that they will reach a critical mass. When these students enter our universities in large numbers, they will make a difference, for that is the nature of their training. I look forward to that day.

NOTES

1 Dalton, James F., *Leadership Skills*, a videotaped lecture, available from the National Society of Professional Engineers, 1420 King Street, Alexandria, VA 22314; (703) 684 2882.
2 Covey, Stephen R., *Seven Habits of Highly Effective People*, New York: Simon & Schuster, 1989, p. 101.
3 Adapted from Ersoz, Clara Jean, M.D., St Clair Hospital, 'TQM: healthcare's roadmap to the 21st century', presented at North Coast Quality Week, New Paradigms in Health, Erie, PA, 2 October 1992.
4 Tribus, Myron, 'Deming's Way', *Quality First*, NSPE Publication no. 1459, 4th edn, National Institute for Engineering Management & Systems, 1420 King Street, Alexandria, VA 22314.
5 *What Work Requires of Schools: a SCANS Report for America 2000*, The Secretary's Commission on Achieving Necessary Skills, US Department of Labor, June 1991.
6 *Learning a Living: A Blueprint for High Performance*, April 1992, US Department of Labor.
7 For an example of how one school system has met this challenge, see *Connecticut's Common Core of Learning*, adopted by the Connecticut State Board of Education, January 1987. The common core does not deal with wisdom and character, but it is a start.
8 Educators will recognize at once the relation of these definitions to Bloom's taxonomy.
9 See, e.g.: Scholtes, Peter R. *et al.*, *The Team Handbook*, Joiner Associates, PO Box 5445, Madison, WI 53705-0445; (608) 238 8134; FAX: (608) 238 2808.
Brassard, Michael, *The Memory Jogger Plus+* GOAL/QPC, 13 Branch Street, Methuen, MA 091844; (508) 685 3900; FAX: (508) 685 6151.
10 Harris, John W. and Baggett, J. Mark (eds) *Quality Quest in the Academic Process*, published by Samford University, Birmingham, Alabama 35229, and by GOAL/QPC (1992).
11 Be aware, however, that some of the changes which occur under TQM will not sit well with all parents. We already know of instances in which parents who are proud of their children's report cards (all As) are upset when grading is eliminated or reduced in importance. Some do not like co-operative learning.
12 See listing of reports on TQM in education prepared by the American Association of School Administrators. Write or call to the editor of the *Quality Network News*.
13 See, e.g., Sachar, Emily, *Shut Up and Let the Lady Teach*, Poseidon Press, 1991.
14 See note 2.
15 Special software for creating these charts on a PC or a Macintosh computer are under development by GOAL/QPC.

6 Is there a place for Total Quality Management in higher education?

Jacky Holloway

The debate about 'quality in education', which has been gathering momentum over the past decade, encompasses a number of complex sub-debates. For instance, what is meant by *quality* in an educational context? Who should measure or control educational quality? Can the interests of diverse stakeholders in education be fairly reflected in definitions of quality? Should quality be assessed differently at school, and at further and higher education levels? Is it more appropriate to measure quality with reference to inputs, processes, outputs or outcomes, and at the level of the educational programme, institution or system? If quality is multi-dimensional, which dimension deserves priority when resources are limited?

Each is a valid question deserving serious exploration in its own right; and none may be amenable to a 'best' or 'correct' answer. To some extent this lack of potential precision reflects the state of the art of quality assessment and management in services generally and in education in particular. More significantly, it reflects the fact that stakeholders in education systems (especially public sector systems) have values and interests which may always conflict or compete in some ways. The challenge for educational providers is to manage their services within such constraints as to negotiate the boundaries of the legitimate interests of external customers, consumers and the wider community, and to operate within these boundaries in ways which also meet the needs of internal customers. The key aim of this chapter is to explore what Total Quality Management (TQM) may have to offer to a range of stakeholders in higher education as they address such challenges.

ISSUES AND QUESTIONS

Much research and documented discussion has addressed the questions introduced above, often in isolation but increasingly in combination. They are mostly questions about 'whats', objectives or ends, still reflecting uncertainty about what comprises 'quality' in education. However, the policy context of the late 1980s and 1990s has forced the pace. While the 'ends' of education are still debated, pressure is on to address the means to measure, improve and monitor quality. This shift of focus onto the 'hows' of quality assessment, assurance, management and related terms is not a peculiarly British phenomenon. It is long familiar to North Americans and is increasingly prominent elsewhere in Europe. (For a brief account, see Burrows *et al.* 1992a.) Some reference will be made to the 'whats', or characteristics, of quality in education, but in the main this chapter will assume that the questions have been resolved sufficiently to enable attention to be focused on one particular contender for providing the means to some agreed ends (the 'hows').

The contender in the spotlight is TQM. Before the momentum for TQM becomes unstoppable or, equally, before TQM is unfairly rejected, this chapter aims to explore its current and potential future roles in the light of concerns about its appropriateness as a route to the high-quality service we all desire.

TQM has an obvious appeal for higher education institutions today as they are being encouraged to compete actively for students (their primary 'customers' or beneficiaries). Furthermore, external stakeholders – employers, government, the quality assessors and the representative bodies' quality assurers – are increasingly looking for systematic and systemic approaches to quality, not *ad hoc* initiatives or post-event corrective action. Students increasingly seek to be reassured that their studies will meet their needs and their qualifications will be valued highly by others. Their concerns about quality have been articulated in terms which have much in common with proponents of quality improvement in other public services (National Union of Students 1992). As external and resource pressures increase, higher education staff will increasingly need new techniques and skills to deliver a quality service in a climate where morale can be very fragile. All stakeholders stand to gain from an evaluation of the concepts and practices of TQM in a higher education context. Whether they hold great promise, or are dangerous, inappropriate or ineffective, it would be nice to know as soon as possible!

TQM IN THE HIGHER EDUCATION POLICY CONTEXT

It is unnecessary to look far beyond the remaining public services to understand why TQM is of rapidly growing interest to managers and decision-makers in British higher education. Those services which have not been subject to wholesale privatization since the early 1980s have none the less had a central government spotlight turned on them to illuminate their performance, with strong emphasis on their efficiency.

During the 80s, government-inspired managerialist internal practices (management budgeting, appraisals, business planning, performance indicators) gradually became commonplace in the public sector. These were accompanied by structural developments which have altered accountability relationships: competitive tendering for a growing range of local government services; general management and the internal market in the NHS;

local management of schools; and so on. Perhaps due to the unpalatable effects of an undue emphasis on efficiency and economy as well as to changing public demands, more recent central and local government policies have placed the stress on the effectiveness of services meeting the needs for which they were established (or, sometimes, changing the definition of those needs). These developments have been well documented by, amongst others, Cave *et al.* (1990), Day and Klein (1987), Henkel (1991a, 1991b), Holloway (1993a), Metcalfe and Richards (1990), Pollitt (1986, 1987) and Pollitt and Harrison (1992).

While efficiency and effectiveness remain requirements, in many services the predominant performance-related concern is now a broader one – the *quality* of services and products. Debates about the definition of 'quality' and approaches to its assessment persist, but few would dispute its multi-dimensional nature (as articulated in an influential *British Medical Journal* article by Maxwell in 1984). Here we will take the 'quality' of a public service's practices to reflect a set of dimensions including effectiveness, efficiency, equity, access and acceptability. The value which stakeholders will place on these dimensions will vary with their interest in the service concerned.

While in some cases 'quality awareness' has been demanded from above, in many a shift in emphasis in advance of policy pressure reflects a desire to retain control over intrinsic service characteristics, or to protect professional domains. The acceptance of clinical audit in the NHS in the late 80s is a case in point, when the pragmatists in the medical profession finally persuaded their colleagues that, unless a routine peer review system was rapidly established, a less acceptable model would be imposed. In some cases pressures from British central government have acted as no more than a catalyst for major investments in quality management initiatives: elsewhere in the NHS, in local government, British Rail and the Post Office, for instance. The spread of such initiatives can only be partially explained by the import of managers from the private sector (relatively few of whom would have had direct experience of TQM anyway), threats of privatization, overseas study tours and the implementation of the government's Citizen's Charter policy initiative. Public sector managers today are well aware of developments in private sector practices and, perhaps with an increased expectation of careers in more than one sector, frequently look outside their own service for new techniques. Their growing interest in TQM can be located within a broader debate about the role of generic and distinctive competences in the 'new public management' of the 1990s.

With such diffusion of experiences from the traditional and newly privatized services, and between public services, it is therefore only to be expected that higher education will be affected by TQM in due course. The management of schools and the nature of their curricula have been subject to major change driven by central government policy over a number of years, although perhaps their size in particular has limited the extent to which fully-fledged TQM has yet been explored (West-Burnham 1992). The beam of the government's quality spotlight has swung onto the higher education sector comparatively recently, following key legislative changes for further and higher education in 1991–92 (see Quality Support Centre 1993, and for a summary of relevant policy and legislative documents from 1985–92, see Harvey *et al*. 1992a). The 'new' universities or former poly-technics, when validated by the Council for National Academic Awards (CNAA), had wide experience of quality assurance and self-assessment. Higher education in Britain is now largely provided by a unified university sector, and responsibility for quality audit and assessment have been vested in two external bodies the Higher Educational Quality Council ('owned' by the university sector collectively) and Quality Assessment Committees linked to the Higher Education Funding Councils. Would the implementa-tion of TQM be an appropriate response by today's universities and colleges to the requirements of these bodies for self-assessment, inspection and con-tinuous quality review?

The adoption of industrially developed quality systems has had a slow start in higher education when compared with British local government and the NHS. *Quality in Higher Education* (QHE), a large-scale study of approaches to quality assessment in higher education undertaken at the University of Central England, found that the number of institutions which by 1992 had embraced TQM explicitly and widely remained at around half a dozen. (See Harvey *et al*. 1992c for a summary of the project, Burrows *et al*. 1992b, and related publications already cited.) This pattern is surprisingly similar to that reported in the United States by Chaffee and Sherr (1992).

A small number of the QHE study's respondents had adopted narrower quality assurance approaches, seeking accreditation to the British Standard for quality systems, BS 5750 (the UK equivalent to the European and inter-national quality systems standards EN 2900 and ISO 9000). At the begin-ning of 1993 the vast majority of the still-small number of educational and training institutions (including further education) registered under BS 5750 had accreditation for the delivery of basic vocational training, or for their administrative functions. There is some interest in quality systems standards in universities in connection with programmes such as management educa-tion, where students may be sponsored by employers who demand quality systems accreditation for all their suppliers. However, accreditation of quality systems very rarely extends to course design or the delivery of non-vocational programmes.

However, there are signs of a rapid growth in interest in TQM and quality systems standards in higher education from 1993 on. This perhaps reflects the UK Department for Education's intention to establish an explicit link between quality assessment and funding. Proxy indicators include the increasingly regular appearance of letters and articles on quality manage-ment in the *Times Higher Education Supplement*, and the readiness of university academics, administrators and managers to participate in seminars and other events with a quality management theme. Following long-standing (and not always fruitful) debates about the definition and measurement of 'quality' in higher education, a new need has emerged for the rapid discovery of how to put theory into practice.

Having flagged up some characteristics of the policy context with potential relevance to quality management in higher education, it is time to revisit the objectives of this chapter and plan the way ahead. It is suggested that interest in TQM may grow very rapidly in higher education in the early 1990s. It is also suggested that translating interest into implementation may be difficult and dangerous, for the following reasons: TQM is a complex approach demanding considerable resources; it is an approach to long-term organizational change, and therefore may not be an ideal response to potentially short-lived political developments. Few models of TQM have been designed with service industries in mind; and its effectiveness in meeting the (sometimes conflicting) needs of stakeholders in public services is as yet relatively unknown.

Defining 'quality' and 'customers' in any educational context can be particularly problematic. It is also likely that some more specific and as yet undiscovered factors will be relevant to successful implementation in higher education institutions. On the other hand, there are features common to most models of TQM identified below, which may appeal to the collegial culture of universities. Other features may be favourably regarded by employers, whose relationship with higher education institutions is likely to become closer through the 90s. In theory at least, some of its most significant benefits may be felt by those groups which traditionally have had least power: students and support staff. TQM can also provide tools and techniques for improving efficiency significantly, although it is the tendency in commercial firms to overemphasize these aspects of TQM which may alienate academic staff in particular. Some of these issues are explored by Geddes (1993), Sallis (1993), and in the North American context by Chaffee and Sherr (1992).

TQM CORE CHARACTERISTICS

TQM has now been referred to frequently as a potential way of enabling the higher education sector to manage all aspects of 'quality' in higher education institutions which are under increasing scrutiny. No distinction has yet been made between the intrinsic quality of students' learning experiences, quality of 'educational products' (course, curricula, physical teaching materials) and the broad field of quality of service: all the human interactions (sometimes involving equipment) involved in the delivery of educational products; individuals' learning experiences and the environment in which teaching and learning take place. Yet clearly all of these inputs and processes are pertinent to 'quality of higher education'. So too are the outputs and longer-term or indirect outcomes of higher education processes;

certainly for many of the QHE study's stakeholder groups, these were the key concerns. Can TQM really have such a wide-ranging impact, or are its potential benefits confined to, say, support services, teaching materials or the physical learning environment?

In this section some core characteristics of TQM are outlined, and distinguishing characteristics of some popular models (or varieties) are suggested. The place of TQM in service management *per se* is considered before focusing on its potential use in higher education.

Based on the substantial research of Oakland and colleagues at the University of Bradford, any model of TQM can usually be expected to involve the following common core:

- recognizing customers and discovering their needs;
- setting standards which are consistent with customer requirements;
- controlling processes and improving their capability;
- establishing systems for quality;
- management's responsibility for setting quality policy, providing motivation through leadership, and equipping people to achieve quality;
- empowerment of people at all levels in the organization to act for quality improvement.

(Dotchin and Oakland 1992: 141)

Equally characteristic is the notion that 'good enough quality' can never be achieved but that improvement must continually be sought. Few practitioners or consultants would dispute the inclusion of such characteristics in a definition of TQM, and there is nothing here to suggest that these are inappropriate for service organizations. Clearly too, this hard core embraces much current thinking on good management practice, which in turn is underpinned by a wide range of theoretical fields (theories about organizational structure, culture, change; systems theories; strategic management; occupational psychology; motivation theories; and so on). It would be difficult to argue that this TQM common core has been explicitly developed as a coherent organizational paradigm, although those who apply it may *perceive* it to be a distinctive approach to performance improvement. Whether there is anything especially problematic about applying this general set of TQM objectives in higher education or other public services is a matter for debate to which we will return.

Most managers who encounter TQM meet it in a form packaged by an advocate of one of the many 'quality gurus', or occasionally by a guru in person. (Some of the distinguishing characteristics of the quality gurus are referred to below, but for a more comprehensive but still brief introduction to their work see Bendell's booklet for the Department of Trade and Industry 1991; Oakland 1989, 1991, also provides accessible introductions to the whole field of TQM.) The original prescriptions of gurus like Deming, Crosby and Juran were developed in the manufacturing sector. This is not surprising, since the development of the early models coincided with the urgent needs for post-war economic reconstruction, Japanese industrialists and scientists being particularly receptive to the concepts of statistical quality control from which today's western TQM models derive. However, services clearly represent the growth area of economic activity for the 1990s in the west.

The quality literature during the 1980s may have been dominated by manufacturing applications (Dotchin and Oakland 1992), but the newer markets for quality management represented by service organizations and functions are being seized upon readily by consultants and trainers. Many base their prescriptions on the gurus' tools and techniques, with their manufacturing origins and with little adaptation to meet the distinctive characteristics and needs of services. Of course, many managers of services are themselves eagerly seeking assistance from the 'quality industry' to help them achieve organizational change, development and performance improvement. In the NHS, for instance, attention was turning to TQM from the mid-80s with the development of general management; deregulation in the personal finance sector brought quality to the fore in bank and building society marketing; quality of produce and service have figured large in the ongoing supermarket war. Even voluntary organizations are exploring what TQM might have to offer them, while Pfeffer and Coote (1991) address issues of power and public service politics in an evaluation which concludes that appropriately designed TQM may have a positive role to play in the public sector.

An important feature of much service activity is its labour-intensiveness. This also characterizes the major part of TQM investment and activity (staff and management time, training, development, communication skills, team-working, for instance). Investment in quality systems hardware is a relatively small contribution even in manufacturing operations today. Indeed, as Deming has argued, the technology employed by the Japanese motor industry is broadly similar to that in the west; the major investment has been in human resource management (and see Holmes 1991).

So is there really any need to doubt the appropriateness of TQM to services in general? Although there is considerable debate about what precisely are the important distinctions between services and other businesses and activities (Dotchin and Oakland 1991; Normann 1991; Zeithaml *et al.* 1990; Gronroos 1984; Gummesson 1991; Shostack 1977), few writers see the essence of the service act as so intangible as to be not amenable to scrutiny. An insistence on the 'intangibility' of 'good teaching' could be interpreted as a convenient way of avoiding any attempt to be responsive to feedback, especially when combined with the 'professional knows best' view.

It does seem worth recognizing that service organizations, and service departments and roles within any organization, have some distinguishing characteristics of relevance from time to time. However, 'services' embrace enormous diversity, and this internal diversity may produce more significant contingency factors than the service/manufacturing split. An appropriate classification framework would be a valuable contribution to the methodology for a systematic and systemic study of TQM successes and failures. Contributions have already been made here by Dotchin and Oakland (1991), Haywood-Farmer (1988) and Fitzgerald *et al.* (1991), amongst others.

In the meantime, the growing service management literature and research continues to provide a number of useful models and concepts for describing and analysing service performance, amongst them the basic concept of the customer-supplier chain, gap analysis (Zeithaml *et al.* 1990), and service repositioning (Haywood-Farmer 1988). Such models can be of practical assistance to managers in the diagnosis of quality problems: for instance, in matching the expectations of their stakeholders with service characteristics; in the design of new or improved services; modelling changes, testing their effectiveness; and in implementation and ongoing monitoring of service efficiency and acceptability. They can also provide data for decision-making involving all concerned: of particular value in an academic institution, perhaps, where decisions are often taken by representative committees rather than by those with a solely management role.

On the basis of available literature it would seem that these bodies of knowledge have not readily been applied in the quest for quality in higher education. However, 'service management' is not necessarily an alternative to TQM; it could readily be incorporated within the long-term processes of TQM development. For such guidance one can of course turn also to other bodies of knowledge from which to select concepts and models relevant to the improvement of quality and any other aspects of performance.

In any event, the value of TQM *per se* can only be assessed in conjunction with the organization's aims and the objectives of its TQM programme. Unless these are clear (and one could say that higher education institutions have not always been crystal clear about their aims), there are limits to the extent to which the potential appropriateness of TQM can yet be judged. This notion of judging an institution's service quality in the light of its own objectives (informed, one would hope, by the needs of its customers) is ostensibly shaping the formal requirements of the new higher education quality assessment machinery in Britain. Whether this will be a precursor to more prescriptive 'gold standards', however, remains to be seen.

PROSPECTS AND ASPIRATIONS FOR TQM IN HIGHER EDUCATION

In the conclusions to the first phase report of the QHE project (Harvey *et al.* 1992b), the growing interest in TQM was noted, together with the need for a careful exploration of its potential value and appropriateness in the higher education context. A key question to be asked is whether the various elements of the above common core, or the (prescribed or DIY) routes to them, are better suited to some organizational contexts than others.

Beyond the higher education context and as a counterweight to the preaching of the converted, more critical evaluations of the various TQM models are now being undertaken. This investigation has often initially involved trying to identify common elements as above (Dotchin and Oakland 1992; Holloway 1991; Saraph *et al.* 1989). Where TQM programmes in education and other sectors have been evaluated systematically (Schofield *et al.* 1991; Coulson-Thomas 1992; Binney 1992; Brunel University 1991; Geddes (1993); Chaffee and Sherr 1992), their findings tend to point towards fairly predictable critical success factors: training, top management commitment, good information and the like. If these are not present, few organizational changes are likely to succeed, let alone TQM; and if they are present, 'TQM success' may be hard to disentangle from 'good management practice'. In many cases studied, it is too early to judge TQM's contribution to sustained organizational competitiveness or development, quite apart from the methodological problems of attributing causation.

Only recently has the focus of TQM research started to include the differences between the models and the implications these may have for their applicability in different contexts. Do the differences indicate particular theoretical underpinnings, assumptions about how people and organizations work? Or are they differences in presentation? In addition, how does the set of common core elements compare with other approaches to organization-wide change and development? Is there anything innovative about TQM, or is it simply 'old wine in new bottles'? If this is the case but the wine happens to meet a need that had not previously been recognized, or is now made more palatable to its consumers, is there a problem? Can a distinctive set of critical success factors for TQM implementation be identified, and if so are they unique to TQM or common to, for instance, organizational development, strategic planning or human resource management (see, for example, Holmes 1991)?

Answers to such questions are urgently required, as signs of TQM failures surface at practitioner events and are reported in the business media. The symptoms include a need to relaunch the TQM programme, abandonment of Quality Circles, vociferous reactions against slogans and gimmicks, and incomplete implementation. Are organizations failing to choose or implement TQM 'correctly', are they victims of unforseen environmental or internal obstacles, or are the TQM models fundamentally flawed? The hypothesis of the research proposed below is that there are some common, systemic causes for problems and failures. Understanding these causes should also have practical relevance to potential consumers of TQM approaches, including many in higher education.

In this final section we will link concerns expressed by higher education stakeholders to such generalized research questions. A framework for addressing such concerns within a time-scale short enough to meet practitioner needs but long enough to produce new learning will be outlined.

The QHE research has shown remarkable consistency in the criteria by which key stakeholder groups judge the quality of higher education. Naturally there are distinctive patterns of concerns within the staff, student, employer, quality assurers, and government and quality assessor groups. But the picture emerging from the many QHE reports is one in which the following ten items were given priority by at least half the stakeholder groups:

- There are adequate physical resources to support teaching and learning.
- There are adequate human resources to support teaching and learning (and staff are properly qualified).
- The programme has clear aims and objectives which are understood by staff and students.
- The subject content relates to the programme's aims and objectives.
- Students are encouraged to be actively involved in, and are given responsibility for, learning.
- The standard of the programme is appropriate to the reward.
- Assessment is valid, objective and fair.
- Assessment covers the full range of course aims and objectives.
- Students receive useful feedback from assessment (and are kept informed of progress).
- Students leave with transferable knowledge and skills.

The researchers conclude: 'Quality in higher education is increasingly focusing on the total student experience. Quality assessment must relate to inputs, processes and outputs. Quality criteria change over time and quality assessment must take into account differences in the mission of institutions' (Harvey *et al.* 1992c: 3).

Taking the above list, it would seem that TQM could offer a great deal to higher education. In addition to encompassing good management practice, the principles common to a number of models of TQM – continuous improvement, responsiveness to a range of stakeholder or customer needs, fitness for intended purpose, the involvement of everybody – could provide additional appeal in the light of these priority criteria. Interestingly, relatively low priority was placed on criteria which most directly relate to subject knowledge and course content, and face-to-face teaching performance *per se*. So the potential of TQM to threaten academic freedom may be low; and the significance of the intangible aspects of 'good teaching' is rather outweighed by the presence of a number of very tangible considerations. This is not to argue against TQMs embracing the teacher/learner interaction. In some models (Deming's, for example), such a limitation would be highly inappropriate, but this interface should be handled with care. So why might staff in higher education, in particular, continue to find TQM unappealing?

The following sorts of fears are amongst those expressed by academic and management staff with direct involvement (most very recent) in TQM in higher education:

- a distaste for evangelism;
- too rapid movement towards 'how to do TQM' without adequate consideration of the objectives of the TQM programme or the institution's aims and values;
- problems with identifying customers, and then prioritizing their competing needs, without market values to assist in the decision;
- resource constraints, sheer inability to meet students' needs;
- reconciling customer-responsiveness with the possession of professional expertise and power – the customer is not always right.

By and large, these are higher education versions of concerns that apply to many if not all public services and are borne out by US evidence too (Chaffee and Sherr 1992). They may be more generic than that; they reflect organizational culture, structure, resources, power distribution, organizational capability, environmental constraints, organizational strategy and TQM objectives, and control. Taken in conjunction with the QHE priority criteria, and the 'success factors' emerging from limited research to date, they start to suggest some contingency factors which might prove fruitful in helping to understand what may make TQM, or particular variants, succeed or fail. For instance,

- the extent to which TQM is integrated with strategic planning;
- the consistency of the chosen approach with the organization's culture(s) and values;
- the effective deployment of management good practice in the name of TQM;
- a conscious effort to understand the objectives of stakeholders when designing and implementing TQM programmes;
- objectives for the TQM programme which reflect its inherently systemic and holistic nature;
- the forms of ownership, power, control and accountability within organizations;
- the relative stability and predictability of the organization's competitive environment.

The comparatively recent growth of TQM applied to services presents new research opportunities. The likelihood of its rapid expansion into higher education, coinciding as it almost inevitably will with rapid externally influenced change and continued resource constraints, makes it imperative that such research is of value to practitioners as well as detached observers. There are many methodological challenges in testing contingency factors in real organizations, but much to be gained for practitioners and customers alike of organizations striving for total quality.

The research opportunities include the feasibility of carefully designed, in-depth evaluation studies as well as large-scale surveys and comparative case studies, perhaps on a collaborative basis. It seems likely that a number of higher education institutions, which have embarked upon TQM, would be interested in charting their own experience, in an action-research mode. From the outset some carefully chosen TQM case studies from other sectors may provide useful pointers. Such research can contribute to more effective practice as well as to the development of firmer theoretical underpinnings for TQM. Maximum benefit may be obtained by combining longitudinal case and cohort studies with survey and secondary data as a means of triangulation. This may increase the prospects of obtaining useful data for practitioners within a relatively short time, particularly if an appropriate communications network were available to facilitate sharing of information. Secondary data may also possibly enable influences of national cultures to be explored.

As one of the characteristics of TQM is its holistic nature, it would not be appropriate to restrict the sources of theoretical insights solely to, for instance, organizational behaviour, educational theories or statistics, but to draw on a wide range of other disciplines as appropriate. Immediately appealing fields include systems thinking, many areas of management theory including organizational change, decision sciences and psychology.

CONCLUSIONS

This chapter has attempted to review the prospects for positive outcomes from the application of TQM to higher education, drawing on the early experiences of several UK universities. It is too early to tell whether certain combinations of contextual factors and gurus' models are promising or portentious, but it is fairly certain that HEIs will turn to TQM and other organization-wide quality systems in increasing numbers during the 1990s in Britain and abroad. Pressures in this direction come explicitly from key stakeholders, within the broader context of the application of post-Fordist and consumerist models to public services (Holloway 1993b). Generic lessons from the experience of other sectors will grow in significance, but the role for TQM at the teaching–learning interface may become a subject for more specialized debate.

What is not at issue is that for a number of higher education institutions, TQM has already found a place. To return to the pragmatic motivation alluded to early in this chapter, even a relatively small study of the impact of TQM as it emerges in higher education institutions should contribute to our understanding of its benefits and pitfalls, and its coherence as an organizational paradigm. Spin-offs should include more effective higher education, and more relevant teaching about total quality management.

REFERENCES

Bendell, T. (1991) *The Quality Gurus*, London: Department of Trade and Industry.

Binney, G. (1992) *Making Quality Work: Lessons from Europe's Leading Companies*, London: Economist Intelligence Unit.

Brunel University (1991) *Evaluation of Total Quality Management Projects in the National Health Service*, First interim report to the Department of Health, Brunel University: Centre for the Evaluation of Public Policy and Practice.

Burrows, A., Harvey, L. and Green, D. (1992a) *International Rise in Interest about Quality in Higher Education: a Review of the Literature*, Birmingham: Quality in Higher Education.

—— (1992b) *Quality Assurance Systems: A Review of the Application of Industrial Models to Education and Training*, Birmingham: QHE.

Cave, M., Kogan, M. and Smith, R. (eds) (1990) *Output and Performance Measurement in Government: the State of the Art*, London: Jessica Kingsley.

Chaffee, E.E. and Sherr, L.A. (1992) *Quality: Transforming Post-Secondary Education*, Washington, DC: ASHE-ERIC Higher Education Report no. 3.

Coulson-Thomas, C.J. (1992) 'Surveying the scene', *The TQM Magazine* (Feb. 1992): 25–31.

Crosby, P.B. (1979) *Quality is Free*, New York: McGraw-Hill.

—— (1986) *Quality without Tears*, New York: McGraw-Hill.

Day, P. and Klein, R. (1987) *Accountabilities: Five Public Services*, London: Tavistock Publications.

Deming, W.E. (1986) *Out of the Crisis*, Cambridge, MA: MIT Center for Advanced Engineering Study.

Dotchin, J.A. and Oakland, J.S. (1991) 'Total Quality Management in the Services, Part 1, Understanding and classifying services', European Centre for TQM, working paper.

—— (1992) 'Theories and concepts in Total Quality Management', *Total Quality Management* 3(2): 133–45.

Fitzgerald, L., Johnston, R., Brignall, S., Silvestro, R. and Voss, C. (1991) *Performance Measurement in Service Businesses*, London: CIMA.

Geddes, T. (1993) 'The total quality initiative at South Bank University', *Higher Education* 25(3): 341–61.

Gronroos, C. (1984) *Strategic Management and Marketing in the Service Sector*, Bromley: Chartwell-Bratt.

Gummesson, E. (1991) 'Truths and myths in service quality', *International Journal of Service Industry Management* 2(3): 7–16.

Harvey, L., Burrows, A. and Green, D. (1992a) *The Policy Background to the Quality Debate in UK Higher Education 1985–1992: a Summary of Key Documents*, Birmingham: QHE.

—— (1992b) *Criteria of Quality*, Birmingham: QHE.

—— (1992c) *Criteria of Quality, Summary*, Birmingham: QHE.

Haywood-Farmer, J. (1988) 'A conceptual model of service quality', *International Journal of Operations and Production Management* 8(6): 19–29.

Henkel, M. (1991a) 'The new "evaluative state"', *Public Administration* 69 (Spring): 121–36.

—— (1991b) *Government, Evaluation and Change*, London: Jessica Kingsley.

Holloway, J.A. (1991) 'Designing for quality models for public services', Paper presented at the European Group for Public Administration Conference, The Hague (Sept.).

—— (1993a) *Managing Organizational Performance*, Open University course B887 *Managing Public Services*, Milton Keynes: The Open University.

—— (1993b) 'Delivering "quality" in distance education: exploring the role for quality management', Open University: Centre for Youth and Adult Studies, Occasional Paper series.

Holmes, K. (1991) *Total Quality Lessons from Japan*, Surrey: PIRA International.

Juran, J.M. *et al.* (eds) (1975) *Quality Control Handbook* (3rd edn), New York: McGraw-Hill.

Maxwell, R.J. (1984) 'Quality assessment in health', *British Medical Journal* 288 (12 May): 1470–2.

Metcalfe, L. and Richards, S. (1990) *Improving Public Management* (2nd edn), London: Sage.

National Union of Students (1992) *NUS Student Charter*, London: NUS.

Normann, R. (1991) *Service Management: Strategy and Leadership in Service Business* (2nd edn), Chichester: John Wiley & Sons.

Oakland, J.S. (1989) *Total Quality Management*, Oxford: Heinemann.

—— (1991) *Total Quality Management for Effective Leadership*, London: DTI.

Pfeffer, N. and Coote, A. (1991) *Is Quality Good for You? A Critical Review of Quality Assurance in Welfare Services*, London: IPPR.

Pollit, C. (1986) 'Beyond the managerial model: the case for broadening performance assessment in government and the public services', *Financial Accountability and Management* 2(3): 155–70.

—— (1987) 'The politics of performance assessment: lessons for higher education?' *Studies in Higher Education* 12: 87–98.

Pollitt, C. and Harrison, S. (1992) *Handbook of Public Services Management*, Oxford: Blackwell.

Quality Support Centre (1993) *A Guide to the Changes in Higher Education*, Milton Keynes: Open University Press.

Sallis, E. (1993) *Total Quality Management in Education*, London: Kogan Page.

Saraph, J.V., Benson, P.G. and Schroeder, R.G. (1989) 'An instrument for measuring the critical factors of quality management', *Decision Sciences Journal* 20(4): 810–29.

Schofield, A., Sheaff, R., Wellstead, L. and Young, E. (1991) *Report for the NHSTA on Total Quality Management*, University of Manchester Health Services Management Unit.

Shostack, G.L. (1977) 'Breaking free from product marketing', *Journal of Marketing* 47(2): 73–80.

West-Burnam, J. (1992) *Managing Quality in Schools*, Harlow: Longman.

Zeithaml, V.A., Parasuraman, A. and Berry, L.L. (1990) *Delivering Quality Service: Balancing Customer Perceptions and Expectations*, New York: The Free Press.

7 Staff appraisal training and Total Quality Management

Jeff Jones and John Mathias

SUMMARY

The purpose of this chapter is to discuss the relationship between staff appraisal and the development of Total Quality Management cultures within educational institutions. It will be argued that a sound appraisal programme will be a necessary foundation for the development of a 'quality culture'. It will be further suggested that the training which underpins the concept of appraisal put forward in this chapter is an essential element in institutionalizing the central principles of appraisal. In other words, as appraisal becomes an integral part of the management of an institution, then quality dimensions will gradually develop.

The first section of the chapter will consider the background to teacher appraisal. The nature of TQM will then be explored. Finally, the role of training within a 'quality appraisal culture' will then be considered, followed by discussion of the central principles which underpin appraisal.

BACKGROUND

The language used within education has changed considerably in recent years. The word 'accountability' was hardly heard in the 1970s. In fact, prior to 1970 the term 'accountability' had rarely been used in government White Papers on education. 'Appraisal' and 'performance indicators' were also not part of common language in the not too distant past. More recently 'quality culture' and 'total quality management' have become part of the language of the education system. Where has this change in language come from? What has happened in educational institutions as a result of these changes?

The move to a more market-led approach has been backed by legislation and government circulars and publications. Implicit within these changes have been demands for greater accountability within the education service. One of the key elements within these demands for greater public accountability has been pressure for the introduction of mandatory staff appraisal programmes within the education system. It is interesting at this stage to look at the main political factors which have underpinned these developments:

1961 Curriculum Study Group, set up to examine curriculum patterns
1974 Assessment of Performance Unit established by DES
1976 The Ruskin College speech which launched the 'Great Debate'
1977 The Taylor Committee
1978 *Primary Education in England* (HMI)
1979 *Aspects of Secondary Education* (HMI)
1981 The School Curriculum (Circular 6/81)
1981 Practical Curriculum
1983 Teaching Quality
1984 Education Observed 3: Good Teachers
1985 Quality in Schools: Evaluation and Appraisal
1985 Better Schools
1985 *Those Having Torches* (The Graham Report)
1986 Education Act (no. 2)
1987 'School teachers' pay and conditions of employment: government proposals'
1988 Education Reform Act
1991 The Education (School Teacher Appraisal) Regulations
1991 Circular 12/91

The arrival of Kenneth Clarke as Secretary of State for Education in December 1990 marked the end of any uncertainty that some had in relation to whether we would or would not have a national scheme for the appraisal of teachers. He soon made use of his powers under the terms of the 1986 Education (No. 2) Act (to be precise, Sections 49 and 63 of the Act) to compel Local Education Authorities (LEAs) to implement a scheme in the schools maintained by them. Governing bodies were given this role in the case of grant-maintained schools.

The School Teacher Appraisal Regulations and the accompanying Circular 12/91 published in July 1991 established a national framework, the main aims from which are set out below:

Aims of appraisal

4 (1) Appraising bodies shall secure that appraisal assists
   (a) school teachers in their professional development and career planning; and
   (b) those responsible for taking decisions about the management of school teachers.
 (2) In carrying out their duty under Regulation 3, appraising bodies shall aim to improve the quality of the education for pupils, through assisting school teachers to realise their potential and to carry out their duties more effectively.

(3) Appraisal procedures shall in particular aim to
- (a) recognise achievements of school teachers and help them to identify ways of improving their skills and performance;
- (b) help school teachers, governing bodies and local education authorities (as the case may be) to determine whether change of duties would help the professional development of school teachers and improve their career prospects;
- (c) identify the potential of teachers for career development, with the aim of helping them, where possible, through appropriate in-service training;
- (d) help school teachers having difficulties with their performance, through appropriate guidance, counselling and training;
- (e) inform those responsible for providing references for school teachers in relation to appointments;
- (f) improve the management of schools.

(The Education (School Teacher Appraisal) Regulations 1991)

These points raise interesting questions about the meaning and purpose of appraisal as perceived by the Department for Education (DfE). The writers of this chapter are clear that the only meaningful and indeed workable form of appraisal stems from and leads to the professional development of teachers.

> Appraisal of performance is an activity which is central to the effective management of the teaching and learning environment. We see appraisal as a right of all teachers, something which is done with people rather than to them. It is therefore important that both appraisee and appraiser are actively involved in the process. Rather than adding to the already considerable pressures faced by teachers, appraisal of performance aims to channel the energies of staff towards the essential rather than the superficial. The principal aim of appraisal is to enhance and maximise the educational opportunities of pupils through the professional development of teachers, thus leading to both institutional and individual growth.
>
> (Mathias and Jones 1989a)

Yet there are features emanating from parallel developments in national education policy which impinge upon this concept. For example:

1 performance-related pay;
2 the use of appraisal to inform decisions related to promotion;
3 the role of appraisal within disciplinary procedures;
4 the tensions between the role of appraisal in terms of professional development and accountability.

The Regulations in these areas are less clear and illustrate the need for the concept and purposes of appraisal, in terms of individual and institutional needs, to be clarified at the outset, before integrating to the management culture of the institution. Failure to do so will create tensions and lack of trust within an institution and will result in appraisal becoming a narrow, instrumental procedure rather than a central management tool:

Use and retention of appraisal records

14 (1) Relevant information from appraisal records may be taken into account by head teachers, Chief Education Officers or any officers or advisers specifically designated by the Chief Education Officer under Regulation 13(1)(b) or (2)(a) in advising those responsible for taking decisions on the promotion, dismissal or discipline of school teachers or on the use of any discretion in relation to pay.

(2) Those responsible for planning the training and development of school teachers in a school (including, in the case of a school maintained by a local education authority, appropriate officers of or advisers to that authority) shall receive particulars of any targets for action relating to training and development.

(The Education (School Teacher Appraisal) Regulations 1991)

It is therefore suggested that appraisal and the broader concept of performance management has the potential to support everyone, within any organization. It involves the development of a positive working ethos deliberately created by the adults who work there, and individual target-setting so that the goals of the organization are met as well as those leading to personal and social development.

In whatever organization, performance appraisal cannot be regarded as either a set of techniques or a discrete process with an easily definable boundary. The principles and practice of appraisal are inextricably linked to the management process in any organization, and to that organization's philosophy towards people, whether it adopts a traditional, paternalistic welfare personnel management approach, or a modern, human resource management approach.

The following quotations highlight the potential of the appraisal process to encourage and support people within organizations to enhance their knowledge and competence by identifying and acknowledging strengths and weaknesses:

You can't develop people. That door is locked from the inside. You must create a climate in which people will develop themselves.

(Townsend 1970)

All personnel development is self-development which happens when people use whatever opportunities are available to increase their skills and knowledge, their competence and confidence.

(John Harvey Jones 1989)

Far from being a panacea, the appraisal process has the potential to provide organizations with the 'climate' and 'opportunities' referred to above. Used effectively, appraisal can serve as the mechanism which enables organizations not only to come to terms with change but also to promote their vision of total quality.

APPRAISAL AND QUALITY

It is self-evident that certain values should be attached to the processes by which education is delivered, as well as to its more discernible outputs and outcomes. Any discussion which focuses on the criteria by which effectiveness of an action, process or outcome is concerned raises an equally interesting debate about the notion of 'quality'. Quality is a valuable criterion for gauging the effectiveness and efficiency of an action since it encompasses both outcome and process: 'The quality of features and characteristics of a service that bear on its ability to satisfy stated or implied needs' (Rooney 1988). TQM can be seen as an approach to improving quality. 'Quality management will include in its totality a continuous cycle of planning, training, actioning, monitoring, improving and reviewing the performance of an organisation' (Stebbing 1990).

TQM has the following characteristics:

- total commitment from all involved;
- active involvement of everyone throughout the organization;
- the breakdown of professional and functional barriers.

It has four main components:

1 problem-solving – the ability to break down complex series of issues to a set of manageable tasks requiring a solution, a decision, a plan or an idea;
2 getting decisions right the first time – decision-making requires a method of organizing information and evaluating the benefits and potential problems of each alternative;
3 preventing problems – through a process of analysis, potential and actual problems can be identified, assessed and eliminated or catered for by contingency planning;
4 establishing an innovative attitude, so that opportunities for making improvements can be identified.

It is vital that appraisal should be seen as an integral part of the management and support of staff, and not as an isolated exercise. It should be carried out against a background of the institution's objectives expressed in the strategic plan. The integration of organization and personal objectives represents the key to successful appraisal of performance schemes. An objective for inclusion in that strategic plan should be to ensure that appraisal operates equitably for all involved in the process.

The concept of strategic planning is relatively new within educational contexts. Within the United Kingdom, the Education Reform Act 1988 provided impetus for improvements in the management of schools:

> For governors, heads and teachers, bringing together all these changes will require, as part of the new partnership, strategies for managing development and change to make the school more effective. School development plans are a means of realising these goals.
>
> (Hargreaves *et al.* 1989)

Strategic or development planning has a number of benefits for an organization. For example, it can help an organization clarify its aims and the way these are translated into practice through the development of curricula and teaching and assessment strategies. The organizational patterns and resourcing needs of an institution can be considered in both the short- and long-term. The training needs of individuals can be matched to institutional goals. And, most importantly, it can involve staff at all levels within an organization in the planning of its goals. Appraisal must be seen as an essential element of this process.

Success is dependent on the appraisal scheme being understood and operated as a process of learning, rather than as a process of direction and control, for the whole organization as well as both appraiser and appraisee. This suggests that appraisal is at the heart of a developing 'quality' environment. The model below puts forward an approach to appraisal which can help to balance the sometimes conflicting demands of public accountability and professional development whilst creating 'quality' dimensions through the matching of individual and institutional goals.

QUALITY CONSIDERATIONS AND ISSUES IN STAFF APPRAISAL TRAINING

Investment in high-quality training is an essential element in developing a 'quality culture' in any institution. In this context, a number of principles underpin a training policy:

- Training is an integral component of managing quality.
- Training should lead to improvement and development of individuals as well as institutions.
- Appropriate training is an entitlement for any individual.
- Training should be specific to the needs of the institution.
- Training comes in a variety of forms.

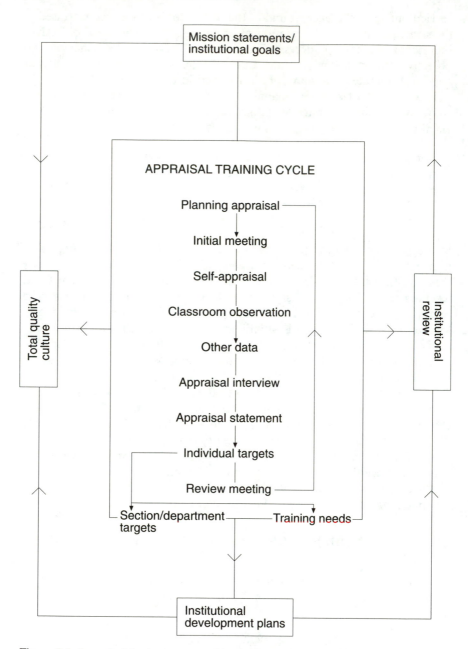

Figure 7.1 Appraisal in the context of institutional development

- Appraisal training covers a wide range of topics, including:
    managing and planning appraisal;
    information collection skills;
    job analysis;
    interpersonal skills, e.g. listening, feedback;
    reviewing skills;
    target-setting and report writing.

A number of issues connected to the relationship of appraisal training and TQM need to be considered. Figure 7.2 highlights these issues and indicates the complex interaction between them:

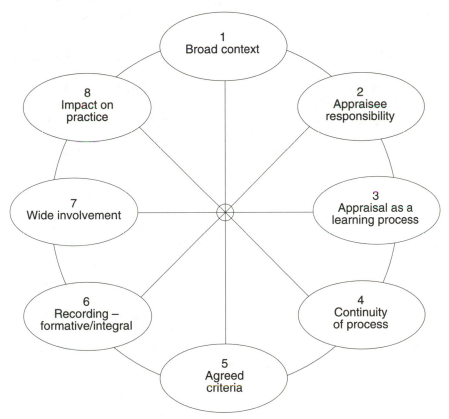

Figure 7.2 Appraisal and TQM: the interaction of the issues

Within the context of teacher appraisal in the United Kingdom, the full capacity of appraisal to bring about development is unlikely to be fully realized until the statutory implementation for appraisal has taken its course; that is to say, until all teachers have been through the first cycle of appraisal. Its introduction in schools will raise a number of issues, however. These issues will centre on:

- the clarity of the institution's values and objectives;
- the effectiveness of the management structures and processes;
- the credibility of appraisers;
- the agreed criteria for defining effectiveness;
- the quality of the relationships;
- the level of commitment to professional development;
- the effectiveness of the training which takes place.

Issue 1

Appraisal schemes should operate within a broad context. The individual needs to be provided with a range of formal and informal opportunities for development. *Quality here is gauged by*:

- the level of involvment of the individual in the institution's development planning;
- the extent to which the institution's development plan might influence the individual's job description/work pattern;
- the extent to which the needs of the institution and the needs of the individual interrelate;
- the range of opportunities offered to the individual to bring about individual and ultimately institutional growth.

Issue 2

Appraisal should encourage the appraisee to take increasing responsibility for the process. The individual should be provided with opportunities to refine the necessary skills. *Quality here is gauged by*:

- the effectiveness of the arrangements for the training of appraisers and appraisees;
- the extent to which opportunites are provided for practice to be developed and evaluated;
- the extent to which existing mechanisms enable the needs of the institution as well as the individual to be met.

Issue 3

The appraisal process represents a learning process for those involved. Opportunities should be provided for all those involved to reflect on the learning which has resulted from their participation in the process. *Quality here is gauged by*:

- the extent to which the implementation of the scheme allows time for appraisee and appraisers to prepare for and reflect upon their experiences;
- the level of understanding of appraisee and appraiser of their responsibilities at each stage of the process;

- the extent to which participants' experience of the process informs the future development of the appraisal scheme.

Issue 4

The appraisal process should be built on structures and procedures which promote continuity of process and practice both within the institution, and between the institution and the LEA/governing body. Since appraisal is about individual development within an organization, these structures and procedures should be capable of refinement and development informed by practice. *Quality here is gauged by*:

- the level of consistency of practice and understanding of the scheme and its intended purpose;
- the extent to which the identified targets of the individual are related to the institution's development plan;
- the extent to which there are common elements to the training of appraisers and appraisees;
- the extent to which there are opportunities for all involved to review the scheme, e.g. organization, training, time-scale, etc.
- the extent to which the lessons learned about the process and practice are shared between the institution and the appraising body, e.g. LEA.

Issue 5

The criteria used for appraisal should be shared by appraiser and appraisee. These need to be acknowledged and agreed at the planning stage and re-affirmed through practice. *Quality here is gauged by*:

- the effectiveness of the process for agreeing criteria;
- the level of involvement of staff in the development of criteria;
- the nature of the mechanism for reviewing criteria.

Issue 6

Recording should be regarded as a formative and integral part of the appraisal process rather than an end in itself. Review and reflection needs to be built in at each stage. *Quality here is gauged by*:

- the extent to which self and joint appraisal has enabled effective evaluation of performance to take place;
- the effectiveness of the recording process above;
- the way in which individual targets are identified;
- the way in which the institution is informed of an individual's progress towards collective targets;
- the extent to which the relationship between the individual targets and the development plan are evaluated.

Issue 7

A range of significant others are potential contributors to aspects of the individual's appraisal. *Quality here is gauged by*:

- the extent to which the appraisee can propose the range of other participants who could be involved in the appraisal;
- the level of objective feedback gained from the exercise.

Issue 8

The learning which transpires as a result of the appraisal process should inform individual, institution and LEA practice. *Quality here is gauged by*:

- the way in which professional practice is reviewed in the light of the experience of the appraisal process in relation to:
    the individual;
    the institution;
    the LEA/governing body;
- the extent to which there are mechanisms in place to ensure that the review of professional practice influences individual, institution and LEA development.

CONCLUSION

This chapter has attempted to show the way in which staff appraisal can aid the development of a quality culture in an educational system. It has suggested that a 'quality' appraisal programme can enhance both individual and institutional development, particularly when it is based upon a concept of staff entitlement and active involvement – in other words, a model which demonstrates trust and which provides some sense of ownership to participants may be the best way of satisfying the sometimes conflicting demands of individual development, institutional growth and public accountability.

It is the contention of the authors that, at its best, appraisal has the potential to set free and direct the creativity of teachers (Mathias and Jones 1989c) to aid both their own development and that of the institution in which they work. It is the *essential* element of a 'quality culture'.

REFERENCES

Great Britain, Department of Education and Science (1991) *School Teacher Appraisal (Circular 12/91)*, London: HMSO.
——, Welsh Office (1991) *The Education (School Teacher Appraisal) Regulations 1991*, London: HMSO.
Hargreaves, D.H. (1989) *Planning for School Development: Advice for Governors, Headteachers and Teachers*, London: HMSO.
Harvey Jones, J. (1989) *Making it Happen*, London: Fontana.

Mathias, J.R. and Jones, J. (1989a) *Appraisal of Performance: an Aid to Professional Development*, Windsor: NFER-Nelson.

——— (1989b) *Appraisal of Performance: Teachers' Guide*, Windsor: NFER-Nelson.

——— (1989c) 'Setting them free', *Education* 173(1).

Rooney, D. (1988) in J. Oakland *Total Quality Management*, Oxford: Heinemann (1989).

Stebbing, L. (1990) *Quality Management in the Service Industry*, New York: Ellis Horwood Series.

Townsend, R. (1970) *Up the Organisation*, New York: Knopf.

Part II
Higher education

8 Total Quality Management in higher education
Learning from the factories

Dean L. Hubbard

If American industries can dramatically improve their effectiveness through the application of TQM principles, would similar improvements result if education adopted the same approach? Are TQM concepts applicable to the unique environment of higher education? If so, what about specific TQM techniques? Can such techniques be applied without compromising traditional academic values, such as academic freedom? In sum, can higher education learn from the factories?

In 1984 Northwest Missouri State University began to explore these questions by extrapolating from what is being done to manage quality in industrial and service settings to an educational environment, particularly the academic side of the enterprise. Northwest is a typical comprehensive, co-educational, publicly supported, regional University. The University has a student enrollment of just over 6,000 and a faculty of 235. The majority of students live in on-campus housing (67 per cent) and come from within a 100-mile radius of the campus, which is located in Maryville, Missouri, a community of 10,000. The University offers 112 undergraduate programmes, 26 master's programmes and the educational specialist degree.

IMPLEMENTING TQM IN A UNIVERSITY SETTING

Benchmarking

The first step in developing Northwest's TQM plan (titled the 'Culture of Quality') involved an approach frequently utilized by industries: benchmarking. Robert Camp defines benchmarking as 'the (continuous) search for . . . (the) best practices that lead to superior performance'.[1] Of all the techniques utilized in TQM, in my judgement, benchmarking is the easiest fit to education and the most important for at least two reasons. First, it raises expectations, and high expectations are the foundation upon which quality is built in any setting. Secondly, without benchmarks, goals have a tendency to be self-serving and preserving of the *status quo*. Stated more bluntly, comparisons of one's students or programmes with those from other institutions is the best antidote for the inertia that plagues most campuses.

In keeping with Camp's definition, Northwest benchmarked several sources, beginning with the institution's own faculty and students, who were asked to submit 'ideas for creating a culture of quality on campus'. While different individuals and groups on campus spent a semester formulating ideas, a steering committee culled ideas from the so-called 'educational reform' literature that had appeared over the previous decade. Various data regarding student characteristics and performance were gathered and compared to national norms. The 200 ideas gleaned from all these sources were synthesized and incorporated into a document entitled 'Reviewing the reviews: suggestions for reforming higher education'. Of course, not all 200 ideas could be applied at Northwest, nor were all of equal value. In fact, some were mutually exclusive. Ultimately, forty-two were selected as the goals which make up the Culture of Quality plan.

Applying the principle of parsimony

Planning efforts in higher education are usually too global, involve too many goals, and fail to differentiate between the crucial and the trivial. One way to overcome this tendency is to apply the principle of parsimony. Although one will not encounter the expression 'principle of parsimony' in the literature on TQM,[2] the concept frequently appears. For example, Dr Nam Suh, Professor of Engineering at MIT, avouched as an axiom: 'The perfect design is associated with the assemblage of the fewest parts.' We take this to mean fewer and more sharply focused goals, clear definitions of quality appropriate to the task at hand, fewer administrative lawyers, fewer programmes and fewer evaluative metrics.

Northwest started by applying this principle to its mission. A sharply focused statement was adopted which commits the University to 'place special emphasis upon agriculture, business, and teacher education, particularly as these professions contribute to the primary service region'. Further, 'All of the University's programs build upon comprehensive general education requirements.'

A sharpened mission provided one-half of the context needed for selecting a mutually supporting cluster of goals that reflect the basic values of the University from the 200 recommendations garnered through the benchmarking process. The steering committee produced the second half by examining fifteen major research reports in order to identify a set of planning assumptions. Their findings were subsumed under six rubrics: demographics, economics, social, political/legal, technological and competitive. Again, the principle of parsimony was applied when five 'mega-trends' particularly germane to Northwest were extrapolated from these assumptions:

- The emerging global economy will give rise to a global community characterized by increased communications across national borders, not only in business, but also in education, entertainment, science and the arts.

- Technology will penetrate even deeper into our daily lives.
- Information increasingly will become the capital, or raw material, of economic activity. The ability to receive, analyse and transmit information in oral, written and numeric form will be crucial.
- The need for specialists will increase since nearly every successful enterprise operates within a rather narrow market niche.
- The rate of change in all areas will accelerate. Those who have learned how to learn will be best equipped to capitalize on such an environment.

A third application of the principle of parsimony was to the organizational structure itself. Concomitant with the announcement of plans to shift to a TQM approach to management, corporations frequently announce plans to 'flatten' the organizational structure by significantly reducing administrative positions. While cost savings are probably the primary driver of such moves, from a TQM standpoint eliminating layers facilitates involving employees in defining and managing quality in their own work setting. (Since line administrators justify their existence by pointing to decisions they make, and since there are only so many decisions to go around, reducing the number of administrators frees up decisions which can then be pushed down.) A secondary, but equally essential, benefit is that pruning generally results in an organizational structure which more sharply reflects the mission.

At Northwest, seven colleges were consolidated into four, which more crisply reflected the commitment to 'place special emphasis upon agriculture, business, and teacher education, particularly as these professions contribute to the primary service region'. Thirty-one programmes were eliminated, along with four full-time dean positions and two vice-presidencies. The result was a reallocation of $1.9 million (over 6 per cent of the Education and General budget) away from administration and academic support areas to qualify improvements in instruction.

Finally, the principle of parsimony was applied to the number of support services the University would attempt to manage. The result was outsourcing the management of custodial, grounds, maintenance and the power plant to Service Master Corporation (food service and the book store had previously been contracted out).

Focus on the customer

Despite the intuitive appeal of adopting a focus on the customer, faculty generally have difficulty understanding how such an approach would play out in the classroom. In fact, at some universities TQM efforts have aborted over this issue. We concluded that in the classroom, the student along with the instructor are 'suppliers' producing a 'product' (knowledge) that a future 'customer' (employer or graduate school) will evaluate. Even as the supervisor (instructor) and worker (student) in a TQM setting co-operate to understand and satisfy the customer, so students are involved in instructional design and evaluation and empowered to assume more control for their own learning. In other settings on campus the student is the customer in the typical sense of the word.

At Northwest, in the support services, a customer orientation was readily adopted. A permanent Continuous Quality Improvement committee was established in order to identify and prioritize opportunities for improvement and to establish expectations. The council, chaired by a department director, includes faculty and students. One of their first accomplishments was to develop and post across campus the following pledge:[3]

Culture of Quality Commitment to Service

Northwest Missouri State University recognizes that quality service is an essential component of a quality University. Furthermore, we acknowledge that all of us – students, faculty, staff, and administration – are at times providers and at other times recipients of services.

Accordingly, we pledge our best efforts to provide quality service to you by:

● Treating you with respect, fairness, and honesty.
   Making you feel important and earning your trust.

● Performing our tasks with competence and skill.
   Giving you confidence in the quality of what we provide.

● Communicating clearly and courteously the services provided.
   Making it easy for you to know what you can expect.

● Listening actively to your request, comments and concerns.
   Making it easy for you to tell us what you need.

● Being flexible and open to new ideas.
   Accepting you and valuing your knowledge.

● Providing what we agree to deliver in a timely manner.
   Enabling you to depend on us to help meet your goals.

Various assessment instruments have been adopted to understand and monitor customer needs, expectations and perceptions, including regular focus group sessions. (The Student Senate sponsors an annual 'gripe day' to garner reactions, plus an 'I Love Northwest week' to celebrate successes.) Maintenance and custodial personnel regularly survey administrators, faculty and students regarding the perceived quality of their services. Additionally, monthly building inspection tours are conducted to sites selected by a member of the President's Cabinet.

Assessment of prevention

Historically, industry assured the quality of its products by placing inspectors at the end of the assembly line. Assessment (to use educational parlance) under such conditions consisted of ranking and sorting what workers produced. Several problems attend such a system. First, it is very expensive. The cost of not making products right the first time includes wasted labour and raw materials, labour and materials needed for rework, warranty costs for marginal products that were shipped, to say nothing of lost customers, damaged reputation and the like. (Ponder the cost to education of remediation, attrition and underdeveloped talent.) Secondly, inspectors at the end of the assembly line suggest to workers that they are not trusted to do the job right the first time, thus lowering expectations and aspirations. As is often the case, expectations become self-fulfilling prophecies. Finally, the presence of inspectors highlights differences between management and labour. Under such circumstances workers tend to focus their attention on turf protectionism, cumbersome work rules and other adversarial strategies. All of these negative consequences can be observed in education.

Yet, it is incontrovertible that assessment and feedback are critical to the improvement of any process. Less obvious is the linkage between assessment systems and attempts on the part of those being assessed to 'beat the system'. Sometimes that means 'cooking' or distorting the numbers. At other times it leads to focusing solely on that which is easily measurable while ignoring more important goals (for example, simple recall rather than critical thinking skills). Or, since assessment *ipso facto* clarifies minimum standards, minimums often become maximums. Once participants – be they students or employees – conclude that the primary reason for measuring how they are doing is so they can be sorted and ranked, they will shift their energies toward finding ways to circumvent the system.

This conundrum led Phil Crosby to advocate that inspectors be taken off the assembly line and that the focus be on prevention. Edwards Deming concurs with Crosby, but goes even further: 'Eliminate quotas or work standards, and management by objectives or numerical goals; substitute leadership.'[4] In higher education, most assessment is 'inspection at the end of the assembly line' for purposes of ranking and sorting; relatively little diagnostic testing is done. Further, the primary beneficiary is the instructor who uses results to assign grades, not prevent failures. The key to at least attenuating these problems lies in shifting the primary focus of assessment away from ranking and sorting towards improvement.

At Northwest, two approaches to assessment were incorporated into the Culture of Quality plan in order to focus the results on raising expectations and preventing errors rather than simple ranking and sorting. First, an assessment programme deliberately designed to raise expectations was put in place. Freshmen are asked to come to campus for a week-long orientation before school begins each autumn. During that time, in addition to being introduced to the Culture of Quality, they are tested along several dimensions using a combination of locally developed and nationally normed tests. The information gleaned is used for placing students in appropriate classes and later as a benchmark against which progress can be measured.

At the end of the sophomore year, a nationally normed test administered during Freshman Orientation is re-administered (to plot progress), and a writing sample is analysed. Various departments also administer their own tests, examine portfolios and the like before the student is formally admitted to advanced standing. Three benefits accrue from such a programme: (1) an opportunity is provided to ameliorate problems while there is still time; (2) a salutary kind of anxiety is induced on the part of freshmen as they look forward to this hurdle; and, (3) a more homogeneous upper-division environment is created which facilitates teaching to higher-order thinking skills such as analysis, synthesis and evaluation. This approach also avoids the practical problem with senior exams which are part of graduation requirements; namely, the reluctance to deny graduation after four years of promotion and presumed satisfactory performance.

At graduation additional tests are given. The results are used to evaluate programme effectiveness. Finally, five years after graduation, alumni are surveyed in order to glean additional 'customer' perspectives.

A second, less traditional, use of assessment focuses on improving both teaching and learning. In his book *Higher Learning*, Derek Bok suggests that testing drives student study habits.[5] The first thing students do when beginning a course is find out how they will be tested. They ask the instructor, they query former students, they study the syllabuses. Once they have a feel for the type of questions they will be asked, they adjust their study habits accordingly. Therefore, if instructors ask questions which force students to use higher-order cognitive skills such as analysis, synthesis or evaluation, students will prepare themselves for those tasks. On the other hand, if all the instructor demands is recall and understanding, students will study in those modes.

Since few college instructors have ever systematically learned how to construct questions which test to different cognitive levels, we focused faculty development on that task. Specialists were brought to campus to hold weekend workshops on the topic of teaching to, and testing for, higher-order cognition. Participation was extensive and enthusiastic. Thus, the stigma often associated with assessment was avoided, assessment was at least moved in the direction of prevention, quality of instruction was improved, and the expectations of students were raised.

Training

Although it would be impossible to implement TQM without training, training should not be treated as an end in itself nor should success be judged by how many participate in specific training exercises. Over the years, Northwest has sponsored a plethora of training programmes dealing with everything from statistical process control to how to handle the telephone. Through the George Washington University National Satellite Network, the University has participated in video conferences featuring Edwards Deming, Peter Drucker, Joseph Juran, Phil Crosby and Peter Scholtes.

TQM in the support services

Most colleges and universities which have attempted to apply the concepts of TQM have started with support services, hoping that the academic side will emulate what they see working successfully in these more amenable areas. In fact, some have advocated that this is where the process should start. Northwest took the opposite approach. We worried that starting with support services might trivialize the whole effort and, in any case, would be akin to General Motors sprucing up the factory and cleaning up the cafeteria while still turning out inferior cars. So, we started with the academic programme. Within a year, the Support Staff Council asked why they couldn't be part of the Culture of Quality. Since that time, all of the support services (custodial, grounds, maintenance and power plant), as well as in the traditional student services (registrar's office, student finance, cashiering and the like), have been involved.

Continuous quality improvement

Continuous quality improvement is one of the pillars of the TQM faith. In that spirit, managing quality, like quality itself, must be viewed as a receding horizon. Hence, we do not claim to have arrived! In fact, the Culture of Quality plan is currently being evaluated and expanded in the context of the latest Baldridge Award criteria. It was anticipated that an improved plan will be completed by the spring of 1993.

Educators, like their counterparts in industry, need to remind themselves that plans are not static, nor are they ever complete. (In this sense, the notion of *total* quality management is a misnomer.) Some action steps involve initiating activities which are ongoing, ergo, never 'completed'. A lecture series which supports general education would be an example. Other action steps are complex and require several years to pilot, test and refine before it can be said they have been fully implemented. Northwest's assessment programme would fit this category. Also, some departments begin implementing some action steps earlier than others. And, of course, in the process of implementation refinements or adjustments are frequently made in the original action step.

RESULT OF TQM AT NORTHWEST

Following is a summary of some of the major accomplishments realized to date as a result of the Culture of Quality programme.

- The first comprehensive electronic campus in the nation was installed, which includes a computer workstation, 2 dedicated television channels, and a telephone which accesses a Touch Tone Talker in each residence hall room. The network includes more than 2,400 terminals, 400 microcomputers in 15 labs, 200 software applications and a computerized videodisk and interactive voice synthesizer tutorial system.
- Major writing assignments have increased 72 per cent as a result of an across-the-curriculum programme and the electronic campus.
- The term was lengthened from 15 to 17 weeks. The net effect of this change was the addition of one month of instruction to the school year, or 16 weeks to the four-year college experience.
- An undergraduate research programme is in place, which has met with remarkable success. Since 1990, top students (called 'Presidential Scholars') are required to participate.
- Over 50 events are sponsored each year designed to integrate the student's extra-curricular life with learning activities. Examples include distinguished lectures, art gallery exhibitors, music master classes, Black history month speakers, guest lecturers, Greek war presentations and residence halls guest lecturers.
- A Student Service Centre was established with the goal that students can transact 90 per cent of their business with the University at a single location. In other words, instead of going to different buildings or offices to cash cheques, pay bills, buy tickets, etc., students can do all that at one centrally located counter.
- Registration, which used to take 1 or 2 days, can now be accomplished from the student's room or adviser's office on the electronic campus in less than 15 minutes.
- Seventeen 'Institution-wide Instructional Goals' were adopted by the faculty. These goals provide a context for all other action steps.
- An assessment programme was initiated, employing multiple measures of student attitudes and performance.
- A general education CORE was adopted which encompasses the basic knowledge and skills necessary for successful completion of college and later functioning as a literate, educated citizen. The CORE must be completed by the end of the sophomore year.
- Freshmen experiencing difficulty in selected courses now have the opportunity to participate in supplemental instruction activities which not only help them in the targeted course, but also provide instruction in note-taking, test-taking, how to use a textbook as a learning tool, and other similar topics. The result is that, instead of spending 3 hours per week in, for example, chemistry, students may spend 4 or 5 hours.

- Advanced standing requirements are being developed whereby students will be formally evaluated at the end of their sophomore year.
- Workshops are regularly conducted to assist faculty in developing pedagogical strategies for extending writing, thinking and listening skills across the curriculum.
- A faculty committee created a uniform course outline/syllabus format to ensure that the University's 'Institution-wide Instructional Goals' are integrated into the objectives of CORE courses.
- An applied research programme encourages faculty to experiment with alternative teaching and learning strategies.
- Over half of all departments have adopted or developed comprehensive senior exit exams.
- Yearly workshops are conducted to assist faculty who are inexperienced with teaching at the college level.
- A new faculty evaluation system was developed by the faculty. Of course, most of these initiatives could have been implemented in the absence of TQM, but they weren't. Also, Northwest's experience suggests that doing things better does, in the end, pay off. Specifically, the dollar impact of Culture of Quality changes are equally dramatic.
- A $962,000 deficit in the Education and General accounts was turned into a $883,000 reserve.
- The number of students choosing to move out of residence halls at the end of their freshmen year dropped by 50 per cent.
- The University went from technical default on its auxiliary bonds to a $1,700,000 surplus; at the same time residence halls were being renovated, new furniture was installed and occupancy rates went from 60 to 100 per cent.
- Faculty salaries increased at nearly twice the rate of inflation (30.3 versus 21.3 per cent), and operating and equipment budgets were substantially increased.
- The portion of the University's Education and General budget allocated to instruction grew from 48.5 per cent (the national average) to over 59 per cent. (According to John Minter, the 75th percentile of the general budget allocation is 51.5 per cent for comprehensive universities.)
- Computed in constant FY92 dollars, $3,100,000 (10 per cent of the Education and General budget) was shifted from physical plant administrative and academic support services into instruction, even as services were improved.
- Despite a severely declining population in its catchment area, enrollment grew 26 per cent until it hit capacity.
- Foundation assets grew from $1,400,000 to $3,700,000.
- A 6- to 18-month backlog on maintenance projects was eliminated. Buildings sparkle and a general campus beautification programme has been introduced. At the same time, campus maintenance costs were reduced by $1,700,000 per year.

OBSERVATIONS AND LESSONS

Colleges and universities are exceedingly complex organizations. A typical campus encompasses a bookstore, dining establishment, hotel operation, police force, construction company, athletic club and entertainment centre, all of which supposedly support and complement a collection of fiercely competitive academic departments (internally) which deliver the institution's core product. Each of these segments share attitudes and technologies common to their industry, albeit tempered by their association with each other and with the traditions and expectations of academia. Beyond the Golden Rule, the assertion that any single concept can be applied in this multifarious environment seems exceedingly heroic. Indeed, any attempt to apply the Deming, Crosby, Juran or any other guru's model slavishly to every segment of an educational institution is probably doomed from the outset. Nonetheless, the system in all of its diverse dimensions – from the registration of students to the presentation of ideas – can be managed in ways that maximize quality outcomes. Furthermore, although there are identifiable differences between manufacturing a product and teaching course or delivering a service, many of the principles and techniques used in managing manufacturing quality can be applied to managing educational quality. Likewise, some of the principles which undergird quality education have trenchant potential for manufacturing (for example, designing assessment to raise expectations).

Education can learn from the factories. Principles for ensuring quality which are grounded in a clear sense of mission, concern for people and high expectations can and should be emulated. John Gardner's observation applies to education just as surely as it does to other segments of society:

> In a society of free men, competence is an elementary duty. Men and women doing competently whatever job is theirs to do tone up the whole society. And the man who does a slovenly job – whether he is a janitor or a judge, a surgeon or a technician – lowers the tone of the society. . . .
>
> Those who are most deeply devoted to a democratic society must be precisely the ones who insist upon excellence, who insist that free men are capable of the highest standards of performance, who insist that a free society can be a great society in the richest sense of that phrase. The idea for which this nation stands will not survive if the highest goal free men can set themselves is an amiable mediocrity.[6]

NOTES

1 Robert C. Camp (1989) *Benchmarking: the Search for Industry Best Practices that Lead to Superior Performance*, Milwaukee, WI: Quality Press, p. 12.
2 The concept of *parsimony* was first set forth as a principle in the book I co-authored with Lewis B. Mayhew and Patrick J. Ford, *The Quest for Quality: the Challenge for Undergraduate Education in the 1990s*, San Francisco: Jossey-Bass, 1990.

3 The committee adapted its pledge from one originally developed by the Business Affairs Department, College of St Thomas, St Paul, MN.
4 Point number 11 of Deming's fourteen points.
5 Derek Bok, *Higher Learning*, Cambridge, MA: Harvard University Press, 1981.
6 John Gardner, *Excellence*, New York: Harper & Row (1961), 2nd edn, 1971, pp. 193–4.

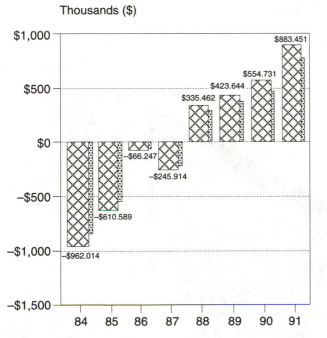

Thousands ($)

Figure 8.1 Education and general fund balances: Northwest Missouri State University
Source: Actual from audited financial statements

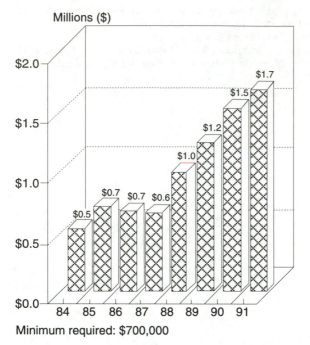

Minimum required: $700,000

Figure 8.2 Auxiliary debt reserves: Northwest Missouri State University

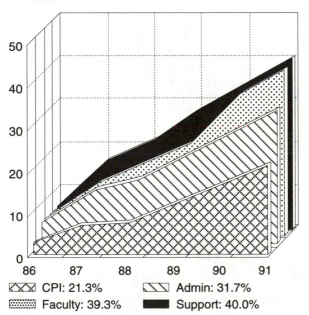

Figure 8.3 Salary increase comparisons: Northwest Missouri State University

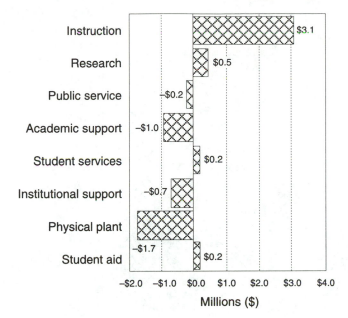

Computed in constant FY92 dollars

Figure 8.4 Constant dollar changes since FY85: Northwest Missouri State University

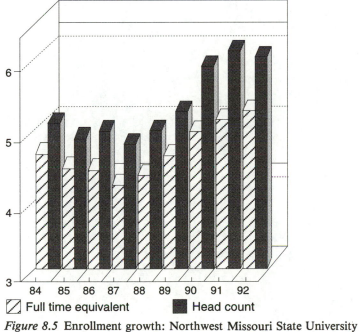

Figure 8.5 Enrollment growth: Northwest Missouri State University

Millions

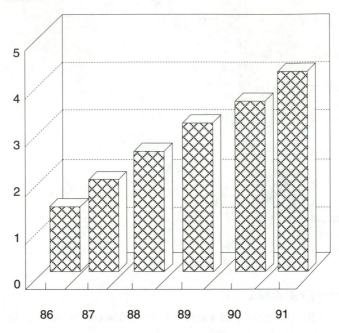

Figure 8.6 Growth in assets: Northwest Foundation, Inc.

9   Bringing total quality improvement into the college classroom

W. Lee Hansen

To learn is to change. Education is a process to change the learner.
(Leonard 1968)

This chapter describes a recent effort to infuse the Total Quality Improvement (TQI) approach, popularized by Deming and others, into an upper division, junior-senior economics course at the University of Wisconsin-Madison. The process of infusing TQI into instruction has received relatively little attention. Most efforts to bring TQI into higher education focus on improving administrative operations and establishing courses and programmes for students to learn how to apply it in their future jobs. Though these activities are commendable, the challenge lies in applying TQI to help students realize their potential for learning in traditional courses.

This presentation is necessarily autobiographical. No manuals or road maps existed to guide in developing and testing this application of TQI. No doubt much can be done to improve on my initial efforts. As experience accumulates on attempts to infuse TQI into instruction, some generalizations and perhaps even principles will emerge to guide faculty members interested in improving their teaching and increasing what students learn in their college courses. Based on my limited experience, it is obvious that TQI embodies an array of techniques for encouraging and facilitating student learning. What may be unique about TQI is the more encompassing framework it provides for combining these techniques and devices, monitoring their effectiveness and stressing continuous improvement.

This chapter is divided into several sections. The first section puts the instructional application of TQI into the wider context of TQI. The second section describes what motivated me to apply TQI to instruction and then reviews the key elements of the course; namely, a customer focus, student involvement and continuous improvement. The third section describes how each of these elements was operationalized: customer focus, through an emphasis on proficiencies in using knowledge; student involvement, through the team-orientated research projects; and continuous improvement, through the use of ongoing course and instructor evaluations. The fourth section assesses the results of these efforts. The last section distils what I learned from this experience.

THE CONTEXT

The barrage of criticism directed towards higher education institutions, their administrators and faculty members, combined with the frustration experienced by public officials in attempting to assess the effectiveness of public expenditures on higher education, has served as a powerful stimulus to colleges and universities to improve the quality of what they do and to document its beneficial effects. The TQI process is seen by many as having an enormous potential for responding to these challenges. This approach carries with it the possibility of producing significant improvements in higher education and how we think about the creation, dissemination and utilization of knowledge.

The TQI approach gained attention in the 1970s as a major force in Japan's emergence as a major economic power (Imai 1986). Since the early 1980s, Deming has pushed for adoption of this approach in the United States (Deming 1986). Because of competitive pressures and the inner logic of the approach, it has been accepted by many American business leaders and, now, is being implemented in many US firms (Walton 1990). The resulting success stories have stimulated growing numbers of government and non-profit organizations to adopt TQI (Spanbauer 1992). Increasingly, academic institutions are demonstrating interest in TQI, and frequently are adopting it (Miller 1991; Sherr and Teeter 1991; Spanbauer 1992).

Why has adoption of TQI lagged in higher education? Perhaps no more than 200 of the approximately 3,400 post-secondary institutions in the United States describe themselves as involved in applying some form of TQI (*TQ Magazine* 1992). The reason there are so few adherents is that many institutions regard TQI as the latest in a series of faddish approaches urged on higher education. In this sense it is reminiscent of the enthusiasm for the long-discarded MBO (management by objectives) approach of the 1970s and the now languishing strategic planning focus of the 1980s (Keller 1983). Many institutions are taking a 'wait-and-see' attitude – and will think about adopting TQI only after other institutions have demonstrated its effectiveness.

The challenge in higher education is to devise a strategy that provides leadership from the top and at various levels throughout the institution, and one that is simultaneously able to draw independent-minded faculty members willingly into the TQI culture. The task is not easy. Indeed, overturning the traditional 'culture' of academe may be more daunting than the admittedly difficult job of transforming the 'culture' of corporations. Thus, the task is to discover how to change the culture and, resources permitting, to use incentives to overcome the barriers.

Meeting these challenges can occur at four levels:

1 The institution's leadership can implement TQI programmes in the non-academic spheres of its operations. The major difficulty lies in providing TQI training to a cadre of current employees so they can proceed, and then in maintaining momentum during the long start-up period.

2 The growing demand for knowledge about TQI and for people who can implement TQI programmes will lead to the emergence of academic courses and programmes in the subject (Finster 1991). There is little need to push on this front. Individual faculty members and departments will respond to this growing demand by creating the necessary courses and programmes. Indeed, it may be impossible and probably foolish to prevent faculty members from responding to this demand.

3 This is more difficult; administrators can encourage academic units – i.e. their various departments, schools, and the like – to apply TQI in organizing their resources to facilitate high-quality teaching and research by their faculties and thereby enhance student learning.

4 This is no doubt the most demanding task of all – encouraging individual faculty members to infuse the key ingredients of TQI to their own teaching and research activities.

Infusing TQI into the academic sphere is complicated because the role of faculty members differs so significantly from those of employees in most organizations. Faculty members operate largely as self-contained production units. Individual faculty members produce courses that, when aggregated, make up what is described as general education, the undergraduate major, and eventually a college degree. They also engage in research and scholarly activity. Finally, they are involved in an array of public service activities that draw on their knowledge and skills.

To carry out these diverse activities, faculty members draw on the existing body of knowledge, including their own. They identify gaps in knowledge that need to be filled through independent research carried out by themselves or others. The resulting knowledge feeds directly back into their own instruction and research. Much of it also feeds into books and articles that constitute the body of knowledge which faculty members throughout academe use in their own teaching and research.

Departmental units, typically, can provide at best weak encouragement for or surveillance of these activities. They are disadvantaged because individual faculty members know more about what is being taught and how it should be taught than do their colleagues, department heads, college presidents and boards of trustees. For these reasons it is difficult, if not impossible, to mandate TQI for the academic side of higher education. Faculty must become convinced of the virtues of TQI before they can be expected to embrace it. One hope is that case studies of the kind presented here will capture the attention of other faculty members and stimulate increasing numbers of them to explore the possibilities of TQI in their instruction and research.

THE MOTIVATING FORCE

Many of us experience difficulty recalling how we developed interest in a topic; that is certainly true of my interest in applying TQI to teaching. It began, I suppose, when I first read Deming (Deming 1986) shortly after his book was published. I had heard about Deming and his approach, and thought I should learn more about it. Additional stimulation came from a colleague and collaborator, Jacob Stampen, who was exploring how to apply TQI in education (Stampen 1987). When in the autumn of 1990 Stampen offered an informal faculty and graduate student seminar on applying Deming to education, I participated and became more deeply interested. Perhaps my economics training made the systematic approach to improvement especially appealing. I also realized that I already practised many of the principles espoused by Deming. This led me to begin thinking about how to apply Deming's approach in my teaching. To deepen my knowledge, I arranged to sit in on a spring semester TQI course taught in the business school by Mark Finster.

While making final plans for my spring term teaching in January 1991, I happened to hear that a colleague in statistics, Ian Hau, was presenting a seminar describing his experience applying TQI in a statistics course (Hau 1991). I attended that presentation, met Hau, and later commented on his draft paper. While listening to his presentation, I suddenly realized how I could implement several aspects of the TQI approach into an upper division labour economics course I was preparing to teach.[1]

I should point out that I was not aiming for doing a full-scale TQI-orientated course. Too much was already on the schedule to allow much, if any, time for imparting the TQI management and planning tools (Brassard 1989) or developing team skills (Scholtes 1988). My focus had to be more limited, with the result a hybrid course. In time, the course may be able to take on a stronger TQI orientation while continuing to serve its purpose within the undergraduate economics major.

Some background on my approach to teaching is helpful at this point. In recent years I had been puzzling over how to build into my course a greater emphasis on the development of the proficiencies that might be expected of graduating economics majors. These proficiencies call for developing in students an ability to *use* their knowledge rather than merely display it in traditional academic fashion, principally through examinations. Under this approach, students would have to demonstrate these proficiencies as part of their graduation requirement. The only way to develop these proficiencies is in courses that give students opportunities to practise these proficiencies. The proficiencies spelled out for the economics major are shown in Table 9.1 (Hansen 1986).

This interest in proficiencies arose because of feedback obtained from department questionnaires sent out, usually in the year following graduation, to former undergraduate majors in economics. The responses revealed

Table 9.1 Proficiencies for the undergaduate major

Gaining access to existing knowledge

- Locate published research in economics and related fields
- Locate information on particular topics and issues in economics
- Search out economic data as well as information about the meaning of the data and how they are derived

Displaying command of existing knowledge

- Summarize (e.g., in a short monologue or written statement) what is known about the current condition of the economy
- Summarize the principal ideas of an eminent living economist
- Summarize a current controversy in the economics literature
- State succinctly the dimensions of a current economic policy issue
- Explain key economic concepts and describe how they can be used

Displaying ability to draw out existing knowledge

- Write a précis of a published journal article
- Read and interpret a theoretical analysis, including simple mathematical derivations, from an economics journal article
- Read and interpret a quantitative analysis, such as regression results, from an economics journal article
- Show what economic concepts and principles are used in economic analyses in newspapers and news magazines

Utilizing existing knowledge to explore issues

- Prepare a well-organized and well-written analysis of a current economic problem
- Prepare a memorandum for a superior that recommends some action on an economic decision faced by an organization

Creating new knowledge

- Identify and formulate a question or series of questions about some economic issue that will facilitate investigation of the issue
- Prepare a 5-page proposal for a research project
- Complete a research study with a polished paper

---

that the jobs taken by these recent job entrants almost universally required them to have well-developed skills in speaking and writing and some sense for quantitative relationships, and the ability to carry to completion larger projects. As employees, they were necessarily required to work closely with fellow employees, often as members of teams, to resolve problems, clarify options and make decisions. Respondents frequently commented on how much they had gained from courses that gave attention to the elements of these proficiencies – namely, writing assignments, oral presentations and acquaintance with regression analysis. Many lamented that they had not had an opportunity to develop these proficiencies to any great extent.[2]

Even before sketching out the proficiencies concept in 1985, I had begun redirecting my teaching to emphasize these proficiencies. The lower-level proficiencies had received most of my attention. Students always had to complete a variety of homework assignments that require them to locate, manipulate and interpret empirical data. We worked through a number of articles in professional journals.[3] They were also given a variety of short writing assignments that tested their ability to express themselves and organize their ideas. On several occasions, I taught upper-division courses on a writing-intensive basis (Hansen 1993).

Despite these efforts, I had done little to stimulate development of the highest-order proficiency, that of 'creating knowledge'. The reason was obvious; with an enrolment of at least fifty and sometimes almost 100 students, the burden of supervising individual research projects and then evaluating the resulting papers is impossibly large. Nor had I done much to help students gain experience working on team projects in an academic setting; this proficiency was not even on my list.

These various ideas gave rise to the following plan: with only minor modifications in the nature and content of the course, students would be organized into four-to-six-person teams, with each team working on one of a pre-selected set of research projects that were directly related to the course and its goals. During the last several weeks of the course, each team would make a collaborative presentation of its findings to the class. Shortly after the oral presentation, each team would submit a collaboratively written report. To help evaluate the effectiveness of this approach, one team would have the task of monitoring the course, and another team would assess the scope of the proficiencies embedded in the structure of the course.

What emerged can be translated into what I call a TQI Instructional Approach (TQIIA), shown in Table 9.2. Its three components which are the hallmarks of the TQI framework include: customer focus, student involvement, and continuous improvement.

Table 9.2 TQI instructional system

Customer focus	–	Proficiencies
Student involvement	–	Team projects
Continuous improvement	–	Ongoing evaluations

Customer focus

Identifying the customer in higher education is difficult. Who are the customers? Are they the students, their parents, taxpayers, prospective employers, the public at large? The proficiencies approach resolves that question in an interesting and useful way. While the immediate customers are students, the real customers comprise two groups with quite similar interests. One is employers who want to draw on the knowledge and skills of new college graduates after their entry into the labour market. The other is the community of taxpayers who want to be assured that the subsidies provided to college students were well spent. These customers want to see evidence that graduating economics majors acquire a substantive knowledge of economics, are proficient in using that knowledge, and display the attributes of educated people through their contributions to their organizations, communities and to society.

What employers as customers want of graduates emerged not only from the questionnaires returned by former students but also from extensive discussions I had with numerous employers, large and small alike, spread over the private, public and non-profit sectors.[4] What, in addition to this, the community of taxpayers wants is necessarily less sharply defined. Some sense for these expectations emerges from survey data on public attitudes towards higher education, comments on higher education published in newspapers and letters to the editor columns, and the writing of scholars who have looked into what are described as the social benefits of higher education (Bowen 1977).

The proficiencies approach offers a unique way of viewing students as customers. It helps them visualize the outside world of employers and the public as their customers whom they must serve. Put another way, students are the customers of their own knowledge. Once they accept this view, they can more easily visualize themselves as customers for my instructional services. In turn, I see them as customers for my instructional services which they must have to develop their proficiencies. The implications are clear. Just as I must satisfy their expectations if they are to be appreciated by employers and others, they must satisfy my expectations if they want to meet the expectations of the three groups of customers for their knowledge and skills.[5]

Student involvement

Much university teaching is dominated by the lecture approach, or in the case of large introductory courses, lectures supplemented by discussion and/or laboratory section meetings led by graduate teaching assistants. Even in small classes, faculty members typically find it easier to lecture than to engage students in probing discussions that help students learn how to think broadly and deeply about the subject matter. This practice continues despite mounting evidence that students will benefit from active involvement in the learning process (Light 1990, 1991). We know from our own experience that collaborating on research, testing our ideas in seminars and public lectures, and teaching itself are all-powerful means of learning and clarifying our thinking. Some of us also know that closer interaction with students in the classroom makes teaching a more interesting and challenging enterprise.

The active involvement appropriate for students in a customer-driven environment had become apparent from the earlier surveys and the resulting list of proficiencies. Our surveys indicate the importance of being able to carry out projects and to do so in collaboration with other employees. The question is how to transfer this approach to the classroom. Small discussion groups may be helpful within the existing curriculum in strengthening the first four proficiencies which get most of the attention.

Relatively little is done, however, to promote the highest-level proficiency, that of 'creating new knowledge'. The solution: to organize students into teams to undertake joint research projects. The benefits are obvious. Many fewer projects and papers need to be supervised and evaluated, thereby making it possible to promote this proficiency in larger classes. More important, the interactions among team members leads to higher-quality research projects because of the advantages that come from collaboration.

Once this position is adopted, the task is to formulate a series of feasible projects, think through the process by which the teams will operate, and decide how to evaluate the success of the teams both in producing a tangible product and in the process enhancing their ability to create new knowledge.

Continuous improvement

Knowing how well the needs of both the immediate and real customers are being met is difficult under our conventional approach to instruction. One, or at most two, within-term examinations enable students and faculty members to assess what is being learned prior to the final examination. Such infrequent assessments are not always informative because they do so little to pinpoint the problems students and the professor may be having. In addition, faculty who require regular assignments typically have a much better sense for what and how well students are learning. The same goes for teaching effectiveness. End-of-term evaluations of courses and instructors provide feedback that is useful for improving *next* term's course; they do nothing to help this term's students.

Two forms of continuous assessment are possible. One is a series of increasingly complex assignments that monitor how well students are mastering the subject matter and developing the proficiencies set out for the course. Acquiring more complex knowledge and higher-level proficiencies requires mastery of what necessarily precedes them.

The other is an ongoing programme of feedback on course and instructor effectiveness. Most colleges and universities require the end-of-term evaluations, but few go beyond that. Ongoing evaluations enable faculty members to respond more quickly and effectively to real or perceived problems. Students, as customers, appreciate being consulted about their reactions to the product and how it is packaged. In my experience, the evaluation process contributes to building a closer and more effective relationship with students.

Because continuous improvement and customer focus are so intimately linked, it seemed useful to expand the scope of ongoing assessment efforts. This called for a process that not only evaluated the course and the instructor but also monitored student gains in proficiencies. It proved to be relatively easy to push ahead with continuous improvement and customer focus on proficiencies inasmuch as I had been building an integrated set of assignments on proficiencies and I had experimented with more frequent evaluations.

PLANNING AND IMPLEMENTATION

With this background, we were ready to examine the planning and implementation of this approach to a specific course.

Course description

Economics 450, Wages and the Labour Market, is an upper division course taken largely by undergraduate economics majors who are third and fourth-year students, juniors and seniors. It also includes a sizeable contingent of master's degree industrial relations students, and a smattering of students from other fields. Typically, about fifty students enrol in this course – twenty to twenty-five of them are undergraduate economics majors, another fifteen to twenty are from industrial relations, and the remaining five to ten are a mixture of graduate and undergraduate students from related disciplines, ranging from sociology to industrial engineering. The purpose of this course, which assumes an intermediate knowledge of economics, is to help students learn how to apply the knowledge they are learning rather than simply regurgitating it in examinations.

The course content is best represented by the texts of Ehrenberg and Smith (1991) or Kaufman (1989). The text is supplemented by several 'real books', not textbooks (Hansen, 1988) that report on current research.[6] Students also purchase a reading packet that includes a collection of journal articles, policy-orientated materials and newspaper articles, all selected to help students see how to apply their knowledge in real world contexts. Considerable attention is given to written assignments as a way of helping students learn and demonstrating their ability to use their knowledge.[7] Several homework assignments require students to think about and work with actual data. Typically, students regard the course as a demanding one. Over my fifteen years of teaching this course, it has evolved away from formal presentations and textbook learning. Much more emphasis is given to involving students in the learning process and using a wider array of reading materials and instructional approaches.

Planning

At the start of every course, I ask students in effect to view themselves as customers. They were asked to indicate what they hope to learn in the course, interest in particular topics, and background information about them that is pertinent to the course. I use these responses to learn more about the students and to tailor the course towards their needs. The first task in the new TQI-orientated version of the course involved identifying a dozen or so research topics of potential interest to students and amenable to completion within the term.

Two types of substantive topics immediately came to mind. One involved updating the results of various empirical studies cited in the course materials, such as the impact of union membership on earnings, the magnitude of salary disparities for female workers, earnings differences by level of educational attainment, an analysis of the wage settlement for postal workers. The other involved working at a conceptual level, focusing on how to think about a topic and establishing its empirical dimensions. Among these topics were the following (recall that the course began in January 1991): what is the likely impact of the current recession on employment and wages in Wisconsin? How would you try to assess the impact of the obsolescence of skills on the earnings of workers? And, if the Gulf War required mobilizing additional forces and re-imposition of a military draft, how could the military draft be integrated with the volunteer force?

Two other sharply different types of topics were needed in view of the objectives of the course. The first called for establishing and implementing a continuous assessment system; the results can be of direct benefit to currently enrolled students. The second called for a review and refinement of the proficiencies in the major. Though not directly focused on the subject matter of the course, this topic was of direct concern to me as a teacher. Perhaps I had not properly framed my list of proficiencies, or I had failed to include one or more proficiencies that students viewed as important. While team participants might benefit directly from thinking about proficiencies, my hope was to learn more and thereby improve the quality of subsequent offerings of this course.

After this list of topics was compiled, brief elaborations of each were prepared for distribution to the students. The purpose was to help them decide which topics were of most interest and then to rank them. Their rankings were to assist me in forming the membership of the various teams.

Special arrangements had to be made for students working on the first set of topics. Doing empirical work requires having access to pertinent data sources, access to a computer, and knowledge of software programs that permit students to perform the necessary statistical analyses. A copy of the March 1988 Current Population Survey was obtained through the Social Science Data and Computation Library which also created a data extract from the CPS files. Arrangements were made for students to use the Social Science Micro Computer Laboratory for their data processing and the Industrial Relations Research Institute's Micro Computer laboratory provided the technical assistance so that teams could use SPSS software to carry out their analyses. Arrangements were also made for the Laboratory

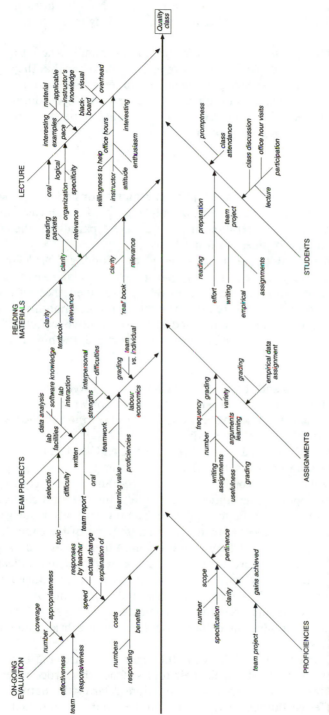

Figure 9.1 Ishikawa analysis for class quality
Source: Townsend 1970

to provide three class periods of familiarization with its facilities and with SPSS, as well as special consulting for teams requiring more time for their data analysis.

The next step required developing a statement explaining how to ensure that the teams operated effectively and re-assuring students that they would be graded fairly. I also needed to engage the interest and enthusiasm of students in practising the team approach. I also wanted to address what students would quickly recognize as a substantial departure from the traditonal lecture-discussion approach.

Implementation

Getting a series of team projects launched requires considerable time and effort. It must be done immediately not only to get students started but also to convey that they are operating under a different paradigm; the course will not be run on a business-as-usual basis.

A good portion of the first class period on Monday was devoted to examining the nature of the course and particularly my plan to experiment, as I described it, with the team approach. I explained that everything possible would be done to assure that the approach went smoothly, that my interest was in having students involved in the substantive aspects of their topic rather than getting bogged down in, for example, learning programming, that I would try to honour the preferences of students for the various projects, and that in grading the team projects I would try to differentiate between their efforts and those of their team-mates. I went over the list of topics, and said that I wanted their top three rank-ordered preferences by Wednesday so that we could have the teams meet during the Friday class and get the projects started promptly.

On Wednesday I collected the preference sheets and worked between then and Friday's class to put together the teams, trying to honour the preferences of students. Several topics drew less interest and were discarded. For oversubscribed topics, some students had to take their second choices.

On Friday we meet in a large conference room where, after our general session, students could meet as teams in different parts of the room for the purpose of figuring out how they would organize themselves and proceed. The team memberships were announced, and a few students indicated a desire to move to different teams. A couple of trades were arranged on the spot. I then instructed the teams on the essential ingredients of successful teamwork. My comments drew on the contents of *The Team Handbook* (Scholtes 1988). I supplemented these comments with a brief handout on working in teams.

With these matters out of the way, the teams convened and began discussing how to define and attack their topics. Once this process began, I moved from team to team to answer questions, clarify the nature of the topic, and offer encouragement. I could not help but be impressed by the vigour with which team members interacted. Students seem genuinely excited at the prospect of working together. They liked the idea of being placed in a problem-solving situation where there was no single correct method of attack and where answers were to be developed through their collective efforts.

The following Monday I announced that the Friday class later that week would again be given over to team meetings. This would enable students to continue defining the project and deciding how to proceed. Once again, we met in the more informal setting of a large lounge. Students took up where they left off last time. I continued making the rounds of the groups, offering guidance as seemed appropriate. At the end of the 50-minute class, most teams seemed to have developed a plan of action. It appeared to me that the project approach was off to an auspicious start.

On Friday of the third week the teams met again. It was clear that most of them had decided what needed to be done, as several concluded their meetings quickly and left to carry out their individual assignments. Several weeks later I had the teams convene during the last 20 minutes of the class. Meanwhile, individual students and the teams often discussed their work before or after class, and sometimes during my office hours, as they struggled to work together and figure out how to deal with difficulties. On several other occasions the last half-hour of the class period was set aside so that teams could meet to monitor their progress and assess what needed to be done next.

Execution

Everything did not go smoothly. The task of getting the data organized in a way that would be computer-friendly for the student teams proved to be a much bigger task than expected. Because the student laboratory assistant with a political science background was not conversant with the approaches used in economics, I spent much more time assisting in the data preparation than I had expected. As a result, students were not able to get to the computational aspects of the assignment until the second half of the term.

A further complication arose because of the heavy demands made by other students on the lab. To ensure that the lab's personal computers would not be tied up for long periods of time cranking out regressions, we greatly reduced the size of the data samples. This compromised the possibility of carrying out one project; as a result, that team's members had to be combined with another team working on a similar project.

When the data were ready, two class meetings were scheduled in the laboratory so that students who needed to could become familiar with the computer system and learn how to use SPSS. Most teams had to spend considerable additional time in the lab, largely because they did not know much about SPSS.

As the frustration level grew among the teams carrying out the empirical replications, I had to do a considerable amount of hand-holding and calming people. The other teams were moving ahead, even though several experienced other frustrations. As the difficulties and frustrations of the various teams became known, everyone became more understanding about the problems that are inevitably encountered in carrying out team research projects.

Presentations

As the term came to a close, the time approached for the oral presentation. To prepare the teams, I offered suggestions about how these reports should be organized and presented. Because time was limited, each team had 15 minutes to make its presentation, with an additional 5 minutes to respond to questions from the class. With nine teams to report, three full class periods were devoted to these presentations.

The presentations, though varying in sharpness and polish, turned out well. One person acted as a moderator and wove together in integrated fashion the contributions of fellow team members. In other cases, each student presented a portion of the team's report. Members of the class were highly attentive and asked good questions. I ended each presentation with a question or two and perhaps a substantive observation about the topic. In several instances, students gathered at the end of class to ask further questions of teams or team members.

The written reports which were to be turned in at the next class meeting also varied in quality, reflecting in considerable part the nature of the topic and abilities of team members. I promised the teams written comments on both their oral presentations and their written reports. These were distributed at the next class. I did not grade until after all the written reports had been completed and turned in.

Team processes

Inasmuch as the team projects differed, their processes necessarily differed. None the less, they fit the *Plan-Do-Check-Act-Cycle*. The processes that applied are illustrated in Figure 9.2.

The teams working on substantive questions followed what might be called an investigative cycle. The steps can be broken out as follows: *P*lan (define the questions, plan the analysis), *D*o (carry out the analysis), *C*heck (assess the results, reformulate the analysis), *A*ct (redo the full analysis), and then *R*eport the results. These steps, which can be phrased variously, amount to application of the several steps in the well-known scientific method.[8]

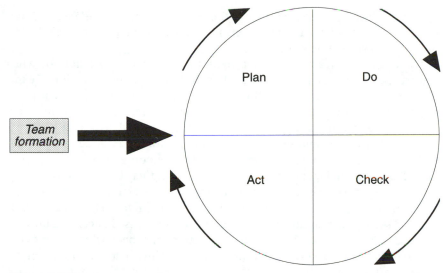

Figure 9.2 Improvement cycle

Flow chart

The flow of activity for all teams except the evaluation team is detailed in Figure 9.3. The flow chart is described as the TQI Team Project System to differentiate it from what might be called the TQI Evaluation System which is discussed later.

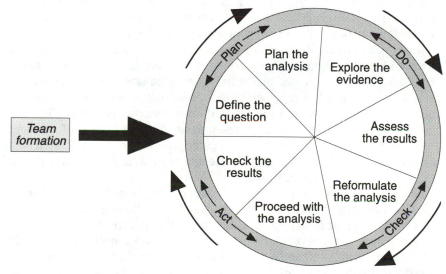

Figure 9.3 Investigative cycle

Evaluation team

This team operated differently from the others because of the nature of its task. We met together early in the term to discuss my views as to what kinds of evaluations were needed.

The evaluation team set up a programme of ongoing evaluation, with feedback to me on the results so that I could take appropriate action. Team members met with me, received copies of other course evaluation forms, and went off to develop their own evaluation form. The plan called for adapting the traditional course evaluation form and administering it both before and after the mid-term exam. A similar form would be used at the end of the term. In addition, more selective responses would be sought periodically, involving a few students each time rather than the entire class. The details of later evaluations were to be worked out as the process evolved. The members of this team were particularly effective, and I enjoyed seeing their enthusiasm and their common sense in deciding how to proceed. Prior to the first evaluation, team members were informally picking up various student reactions and conveying their interpretation of them to me without naming names. I found this informal feedback useful, and looked forward to the results based on responses to the initial and post-mid-term exam evaluations.

The team began by devising a survey for administration during the sixth week of the course. After reviewing the survey with them, they administered it and analysed the results.

The most prominent concerns were the fast pace of the course, some difficulty with concepts, and a sense that class discussion was not always focused enough to be useful. I relayed these comments to the class, and indicated my intention to be responsive to these customer concerns. It was obvious from their reactions that the students were intensively interested in the feedback from the survey and in my reaction to the results.

It was quite evident that the mix of students – economics undergraduates, master's-level industrial relations students, and an assortment of students from other majors – created difficulty. Undergraduate economics students were more technically adept, while the master's-level students were more knowledgeable about labour market and wage phenomena. This difference has always been of concern and represents one of the challenges of teaching this course. These differences are highlighted with several sets of histograms shown in Figure 9.4. No attempt is made here to analyse these patterns or to report a variety of other responses.

Because students are always apprehensive about the mid-term examination, the evaluation team prepared a follow-up survey to be administered immediately after the exam. The nature of the negative feedback was not unexpected; the exam contained too many questions. This is a frequent complaint, and I responded by reducing slightly the number of questions into the final examination. As a general rule, however, I believe it is better to ask more rather than fewer questions, because I can get a better sense of each student's mastery of the subject. Students report feeling pressured by the number and variety of questions, and often the difficulty of being forced to apply rather than feed back their knowledge.

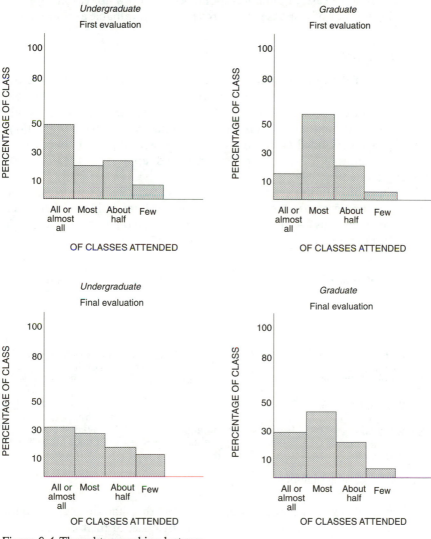

Figure 9.4 Thought-provoking lectures

The team then decided that it would try to monitor student responses to the course on a continuing basis. To get feedback, team members talked with students before and after class. The team also produced quick response sheets so that students could jot down their reactions to each day's class. These responses were read and summarized by the team which before the next class meeting could alert me to student problems and concerns. This proved to be enormously effective as teams ran into unanticipated difficulties with their projects and may have been too bashful to approach me directly. To the extent possible, I tried to respond as these concerns became apparent. In some cases, I did not respond because I saw no reason to do so; explaining my lack of response often proved to be as valuable as responding.

EVALUATION

As the end of the term drew near, it became important to co-ordinate the information-gathering efforts. Four instruments were to be used. The goal was to maximize the effectiveness of the information-gathering effort while holding down the amount of time students would need to do the evaluation. The objectives included evaluating the course, assessing the impact to the teams, monitoring gains in proficiencies and appraising the value of ongoing evaluation.

Members of both the evaluation and proficiencies teams were asked to assist, and the class was asked to offer any advice it might have either to me or to the two teams. A flow chart of the full schedule of evaluations is shown in Figure 9.5.

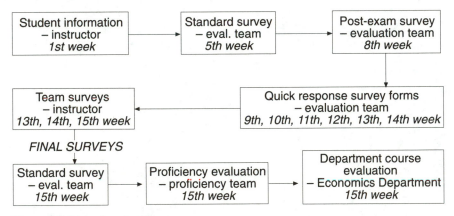

Figure 9.5 List of evaluations

Students obviously wanted feedback on what they had done as a group. They were also interested in their 'grade' on this part of their course work. Though Deming may argue that team participants should be rewarded as a group, the reality of submitting a final course grade for each student necessitated a different approach. As noted earlier, students had been told that some method would be used to evaluate both their performance as a team and their individual contribution to the team effort.

Evaluating the work of the teams and their individual members was complicated. Not only did the input of individual students vary, but also some students were obviously more capable than others. Moreover, the team projects differed in complexity and difficulty. Rather than attempting to divine exactly who did what, I decided to involve the team members in the process.

I began by preparing a team evaluation sheet. It asked each student to apportion among the various team members, including themselves, the total time and effort devoted to the team project, or at least their perceptions of that effort. Thus, if a team's four members made approximately equal contributions, each member would be assigned 25 per cent of the credit going to the team. If the contributions of individual team members differed, as was usually the case, and the allocation of individual team members differed, as was usually the case, the allocation of individual rewards also varied.

These evaluations yielded two interesting results. One was the general agreement among team members about the relative contributions of other team members, whether the contributions turned out to be relatively similar or quite different. Another was the similarity of their assessments with my perceptions of the relative contribution of each team member. My perception was formed by having observed team members at their meetings (at least those held during class periods and sometimes those held after class), talking with students, and knowing how students were performing in other course activities, such as writing assignments. With this information and my evaluation of each team's oral presentation and written report, I assigned a grade to each team's project. I recorded this grade and then indicated on a special form for each student the extent to which their individual grade deviated from the overall team grade. Thus, the team might have earned a grade of AB on its project, with some individuals receiving As, others getting ABs, still others getting Bs, and perhaps a few others getting BCs.

In a final effort to be as fair as possible, I allowed students to indicate if they wanted their grade on the team project to carry somewhat more or somewhat less weight in their grade on class assignments, which in turn would filter into the course grade. As might be expected, students who scored low on the team project opted to have more weight put back on their other work, and vice versa. Generally, students were satisfied with the evaluation of their projects.

Evaluating proficiencies

Information on proficiencies came from two sources. One was the team evaluation form that I devised in consultation with both the evaluation and proficiencies teams. It asked team members what level of proficiencies they had drawn on in working on their team project. The other was the proficiencies questionnaire developed by the proficiencies team. It asked students what particular skills they had developed and/or utilized in connection with each of the proficiencies.

Evaluating the ongoing evaluations

The evaluation team asked in its form for students' reactions to the process of ongoing evaluation, using an open-ended question.

When the official departmental course evaluation was to be administered, I worked with both teams to be assured that the overall evaluation of the course would be comprehensive and at the same time minimize the overlap amongst the various evaluation instruments. Through lack of full communication there was some overlap but it was not substantial. In any case, on the day of the evaluation during the last week of classes I asked students to pick a 4-digit number and put it on each of the various evaluation sheets. I indicated that this would help me carry out a thorough evaluation of the course and their progress in mastering the proficiencies in the major. I also promised anonymity, assuring them, lest they were concerned, that the various forms would not be turned over to me until after the final grades had been submitted to the Department of Economics.

End-of-course evaluation

The traditional formal procedure for evaluating instructors and courses is through the department's end-of-term course evaluation questionnaires.[9] The difficulty with this approach is that the results come too late to help improve the course or its instructor. Although there is no reason why faculty members could not mount earlier course evaluations of their own, this is rarely done. The earlier feedback I obtained from more frequent evaluations proved useful in fine-tuning the course and identifying problems experienced by students.

Linked responses

The linking of student responses at the end of the term proved useful in giving me a more complete picture of what went on. Immediately after the course ended I had all of the responses entered on a disk, so that they would be available for analysis. There was no way to link up the earlier evaluations carried on by the evaluation team except by grouping the responses for similar categories of students; for example, undergraduate versus graduate students.

Unfortunately, I was unable to obtain from the team either its data disk or the completed surveys from its several evaluations. Hence, my hopes of linking the end-of-course evaluations with the earlier evaluations was thwarted, except for what the team provided in its written report.

WHAT WAS LEARNED

What did I learn from this experience? How can this course be improved? How can my teaching benefit from this experience? How can student learning be enhanced in future offerings of this course? These are several of the many questions that came to mind as the course ended and in subsequent reflections.

Much was learned from what was tried. The most important lesson is that teaching this kind of course, with its multiple goals and objectives, emphasizes the instructor's role as a manager of resources. The many different activities designed to help achieve the goals and objectives of the course require a well-thought-out, term-long plan of action, continuing coordination of these activities and flexibility in adapting to problems as they arise. The use of team projects makes everyone particularly conscious of the time of students, individually and in teams. Because students have a heavy workload in other courses, it is important to see that their time is well used. Of direct interest is student reaction to the proficiencies approach, team projects and ongoing evaluation.

Proficiencies

The evaluation information on proficiencies can be grouped into several categories: open-ended comments about the skills gained in dealing with each of the proficiencies; a numerical rating of the extent to which team projects drew upon each of the proficiencies; and miscellaneous comments scattered through the surveys.

In their open-ended responses, students seemed impressed with the gains they achieved in improving their proficiencies. Because of the structure of the questions, the responses proved to be far more specific and revealing than those I have received in previous course evaluations. It was apparent that students were thinking about the gains they achieved in being able to use their knowledge. I came away with the sense that these students had been pushed to develop their proficiencies and that they not only responded, but also were able to assess their progress.

Team involvement

Information on team involvement came from open-ended questions asking what was positive and what was negative about the team projects. Students were almost unanimous in favouring continuation of the team projects. At the same time, they qualified their responses by suggesting various improvements, among them better organization of the projects (particularly those involving data tapes and the computer). The sense of their comments is that if these improvements were made, the team approach could be a highly valuable learning experience.

What students found positive about the projects was working with others, finding complementary strengths among team members, exchanging ideas about the project, and realizing that the team skills acquired would be valuable after graduation. The negatives divided into two categories. One

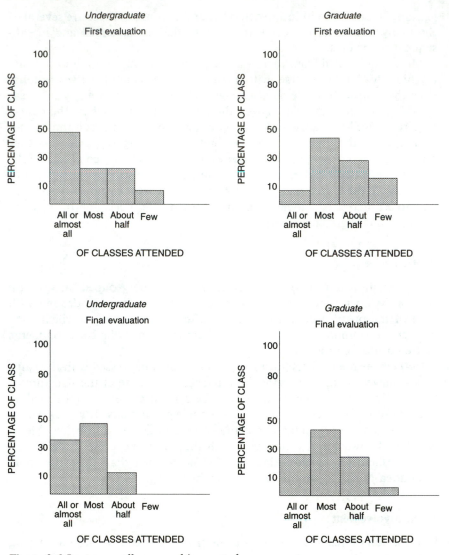

Figure 9.6 Lectures well-prepared/presented

focused on teams: the diversity of knowledge, skills and interest among team members to participate fully, and difficulties in scheduling team meetings to carry on the work. The other concerned the projects, centring on their difficulty and/or ambuguity, lateness in getting the data ready for the computer, and problems in mastering the computer software needed to manipulate the data.

These generally favourable views indicate that team projects should be continued. The comments also indicate that the projects need to be more sharply defined, and the data and computer set-up needs to be better organized.

Concluding comment

Teaching this course proved to be enormously stimulating. Several factors accounted for this. The special focus on creativity and the discovery of new knowledge made the course more challenging to students and seemed to energize them in new ways. I found this focus satisfying for the stimulus it provided in watching students work as teams in carrying out their research projects. I learned much about the challenges of trying to emphasize proficiencies, particularly that of creativity and the discovery of new knowledge. Though this focus required some extra work on my part, my view is that the benefits exceeded the costs. Based on the survey responses and the informal comments made by students after the course ended, I believe they held similar opinions.

Working with students as team members also provided an easy opportunity to know them better and observe more closely what they were learning. The ongoing surveys provided useful feedback that enabled me to keep in close and regular touch with their reactions and problems.

Much remains to be learned about how to infuse TQI into individual courses. The most immediate task is deciding how much to emphasize instruction in teamwork and use of the seven key tools of the Deming approach in a course that is already packed with content and assignments to enhance student proficiencies. The longer-run task is to develop more effective methods for enhancing student proficiencies and for assessing the level of proficiencies they attain.

The prospects for quickly resolving these varied issues are unclear. My efforts to infuse TQI into this course yielded valuable insights that will help improve what I do next time. That next effort, in turn, will yield still other insights, in the spirit of the never-ending *Plan-Do-Check-Act* cycle. With time, the vision of how to help students attain the proficiencies expected of economics majors should come even closer to realization.

NOTES

1 I became even more convinced after Hau digressed to describe using TQI in coaching a soccer team of 10-year-old girls; he brought the team from the bottom of its league to the state championship play-offs within the space of a single season.
2 More details are available in old files which I have not yet re-examined.
3 Considerable time was devoted to class discussion, working through empirically orientated articles from professional journals, and engaging in policy analyses.
4 Over the previous years, I had exploited a wide network of friends in business, government positions and elsewhere to find out what they and their colleagues looked for in new college graduates. From these contacts, and based on what most

economists and teachers would see as what it is we should be doing (even if we are not), these proficiencies began to take shape.

5 In this setting students may be viewed as analogous to apprentices rather than workers.

6 Amongst the books used recently are Freeman (1975), Bawden and Skidmore (1989) and Burtless (1990).

7 Students have always been required to write a variety of short papers even when the course is not taught on a 'writing-intensive' basis (Hansen 1993).

8 For the evaluation team involved in monitoring course quality, I stayed with the modified Plan-Do-Check-Act Cycle rather than Hau's adaptation: *S*tudy the current situation, *I*dentify vital problems, *A*ct on problems, and *M*onitor progress.

9 A departmental questionnaire is administered by the undergraduate adviser's office toward the end of the term. The results are not available to the individual instructor until after final grades have been turned in. The course evaluation results are open for inspection by students and others, although requests to see the results are infrequent. Students are asked to respond to a series of questions about the course and instructor, culminating with questions about the respondent's enthusiasm for recommending to a friend the course and the instructor. For almost twenty-five years the Department of Economics has evaluated its courses, long before such evaluations were mandated by the Board of Regents. For details, see Hansen and Kelley (1973).

REFERENCES

Bawden, D. Lee and Skidmore, F. (eds) (1989) *Rethinking Employment Policy*, Washington, DC: Urban Institute Press.

Bowen, H.R. (1977) *Investment in Learning: the Individual and Social Value of American Higher Education*, San Francisco: Jossey-Bass.

Brassard, M. (1989) *The Memory Jogger Plus +: Featuring the Seven Management and Planning Tools*, Mentuen, MA: GOAL/QPC.

Burtless, G. (ed.) (1990) *A Future of Lousy Jobs: the Changing Structure of US Wages*, Washington, DC: Brookings Institution.

Deming, W. Edwards (1986) *Out of the Crisis*, Cambridge, MA: Massachusetts Institute of Technology, Center for Advanced Engineering Study.

Ehrenberg, R.G. and Smith, R.S. (1991) *Modern Labor Economics: Theory and Public Policy*, (4th edn) Glenview, IL: Scott, Foresman & Co.

Finster, M.P. (1991) 'The quality revolution at a school of business', *ASQC Quality Congress Transactions – Milwaukee*.

Freeman, R. (1975) *The Overeducated American*, New York: Academic Press.

Hansen, W. Lee (1986) 'What knowledge is most worth knowing – for economics majors', *American Economic Review* (May).

—— (1988) ' "Real" books and textbooks', *Journal of Economic Education*.

—— (1991) 'The economics major in liberal arts education', in Carol G. Schneider (ed.) *Liberal Learning and the Arts and Sciences Major*, vol. 2, Washington, DC: Association of American Colleges; for an abbreviated version, see 'The economics major: can and should we do better than B–?' *American Economic Review* (May).

—— (1993) 'Teaching a "writing-intensive" course in economics: an evaluataion', forthcoming, *Journal of Economic Education*.

Hansen, W. Lee and Kelley, A.C. (1973) 'The political economy of course evaluations', *Journal of Economic Education*.

Hau, I. (1991) *Teaching Quality Improvement by Quality Improvements in Teaching*, Madison, WI: Center for Quality and Productivity Improvement, College of Engineering, Report no. 59 (Feb.).

Imai, M. (1986) *Kaizen: the Key to Japan's Competitive Success*, New York: McGraw-Hill.

Kaufman, B.E. (1989) *The Economics of Labor Markets and Industrial Relations*, 2nd edn, Hinsdale, IL: Dryden.

Keller, G. (1983) *Academic Strategy: the Management Revolution in American Higher Education*, Baltimore, MD: Johns Hopkins University Press.

Leonard, G. (1968) *Education and Ecstasy*.

Light, R.J. (1990) *The Harvard Assessment Seminars, First Report*, Cambridge, MA: Harvard Graduate School of Education and Kennedy School of Government.

—— (1991) *The Harvard Assessment Seminars, Second Report*, Cambridge, MA: Harvard Graduate School of Education and Kennedy School of Government.

Miller, R.I. (ed.) (1991) *Applying the Deming Method to Higher Education*, Washington, DC: College and University Personnel Association.

Pirsig, R.M. (1974) *Zen and the Art of Motorcycle Maintenance: an Inquiry into Values*, New York: Bantam Books.

Scholtes, P.R., and others (1988) *The Team Handbook: How to Improve Quality with Teams*, Madison, WI: Joiner Associates.

Senge, P. (1991) *The Fifth Discipline*, New York: Doubleday Books.

Sherr, L.A. and D.J. Teeter (1991) *Total Quality Management in Higher Education*, New Directions in Institutional Research, San Francisco: Jossey-Bass.

Spanbauer, S.J. (1992) *A Quality System of Education*, Milwaukee, WI: ASQC Quality Press.

Stampen, J.O. (1987) 'Improving the quality of education: W. Edwards Deming and effective schools', *Contemporary Education Review*.

Townsend, R. (1970) *Up the Organisation*, London: Michael Joseph.

TQ Magazine, 1992.

Walton, M. (1990) *The Deming Management Method*, New York: Putnam.

10 Doing Total Quality Management the hard way

Installing BS 5750/ISO 9001 at the University of Wolverhampton

Susan Storey

The University of Wolverhampton is a large (by UK standards) higher education institution offering undergraduate and postgraduate degrees, certificates and diplomas, professional courses, short courses, training, contract research and consultancy. It is organized into four faculties and ten academic schools over five sites in the West Midlands and Shropshire, and has a growing off-campus and overseas operation. The majority of taught programmes are within the University's Modular System.

At this time, summer 1993, the university has been pursuing total quality and developing its quality system to BS 5750 for three years. A full account of the strategic reasons for adopting TQM and the planning behind the implementation strategy is given in 'Towards Total Quality Management in higher education: a case study of the University of Wolverhampton' (Doherty 1993). The university has applied for registration to BS 5750, Part 1, for the design and delivery of 'Learning experiences, delivered by means of courses, research and consultancy', and has included the whole institution in the scope of its application.

TQM development that is not directly linked to BS 5750 implementation continues, although it is currently taking something of a back seat to the installation and evaluation of systems and procedures and internal quality system audit.

REVIEW OF BS 5750 IMPLEMENTATION

Target slippage

The most obvious feature of the University of Wolverhampton's implementation of BS 5750 is the very slow progress we have made towards registration. The eighteen months it took educational pioneers Sandwell College to get their system installed, tested and assessed makes our three years (and we're not there yet) look very long-winded.

I would suggest that this is a reflection both of the state of the (then) poly-technic's academic infrastructure at the outset and a consequence of the teamwork methodology we adopted to get procedures written.

Documenting procedures

The intention was to use the installation of the BS 5750 quality system to create more robust systems that actually worked and that were both user- and customer-friendly. The use of cross-functional and cross-departmental teams to document and critique existing procedures was designed to heighten awareness of internal client chains and create a more customer-orientated culture. As an act of commission, the functional managers were part of the team but did not lead it.

As a device to improve communications, create a sense of ownership of systems amongst operational staff and involve many people, the Quality Improvement Teams (QITs), or 'Magic Circles' as they came to be known, were entirely successful. The greatest success of that methodology was that the teamwork approach to tasks and to development projects has passed into the culture of the institution. There are now project groups for the development of performance indicators, centralized admissions, academic development, the 'Command Module' for the management of the admissions, enrolment and module/award registration processes, and school, department and faculty QITs are commonplace. As a means of achieving consensus in the development of the most sensitive and difficult procedure of all, the Procedure for Teaching and Learning Delivery, the QIT approach was essential. However, as a means of producing effective and auditable procedures to a timetable, initially, the 'Magic Circles' were not particularly effective. Let it be said: this reflected failures on the part of the implementation team – the Pro Vice-Chancellor (Quality Assurance) and the Head of the Quality Assurance Unit – and the Senior Management, not the participants. The reasons why the majority of QITs did not deliver were primarily:

- *Lack of trained facilitators* The team leaders were given no training in group facilitation. They and the procedure 'scribes' received training in the requirements of the Standard and in Procedure Writing, but the need for QIT facilitators to have a very clear role definition and particular interpersonal and technical skills was overlooked.
- *Reforming zeal* Several QITs faced with the task of documenting the existing procedure flatly refused to do so on the grounds that the current system was 'rubbish'. They started from scratch with sky-high aspirations and created new procedures that, in a perfect world, would certainly deliver a quality service. These procedures had the virtues of logic, high standards and group consensus. Unfortunately, what had been overlooked was the reasons why the existing procedures were as they were. The QITs were right that the procedures did not work but, we now know, the reason why was not always a faulty procedure. Sometimes the problem was faulty implementation because of lack of training or lack of ownership. Often, the aspects of a procedure that caused most irritation were legal, constitutional or fiscal requirements and could not be

changed without the approval of the university's Board of Governors or an Act of Parliament.

- *Lack of clarity of the institutional framework*   The institution had always operated on a 'need to know' basis with respect to policies and regulations and, even as recently as two years ago, it was rare to find a clear articulation of the rules in a definitive version marked with its approval status. The financial regulations are a case in point: every budget holder is under obligation to abide by the financial regulations, but until a few months ago budget-holders did not have a copy of the regulations.

- *Confusion over what constitutes a procedure*   There has been, and remains, great confusion concerning the distinction between procedures and work instructions and what should and should not be in a procedure. Explanations, definitions and a multiplicity of training activities have not resolved the difficulty for most people, because the culture of the university (*any* university) militates against genuinely mandatory requirements. There is an in-built feeling that saying 'must' is rude. There are few rules: handbooks, guidelines and notes abound. On the other hand, there is a reluctance to let people off the hook with respect to deadline dates that nobody has ever met. Deadlines are used by administrators as targets *after* which they will start to get excited.

- *Gatekeepers and stumbling blocks*   These have been many and varied. Some have had legitimate concerns that legislation and regulations were being ignored. Some have been responding to a perceived threat to their power base. Responses to the new procedures have included insistent assertions that a procedure already existed, bald and unqualified statements that 'You can't do that', references to various policies, regulations and minutes that were nowhere to be found in any definitive state and, most effective of all, blank incomprehension.

- *Lack of incentives*   The voluntary status of the QIT leaders was beneficial in many respects in that they were committed enthusiasts. It was not, however, their job to write procedures for other people, and we felt that we had no right to press them for a result. Many also became disillusioned by the length of time it took to get their procedures edited, approved and published.

In the end we have had to pass the buck right back to the corporate managers whom we have identified as procedure owners to produce the generic, or university-wide procedures and to the heads of schools, departments and units to produce local sub-procedures and work instructions.

It is my belief that the teamwork method was the best approach for the institution in the state of development that pertained at the time, although we could have given the groups a much tighter specification and more relevant training. Facing managers with the doers and the done-unto had a very marked and beneficial effect on internal client chains and the degree of co-operation that took place between sections.

Defining procedures

The *Concise Oxford Dictionary* definition of procedure is 'a mode of performing a task; a series of actions conducted in a certain order'. BS 4778 Glossary of terms used in quality assurance contains references to but no definition of 'procedure'. BS 5750, Part 4, Guide to the use of BS 5750: Part 1 section 4.5.2 states:

> Procedures may be separated into two categories: 'general' and 'detailed'. General procedures are those that pertain to departmental or interdepartmental methods of operation and that, normally, remain relatively constant. . . . Detailed procedures are those that are created for and pertain to, for example, a specific product, test device, production technique, special packaging or handling instructions. Documented detailed procedures are job or work instructions that describe in detail what is to be done, who should do it, when it should be done, supplies, services and equipment to be used, criteria to be satisfied etc. . . . The ultimate test of a procedure is its ability to provide the control to achieve the result for which it was created.

The generic procedures that are evolving within the university are more in the style of regulations or customer charters than a blow-by-blow account of a process. There are still, however, a number of procedures that are extremely prescriptive and specific: these are mainly in areas where there is, or it is desired that there should be, a tight central control over local operations. The main difficulties that the university generic procedure writers have encountered have been:

- attempting to reconcile differing practices across the institution;
- specifying the location of responsibility for stages of the procedure;
- clarifying what is mandatory and what is guidance;
- keeping procedures simple whilst including all essential stages;
- persuading senior managers to approve them.

THE AUDIT EXPERIENCE

After a year of trying, unsuccessfully, to get a set of Generic Procedures installed, the implementation team decided to begin the process of internal quality system auditing; as much as anything to find out what systems were in place, to what extent they were documented and how effective they were. This caused some of the university's trained internal quality auditors to experience cognitive dissonance as they had successfully internalized the concept of auditing against known and documented procedures and felt at a considerable disadvantage 'auditing in the dark'. Most of the early audits were carried out by teams comprising a Lead Auditor, normally the Head of the Quality Assurance Unit, a trained internal quality auditor and a trainee auditor. The success of the audit depended on the willingness of both auditors and auditees to regard the exercise as developmental. Even in the most favourable circumstances, however, the Audit Teams encountered some nervousness and, very occasionally, covert hostility and obstruction from auditees. Despite this, many auditees agreed that the audits had been useful and conducted in a positive spirit, and it was noticeable that recruitment to internal auditor training received a considerable boost from staff who had been on the receiving end of an audit.

Corrective Action Requests (CARs) were issued from this first round of audits where a non-compliance was found against a local or university procedure, where the procedure in operation (whether documented or not) did not meet the requirements of the Standard and where there was an obvious system failure. Three early CARs were sent to the Directorate, much to their astonishment, because the system failures at school level were considered to have university-wide policy implications.

At the end of each audit, the auditees were asked to feed back to the Audit Team on their view of the audit process. On the whole, feedback was positive, with comments such as 'We were pleased to see the system tested and found to work', 'It's nice to have the opportunity to put quality problems at school level on the institutional agenda', 'Not as bad as I thought it would be', but there were concerns that CARs would bring down retribution from on high and the implementation team was half amused and half worried (our usual state of mind when I think about it) to learn that some kind of inter-school tally was being kept of numbers of CARs received.

SYSTEM BENEFITS, PERMEATION FAILURES

There have been considerable system improvements within the university and between the university and its partner institutions over the last two years. It would be difficult to prove that they all result from the attempt to implement BS 5750, but it is certainly the case that some of them are directly attributable to the development of the quality system and that others spring from the same institutional commitment to quality improvement. Many developments have been complementary, and it is gradually becoming clear to those staff who are immersed in the heartland of developments that there is a coherent institutional strategy and not just a series of 'flavours of the month'. It is unfortunately also the case that it is only those staff who are right in the thick of it who have this perception, which reveals a major communications failure on the part of both the implementation team and the senior managers of the university.

I can do no better here than quote the views of some colleagues:

> I've heard of it (BS 5750) but what exactly is it? Is it the training courses? If it is then it's beneficial. [This referred to courses on health and safety, first aid, etc. as part of the Corporate Staff Development Programme.]
>
> (Caretakers)

It's brought the customer nearer to what we are doing [but] there is more paperwork flying about. People have got the bug and are creating procedures all over the place.

(Site Manager)

What is it?

(Student)

We've used it to open up administration. It has been a useful tool to give academics a reason why we wanted things from them: they always want a reason.

First we used it as a stick and then we publicized the carrots, the benefits. We said 'This is what you got out of it'.

(Faculty Administrator)

Not more bloody procedures!

(Anon)

It has highlighted the similarities and the differences [between working practices]; made us aware of the need for liaison.

(Faculty Manager)

It has been a lot of work. I would have liked time off to do it.

(Faculty Manager)

Say what you do and do what you say. Not having previously *said* what we did led to a lot of work.

(Faculty Administrator)

To be quite frank it [BS 5750/TQM] has made no difference whatsoever to the staff in my section. I only know about it since I have been on FQAC [Faculty Quality Assurance Committee]. If they have heard about it it hasn't really touched them.

(Principal Lecturer)

Before the University went for BS 5750 I had the strong impression that the administration was very weak across the institution. There has been a very noticeable improvement. My perception is that the system is now so tightly run that mistakes are unlikely. However, the amount of paper that comes out is adversely affecting everything else. Academic staff are neutralized by bureaucracy and there is an immense feeling of frustration. This is reinforced by the culture of senior academics being administrators: staff are aware that if they do not have an administrative role they are sidelined, not part of the power structure.

(Principal Lecturer)

Managers who believe BS 5750 is a way of getting everyone else to do their job properly are in for a shock. Going for BS 5750 will reveal to everyone at every level in the organization just how good or bad at their jobs managers at every level in the organization are.

(Head of school)

MEETING THE REQUIREMENTS OF THE STANDARD: WHICH CLAUSES HURT?

Each organization has its own unique character even within general type. The University of Wolverhampton was once described by its Vice-Chancellor as having an 'innate incoherence': a characteristic of creative organizations. Getting this innately incoherent organization into a sufficiently coherent state to enable it to achieve BS 5750 whilst protecting its necessary freedoms has highlighted the importance of certain of the Standard's clauses and the difficulty of reconciling their requirements and the traditionally *laissez-faire* culture of higher education.

Clause 4.1.2.1: Responsibility and authority

'The responsibility, authority and the interrelation of all personnel who manage, perform and verify work affecting quality shall be defined.' This is a key requirement for the university, and defining the responsibility and authority of staff has been of considerable benefit, not least to the staff themselves. Where we have experienced most difficulty has been in the area of 'interrelation': this is graphically illustrated in our functional organization charts which are out of date as soon as they are printed and some of which bristle with dotted lines denoting the functional co-operation and communications much more relevant to achieving quality than the solid lines denoting line management. It is perfectly possible to describe an organic organization: the problem with the University of Wolverhampton is that it behaves like an organic organization but still has a traditional, hierarchical management structure.

Clause 4.3: Contract review

In a straightforward manufacturing context contract review requires the supplier to review the contract with the customer regularly to ensure that the contracted product specification is being delivered and that it is still what the customer needs. In the context of the University of Wolverhampton, the product is the learning experience and the customers are the students (the consumers), the students' sponsors, qualification-awarding and professional bodies and funding bodies. The nature of the contract to provide learning experiences is, therefore, complex and a range of 'customers' is involved. The factors which have needed to be taken into account are:

- promotional material – that it is not misleading;
- admission – criteria for entry and how an applicant's 'ability to benefit' is assessed;
- enrolment and registration – that students are fully informed of their rights and responsibilities and that changes to registration are fully, accurately and promptly recorded;
- student tracking – that it is possible to find any student in the system by consulting the record of her or his registered programme;
- attendance – that it is known whether or not a student is still pursuing her or his registered programme and that appropriate evidence of attendance is supplied to sponsors;
- student progress – that the continuing ability of the programme to meet the student's needs and the student's continuing ability to benefit are assessed.

None of these concerns was new, but the contract review requirement brought them into sharper focus, particularly:

- evidence – the need to provide positive evidence that parts of the admissions and registration processes had been carried out rather than it being assumed that, if the student was registered, all necessary procedures had been carried out correctly;
- registers – for many programmes there was no attendance requirement and no requirement upon staff to keep registers (although many staff did keep registers). With class sizes of 100 or more students as the norm, it was impossible to know, other than by keeping a register, who was 'in attendance' until assignments were or were not submitted. With the university's previous management information system it was impossible to produce accurate class lists for registers in time to be useful. At the time of writing this issue has not been resolved. For the future, a system involving 'smart' student identity/library cards (bar-coded and read by laser or light pen) is under consideration. For the present, registers must be kept for certain full cost courses and where attendance is a require-ment either of the awarding body or of the sponsor, but for other pro-grammes, particularly those involving student managed learning, the responsibility to demonstrate that the student is still in attendence rests with the student.

Clause 4.16: Quality records

The most revealing outcome of the BSI (QA) pre-assessment audit was the university's inability to produce objective evidence of the existence and effectiveness of its systems. Most critical procedures appeared to operate on trust, assumptions and negative evidence – that is, if nothing was recorded it meant that everything was all right – only problems and anomalies were noted. The concept of *evidence* has been alien to the 'professional' academic culture, and staff have been surprised to be asked for proof that they had carried out certain activities.

MANAGEMENT REVIEW

The Management Review Team (MRT), consisting of the Vice-Chancellor, Deputy Vice-Chancellor, Pro Vice-Chancellors, the Director of the Corporate Enterprise Centre and University Trading Companies, the Finance and Personnel Services Managers and the Head of the Quality Assurance Unit, was formed to meet the requirements of clause 4.1.3 of the Standard: 'The quality system adopted to satisfy the requirements of this International Standard shall be reviewed at appropriate intervals by the supplier's management to ensure its continuing suitability and effectiveness.' The MRT has two routine functions: it receives and considers the reports of internal quality system audits and it approves additions and major changes to the quality system, normally reflected in the Quality Manual and new generic procedures. The demarcation between the MRT members functioning as the MRT and most of the same individuals functioning as the directorate is, appropriately, hardly visible. The whole point of management review is that the individual or group has the power to make necessary changes to the quality system. In effect, the MRT is a slightly expanded directorate group with an agenda explicitly focused on quality.

The guiding principles, in my experience, upon which most UK higher education management practice is based are:

- getting by;
- getting away with it;
- getting the money.

The tendency of MRT members, functioning as directorate, towards managerial expediency could not survive being faced at every meeting with their own stated commitment to put quality first. Over the last eighteen months the tenor of the meetings has changed from 'kill the messenger' to a real willingness to tackle quality problems at their point of origin.

The first round of audit reports contained detailed accounts both of observed and verified activity and the views of staff who were interviewed. At first MRT members protested every time that a misconception or unsubstantiated statement occurred in a report, although an attempt had been made to differentiate clearly between statements that were verified and those that were not. It was pointed out to them that it was just as important for them to understand what staff thought as find out what staff did: it was beside the point for the MRT to sit in the council room demanding that 'misleading' statements be removed from audit reports when the reports merely reflected what staff genuinely believed to be the case. Neither was it certain that MRT members, having agreed that their staff were in error, would agree amongst themselves on the correct procedure or terminology.

The following are fairly typical examples of the gap between the various staff and management views of the world as revealed through internal quality system audit:

- *Job titles*

    Staff had a rough idea of what their job titles were but because, in many cases, their jobs had changed since their original appointment and they had not usually had an updated job description, they called themselves whatever seemed to them to describe what they did most accurately. Titles like 'Chief', 'Senior', 'Head', 'Leader', 'Co-ordinator' were used variously and inconsistently across the institution.

    Heads of schools, departments, units and centres also had a rough idea of the titles of their staff since they had been responsible for inventing many of them

    Senior management believed that there was systematic use of nomenclature over which some form of corporate control was exercised. As far as they were concerned, certain job titles carried contractual implications and a particular pay scale, and were not to be used in any other circumstances.

    Resolution: there are now generic basic job specifications for certain grades of staff (Principal Lecturer; Senior Lecturer; Administrator; Secretarial/Clerical Assistant) and other grades are being brought into line. New posts are subject to grading review at which the job specification, title and grade are approved.

- *Budget allocation and devolution*

    Staff had very little understanding of budget devolution and the fact that their Head of school/department had the major role in determining the priorities that affected their lives.

    There appeared to be no understanding that Heads bid for an annual budget which they then had authority to allocate more or less as they saw fit within their schools.

    Heads understood the bidding process but held to the belief that the allocation system to schools/departments was unfair to their particular school/department.

    Senior management believed that Heads understood the budgetary system very well and that they sometimes chose to obscure its workings from their staff.

- *Management and functional structures*

    Staff and *Heads*: structures were clearly described and understood at school/department level but were frequently challenged by senior managers reading the account of the operational system in an audit report.

    Senior management varied in its response depending on the strength of individual members' corporate versus faculty/site loyalties. On the whole, there was a desire to standardize operations as far as possible, or at least to have a corporate standard from which variations would have to be approved and known.

- *Policies and regulations*

Staff were well aware of regulations that directly impacted on their subject or work area: e.g. science technicians knew what the rules were for the disposal of hazardous waste; finance officers knew the requirements of the tendering procedure; BTEC course leaders were in possession of the latest BETC subject guidelines. At the immediate, operational level staff generally had access to the regulations they needed. What they lacked was an understanding of the university's policy framework and where there was a conceptual or policy gap it was filled by myth.

Heads had sufficient understanding of the institutional policies and regulations to enable them to work within them if they wished to conform, but also sufficient guile to take advantage of the lack of clear articulation of policies and ambiguous status of regulations if they wished not to conform.

Senior management, on the one hand, resisted being tied to firm statements on policies that they were attempting to introduce incrementally, and, on the other, had a certain belief in the existence of policies unknown outside the directorate sphere.

Resolution: the status of all policies and regulations is now clearly identified. The principle of incremental introduction of new systems and changes, piloting and testing, is accepted as entirely legitimate, provided that draft procedures or regulations are not passed off as approved, and it is understood that a state of change is the norm. However, at any given point in time it is possible to say 'This policy is in force: these regulations apply.'

'QC cannot progress if policy is not clear' (Ishikawa 1985).

- *System failure*

An early surprise for the MRT was the report of objective evidence of system failure. The system failure had manifested itself previously in grumbles from the schools about uncertainty over student numbers and the inability of the university's management information system to provide accurate class lists, but everything always settled down by the second or third week of the term and everyone always coped. What emerged through audit was that there was a fundamental flaw in the (then) polytechnic's management of first-level student programmes within the modular system, that is, the management was left very substantially to the student. Admission and enrolment were carried out on the basis of the intended eventual award but students were required to register, separately from the enrolment process, for a programme of modules that would gain them the award for which they were enrolled. In some cases, core modules were specified and choice was limited. In many cases there was a bewildering array of module choices and students were not only allowed but encouraged to take an option module from an area other than their main study – e.g., business studies or a modern language. In theory, it was a flexible and student-responsive system: in practice, it caused the schools untold headaches over staffing, rooming and timetables.

The initial response of the MRT to the CARs issued by the audit team was to pass the problem back to the respective QITs responsible for the module registration procedure and the student management systems (the so-called 'Command Module'). Members were unanimous that it was a student management system problem. At subsequent meetings, however, members began to acknowledge the possibility of the systems failure having academic policy implications. Rather than compromise the institution's commitment to student choice and flexibility, it was agreed to compromise by presenting first-level students with a pre-determined programme which they still have the facility to change, exceptionally. The agreement to manage student choice more actively and to pre-determine the first semester's diet represents a major attitudinal shift. Furthermore, the will is there to change policy if it is found that the agreed corrective action is not effective.

BS 5750 AND PRODUCT QUALITY

The 'product' of the University of Wolverhampton is defined as 'learning experiences', but whether the 'product' of a college or university is defined as the learning experience or as some form of added value to the student, it is likely that the same processes and procedures will be included in the quality system and that the purpose of the quality system will be to improve the institution's effectiveness and consistency in delivering its product. Detractors criticize BS 5750 because it does not specify a quality standard for the product or service. This reveals a fundamental misunderstanding of the purpose of the Standard and its application. For very many manufacturing companies BS 5750 is applied in conjunction with the specified British Standard for their product. In a service context it is incumbent upon the organization to define its own service standards, and it is this absence of a requirement for consistency of standards between organizations which causes many educationists to challenge the appropriateness of BS 5750 for education. Hingley and Sallis (1991) in the Mendip Papers state:

> BS 5750 only sets the standard for the system, not the standards which the college should be achieving. The college, together with its customers, is the arbitrator of standards. . . . Some critics argue that because colleges set their own standards some could set deliberately low standards. However, this is not even a theoretical possibility because one of the elements in BS 5750 is contract review, and it is unlikely that customers and potential customers will demand anything but high standards from a college. What BS 5750 does not guarantee is consistency of standards between colleges.

I would question whether there has ever been consistency of standards at any level in education, and least of all in higher education. At best, peer review, comparative performance indicators and systems of moderation have provided a crude assurance of comparability. The methodology of the Higher Education Quality Council's (HEQC) Division of Quality Audit (DQA) explicitly recognizes the differences between institutional mission aims and measures the effectiveness of the institution's systems and processes in delivering its claimed outcomes. There are striking consonances between the requirements of a BS 5750 quality system and the HEQC (DQA), as we have found in preparing documentation for our first HEQC (DQA) visit. There is the same need to have a described quality assurance system and to be able to provide evidence of its operational effectiveness. The emphasis on evidence is carried through into the quality assessment activities of the Higher Education Funding Council for England (HEFCE): claims for excellence are assessed by observation and whether they are sufficiently supported by objective evidence. The only difference between this and BS 5750 quality system audit is the element of subjectivity introduced by the pre-judged expectations of assessors: assessors, unlike auditors, are expected to have a view of what constitutes 'product' quality.

There is no doubt that the process of installing BS 5750 at the University of Wolverhampton has resulted in considerably improved internal services, but it is, as yet, unproven that these administrative improvements have materially affected the quality of the student learning experience. It would be reasonable to suppose that smoother and more effective processes would release teaching staff time for more research and tutorial activity but this is not currently their perception. This could be because there is still so much groundwork to be done at school level in establishing documented procedures and the discipline of recording compliance is not yet internalized. 'BS 5750 places a considerable discipline on those intending to use it. . . . It involves a considerable investment of college resources and staff time' Hingley and Sallis (1992). At Wolverhampton there has been a very considerable investment of resources and time at the centre and in central administrative functions, but it is only now that the implementation effort is impacting directly on the majority of academic staff in the requirement for conformance to procedures and the documentation of work instructions. This has led to a perceived increase in bureaucracy: perceived because, when pressed to be specific, the bureaucratic impositions named by staff have been brought about by a tightening of infrastructure systems that were necessary to support a large, multi-site organization and not specifically to meet the requirements of BS 5750. Indeed, I would go so far as to say that we are not doing anything special for BS 5750: it is all work that was needed anyway.

Most, if not all, TQM models focus on improving the process instead of 'inspecting in' product quality at the end of the process. All the evidence in the manufacturing models of TQM as described by Deming, Juran and Ishikawa is that attention given to improving the process results in an improved, more consistent and more cost-effective product. BS 5750 is all about improving process.

TQM AND BS 5750: CHANGING THE CULTURE

Two major staff attitude surveys have been carried out, two years apart, since the beginning of TQM and BS 5750 development within the university. The second survey contained additional questions, and was better structured to gain a response from other than academic staff. There was, however, sufficient commonality to enable a comparison to be made, which has inspired cautious optimism in the implementation team. The attitude of staff towards institutional management and corporate developments is still negative, but it is markedly less negative than it was two years ago. The results of the attitude survey were cross-referenced with the results of a training needs analysis survey of senior and middle managers, and it was clear that one of the major deficiences of implementation had been the failure to gain the commitment of academic staff in particular to BS 5750 and to prepare Heads, Associate Heads and Deputies adequately for a role in gaining the commitment of their staff. Middle managers are often the most resistant group and the most badly handled.

> Leading the TQM initiative cannot be delegated by the top managers. Without their active leadership the efforts to introduce a programme may succeed for a while but will not last. . . . Resistance to new ideas . . . is to be expected. What is needed is for middle management to be:
> (a) fully committed to the proposed approach;
> (b) given the organisational power to implement the change; and
> (c) supported by senior management by their active involvement in the TQM programme.
> Unfortunately not all companies realise this.
>
> (P. Nesbitt 1992)

I do not believe that this is unique to TQM but would apply to the successful management of any major corporate change.

There have been numerous seminars and training activities undertaken jointly by the senior and middle managers of the university focused on quality, customer care, TQM and BS 5750 but it would be fair to say that, between seminars, the teamwork effort has been less than sustained.

It is possible to have TQM without BS 5750 and BS 5750 without TQM. There are those in higher education that consider TQM, Continuous Qality Improvement, Kaizen and, more recently, Investors in People as appropriate for education where BS 5750 is not, because they believe that they are people rather than system-orientated. There is a collegial preference for a bottom-up approach and a suspicion of management-driven quality improvement initiatives: they are felt to be too 'hard'. Nesbitt states, 'People talk about and try for "bottom up" change. There is no history of this ever happening.' However, 'Change cannot be implemented through fear, or just absorbing the messages, nodding, then doing nothing. "Top down" orders will get ignored, sabotaged or re-interpreted in many ways. In an authoritarian organisation, much of the creativity goes into designing ways to circumvent authority.' The great challenge for the university's senior managers is to bring about the effective quality system required to serve the needs of a large, multi-site and diverse organization without resorting to authoritarianism.

SUMMARY

In evaluating progress since the start of our TQM drive I have become conscious that we have done a great deal and that there have been some real achievements:

- teamwork culture;
- administrative process improvements;
- Senior management willingness to meet quality problems head-on;
- Senior management focus on facts as a basis for decision-making and results as a measure of progress;
- greatly improved cross-functional systems and interface communications;
- a clearer and more rational, if still traditional, management map of the organization;
- growing staff confidence in management and growing management belief in the good intentions and abilities of staff;
- a real staff commitment (emerging from the recent staff attitude survey) to customer satisfaction and belief that the university is customer-orientated.

I would also honestly say that there have been no failures, only learning experiences. It is possible to say, with hindsight, that certain things could have been achieved more quickly, more cheaply and with less *Angst*, but I am reviewing them from a very different organizational culture than the one in which the delays, blind alleys and obstacles were experienced. There is a sense in which the mere passage of time, provided that you do not lose heart, is a positive contributory element in the change process. People get used to the idea of TQM and BS 5750 and feel less threatened. Provided a steady pressure is maintained by product champions and the evidence of improvements is publicized, the critical mass moves towards the positive. With a positive recruitment policy, new staff expect to be actively involved in quality system developments and exhibit behaviours appropriate to a total quality organization. It all builds up.

Having said that, delegates at our annual senior staff seminar (reflecting on the results of the Heads' and Deputies training needs analysis which put 'quality' as a low-priority job role but urgent training need) suggested that staff may have become somewhat overexposed to 'quality' as a concept and were switched off by it. They felt that there was a need for staff at all levels to be 'walked through' the quality system to understand what it meant for them in the reality of their day-to-day jobs. Perhaps we are suffering from Excess Activity Syndrome as described by Chang (1993). Certainly we are exhibiting two of the symptoms he describes: 'high count of quality-improvement teams' and 'persistent process-measurement cough' (signifying embarrassment because we are not systematically measuring process). His message, and that of Kearney in 'Total Quality: time to take off the rose-tinted spectacles' is that, unless a TQM system is focused on measured *results*, it will go nowhere. The staff attitude survey measures management culture change and is the only systematic TQM measurement we have carried out so far and, although we have the usual range of product measures (student feedback; external examiners' feedback; student input, process and output indicators and so on), it is only now that we are in a position to take a serious longitudinal view of product life. With the development of the new quality measurement division of the Quality Assurance Unit (providing technical services, surveys, advice and training) and the installation of the new Management Information System, it is now possible, and is our intention, to prioritize both product and process measurement. Kearney states:

> To know if you are improving you must measure. . . . What gets measured gets done . . . (unsuccessful) companies appear to be approaching Total Quality as if they are wearing rose-tinted spectacles. Despite having achieved no tangible results to date, they continue their programmes and 50% view them as successful. Such optimism suggests a triumph of hope over objectivity.

REFERENCES

BS 5750: Part 1: 1987, BSI Standards.
Guidance Notes for the Application of ISO 9000/EN 29000/BS 5750 to Education and Training, BSI Quality Assurance, 1992.
BSI Handbook 22: 1983, Quality Assurance, BSI.
Chang, R.Y. (1993) 'When TQM goes nowhere', *Training & Development* (Jan.).
Deming, W.E. (1964) *Statistical Adjustment of Data*, London: Constable.
Doherty, G.D. (1993) 'Towards Total Quality Management in higher education: a case study of the University of Wolverhampton', *Higher Education* 25.
Hingley, P. and Sallis, E. (1992) 'College quality assurance systems', Staff College (Mendip Papers).
Ishikawa, K. (1985) *What is Total Quality Control? the Japanese Way*, Englewood, NJ: Prentice-Hall.
Juran, J.M. (1988) *Juran on Planning for Quality*, New York: The Free Press.
Kearney, A.T. (1991) 'Total Quality: time to take off the rose-tinted spectacles', London: Kearney Ltd and IFS.
Nesbitt, P. (1992) 'Common barriers to successful Total Quality Management implementation', *Quality Forum* 18 (June).

11 A foot in two camps

Doing BS 5750/ISO 9001 in higher education and industry

Helen Stott

This chapter is simply a practitioner's reflection on current professional activities and is intended as a protocol rather than a piece of research. I am fascinated by human behaviour and welcome any opportunity to study people, particularly the behaviour of people at work. This chapter is, therefore, an echo of impressions rather than facts, of glimpses into people's values and beliefs rather than theory.

I am currently employed as a Senior Lecturer in the Centre for Educational Development, which is part of the Faculty of Education, based at the Walsall Campus of the University of Wolverhampton. I am based here for the majority of my time, co-ordinating, selling and carrying out a variety of training courses and workshops on Total Quality Management (TQM) and BS 5750 to any organization which is willing to pay for them. In addition to this, I act as a consultant for part of my time, helping organizations to implement BS 5750.

For the remainder of my time, I am BS 5750 Co-ordinator, charged with co-ordinating the University's bid to achieve registration to BS 5750, Part 1, for the whole of its operation, comprising five campuses, some 1,500 full- and part-time staff and some 19,000 students. We are currently one of the largest educational establishments in Britain, so the task is enormous.

My current expertise grew out of a deep interest in quality assurance which has grown over the last few years. My Unit depends entirely on externally generated funding, which involves selling a variety of training courses to education, industry and service organizations. With the explosion in interest in TQM and BS 5750, I was chosen to be trained to deliver this type of work because of my deep interest in the subject. I am now a Lead Assessor for BS 5750 and have experience of training managers at all levels in Britain and Europe, in many different types of organizations, including local education institutions, the police service and several production companies. I trained staff in the first primary school to achieve registration to BS 5750, Part 2, and am currently acting as consultant to several diverse organizations, including a local borough council, a distribution company and an iron foundry.

My division of responsibilities gives me an excellent opportunity to make observations related to quality improvement methodology in a number of organizations, and to feed back the results of those observations to enrich both my training courses and workships and the university itself, where I have the fascinating opportunity to study the awakening of a customer-orientated culture. Like the proverbial tanker turning in mid-ocean, we move ponderously but surely from our previous academic elitism to a vision of increased access, flexible, modular routes to accreditation and increased responsiveness to our students. The learning curve I experienced is the basis of what I will describe, together with some personal views on the benefits of a systematic approach to quality management.

Charles Handy (1985) defines organizational culture as 'sets of values, norms and beliefs' which are reflected in different structures and systems. He believes that cultures are affected by events of the past and by the climate of the present, by the technology of the type of work, by their aims and the kind of people that work in them.

In short, culture is about people. To change the existing culture of any organization, we need to change the existing behaviour of the people who are employed there. To change their behaviour, we must first identify what is wrong with that behaviour, then communicate this to the employees in such a way that we enable them to become self-critical and begin to reject past behaviour as undesirable. Only then can we discover the path to continuous quality improvement. Until we are ready to reject the sets of values, norms and beliefs which have caused existing quality-related problems, the organizational culture cannot change.

In education, we face the additional problem of a workforce largely consisting of experts who believe that they are already offering a quality service, blaming the organization or senior management, or both, for existing problems. Rather than accept that crisis management or simply lack of responsiveness to the client may be the cause of student discontent or costly rework, the blame is placed on lack of resources, staff shortages or lack of management support. The academic cohort of the organization is therefore resistant to change, preferring 'academic freedom' to the perceived restrictions of a systematic approach to quality improvement.

Because TQM is largely based on theory and is open to individual interpretation, it may be more widely acceptable to academic staff in many educational establishments than the system-based BS 5750 approach. The idea of working to documented procedures is abhorrent to many academics, and is perceived as inhibiting that freedom which is, in reality, the root cause of poor quality. Try to gear any appraisal system to include observation of lecturers performing in the classroom and watch what happens! Industry, however, is well versed in work-study techniques, accepting them as the norm, and is therefore more open to constant observation and subsequent change to find better ways of working.

Are the problems and frustrations we face in educational establishments really so different from those faced in a typical large manufacturing company? Is the culture change necessary to achieve total quality really miles apart from that faced by colleagues in industry? I am fortunate enough to have had the opportunity to study both over a protracted period, as a player rather than an observer, being able to influence thinking in both a large university and the British division of a multi-national manufacturing company in which I had a recent long-term training and advisory involvement – let's call it Gorway Tyres Ltd.

The conclusion: the differences are based on perceptions rather than reality. Both see themselves as being different, both in culture and in the day-to-day problems they face; and therefore are. Yet scratch the surface and you will find endless similarities. By opening our minds to the lessons we can learn from industry, we can draw enormous benefits and start to change our ivory tower culture.

Let me say at this point that I do not believe that BS 5750 is a magical formula for all ills, nor that it is suitable for all organizations. Its strength lies in the process which organizations must pass through to gain registration. There are three basic reasons why organizations may choose to go through the BS 5750 registration process.

1 for the intrinsic value gained from meeting the challenge;
2 to meet the requirements of a single large customer, such as some government agencies which are requiring BS 5750 registration for large contracts;
3 to maintain or gain access to markets, especially in Europe where quality plays a special role in the emerging set of harmonized product safety standards.

For educational establishments, and particularly further and higher education, the first is the most valuable. In the University, the process has enabled management to obtain feedback on our present state of quality from a variety of sources and to take the opportunity to involve large numbers of staff at various levels within the organization to define and quantify previously unresolved problems.

Total Quality Management is a concept, based on the research of Juran, Deming and others, which states that only the collective efforts of individuals within any organisation can bring about change. At every level in the organisation, each member of staff must take personal responsibility for the quality of his or her work and seek to improve it through constant innovation. TQM is a means for improving personal effectiveness and performance and aligning and focusing all individual effort throughout an organisation. It provides a framework within which the individual may continuously improve everything he or she does and everything which is affected by the quality of his or her work. It is a way of leveraging individual effort and extending its effect and its importance throughout an organisation and beyond.

In short, it is continuous quality improvement, involving everyone in the organisation, managers and workers alike, in a totally integrated effort towards improving quality and performance of every process at every level. The ultimate focus of every process improvement is increased customer/user satisfaction.

Whilst academically acceptable, there are great problems in knowing where to start or which areas to target. BS 5750 has provided us with a route map to our goal. We may never reach it, but it has enabled us to start along the road.

> Without a system to manage and target quality improvement, TQM is often doomed to failure. It is estimated that 80 per cent of companies who implement a quality improvement programme will fail, either because they do not have commitment (at senior management level or throughout the company), or because they do not have an adequate system to manage and structure quality improvement.
>
> (Atkinson 1990)

In addition to the value of the process, BS 5750 has another transparent advantage. It is a tried and tested quality management system which has been developed and refined over many years and is recognized in every country in the world as such. It therefore has universal acceptance in industry and commerce and the process of registration is common to all. More than 17,000 companies in Britain alone are now registered to the standard.

Working with Gorway Tyres Ltd I learned one hard lesson very quickly: you don't get respect from industry simply by being a university lecturer, and being female is no excuse for anything less than perfect. I had to win the respect of every one of the 500-plus managers I trained, and I could only do that by demonstrating an understanding of both their industry and their problems and frustrations. However, from the beginning of the first course I ran in the company, I was treated with the utmost courtesy and patience.

At the time of my first involvement, the managers had been subjected to many failed attempts to implement quality improvement over a period of several years, and were already working to not one but several systems which were designed to ensure quality by both the company itself and major customers. Compare this with the situation existing in many educational establishments, where, often due to pressure exerted by local Training and Enterprise Councils, an almost reluctant awakening of interest in BS 5750 and TQM has stirred for the first time.

Which of these has the advantage? Is it the manufacturing company, which can draw on its past experience of implementing quality improvement and bring diverse existing systems together to meet the exacting requirements of BS 5750, or is it the educational establishment, looking with new eyes at a customer-orientated system where previously no formal system for quality improvement existed?

If my anonymous company and current employer represent typical examples, they both face very similar problems. Success depends on winning the hearts and minds of each employee who will be involved in the system. A documented system can look wonderful on paper, but systems must be living and constantly evolving if they are to work. Unless each employee accepts the system as meeting his or her own needs, not the imposed needs of the organization which restrict and inhibit quality improvement and new ideas, registration to BS 5750 is a costly and useless exercise.

Where staff in any organization perceive that existing systems have failed to improve quality, in their eyes registration to BS 5750 is yet another system imposed by management which will fail just as the others did. Where no formal system previously existed, we in education resist new customer-centred approaches, seeing them as smacking of industrial models. And what could education and industry possibly have in common?

Well, to begin with, we can learn many lessons from industry, both from its successes and its failures. An example of this is in the measurement of quality and conformance to specifications. Statistical process control (SPC) was implemented some years ago in Gorway Tyres Ltd. Look at almost any machine and you will see equipment which measures length, width or depth. On one of my first workshops, I made the mistake of giving an example from one of Philip Atkinson's books (1990).

The example was this. Observing an employee working on a machine, a consultant asked the man why he was not plotting any data on the graph in front of him. His honest reply was 'Today is Tuesday, the man from . . . (the customer) doesn't come until Friday. The chart will be marked up then.' In another case, an employee refused to complete the charts, saying, 'They're a waste of time. I've been filling them in for the last 3 months. There are many times when there have been problems and these are recorded. But no-one takes any corrective action. Why should I waste my time?'

Instead of laughter, I was greeted by deathly silence. I quickly moved on to my next point. At the end of the workshop, I asked one of the delegates why no one had appeared to enjoy my anecdote. With some embarrassment, he told me that I had 'hit too close to home', as this was almost common practice in the plant. I then undertook some research and found that, in their belief that they had now found the answer to all quality problems, management had attended a course on SPC, then had installed SPC equipment on almost every piece of machinery, whether or not that measurement was crucial to the quality of the product. Moreover, since operators were not fully trained in the operation of the equipment, nor realized its role in reducing non-conformance, and since stopping production was tantamount to treason, the charts were largely ignored. Scrap levels did not decrease and therefore the system was perceived to have failed.

With hindsight, if management had carefully analysed the process and installed SPC equipment only at critical stages, if operators had been effectively trained to use the equipment and if levels of non-conforming product had been carefully monitored, the story might have been different. A valuable tool for quality improvement had lost all credibility. The lesson is there for all to see.

Again and again in Gorway Tyres Ltd, I heard the same comment on my awareness-raising workshops. 'What's so different about this system? We've heard it all before. We attend training courses about the latest seven-day wonder which is going to solve all our problems, then we wait . . . and wait . . . but nothing ever changes. We still face the same problems and no-one ever listens to us. After all, we're only the workers.'

I kept stressing the point that there was one vital difference between an in-company quality management system and BS 5750. The International Standard is a public standard. Once registered, a company has proved to the world that its system for managing the quality of its products or services meets the exacting requirements of the Standard. The company is therefore more likely to demonstrate continuing commitment to retaining registration. The company cannot afford to lose its registration, otherwise its customers and its competition would know immediately. BS 5750 forces the company to maintain continuous quality improvement by taking corrective action to solve known problems, or problems identified through internal audit and internal and external failure.

It was not an easy task to convince middle managers in Gorway Tyres Ltd that here was a system which guaranteed commitment from their senior management. The managers even had their own term for the management style which existed in the company. They called it *'Sod-it-and-send-it'* management. It didn't matter if the product was designed well or made well; as long as production kept up with the numbers required, management was happy. But if the customer complained or sent the product back, the wrath of senior management descended on the production managers, and the question was 'Who let that junk get past final inspection?' Quality through catastrophe!

Are we in education so very different? Being part of an externally funded unit, I face the same pressures: sell my courses and earn my salary. But who bothers to look at the feedback from my clients to examine the quality of the courses I offer? I have only ever had two complaints from clients; they were passed to me for my attention without even a covering memo, and no one ever asked me if I had satisfied the complaints or even responded.

I tended to think of myself as unique in my quest for continuous improvement of the work I did, but in the two years I have been involved in Gorway Tyres Ltd, I have been forced to change my views. Fiercely loyal to the company, managers echoed the same feeling almost without exception. They want to take a pride in the products they produce and feel a personal responsibility when they are forced by circumstances to pass on something less than perfect to the next stage in production, often at the demand of a more senior manager who himself is under pressure from corporate management.

I vividly remember the day when all the area managers on my course disappeared during the lunch break, arriving back with new jerseys, which they proudly displayed, saying that they were a token of thanks from their manager for a job well done. A large order of tyres which was urgently required by an important new customer had been completed in record time and they were justifiably proud of their achievement. Next day, a very crestfallen group arrived, minus jerseys. A large number of the tyres were outside the customer's exacting specifications and had been scrapped. The irate management duly reclaimed the jerseys. Yet in the eyes of the area managers they had achieved the objective – to produce the tyres in record time. They had been constantly harassed by their manager to meet deadlines, not to produce quality tyres meeting exact specifications.

Drawing a parallel in education, in 1987 five projects involving a variety of colleges produced comparable results (Theodossin 1989). Some 1,500 employers, mainly in the engineering industry, took part in the survey. The results of the projects indicated growing evidence of employer disapproval of colleges, under four general headings:

1 There was a fundamental incompatibility between colleges and business 'cultures', so that the classroom and workplace are seen as different worlds. Employers detected in colleges evidence of an ivory-tower existence: short working weeks and years, job security and salary guarantees protecting staff from market-place risks, out-of-date lecturers unaware of today's business world, old-fashioned equipment, ideological commitments which were anti-commerce and contemptuous of the world of work.

2 Colleges were unbusinesslike at the operational level. They were unorganized and unsystematic. Decision-making was tortuously slow and involved elaborate committee structures. Lead times were protracted. It was difficult to make contact with individuals who had answers.

3 Too often, colleges expected their customers to fit into what was on offer. Colleges liked selling long, award-bearing courses which start in September, take place during workdays (but not Christmas, Easter, July or August), are constructed in multiples of years and are concerned to 'educate for a lifetime'. Industry wanted short courses available round the calendar and focused on the company's immediate training needs.

4 The college may have been an appropriate place for school-leavers, but it did not offer an adult environment. The physical setting gave evidence of another culture clash, between teenagers and adults. The buildings were dirty and untended. There were broken windows and furniture. Heating was erratic. The ambience was adolescent.

The important question to ask is 'How were the results of the surveys received by college staff'? Perhaps not surprisingly, they were greeted with anger by academic staff, who insisted that the comments were unfair, untrue and unsubstantiated. Pressure was exerted for the feedback to be presented 'more positively'.

Like my area managers, these staff perceived that they were offering a quality product. Yet instead of learning lessons for the future from their mistakes, or lack of responsiveness to their customer requirements, they blamed both the customers for making unfair demands and the researchers for the way in which they had presented the findings. In short, none admitted responsibility for the damning feedback, but, unlike my managers in Gorway Tyres Ltd, blamed the customers for making unfair demands and the researchers for unfair reporting.

But, I hear you say, how does this compare with your own organization? After all, you work in a university, not a college, and surely things have improved since 1987. Since privatization, the university has spent some £4 million on environmental improvements. Student accommodation has improved greatly and great strides have been taken in bringing teaching accommodation up to standard.

On the campus where I am based, largely due to the energy and commitment of our site manager, I must admit that we no longer have broken windows or erratic heating, and buildings in general are no longer dirty and untended. In short, one individual, with the support of management, has listened closely to student and staff complaints and has improved everything which he had the power to improve out of all recognition, often fighting every step of the way to obtain the necessary resources.

More importantly, bearing in mind Handy's definition of organizational culture, our site staff now take a pride in maintaining the site manager's exacting quality requirements. For example, we have recently opened a new Conference Centre. Prior to each event, site and catering staff are given a work instruction, detailing the client's exact requirements. The client (both internal and external) also receives a copy, so that he or she can measure the standard of service given. Each time I use the Centre for a training event, I find that some improvement, however small, has taken place.

At the beginning of our move to implement BS 5750, it was essential to define our product. This proved amazingly difficult. Is the product the course, or the enhancement of learning which takes place during the time a student spends with us? We finally defined it as 'learning experiences'. Having defined our product, we then moved on to defining the variety of clients who purchase our product. These were defined as:

1 students following programmes of study leading to qualifications up to and including first degree and master's degree level where taught elements are involved;
2 students following programmes of study leading to higher degrees which may or may not involve original research;
3 other purchasers of short courses, consultancies or projects.

By defining our clients, we could complete the process by agreeing on the requirements of each defined client, set our quality standards and define responsibility at each stage of the process, from design, development and validation through to monitoring and review. We had begun the process of continuing quality improvement.

Having defined product, customers and requirements, we could then move on to document our quality management system. There was relatively little problem in drafting procedures for course design, because this has been an integral part of our business for many years. Administrative and site procedures were relatively easy to draft, although drafting one effective generic procedure which would be equally applicable on each campus proved more difficult. But no two academics could agree on the content of a procedure which defined delivery styles, or laid down the parameters for quality of teaching. After almost two years, the procedure is still in the debating stage, although a quality improvement team is currently yet again attempting a first draft.

Why is it that measurable quality improvement is so difficult in an educational establishment? I have worked with many colleges and some higher education establishments and ponder on the prevailing culture which exists in them. Instead of perceiving themselves as a team working together to meet the needs of a wide and diverse student profile, academics, administrators and site staff are divided by a class war. Administrators and site staff are often treated as lesser beings, placed there to serve academics who are, in their own opinion, the intelligentsia on whom the future of the organization rests. A blame culture exists, where each blames the other for existing problems. Students are confused by conflict.

To give just one example, if a student's assignment is not marked and returned by the due date, who is he or she to blame? The lecturer, who places the blame on the administrator whose duty it is to collect and return the assignment, or the administrator who places the blame on the lecturer who has neither collected the assignment on time nor returned it on time for return to the student? In the perception of the student, it is largely unimportant. He or she simply wants the assignment back, duly marked and with constructive feedback. If the lecturer and the administrator are not working together as a team to an accepted and acceptable procedure, quality will suffer. In the eyes of the student, the organization is to blame, not the individual.

In Gorway Tyres Ltd, employees realize that the future of the company depends on future sales of its tyres. Customers have choices, and if they perceive that they have purchased a sub-standard tyre they will buy from the competition. Sales will drop and employees will face redundancy. Therefore their future depends on producing consistently good tyres.

This is relatively simple. Customer requirements are known. Energy can therefore be expended on improving the quality of the product against set parameters. But the company faces a similar problem to that of the university. Production staff see themselves as the elite, and staff in support functions such as purchasing and sales are largely perceived as lesser mortals who eat into the profits made through the efforts of production staff. Problems exist at the interfaces between support staff and production staff. Unless good-quality raw materials are purchased, the quality of the tyres will suffer. Unless customers are invoiced correctly, or their tyres delivered by the due date, their perception will be that they have received a poor-quality of service from the company. Unless the sales staff supply production with accurate information about customer requirements and delivery dates, production cannot plan or produce accurately. Just as the university falls down at the interface between academic and administrative staff, so the company falls down at the interface between production and support functions. The same blame culture exists and must be overcome.

This is where one of the major advantages of BS 5750 can be seen. Costly rework is usually created by colleagues earlier in the process who have given you information, decisions, materials or resources which do not meet your requirements. You in turn can create this same costly rework for others who depend on the quality or accuracy of what you produce. The system depends on a system of documented procedures, with responsibility for each task defined and documented. All staff must be familiar with procedures and each one given the necessary training in order to fulfil his or her duties.

If there is a fault in the procedure, or the department or the individual does not have the capacity to comply with the requirements of the procedure, this can be readily identified and remedied. If the fault lies in the attitude of a particular member of staff, be he or she academic or administrative, the necessary steps can be taken. One of the first steps in improving quality is the knowledge of where the problem lies and the planning of how that problem can be overcome.

In Gorway Tyres Ltd, a culture of 'customer visits' has existed for some years, if somewhat haphazardously. This involves employees from one department visiting suppliers in another department which may supply them with raw materials or part-completed products. This happens throughout the process (but unfortunately is only in its infancy in service departments or at the interface between service and production departments). Each is encouraged to identify quality problems potentially caused by their supplier and to work with that supplier to identify causes and solve problems. These customer visits are now becoming the norm and, since commitment to registration, are handled enthusiastically by all involved. In turn, this has led to the identification and solution of seemingly small and unrelated problems.

Because the company also employs statistical techniques to identify waste levels, and so on, it has been able to document improvements. These in turn are published in the company magazine and on notice boards in various areas, so keeping quality improvement to the forefront in every employee's mind. The company as a corporate whole is perceived to be improving and company loyalty is paramount. The objective of the company is to make profit and produce quality tyres, and the mission statement, again widely publicized, echoes this (in that order!) everywhere we step.

Here we can learn from industry. We can formulate and publish our mission statement and constantly aim to improve quality in the organization as a corporate whole. This means yet another change in thinking, for we tend to be departmentalized, with our loyalty given to the faculty or department in which we work. We tend not to see everything we do as benefiting the whole organization or helping to fulfil the mission statement. We cannot measure quality improvement. We have not yet taken on the concept of internal customers and suppliers, nor of working together to improve the quality of the whole.

Here, incidentally, is another lesson to be learned from industry. I recently counted the number of internal memos I received and responded to in one month. The total was forty-three. The time taken to write each memo, distribute it, read it, take action to find out information from others and respond to it, multiplied by forty-three, cost the university a tidy sum and cost me valuable hours when I could have been more gainfully employed. I cost my time at £27.60 per hour. Most of the memos originated from managers, and were typed and distributed by administrators. Add their time to mine, then multiply by the number of staff employed – not to mention the cost of the paper. Then multiply this by forty-three and you have several thousands of pounds per month – and all because we don't talk to one another. In Gorway Tyres Ltd, they don't talk to one another either, but all staff use electronic mail. Memos are restricted to one page. One memo can be quickly typed in by a manager, read 5 minutes later by all recipients and the computer cleared daily. Managers can travel to any part of the organization, in any part of the world and find a computer screen waiting with their messages.

Yesterday, I obtained a copy of the company's magazine and read it with interest. Let me tell you about the content. About 10 per cent of the magazine is devoted to facts about corporate news and another 40 per cent to photogaphs and stories about quality improvements and achieving targets in the company. All employees, from chairman to shop-floor operator, are called 'associates'. Only two stories are about managers; the rest are concerned with the attainments of shop-floor workers, all pictured and named, all smiling. The impression given is that everyone in the company is treasured, as is the part each plays in producing the product. One whole page is devoted to the company's suggestion scheme and the growing amount of suggestions received that month. The majority of suggestions have been adopted and all associates putting forward suggestions have been financially rewarded.

The other 50 per cent of the magazine tells stories of the social side of the company. There are summaries of social evenings held for former company associates and the latest about events held in the company's social club and sports clubs, including rugby, football, cricket, angling and chess. A 'What's On' section gives forthcoming events in the social club; a pensioners' evening, a disco, the Caravan Club social evening and the Bowls Section dinner. One page is devoted to the children's Christmas party. In short, not only are associates treasured; it seems that their families are also. Need I say more? We have only to examine the motivation theories of Maslow (1954), Herzberg (1966), Vroom (1970) and others to recognize that all the ingredients are there.

But to return to the university. Since we embarked on our quest for BS 5750 registration and quality improvement, we have taken enormous strides. Since the germ of the idea of registration sprang from directorate some two years ago, BS 5750 registration has consistently been heralded as the raft on which TQM will be built. The more traditional, and acceptable, theories of TQM are now an integral part of our registration effort. The implementation of BS 5750 has enabled directorate to be better informed about specific quality-related problems, and by improving those areas where the university does not meet the requirements of the clauses of the Standard, definable improvements are beginning to be seen.

Quality improvement teams now exist throughout the institution, looking at specific problems and possible improvements. These were born from 'conscripted volunteers' drawn together from all parts of the organization to try to draft generic procedures common to all campuses. Generic procedures are broad-based and will be turned over to specific departments and schools so that they may personalize them, whilst still remaining within agreed guidelines. In this way, we can now begin to standardize practice. Since then, some have chosen, quite voluntarily, to meet regularly in order to try to find better ways of working.

We have started to train staff in problem-solving and statistical techniques so as to equip them with the skills needed to quantify and improve known problem areas. We are also beginning to train quality facilitators, with the aim of having a trained facilitator in each department.

One of the most astonishing developments arose from the training of internal auditors. BS 5750 requires that an organization regularly and systematically audits each department to ensure that it is complying with procedures. The result of each audit is brought to the attention of the manager of that department, who has defined responsibility for quality, and an agreement is sought on corrective action to remedy the non-compliance and ensure that the cause of the problem is found and removed. On a regular basis, senior management will review the results of all audits and corrective action taken.

In general, the first audit identified six main areas for improvement:

1 Lack of corrective action in schools to resolve identified problem areas, particularly those identified by student feedback and external examiners.

2 Lack of availability of records due to staff holidays or lack of identification of responsibility for maintaining those records; no central record-keeping facility.
3 Reports were not in the prescribed format.
4 Failure to meet required deadlines.
5 Lack of signatures denoting approval before passing to next stage.
6 Lack of information and communication to ensure that necessary staff received vital information.

A de-brief was held after this first audit, and feedback was sought from both auditors and auditees. On the whole, all expressed enthusiasm for the process. The internal audit team recognizes that it has a valuable part to play in quality improvement, as it can work with colleagues to identify causes of problems and possible corrective action, which can then be monitored for effectiveness.

By using a systematic approach, the University is accelerating the process of continuous quality improvement, much as Gorway Tyres Ltd has been able to do. In the company, years of wasted effort in attempting to implement TQM, de-motivation and suspicion of the workforce and pouring money into problems with little success have now been replaced by pride and commitment since the company achieved registration some weeks ago. Success has been seen to be achieved and they are going forward with enthusiasm. Every employee recognizes registration to the Standard as the basis for TQM and commitment to this throughout the company is very strong. TQM techniques, including systematic training in problem-solving, have been implemented at every level and this is proving successful, particularly since recent cross-functional team efforts have solved two particularly costly and frustrating problems.

However, the University is still in its infancy when dealing with customer responsiveness and commitment to quality improvement. We have too few monomaniacs with a mission. But we have started and are gaining momentum with every step nearer to registration. There is no turning back and we will get there in the end, because we have all the ingredients for success. Like Gorway Tyres Ltd, we know that registration to BS 5750, whilst laudable, is not the end of the process, but merely the spearhead of our drive to implement TQM. It may take us several years before all staff accept ownership and we begin to feel the real benefits of our quality management system, but we have known and publicized this from the beginning.

Finally, to return to the first of our reasons for choosing to go through the BS 5750 registration process – that is, for the intrinsic value gained from meeting the challenge – tangible improvements to present are:

1 A defined mission statement, documenting the University's objectives and long-term plan.
2 An approved and circulated Quality Manual, defining the University's

policy and commitment to quality of its defined product to recognized client groups.

3 A system of draft documented procedures, standard to all campuses, yet able to account for geographical and course specifics, constantly evolving as we improve what we do.

4 Clear work instructions for complex technical steps in the procedures, or those where accuracy is essential, available to all appropriate staff where and when they need them.

5 A system of internal auditing which identifies problems, negotiates corrective action to solve them, feeds into reviews by senior management to plan improvements and disseminate good practice to all parts of the University.

6 A strong Quality Assurance Unit led by a head who is totally committed to BS 5750 and TQM and who demonstrates visible support continuously.

7 Cross-functional quality improvement teams beginning to operate, often voluntarily, to improve recognized quality-related problems.

8 The introduction of a corporate training programme to train staff in TQM tools and techniques for measuring and improving quality.

9 Systematic methods of collecting and analysing student feedback on modular programmes.

10 Clear definitions of University-wide responsibility and reporting lines.

To return to my original hypothesis, in order to change the existing culture of any organization, we need to change the existing behaviour of the people who are employed there. The two organizations I have described, so very different in culture and products, have, completely independently of the other, chosen almost identical routes to a TQM-orientated culture. Where Gorway Tyres Ltd had previously failed to make progress, registration to BS 5750 gave it the focus for quality improvement. The quality of the products was seen to improve as a 'right-first-time' culture gradually grew and rework and scrap levels dropped. In the perception of the workforce, this customer-led team effort to gain registration gave visible results and promoted even greater team efforts, as no department wished to be the one to hold back registration. Once this culture was born, it gained momentum through the commitment of the core team and senior management, constantly repeating the message that this was only the first step to TQM. If that commitment had wavered, or if the enormous cost of training and implementation had not been carefully budgeted for, I hesitate to say that success would have been so readily achieved. But as one senior manager said to me,

The cost of poor quality in the company in 1990 far outweighed the costs of implementing our TQM programme. Now we can really start to save money. To put our total expenditure on BS 5750 and TQM in proportion, we would expect to invest a similar amount on the development of just one new label for our tyres.

I know that it may take us a little longer, but we will achieve similar success in the University.

REFERENCES

Atkinson, P.E. (1990) *Creating Culture Change: the Key to Successful Total Quality Management*, Kempston: IFS Publications.
Handy, C.B. (1985) *Understanding Organisations*, 3rd edn, Harmondsworth: Penguin Books.
Herzberg, F. (1966) *Work and the Nature of Man*, Cleveland, OH: World Publishing Co.
Maslow, A. (1954) *Motivation and Personality*, New York: Harper & Row.
Theodossin, E. (1989) *The Responsive College, Crown Copyright*, London: HMSO.
Vroom, V.H. and Deci, E.L. (1970) *Management and Motivation*, Harmondsworth: Penguin Books.

Part III

Further and vocational education

12 A quality journey

The experience of Avon Training and Enterprise Council

John Marsh

SUMMARY

This chapter presents the actual experiences of a mainly government-funded, 'not for profit' organization implementing total quality. It covers the first two years of the organization's existence and highlights the failures as well as the successes, showing how an attitude of continuous improvement has been applied to total quality itself.

The experience has shown the importance of adapting the total quality methods and tools to the individual organization. This is best done by the staff, customers and suppliers themselves. However it is very important to have clear, fixed, principles underpinning all of the activity.

INTRODUCTION

Avon Training and Enterprise Council (TEC) is an independent company mainly funded by the Employment Department. Its mission is to improve the quality of life and prosperity of all the people of Avon by promoting, in partnership with others, education, training and enterprise.

Avon TEC is one of eighty-two similar regional bodies throughout England and Wales. It is led by a Board of Directors, made up of volunteer leaders of local organizations, and a full-time Chief Executive. The Board has representatives from industry, commerce, the voluntary sector, the TUC and local government.

The TEC movement originated from the privatization of the Training Agencies, which in turn had their roots in Manpower Services. Many of the employees are seconded from the Department for Employment. Handing control to local directors has led to the meeting of two very different cultures; the Civil Service culture and the business one. At the time of formation Avon TEC recruited several key managers from industry, and one challenge was to achieve integration whilst retaining the best of both worlds.

At present Avon TEC employs just over seventy staff, of whom half are secondees. The current budget is approximately £30 million per annum. This is used to fund the following:

1 The development and support of a county-wide vision.
2 The provision of training programmes for young people and adults.
3 The promotion and implementation of the Investors in People standard.
4 The support of Education and Business Partnerships.
5 The provision of a full range of business support services.
6 The promotion and support of National Vocational Qualifications.
7 The provision of Labour Market Intelligence.

Avon TEC began operating in April 1991. Its total quality initiative commenced shortly after this, in June.

The initial structure of the TEC was based around the different services with five Operations Managers reporting to the Chief Executive.

The total quality processes are designed and implemented by the Total Quality Manager and a Co-ordinator reporting to him. Quality Assurance functions are kept separate and are the responsibility of another manager. Obviously there is very close liaison between improvement and assurance work. Both quality professionals report to the Standards Operations Manager.

The Total Quality Manager had six years' experience of implementing total quality prior to joining the TEC. This included several years as an engineer in computer manufacture and the remainder in sales support, consulting for manufacturing customers. He had no previous experience of 'not for profit' organizations.

THE INITIAL APPROACH (JUNE 1991–JANUARY 1992)

Previous experience

Six years' experience of implementing total quality had raised some important questions which had to be answered before the initial plan for the TEC could be produced.

The key question was 'Why could there be such a large variation in progress across one company implementing the same method'?

Something that was common in all successful implementations was enthusiasm and commitment from the most senior managers. It is often said that lack of management commitment is the biggest restriction to quality. However, this is not a root cause. Why are senior managers not committed?

The answer lies in the fact that they do not see 'what is in it for them'. For senior managers that has to be achievement of strategic objectives. Implementation of total quality has not been linked closely enough to strategy for the senior managers to become excited. To correct this, the first priority in the TEC was to develop a method to link the total quality plan to the corporate strategy.

It is also noticeable that the majority of successful total quality occurs in manufacturing. There are many reasons for this, not least the fact that total quality was developed in manufacturing. The further one gets from the shop floor, the harder implementation becomes. One reason is that in sales, research, marketing and so on, issues are not so black and white. Precise specifications do not exist. Many of the concepts on the shop floor become meaningless. The language of manufacturing also creates barriers. It therefore became apparent that any single method, without flexibility, could not be implemented in all areas within the organization. In fact, the key was to get those people working in an area to bespoke the concepts themselves using their own language but not losing the key principles. Gimmicks and jargon also had to be avoided as they are easily seen through.

Original plan

It is very important to design a total quality process on clear, proven principles. There are many concepts promoted by the 'quality gurus'. It is dangerous to assume they are all basically the same. One needs to study the ideas carefully. Religious devotion to one guru is dangerous, but 'mixing and matching' should be done with care.

Having come from an organization that adopted a method from Philip Crosby (1979), the TQ Manager was keen to find a more deep-rooted approach to build on. Concepts such as *zero defects* and *cost of quality* had proved difficult enough on the shop floor, and this method's dependency on jargon was a 'turn-off' to many.

The fourteen points developed by Dr Edwards Deming (1986) were chosen as the best set of principles to adopt. Key activities, compatible with the fourteen points, were then identified and an initial flow chart produced. This can be seen in Figure 12.1. These activities were implemented over three months and will be considered in turn.

Strategic planning

A simple means of linking strategy to total quality goals needed to be developed. This was done over a period of a few weeks using some of the readily available Quality Tools (Marsh 1993). The following questions need to be answered by the senior management team and other stakeholders.

- Who are the customers of the organization?
- What are their requirements?
- What is the purpose (vision and mission) of the organization?
- What are the underpinning values or principles?
- To satisfy customers, and the purpose statement, what does the organization have to be good at?
- What are the critical factors for success?
- Which processes, if improved, will most contribute to this success?

Figure 12.2 shows the flow of the process and the key outputs. This was completed in one, intensive, day off-site. The session was incredibly productive, raising and resolving all sorts of latent issues. One major mistake was made. It was designed for the senior management team. It should have involved all stakeholders such as the directors, staff, key suppliers and if possible customers. By excluding the representatives of the directors, some of the results, which conflicted with existing strategy, were not adopted for several months.

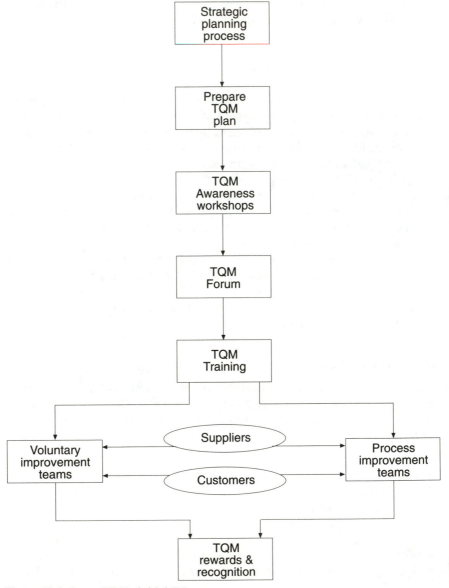

Figure 12.1 Avon TEC's initial TQ process

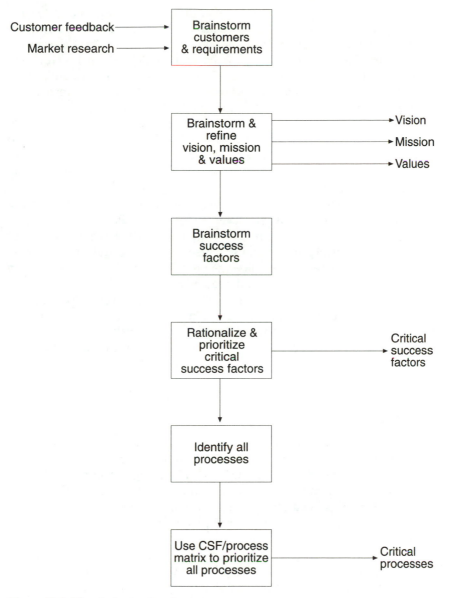

Figure 12.2 The strategic planning process

Awareness workshops

Real commitment to total quality requires the active participation of all of the stakeholders of an organization. Therefore it was decided to start communication with the staff in a series of awareness workshops early in the process.

These workshops were very informal, discussion-based, and lasted for about two hours. They were organized around departments and started with an introduction and statement of support from the TEC Chief Executive.

The ideas of total quality were outlined, and people's comments requested regarding applicability to the TEC. Each group brainstormed the differences between a TEC and a manufacturing company. This list was invaluable, highlighting potential pitfalls and enabling them to be designed out.

The success of these sessions varied a great deal. Some groups were highly articulate and challenged and discussed ideas, whilst others expected only to receive information. This difference tended to reflect the different cultures within the TEC. The seconded civil servants were used to receiving, whilst the commercial people were used to challenging and interrogating.

Later it became apparent that very little knowledge had been transferred in the awareness workshops. However, that was not the real objective.

First, goodwill was gained by involving staff early on. Secondly, clear allies emerged during the sessions. These were the people who showed excitement and interest. In a deliberate policy these people were supported and encouraged to learn more and become champions.

An extensive TQ Library was established, and staff were encouraged to use the books, videos, magazines, case studies and other material, if they were interested. The use of the library has grown consistently.

All staff, without exception, went through the awareness workshops. Currently, all new employees go through a slightly shorter version as part of their induction to Avon TEC.

TQM Forum

To ensure continuity of the work started on the strategic workshop, the management team agreed to form a TQM Forum. Avon TEC was unusual because, in a former existence as the Training Agency, it had been subjected to an abortive attempt to implement total quality. This had combined many of the worst aspects of current practice, including encouraging staff to write slogans of the week! This seriously reduced the chances of getting a second attempt started.

Fortunately, during awareness sessions, it was possible to show the differences in the new approach from that of the old. Many of the staff still believed in the concepts and realized that the previous attempt had reduced these to trivia. With the new management team it was possible to get enough support to try again. Obviously there were those who were extremely cynical, there always are.

The previous attempt had been centred on a Quality Steering Committee. The minutes showed this to be controlling and bureaucratic. It was important to have a different name and style to this new body, so it was called the TQM Forum.

This Forum had clear terms of reference, although in hindsight these were not supported very well early on. Basically it exists to support, provide strategic direction and monitor progress on all aspects of total quality. It is not directive and controlling.

An early problem was the difference in style between the Forum and other management meetings which were target-driven. The Forum depends on debate and innovation and not just ticking boxes. This proved a frustration to some, although attendance was excellent.

Each member of the Forum had ownership of a key step in the total quality plan. In reality, the TQ Team did most of the work, but the step-holder often provided good guidance and support. This also encouraged the spreading of responsibility for quality.

The Forum has become more effective over time. This has reflected the learning curves of the management team. Recently the terms of reference were completely reworked by brainstorming. The outcome was not very different from the original but the commitment to the new terms of reference is much greater.

TQ training

Phil Crosby used to state that training was imperative prior to implementation. Avon TEC found this to be untrue and ineffective. Many total quality packages are training 'sausage factories'. Trainees go in one end and total quality practitioners come out of the other end. If only!

The reality is very different. The cost of failure associated with TQ training could be very high. Most people need to see the real benefits before they will commit themselves to learn and apply this new knowledge. Training must be relevant and can only come after the trainee sees the need. The material then needs to be designed around the individual's requirements.

For these reasons Avon TEC delayed the training programme and started implementing improvement teams with the expert support of the TQ Manager.

After six months of success, and some failure, the members of these teams had applied many of the principles and tools of total quality to their own work processes and were asking for more support and knowledge. The training process was driven by their requirements.

Initially, potential suppliers of training were evaluated. Few showed the flexibility that the TEC required. It was decided to develop the TEC's own course. First, prospective trainees and their managers were consulted to identify their requirements. This led to the decision to develop a 'sandwich' course based around a real project. The final structure is that of five days' theory and two days' review and evaluation spread over six to nine months, depending on the complexity of the projects. Trainees work in pairs but must both be active within the process selected for their project.

The theory is taught in highly interactive ways based around the Quality Toolkit (Marsh 1993a).[1] No more than ten people are trained at one time.

The selection process is mainly based on a desire to do the course. Twenty out of seventy TEC staff have been trained as TQ Facilitators to date. Most are waiting, and some have requested a fast-track version for their own use rather than for facilitating improvement teams.

Improvement teams

Initially, two types of teams were established. Voluntary Improvement Teams (VITs) and Process Improvement Teams (PITs). It was thought that the differences were important.

PITs are multi-functional, and sometimes multi-organizational, focused on achieving specific improvements on a strategic process. The first PITs addressed the critical processes identified in the Strategic Planning Process. Other early PITs were formed for all new processes on the basis that it is easier to design quality in at the start. These PITs were management-guided and had clear objectives.

VITs were more like Quality Circles, being departmental, voluntary and self-directed.

The style of support from the TQ Forum was intended to be different, according to the type of team. However, in reality, this distinction added no value at all, and rapidly all teams became known as PITs.

Prior to the training all PITs were facilitated by the TQ team. This effectively meant that the facilitator was also the leader. As the confidence of other team members grew, roles and responsibilities were handed over. Now each team has its own trained facilitator.

Also at this time a TQ Centre was created. A major restriction to successful teams is lack of facilities. Therefore a large room was created solely for the use of TQ initiatives. The room is laid out in a U-shape and can accommodate fifteen comfortably. It has a very large wipeboard, flipcharts and storage, video and OHP. This room has made the operating of improvement teams much easier. It is also a statement of management commitment.

Awards and recognition

Anyone who has studied total quality will know that this is a controversial subject. Discussion of this at the TQM Forum coincided with the drive for Performance Related Pay (PRP). The author's personal view is that PRP is a very dangerous tool within a quality culture.

For total quality it was decided to offer recognition, not rewards. A letter of thanks from the Chief Executive goes to individuals or teams which have exceeded expectations.

A COMPLETE REVIEW (JANUARY 1992)

The end of 1991 provided an opportunity to review and take stock. In hindsight it marked a move into a more structured, integrated approach.

The problems

Old habits die hard. A key frustration was how to encourage the changing of behaviour. It seemed that the people who desired change and self-development were the ones excelling in total quality, whereas those who did not were avoiding total quality or participating grudgingly.

This is the main reason why total quality is not a quick fix. It requires individuals to challenge their ways of working and assumptions. In fact Covey (1989) refers to quality improvement as an inside-out process; that is, it comes from within the individual to influence the processes.

This is not such a problem as long as the managers lead through this process by example. However, management commitment is not a 'go/no-go' issue. This commitment varies from very high to non-existent. The real difficulties came in areas where the line manager was not leading by example and emphasizing quality.

Larrae Rocheleau, Superintendent of Mt Edgecumbe High School, Alaska, has stated that one only requires the square root of the total number of employees to be 'disciples' to ensure a momentum that is difficult to stop. This was heartening news, because in the TEC we have at least seven of these people, several of whom are very senior.

However, there is still a requirement for more work to be done in the psychology of total quality to address the issue of personal change.

Is total quality a field-day for whingers? Another key problem was that some people were loving analysing problems but using this to reinforce their personal belief that nothing would change. This wasn't 'analysis paralysis' but 'whinging'. These teams had to be facilitated firmly into solution mode.

In many respects the whingers are not so damaging. At least they are raising opportunities for solution. These people need to be encouraged and to be shown that they can solve problems. The real danger comes from the underminers. These people often talk quality, but their actions are subversive and detrimental to others. 'Know your enemies' is the answer. Sometimes 'getting them into the camp' is a good idea by asking them to be trained, and so on. At the end of the day, however, there may be some hard decisions to be made if people continue to work against the direction of the organization.

Avon TEC is fortunate in that the staff are generally highly committed to what they see as a worthwhile task. This is often the case in the public sector and this commitment is powerful for implementing quality.

On a more technical front, several problems had emerged. First, some of the intellectual or theoretical issues were not adding much in reality. The distinction between VITs and PITs turned out to be of no importance in day-to-day operation. In fact, it probably confused people, so the term 'VIT' was dropped.

On a positive note, it became apparent that members of staff were seeing new applications for tools and techniques. This was encouraged and some of the early methods were made more flexible.

Probably the most serious problem was that of 'overheating'. It had always been an objective of the Total Quality Manager to work on all new processes as well as the strategic ones. The reasons are quite obvious. It is a lot more cost-effective as well as easier to incorporate total quality principles at the start of designing a new process. As a result the TEC had seventeen Improvement Teams running at one time. This put pressure on staff to attend as well as complete other tasks. It also created the image that total quality was just about Improvement Teams. Eventually certain teams were allowed to slow down and some to stand down. This was done very carefully to avoid the misinterpretation that management were reversing commitment to total quality.

The opportunities

The complete review led to some direct and immediate improvements. The first was that the TQ Manager used the criteria of the US Baldrige Award[2] to judge progress to date. This is a national award for total quality, and consists of some excellent guidelines which are of value whether the organization is eligible for the award or not.

The guidelines define what is expected for each of the seven categories. These categories carry points depending on their relative importance. In this way the TEC was shown to score 4 out of 10 at the end of the first year. The guidelines also showed gaps in the TEC quality strategy. The TQM Forum developed a new quality plan that by mid-1993 would mean a score of 8 out of 10. This plan is detailed in the next section.

At this time another review was carried out. It involved a brainstorm with all the front-line staff. These are those members of staff who regularly interface with the customers. The aim was to see how the TEC was satisfying its many customers. Twenty staff were present, and the half-day session started with brainstorming all the requirements of the local employers. A list of eighty requirements was rationalized into eight, and the team voted to generate the top three. This clearly highlighted something that many of the staff suspected, that the structure of the TEC was inadequate to achieve the real customer requirements.

The staff were then split into five teams. Each was given a different type of organizational structure to consider. Each team had to identify the strengths and weaknesses in line with the customer requirements. They also had to estimate cost implications and any other key constraints such as skills shortages.

After two hours each team presented back. Three options were rejected by the group as failing to meet the requirements. The final idea was a hybrid of two concepts. This was taken away to be developed.

Within three months this new structure had been designed, proofed and implemented using a whole raft of the Quality Tools.[3] Because the staff were involved from the start the implementation was relatively smooth. The customers' responses were favourable and the process has been improved continuously.

AN IMPROVED APPROACH (JANUARY 1992 ONWARDS)

The review using the Baldrige Award criteria led to the development of a new quality plan based on the categories of the award.

The TEC had already been strong on the Strategic Planning and Leadership for Quality categories of the award. The areas for development were as follows.

Human resource development

Fortunately all employers in the United Kingdom have an excellent, ready-made standard to follow in meeting the requirements of staff development. This is the Investors in People (IIP) endorsement (The Investor in People Toolkit 1991) promoted and managed by TECs.

Avon TEC had already committed itself to achieving this by mid-1993, but now it became apparent to all how this integrated with the total quality strategy.

The development and delivery of facilitator training was carried out in line with the guidelines of IIP. It was need-driven and based on action learning. The demand internally has been very high, even though the course requires considerable effort over 6–9 months.

Recently a common set of total quality objectives has been added to all staff members' job objectives. These are reviewed quarterly in appraisals.

Quality assurance

Another goal was to fully integrate total quality and quality assurance. The TEC's customers seemed to be getting very confused between the two subjects. They are in fact inseparable, but the total quality and quality assurance managers set about producing a detailed, integrating model.

This was worked out by trial and error through PITs. The overview is shown in Figure 12.3. Both process improvement and quality assurance are driven by the strategic plan. The two branches then closely liaise as one sets about achieving customer-driven continuous improvement and the other about assuring that the standards set are actually achieved.

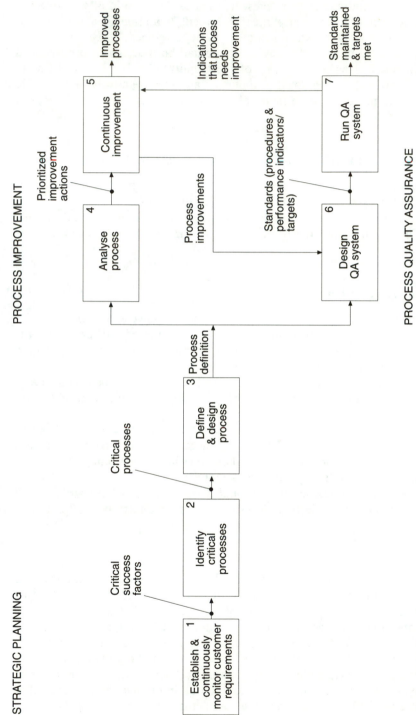

Figure 12.3 Integrating total quality and quality assurance
Acknowledgement: Colin Broom, QA Manager

Customer care

The Baldrige Award,[4] rightly, puts much emphasis on whether the organization is customer-driven or not. This coincided with the emergence of the Citizen's Charter (1991) which reinforced the need to put in place processes to respond to customers.

As a result, the customer care processes were overhauled. The emphasis was on feedback of any kind. This can be formal, through surveys, or informal, through individual comments. All information is collected at one point and communicated to all staff through electronic mail. The feedback consists of three types; complaints, comments and compliments.

Complaints are responded to immediately with targets for resolution. It has not been uncommon for the Chief Executive to respond personally by phone.

A key problem has been how to collect informal feedback where individuals may feel threatened. Even though the total quality function has stressed the fact that the processes are to blame, not people, still the problem exists.

Recently the collection has been delegated to individuals in each department in order to try and improve response time and reduce the fear of reporting bad news.

Principle-centred leadership

A shift in thinking also occurred at this time with the discovery of the American psychologist Stephen Covey. His books (1989, 1991) struck a chord with several of the TEC's Managers who were struggling with how to encourage change from the inside out.

Covey introduced a new dimension to Deming's concepts. Deming correctly states that 94 per cent of root cause problems come from management processes and not people. Hence quality improvers attack processes not people. However in a non-total quality culture only a very few people design the processes. Covey has discovered that process designers incorporate their values into the design. For example, an autocratic manager, who in his heart believes people are basically lazy, will design a very different system from a manager who believes that systems prevent people doing the good job they want to.

Covey's book (1989) was devoured by several senior TEC Managers because it addresses the problem of change from the inside out and helps identify the real values of the people in the organization. This was put into practice immediately on the detailed design of the new organizational structure identified by the staff brainstorm. Before any work commenced, the small team of process designers brainstormed five fundamental principles or values to be adopted throughout. This list included driving out fear and open and honest communication. Force field analysis (Marsh 1993) was also used to assist.

At every stage of the design the team compared the proposed solution to see how it measured up to the principles. It was alarming how quite innocent decisions could have led to very negative effects. It is by not analysing the principles underpinning a process that often discrimination or fear is provoked when the designers are not intending to have this effect. Several of the senior staff at the TEC now believe that values and principles have to be managed as carefully as budgets and performance targets. Adopting and implementing positive principles makes good business, as well as ethical, sense.

DEVELOPING PARTNERSHIPS (JANUARY 1992 ONWARDS)

Avon TEC realized the importance of effective partnerships right from the start, and this is a cornerstone of the vision. However, total quality started to provide principles and new tools to develop much deeper and more meaningful partnerships.

Because of a developing reputation for total quality, several organizations asked the TEC for direct support. This was given on a pilot basis and helped both partners.

A further education college

The first major recipient of support was a further education college. In conjunction with an LEA adviser and the Director of Curriculum, a strategic workshop was delivered. Learning the lessons from the TEC, several governors were present throughout. The addition of customers to these workshops was to come later with a school.

The initial work led to the college committing itself to a five-year process with the support of an American consultant introduced by the TEC.

Local government

The next recipient was a department within a city council. Again the strategic workshop was the starting point. The session got off to a very poor start due to a lot of underlying fear and confusion. The results were useful but probably of limited impact because of the departmental focus. The work was useful as it helped lead the whole council in progressing towards the Investors in People standard. It also highlighted the potential benefits of the TEC and the council working more closely together with the same language and toolkit.

A comprehensive school

The next request for support came from a local comprehensive school. The commitment and enthusiasm was very high, helped by an aware management team and key industrial governors.

The strategic workshop was run in June 1992. This time all stakeholder groups were present. The attendees included representatives from the students, parents, staff, governors, local employers and the local community. The results were very satisfying.

The vision statement was excellent, being formed by all, particularly the students. Critical areas for improvement were highlighted. The workshop worked well because of the considerable effort spent beforehand predicting problems and designing them out. This school now has improvement teams working on processes such as policy and planning and communication. Governors, parents and students are giving up their free time to be involved. Very shortly formal tools and techniques training will start for people in the new teams as well as the existing team structures.

Employers are now starting to take an active role, and this is leading to the school's being in a position to implement the first Community Quality Partnership in this country.

Community Quality Partnerships

The best total quality practitioners, such as Motorola, are starting to help to drive the principles through their most important suppliers: schools, colleges and universities. In the United States employers, educationalists and government leaders are starting to apply the total quality tools to work, in partnerships, to solve common local problems.

This fits with the vision for Training and Enterprise Councils, and Avon TEC is using the school, previously mentioned, to pilot these ideas in the United Kingdom (Marsh 1993b). The early results are promising, but if changing the culture of an organization takes years, applying these ideas throughout a community may take a little longer!

Probably the furthest along this path is Mt Edgecumbe High School, Sitka, Alaska (Rocheleau 1991, Tribus 1992).[5] Avon TEC has been able to liaise regularly with the Superintendent of this school. The transformation of the school has been remarkable, and is reflected in 'hard' measures such as employment as well as 'softer' ones such as the student and staff opinion surveys.

Less global partnerships

Whilst the Community Quality Partnerships present an enormous challenge, the TEC has been implementing some more immediate collaborations. The first was to develop a 'new' service in conjunction with the Guidance Service and the Employment Service. By using the Quality Toolkit (Marsh 1993a) the three organizations were able to design the whole process within four hours. It was then sold almost immediately on the basis of this work. This showed the huge potential of three very different organizations working together with a common purpose, language and tools in a short period of time. Total quality doesn't have to take years if done properly.

The second partnership activity developed out of the TEC's programme to reduce its number of providers of Government Training Programmes from seventy-two to ten. The process of rationalization was developed by the TEC Quality Assurance Manager and led to the possibility of closer and deeper working relationships. Joint Improvement Teams already existed looking at the youth training and special needs training processes. It was decided to offer free total quality training to representatives from each of the ten providers. The training has been delivered to two groups of ten with the providers being trained with their counterparts in the TEC. The cost is minimal but the benefits of better communication and joint problem-solving are already being witnessed.

THE REAL BENEFITS (JANUARY 1993)

How should the benefits of total quality be quantified? First, one needs to consider both the quantitative or 'hard' benefits and the qualitative or 'soft' benefits. Both are just as real. The 'softer' results often have more profound benefit in the long run but are difficult to prove and probably impossible to quantify. 'Hard' measures can often oversimplify a situation, particularly in the service sectors.

'Hard' benefits

- The development of a new organizational structure, implemented in a record time with minimal disturbance and to wide customer acclaim.
- Quantifiable achievements of Improvement Teams including reduced costs of failure and improved customer satisfaction.
- Avon TEC's achievement of top position in government league tables measuring promotion of Investors in People.
- Customer complaints reduced in number and being resolved in record times.
- Customer compliments as well as informal customer benchmarks with other TEC's.
- The development of a 'new' service with the Employment and Guidance Services within 4 hours. Sold within two weeks and demand outstripping supply.

'Softer' benefits

- All staff actively involved in strategic planning, leading to greater understanding of purpose.
- Staff survey and comments generally reflecting greater pride and enjoyment.
- Improving credibility in the community, locally, nationally and internationally.

- The use of a common Toolkit improving efficiency and effectiveness.
- Much greater empowerment and involvement of staff, customers and suppliers.
- The integration of all TEC services in a comprehensive, focused package.
- The provision of a model of understanding for the plethora of quality initiatives, e.g. total quality, IIP, BS 5750, Citizen's Charter.
- Better communications internally and externally.
- Finally, it was summed up when a secondee was asked whether she would like to go back to the old style of management with the managers doing the thinking and the rest obeying orders. 'Things aren't perfect yet. We have a long way to go but no way,' was the answer.

WHERE NEXT (JANUARY 1993 ONWARDS)

The strategy for the future is centred on three interrelated subjects.

First, more emphasis is to be placed on individual responsibility for quality and integrating quality thinking into regular activities. By promoting Process Improvement Teams, quality improvement became highly visible and team-based. However, a tendency has emerged to see Improvement Teams as when 'we do quality'. The plan was that the principles and tools learned in the PITs would filter through into other mainstream activities. There may even come a time when they are so integral that highly visible Improvement Teams become a thing of the past and it can be truly said that total quality is just the 'Avon TEC way'.

To move towards this goal, based on a firm foundation of management leadership, training and coaching, individuals are being encouraged, more strongly, to apply their knowledge on a day-to-day basis. Individuals' objectives now all include customer satisfaction and continuous improvement goals. It is now time to 'turn up the throttle', gently but firmly.

The second emphasis is towards the integration of Process Management into the lifeblood of the organization. Most members of staff regularly refer to process. All Improvement Teams use process tools (Marsh 1993a). The ideas and principles have started to infiltrate issues such as organizational and costing structures as well as quality assurance. Greater emphasis will be placed on improving the TEC's sophistication in this subject.

The third area incorporates many of the points of the first two, and that is the drive towards a true learning organization. The TEC movement's ultimate goal is to encourage employers to model the type of organization detailed in Senge's book *The Fifth Discipline* (1990). Therefore the TECs themselves have to take the lead and set an example. Many of the ideas of the learning organization are a natural extension of total quality.

Simply put, if all organizations implement total quality principles, the key differentiator will become the staff's ability to innovate and anticipate the future. This concept is articulated in Barker's book *Future Edge* (1992). Avon TEC needs to continue to find ways to release the 'creative juices' of its staff to anticipate and respond to a world of ever-increasing political, economic, social and technological change.

Avon TEC is currently applying many of these principles to the new government-led initiatives which will take the United Kingdom into the new millennium.

CONCLUSIONS

Probably the most fundamental conclusion is to base any total quality initiative on solid principles such as Deming's fourteen points, then understand the 'big picture' of how the plethora of current initiatives fit together. Think holisitically but be wary of any initiative that goes against the organization's principles. The national and international quality awards provide useful frameworks.

Set in place processes for continuous learning. Study as much about the subject as possible. Visit practitioners. Find out about failures as well as successes. Then start with an attitude of continuous improvement to the total quality processes as well as all other processes. Establish good review and evaluation mechanisms.

It is imperative to align total quality improvements to the organization's strategy. The best way to do this is to involve all of the stakeholders, including customers. This is the best way to achieve consistency of purpose.

Avoid over-optimism and cut out the jargon. Stress that management is learning as much as anyone else and manage expectations carefully.

Communicate, communicate and communicate again. An organization cannot overdose on effective communications.

Be wary of rushing training for all. Identify training requirements carefully. Deliver bespoke training just in time and evaluate its effectiveness thoroughly. Provide adequate facilities for team improvement. This shows much greater evidence of management commitment than posters on the walls.

Concentrate on process improvement and use a common set of tools. Build partnerships with customers and suppliers based on process management.

Be proud of soft benefits as well as the hard ones and do not oversimplify measuring complex quality issues. As a general rule, do not expect too much too soon. Be slow to be fast.

And finally above all remember that people count.

ACKNOWLEDGEMENTS

I wish, first, to recognize all of Avon Training and Enterprise's employees. Without their commitment and enthusiasm there would be no story. I also want to thank many of the TEC's customers and suppliers who have been directly involved with the total quality experience.

Because of the importance of management commitment to total quality I want personally to thank George Irvine, Chief Executive, and Martin Sandbrook, Operations Manager, for their patience, strategic vision and willingness to try new things.

I am also indebted to Colin Broom, QA Manager, for his determination to link total quality and quality assurance activities through a rigorous methodology.

NOTES

1 The Quality Toolkit comprises the basic tools such as brainstorming, fishbone diagrams, histograms, process definition, etc. as well as some of the more specialist ones such as process modelling, statistical process control and failure mode effect analysis.
2 The Baldrige Award is assessed using seven criteria. These are: Leadership, Information and Analysis, Strategic Quality Planning, Human Resource Development and Management, Management of Process Quality, Quality and Operational Results, and Customer Focus and Satisfaction. However, the Avon TEC is now using the European Quality Award as the design framework.
3 See note 1.
4 See note 2.
5 *Editor's note*: Tribus 92, referred to here, is Chapter 16 of this book.

REFERENCES

Barker, J. (1992) *Future Edge*, New York: Morrow.
Covey, S.R. (1989) *The Seven Habits of Highly Effective People*, New York: Simon & Schuster.
——— (1991) *Principle Centred Leadership*, Summit.
Crosby, P.B. (1979) *Quality is Free*, New York: New American Library.
Deming, W.E. (1986) *Out of the Crisis*, Cambridge: Cambridge University Press.
Marsh, J. (1993a) *The Quality Toolkit — an A to Z of Tools and Techniques*, Kempston: IFS International Ltd.
——— (1993b) 'Quality within the Community', *Managing Service Quality*, IFS Ltd (Jan.): 453–6.
Rocheleau, L. (1991) 'Mt Edgecumbe's venture in quality', *The School Administrator* (Nov.): 14–19.
Senge, P.M. (1990) *The Fifth Discipline*, New York: Doubleday.
The 1992 Award Criteria — Malcolm Baldridge National Quality Award, American Society for Quality Control (1992).
The Investors in People Toolkit (1991) London: Employment Department.
The Citizen's Charter (1991) London: HMSO.
Tribus, M. (1992) *The Application of Quality Management Principles in Education at Mt Edgecumbe High School, Sitka, Alaska*, Quality First, National Institute for Engineering Management & Systems California.

13 From systems to leadership

The development of the quality movement in further education

Edward Sallis

THE DEVELOPMENT OF THE QUALITY MOVEMENT IN FURTHER EDUCATION

The development of quality assurance has made enormous strides in further education in recent years. Quality is an idea whose time has come, and the incorporation of colleges will act as a spur to further development. Further education colleges are reviewing their role and mission. Most have recognized the importance of quality to their survival and future success. The pressure of recent change has forced the pace. Colleges' changing status has exposed them to new realities. No longer can they assume that the future will be like the past, and none can afford to rest on past achievements – as W. Edwards Deming has put it, in his now famous phrase, 'Survival is not compulsory'. This now applies to colleges as much as to any other organization.

Quality developments in further education are mirroring the activity which is taking place elsewhere, both in the public and private sectors. A range of initiatives have been developed to meet the public demand for a consistently high quality of goods and services. There is a growing recognition that quality is the key to competitive advantage. Investors in People, the Citizen's Charter, the Parent's Charter, the European Quality Award, British Standards BS 5750 and International Standard ISO 9000 have been introduced to promote quality and excellence. Of course, further education has long had quality mechanisms in place. Most of these, though, have been external to the colleges and have mainly been the quality control tradition. HMI and local authority inspectors, and the systems operated by examining and validating bodies have all been important for the pursuit of quality. The National Council for Vocational Qualifications are now adding their own quality processes. The difference is that these approaches are external and imposed, whereas quality assurance is internally generated. Colleges are now taking the responsibility for the assurance and development of their own quality. They have recognized the need to demonstrate publicly to their many and diverse customer groups that they can deliver a quality education and training service. A number of institutions are also looking beyond quality assurance at developing total quality approaches aimed at creating a quality culture.

The motives for devising quality systems in further education is complex. It has become a requirement of funding and validating bodies, although for many colleges the initial motivation for introducing a quality system was its benefits as a marketing tool. However, these were not the only reasons for introducing quality assurance. College staff have a strong professional pride. Delivering the best to their students is an important aspect of the professional ethos. Quality assurance draws on this professional tradition and enhances it. In the *National Quality Survey*, which I carried out in 1990, the impetus for introducing quality systems into colleges was explored. The motivation varied considerably between institutions. Some colleges wanted to satisfy the requirements of external agencies; others were concerned to improve their marketing effort; whilst a third group gave priority to better management and administration. However, the primary reason which the majority of colleges gave for putting time and effort into quality initiatives was the improvement of the provision for their students (Sallis 1990b).

Quality assurance developments started in colleges in the late 1980s. A great deal has been achieved since then. Further education is the sector of education which has pioneered many interesting quality developments, including, most importantly, the adaptation of industrial models. However, the quality movement is still new, and ideas and systems of quality assurance are still developing. Despite the mushrooming of activity there has been little academic analysis of quality initiatives in further education, and no major evaluation has been undertaken of the effects on institutional performance and student learning of the many quality initiatives. There has been a range of approaches, but no analysis of the impact which they are having in colleges. The *National Quality Survey* was the first, and to date the only attempt, to map the dimensions of quality in the United Kingdom. The survey found colleges to be strong on enthusiasm, but with little consensus on direction, especially around the issue of the appropriateness of BS 5750. This is a debate which continues today. The regional dimensions of quality were mixed. There was a stronger interest in the tertiary sector and the larger colleges in England and in Scotland than elsewhere, with the level of quality awareness being lowest in Northern Ireland. The survey has not been repeated, but the evidence is that the development of quality systems has been patchy. A number of institutions have developed interesting and purposeful schemes, including work on TQM, and a small number of colleges have been accredited to BS 5750. However, the quality message has not been universally listened to despite the time and effort put into the development of college schemes. A report by Her Majesty's Inspectors entitled *Construction in Further Education*, published in 1992, based on an analysis of construction courses in 270 colleges, makes the telling point that 'few departments produce annual review and evaluation reports. . . . few departments had a mechanism for measuring performance against stated criteria. For example, many departments do not analyse and evaluate examination results and wastage figures' (HMI 1992: 9). The initial work on quality was largely about review and evaluation, and if this message has not been embedded in an area of work in which there are some 130,000 students then clearly quality still has a long way to travel. Gerard Devlin in his 1992 quality survey in Northern Ireland found a similar lack of progress in the Province (Devlin 1992). Nevertheless, there are also many encouraging developments, and a number of important national initiatives have carried the quality message. The Department for Education has sponsored the production of an education and training guide to ISO 9000, which will parallel a similar development from the British Standards Institution for BS 5750. The Training Enterprise and Education Division of the Department of Employment has supported a wide range of initiatives, including the influential Consultants at Work materials on Strategic Quality Management (Miller and Inniss 1992). The Scottish Further Education Unit, in conjunction with Glenrothes College, has published a useful staff development pack on TQM (SFEU 1992), while Bob Havard from the Staff College has produced an educational guide to the Investors in People standard (Havard 1992). The Further Education Funding Council, in Circular 92/18 on college strategic plans, requires that colleges produce a statement on quality as part of their strategic planning process (FEFC 1992), and it has also established its own Quality Assessment Committee. There are a number of active regional and national groups, including the British Quality Foundation's Education and Training Committee, the National Quality Development Support Network, and the North West Quality Network.

The National Quality Survey also showed how isolated developments are in the different sectors of education. There is much less cross-fertilization between them than might be expected. With the exception of colleges with Council for National Academic Awards work, the processes which that body had pioneered on validation and peer review appears to have had little direct influence on most colleges. Similarly, the work on school effectiveness is completely absent from any discussions on quality in further education, and further education work on quality has similarly had little impact on schools. British education has again shown itself to be highly compartmentalized, and it will be interesting to see how the Quality in Higher Education Project will influence thinking in further education, and whether developments in further education will impact on it. The two sectors are moving in somewhat different directions with the Further Education Funding Council retaining the inspectorial system, and many colleges adapting industrial quality models, whilst universities are favouring peer review processes of self-evaluation. As partnerships develop between further and higher education with the acceleration of franchised programmes it will be interesting to see whether a common vocabulary of quality develops.

Despite the work which has been done, there is still much important thinking which needs to take place in the field of quality, and there are a number of potentially fruitful avenues which have almost been completely unexplored. With the possible exception of Kevin Conway's pioneering work on value-added in A levels, and Bert Roberts' on student perceptions there have been few attempts to take quality measurement seriously and to use it to guide institutional practice (Conway 1992; Roberts 1992). What in industry is known as Statistical Process Control (SPC) is largely absent from the thinking on quality. It might have been expected that this would be a major area of activity, both because of the extensive provision of Management Information Systems and the importance of engineering in further education (SPC having had its origins in manufacturing). Besides statistical approaches, there are many other underdeveloped areas worthy of exploration. These include Quality Circles; the use of 'quality tools'; quality audits; the application of quality costings, the use of the methodologies of the various 'quality gurus', including Philip B. Crosby, Tom Peters, W. Edwards Deming, Kaoru Ishikawa, Shigeo Shingo and Joseph Juran; and the rigorous application of TQM linked with a methodology such as that of the US Baldridge Awards or the European Quality Award (see Sallis 1993: 72–6). Many of these approaches are both sophisticated and expensive, but could have important applications for the future. Above all, there is one important dimension that has been largely missing. It is the basic understanding that, whilst quality assurance systems can guarantee a degree of consistency of service, the creation of a truly quality organization involves the development of a particular type of institutional culture. This culture requires strong and purposeful leadership linked to staff taking a greater responsibility for their own quality (Spanbauer 1992: 55–7, 128–31).

The upsurge of interest in quality in further education coincided with the passing of the Education Reform Act in 1988. ERA placed considerable emphasis on monitoring through the use of performance indicators. However, it quickly became apparent to many in colleges that PIs are of limited value in either judging quality or as an aid to improving it. They are primarily a guide to efficiency of the process. They provide little insight into how effective a college is in meeting its customers' needs, nor do they provide evidence about the quality of the learning process. There was a need to look beyond PIs and to look for means which could provide real quality improvements. At the same time the Training Agency was acting as an important midwife to quality development by its sponsorship of a number of large-scale projects. These included the Staff College's *Responsive College Project* and the evaluation initiatives in Avon, Bedfordshire and Birmingham. These drew on the work in marketing, which was a major further education development theme of the early and mid-eighties, particularly the use of student and employer questionnaires. Marketing initiatives helped many colleges to focus their attention on customer requirements. Quality assurance was, in part, an attempt to ensure that customer needs and wants were being met. These initial quality projects also integrated the notion of course team responsibility for evaluation and improvement which had been pioneered by the Business and Technology Education Council. From it they developed a range of review and evaluation strategies for assessing the success of the delivery process. The Further Education Unit in 1989 published a useful document, *Towards an Educational Audit*. It provided a framework for evaluating the performance of colleges which took into account a much wider range of factors for judging effectiveness than the narrow range of PIs published in the Department of Education and Science and Welsh Office's *Managing Colleges Efficiently* of 1987.

THE INFLUENCE OF INDUSTRIAL MODELS OF QUALITY

It was a natural development for colleges, with their extensive business links, to look towards industry models of quality. British Standard 5750 'Quality Systems' was the starting point. The work on BS 5750 was originally supported by the Training Agency through its sponsoring of the pioneering project in Sandwell College of Further and Higher Education on the application of BS 5750 (Collins *et al.* 1990, 1991). The Training Agency's publication *The Management of Quality BS 5750 and Beyond*, in 1990, gave many colleges their first insight into industrial quality models. Industrial models in the form of TQM and BS 5750 received official sanction in the White Paper *Education and Training for the Twenty-first Century*. It contained the expectation that the newly incorporated further education and sixth-form colleges would each have a system of quality assurance, although it was not prescriptive as to the system or the methodology they should employ.

The movement for TQM was later in coming into the picture. The adaptation of the ideas of W. Edwards Deming, Tom Peters, Philip B. Crosby and Joseph Juran, combined with Japanese approaches to quality, was pioneered in some US community colleges in the mid-1980s, principally by Fox Valley Technical College in Wisconsin. In Britain, East Birmingham College is generally recognized as the first further education college to adopt this approach. In the *National Quality Survey* eighty-six colleges said that they were or were intending to following the TQM route, with twenty-seven which were intending to blend TQM with BS 5750.

Quality development in further education is characterized by the breadth and diversity of the provision. Although many colleges are following BS 5750 or TQM, models many others are pursuing systems of their own, or on ones based on the pioneering work of the Avon, Bedfordshire and Birmingham models or on the work of the Consultants at Work, who have pioneered a useful methodology known as Strategic Quality Management.

WHAT DOES QUALITY MEAN IN THE FURTHER EDUCATION CONTEXT?

This is not the place to enter into general philosophical discussions of quality. I have analysed the concept of quality elsewhere (Sallis 1993). Nevertheless, something must be said about what quality means in further education. A college's definition of quality will in part determine the strategies it will employ to assure or improve it. However, the elusive but powerful nature of the concept of *quality* causes difficulties and problems. It is easier to say that 'we are striving for quality' than to describe what quality means. Quality is an extremely enigmatic concept. Describing and defining quality is not easy. Robert Pirsig in his quest for quality in *Zen and the Art of Motorcycle Maintenance*, sums it up thus:

> Quality . . . you know what it is, yet you don't know what it is. But that's self-contradictory. But some things are better than others, that is, they have more quality. But when you try to say what quality is, apart from the things that have it, it all goes poof! There's nothing to talk about. But if you can't say what quality is, how do you know what it is, or how do you know that it even exists? If no one knows what it is, then for all practical purposes, it doesn't exist at all. But for all practical purposes it really does exist. What else are grades based on? Why else would people pay fortunes for some things and throw others in the trash pile? Obviously some things are better than others . . . but what's 'better-ness'? . . . So round and round you go, spinning mental wheels and nowhere finding anyplace to get traction. What the hell is Quality? What is it?
>
> (Pirsig 1974: 187)

Quality is a slippery idea with a variety of contrary meanings. If one is not careful, the debate about what it is can degenerate into a sterile discussion about definitions. I am inclined to agree with Karl Popper that 'one should never quarrel about words . . . one should always keep away from discussing concepts' (Popper 1963: 3–30). However, it is necessary for a college to have a clear idea of what it wants to achieve from a programme of quality development, and to do this it is important to understand the dimensions of quality. To understand quality it is necessary to recognize that it does have contradictory meanings which can lead to different practical outcomes. These different dimensions need to be reflected in the way in which a college approaches quality development. Some of the contradictions in quality can be listed as follows:

- Quality is both a strategic and an operational concept.
- Quality is both a visionary and a practical idea.
- Quality is both an absolute and a relative concept. It can mean both 'high quality' and 'fitness for purpose'.
- Quality is about both ends and means.

- Quality is about both people and systems.
- Quality has to be defined both by the institution and its customers. The views of each may be very different.
- Quality can be allied to both 'hard' and measurable standards as well as to 'soft' and more intangible standards about care, courtesy, concern and compassion.
- Quality cannot stand still. The definition is never static. Today's high quality maybe tomorrow's poor quality.

Colleges themselves have defined quality in different ways. In 1991 I reviewed more than fifty schemes from individual colleges and LEAs, and in these were a range of different definitions. Below are a selection of these which reflect a diversity of approaches. There is a clear distinction between those colleges for which quality is about meeting internally set standards, and those which define it from the point of view of the customer. There is also a difference between those who view quality as being about the core activities of teaching and learning and those who see it as about the total college. Some of those definitions of quality are listed as follows:

- 'delighting the customer'
- 'the elimination of errors and the prevention of waste'
- 'It includes the complete service provided by the institution and its staff. It also refers to the teaching and learning experience that must be at the centre of our professional relationship with our students.'
- 'fitness for purpose'
- 'improving the teaching and learning of our students'
- 'excellence, customer focus, flexibility, relevance, effectiveness, efficiency, conformance to standards'
- 'the ability to satisfy the stated, or implied, needs of our students and their sponsors'
- 'conformance to specification'
- 'improved client satisfaction'
- 'ensuring the accessibility, effectiveness and validity of our programmes'
- 'Quality is everyone's business.'

In discussions of quality there are two major strands to the debate. On the one hand there are systems methodologies and on the other the quality culture approach. The quality culture approach sees people as the producers of quality and directs quality initiatives to improving management, leadership, teamwork and attitudes, and makes the customer the focus of attention. This is the tradition from which TQM stems, and which can broadly be identified as the Japanese approach to quality. The aim is to develop a culture within the organization in which quality improvement is a way of life. The systems approach, by contrast, which is the dominant industrial approach in the United Kingdom, is concerned to improve the systems and procedures by which products and services are produced.

It aims to produce a consistency of product to a pre-defined standard. It has its origins in manufacturing, and is the approach enshrined in BS 5750. Of course, it is possible to combine these approaches.

The systems approach – BS 5750 and ISO 9000 and their place in the quality debate

There is considerable interest in BS 5750 and its international equivalent, ISO 9000, as the means of assuring quality. A number of colleges, including Sandwell College of Further and Higher Education, East Birmingham, Cannington, and Stoke-on-Trent, have been accredited to BS 5750. The Department for Education has commissioned the National Accreditation Council for Certification Bodies to design an education and training application of ISO 9000. As some 17,000 British companies are BS 5750-registered it is not surprising that further education has shown an interest.

BS 5750 places a considerable discipline on those intending to use it. Putting a system in place is not easy or straightforward. It involves a con-siderable investment of college resources and in staff time. Everybody in the institution needs to understand its implications and to work the systems and follow the procedures which have been put in place. BS 5750 only sets the standard for the system, not the standards which the college should be achieving. The college, together with its customers, are the arbitrators of standards. BS 5750 assures that there are systems in place to deliver those standards. What BS 5750 does not guarantee is a consistency of standards between colleges.

Ensuring that a college complies with the Standard is carried out by both internal and third party auditing. An external audit establishes the initial registration. If a college cannot maintain the standards of their systems and procedures, then registration can be withdrawn. A number of accreditation bodies can undertake the audit, and these are registered with the Depart-ment of Trade and Industry as being fit to undertake audits. The bodies which can audit colleges are BSI Quality Assurance, Lloyds Register Quality Assurance, and Yardsley Quality Assurance. Colleges whose quality systems achieve registered firm status can use their accreditation bodies' BS 5750 quality systems logo for marketing and publicity purposes.

BS 5750 has aroused some strong feelings as to its applicability. There is a view that a rigidity applied BS 5750 system can be counter-productive in colleges with their professional and well-educated staff. The concern is whether the heavy extra work-load and the need to work strictly to systems and procedures, albeit internally generated, could damage staff morale. It is argued that it could undermine both creativity and the spirit of entrepreneurialism which are further education colleges' sources of strength.

TQM and the development of quality culture models

The movement for TQM in further education is of more recent origin. Much of the pioneering work of reorganizing work practices on TQM lines has been carried out by a small number of community colleges in the United States, led by Fox Valley Technical College in Wisconsin, and by some UK further education colleges. The initiatives in the United States developed somewhat before those in Britain, but in both countries the surge of interest occurred from 1990 onwards. East Birmingham College is generally recognized as having pioneered this approach in the United Kingdom.

A key element of TQM is the notion of the internal/external customer chain. The idea is that everyone in an organization is a supplier who has customers who may be internal or external. The idea emphasizes the service-giving in everyone's role regardless of their status within the college. The customer chain idea emphasizes that quality is only as strong as the weakest link, and that staff relationships and attitudes are the essential element in building a quality college. It is also implicit that a strong chain cannot exist unless all staff are able to see themselves as the 'managers' of their own quality. The 'management' in TQM often gives rise to misunderstanding. In a TQM culture all staff are managers of their own areas of responsibility and are ultimately accountable to their customers for the quality of the service they deliver. Much work needs to be carried out on the organizational climate and culture of our colleges, and changes to the structure of employee relations need to take place so as to enhance this notion. Nevertheless, even in the present climate positive leadership can enhance the notion of the customer chain by enhancing teamwork, and ensuring that teams have delegated to them the authority they require to make quality improvements in their sphere of operation.

TQM is accomplished by a series of small-scale incremental projects. The Japanese have a word for this approach to continuous improvement – '*kaizen*'. This is most easily translated as step-by-step improvement. The philosophy of TQM is large-scale, inspirational and all-embracing, but its practical implementation is small-scale, highly practical and incremental. Grandiose schemes are not seen as the way forward because often they founder for lack of resources, and their demise can breed cynicism and discontent.

The primary mission of a TQM institution is to meet the needs and wants of its customers. Excellent organizations, both public and private, keep 'close to the customer', in the words of Peters and Waterman, and have an obsession with quality. They recognize that growth and long-term survival come from matching their service to customer needs. Quality must be matched to the expectations and requirements of customers and clients. Quality is that which the customer wants and not that which the institution decides is best for them. Without customers there is no college. The college though should not stop at satisfying customer wants. It should take the next step and aim to delight their customers with their quality.

INVESTORS IN PEOPLE AND TQM

Investors in People (IIP) was launched by the Department of Employment as a national standard in training and development in October 1991. It is different from BS 5750, although it can complement it. As a standard for human resource development it sits easily alongside TQM. Its standards have been developed by the National Training Task Force, and it is administered and assessed locally by Training and Enterprise Councils and Local Enterprise Companies in Scotland. IIP is based on the experience of successful organizations in the United Kingdom which have recognized that a skilled and motivated workforce is crucial to their success. IIP provides a methodology for developing staff in ways which assists in the achievement of organization goals. The essential elements which have to be satisfied for a college to become an Investor in People are, first, a public commitment from the top to develop all staff to achieve the organization's objectives; second, a written institutional or strategic plan which identifies organizational goals and the resources available for it. The strategic plan has to be available to staff and understood by them. The third element is the establishment of regular reviews of the staff training and development. This needs to be followed by action to train and develop individuals throughout their careers. The last element is the evaluation of the investment in training and development and a review of the effectiveness of the staff development process.

Like BS 5750 and ISO 9000, Investors in People does not guarantee quality. However, its achievement can be an important indication that a college is developing a systematic management process to improve the effectiveness of its most valuable resource – its staff. IIP is concerned with developing all employees, and this will mean that colleges will have to give equal attention to the development of support staff as well as to academic staff. While IIP is not a complete TQM standard, it can be a useful marker along the road to total quality. TQM strategies require vision, commitment and the participation of all employees, good communications and a process of evaluating progress. These are all essential features of Investors in People.

THE RELATIONSHIP BETWEEN BS 5750 AND TQM

The relationship between TQM and BS 5750 is a topic of considerable debate. The actual relationship between them will be peculiar to each college. TQM does not force off-the-peg solutions. Each college has its own unique culture, its own needs and has to operate in a particular external environment. However, it needs to be stated that, whereas TQM and BS 5750 can easily co-exist and extend each other, the one does not require the other. BS 5750 and ISO 9000 are not TQM standards. TQM is a larger enterprise than establishing a quality system and does not necessarily require the application of an external standard.

There are a number of possible ways of looking at the links between TQM and BS 5750. In *Total Quality Management* Peter Hingley and I identified four models of the relationship between BS 5750 and TQM (Sallis and Hingley 1992b: 50–1). There is the 'first-step model', which sees BS 5750 as the starting point for TQM. BS 5750 can be an attainable first step on the road of total quality. BS 5750 tackles the procedural infrastructure which precedes the more difficult changes of culture and attitudes. Obtaining BS 5750 or ISO 9000 provides the institution with 'kitemarked confidence' to go forward to tackle the larger issues associated with TQM. There are plenty of industrial examples of companies using BS 5750 and ISO 9000 in this way.

The second model is closely aligned to the first. It positions BS 5750 at the heart of total quality. In this model BS 5750 holds TQM in place and provides it with a solid foundation for continuous improvement. This is the view taken of ISO 9000 by John S. Oakland.

In the third model the relationship is seen differently. It gives BS 5750 only a minor role in the larger TQM enterprise. BS 5750 is seen as only one element in a more important venture. Its role is little more than a useful means of assuring the operational consistency of the institution's procedures. In this model quality is delivered by the active participation of the workforce in improvement teams and not by paper-based procedures.

The fourth model takes a different view of the relationship between TQM and external quality standards. In this model BS 5750 and ISO 9000 are considered as either irrelevant or even antithetical to the pursuit of quality. BS 5750 is viewed as a bureaucratic intrusion into the world of education. BS 5750 has aroused some strong and hostile feelings in further education. It is considered by some colleagues as at best a costly distraction, and at worst an anti-educational concentration on bureaucracy at the expense of desirable goals concerned with learning. The industrial language of the Standard does not help its case. At first reading the language appears to have little relevance to colleges and needs considerable translation to make it relevant. There is a concern that a rigidly applied BS 5750 system could be counter-productive in colleges with their professional and well-educated staff. The concern is whether the extra workload and the need to work strictly to systems and procedures, albeit internally generated, could damage staff morale and creativity.

WHAT MIGHT A QUALITY SYSTEM FOR A FURTHER EDUCATION COLLEGE LOOK LIKE?

Further education is too diverse for there to be a congruence of quality systems, but it is clear that no college in the future will be without its system of quality assurance. It is important to ask whether as the result of the progress which colleges have made towards implementing quality systems there are any general principles which can be drawn together as the essential elements of a quality system. A number of essential points stand out as being central to the process of developing quality regardless of the approach being pursued:

1 There must be a means of addressing the quality of learning.
2 It is essential to ensure that quality is maintained at all stages in the learner's progress through the institution. It must deal with the questions of the quality of the pre-entry, entry, delivery and learning, and exit stages.
3 There must be a whole-institution approach to quality, and any system needs to ensure that, whilst the quality of learning is covered by it, so are the rest of the college's activities. The quality of student services, management information, publicity, etc. must be covered.
4 Quality needs a strategic dimension, and the quest for quality must be an integral part of the mission of the institution.
5 A means of determining customer needs and wants must be established. These can include exit interviews, questionnaires, audits, feedback from tutorials, focus groups, evaluation exercise, performance indicators on retention rates, etc.
6 All the processes must be valid and be capable of evaluation.
7 Staff at all levels must take an active part in improving quality.
8 The quality system must be credible to outside organizations to which the college is accountable.
9 The quality system must contain mechanisms which lead to demonstrable quality improvements.
10 The quality system must give as much attention to the human dimensions of quality, such as service, care and courtesy, as to paper-based systems and procedures.
11 Quality must be based on strong leadership from the senior management of the institution.
12 The quality system must encourage teamwork and provide means which allow teams to take responsibility for their own quality.

LEADERSHIP AND TOTAL QUALITY

The function of leadership in a college is to enhance the quality of learning and to support the staff who deliver it. Although this sounds obvious, it is not always the way management functions are viewed. Traditional notions of managerial role and status can lie uneasily with the total quality approach. TQM turns the traditional institution on its head and inverts the hierarchy of functions. It should empower teachers and provide them with greater scope for initiative. It is for this reason that it is often said of

TQM institutions that they require less management and more leadership.

Leadership has not been given the prominence it deserves in the quality debate. There has been an overconcentration on quality systems and insufficient attention has been paid to the management of quality, and in particular to the nature of the leadership required to develop a quality college. A quality culture involves strong and purposeful leadership at all levels. It requires all of its members to take a personal responsibility for quality. It needs colleges to invest in their staff because the bottom line in education is that it is people who deliver quality. This is not to deny the importance of the work that has been carried out on quality systems and procedures. It is, rather, to paint a larger canvas. Quality assurance is a core element of total quality, but it is nevertheless only a part of a much larger enterprise. The challenge is to develop a quality learning culture.

Kaoru Ishikawa has argued that total quality involves a thought revolution by management. In his writings he makes it patently clear that total quality is a humanistic philosophy which makes the manager the servant of his or her customers. The task of the management is to find ways of better serving customers' needs and wants. However, management cannot succeed without leadership, and this consists of enthusing others in the organization so that they similarly want to serve their customers, internal and external, with a similar devotion. What is the role of the leader in an institution undertaking a total quality initiative? No list of attributes says it all; however, the major functions of quality leadership can be listed as follows: A leader must:

- have a vision of total quality for his or her institution;
- be visible and accessible to staff and students;
- have a clear commitment to the quality improvement process;
- communicate the quality message;
- ensure that customer needs are at the centre of the institution's policies and practices;
- ensure that long-term strategic planning takes place;
- ensure that there are adequate channels for the voices of customers;
- lead staff development and invest in training;
- be careful not to blame others when problems arise without looking at the evidence – most problems are the result of the policies of the institution and not the failings of staff;
- lead innovation within their institutions;
- facilitate the process of continuous improvement;
- ensure that organizational structures clearly define responsibilities and provide the maximum delegation compatible with accountability;
- be committed to the removal of artificial barriers, whether they be organization or cultural;
- build effective teams and motivate employees;
- develop appropriate mechanisms for monitoring and evaluating success;
- develop effective quality systems and procedures.

A major aspect of the leadership role is to empower teachers to have the maximum opportunity to improve the learning of their students. Stanley Spanbauer, the President of Fox Valley Technical College, who has taken a lead in introducing TQM into vocational education in the United States argues that

in a quality-based approach, school leadership relies on the empowerment of teachers and others involved in the teaching/learning process. Teachers share in decision-making and assume greater responsibilities. They are given more power to act and greater autonomy in almost everything they do.

He goes on to elaborate his belief in the importance of leadership with these words:

Commitment means much more than giving an annual speech on how important quality is to our school. It requires unending enthusiasm and devotion to quality improvement. It calls for an almost fanatic promotion of and attention to new ways to do things. It requires constant review of each and every action.

(Spanbauer 1992: 15)

In the Japanese approach to quality the total commitment and leadership of senior management on a long-term basis is always advocated as the key to the successful implementation of TQM (Dale and Cooper 1992: 145). The purpose of management is to lead a college devoted to producing a quality learning environment for its students. In the midst of all the problems and changes facing further education that remains the challenge for the quality movement.

REFERENCES

British Standards Insitution (1990) *Quality Systems*, Parts 1–3 (1987), Part 4, Milton Keynes: BSI.
—— (1991) *BS 5750 Guidance Notes for Application to Education and Training*, Milton Keynes: BSI.
Collins, D., Cockburn, M. and MacRobert, I. (1990) *The Applicability of BS 5750 to College Operations*, First Year Report (Nov. 1989–Oct. 1990), Sandwell College of Further and Higher Education.
—— (1991) *The Applicability of BS 5750 to College Operations*, Second Year Report (Nov. 1990–May 1991), Sandwell College of Further and Higher Education.
Conway, Kevin (1992) *A-Level Analysis for Value-Added – Good Value for . . . Students*, Greenhead College, Huddersfield.
Dale, B. and Cooper, D. (1992) *Total Quality and Human Resources*, Oxford: Blackwell.
Deming, W. Edwards (1982) *Out of the Crisis*, Cambridge: Cambridge University Press.
DES and Welsh Office (1987) *Managing Colleges Efficiently*, London: HMSO.

Devlin, G. (1992) 'The Northern Ireland further education quality assurance survey', Mendip Paper MP045, The Staff College, Blagdon, Bristol.

Fox Valley Technical College (1991) *Quality First Process Model*, 2nd edn, The Academy for Quality in Education, Fox Valley Technical College Foundation, Appleton WI.

Further Education Funding Council (1992) 'College strategic plans' Circular 18/92.

Further Education Unit (1989) *Towards an Educational Audit*, London: FEU.

Harvey, L., Burrows, A. and Green, D. (1992) *Criteria of Quality Summary*, Quality in Higher Education Project, University of Central England in Birmingham.

Havard, B. (1992) *Investors in People*, The Staff College, Blagdon, Bristol.

Her Majesty's Inspectorate (1991) 'Quality Assurance in Colleges of Further Education', Reference 92/92/NS, Department of Education and Science.

—— (1992) 'Construction in further education', Reference 256/92/NS, Department of Education and Science.

Ishikawa, K. (1985) *What is Total Quality Control?* Englewood Cliffs, NJ: Prentice Hall.

Miller, J. and Inniss, S. (1992) *Strategic Quality Management*, Ware, Herts: Consultants at Work.

Oakland, J.S. (1989) *Total Quality Management*, Oxford: Heinemann.

Peters, T. and Waterman, R.H. (1982) *In Search of Excellence*, New York: Harper & Row.

Pirsig, R.M. (1974) *Zen and the Art of Motorcycle Maintenance*, London: Vintage.

Popper, K. (1963) *Conjectures and Refutations*, London: Routledge & Kegan Paul.

Roberts, A. (1992) 'Establishing customer needs and perceptions', Mendip Paper MP031, The Staff College, Blagdon, Bristol.

Ruston, R. (1992) 'BS 5750 in educational establishments', in Edward Sallis and Peter Hingley *Total Quality Management*, Coombe Lodge Report 23(1), The Staff College, Blagdon, Bristol.

Sallis, E. (1990a) 'The evaluation of quality in further education', *Education Today* 40(2).

—— (1990b) 'The National Quality Survey', Mendip Paper MP009, The Staff College, Blagdon, Bristol.

—— (1992a) 'Total Quality Management and standards in further education', in Harry Tomlinson (ed.) *The Search for Standards*, Harlow: BEMAS/Longman.

—— (1992b) 'Total Quality Management and further education', in Tim Simkins, Linda Ellison and Viv Garrett (eds) *Implementing Education Reform: the Early Lessons*, Harlow: BEMAS/Longman.

—— (1993) *Total Quality Management in Education*, London: Kogan Page.

Sallis, E. and Hingley, P. (1991) 'College Quality Assurance systems', Mendip Paper MP020, The Staff College, Blagdon, Bristol.

—— (1992) *Total Quality Management*, Coombe Lodge Report 23(1), The Staff College, Blagdon, Bristol.

Scottish Further Education Unit and Glenrothes College (1992) *TQM in Training: the Practitioner's Guide*, Glasgow.

Spanbauer, S.J. (1987) *Quality First in Education . . . Why Not?* Fox Valley Technical College Foundation, Appleton, WI.

—— (1989) *Measurement and Costing Quality in Education*, Fox Valley Technical College Foundation, Appleton, WI.

—— (1992) *A Quality System for Education*, Milwaukee, WI: ASQC Quality Press.

Training Enterprise and Education Directorate of the Department of Employment (1990) *The Management of Quality BS 5750 and Beyond*, Training Quality Branch, Training Enterprise and Education, Directorate Employment Department Group, Sheffield.

14 Listening to the voice of the customer

Sam Schauerman, Donna Manno and Burt Peachy

SUMMARY

This chapter explains the concept of *Quality Function Deployment*, developed by Professor Yoji Akao in 1978, and how it can be utilized to centre your institutional improvement efforts on customer needs. In addition, the chapter describes how El Camino College is using this process to match constituent needs to college functions as part of the institutional planning process.

In the last decade major industries, service organizations and educational institutions have been implementing the concepts and practices of Total Quality Management to improve the quality of the goods and services they produce. One of the major tenets within the principles of Total Quality Management/Continuous Quality Improvement is the need for organizations to adopt a strong customer focus as one of their major initiatives in the transformation of their organizational culture towards quality. It is surprising to us in our quality consulting that many organizations do not know who their customers are! What is equally surprising is that many organizations, once they have identified their customers, lack strategies to survey customer needs on an ongoing basis and are frustrated in making organizational improvements that truly address customer requirements. The initiatives and tools discussed in this chapter will expose the reader to a continuous improvement strategy called 'Quality Function Deployment' and its application within a higher educational setting.

CUSTOMER STORIES

Everyone has good and bad customer stories. Most of us have experienced the thrill of superior service and the disappointment and frustration when a service fails to meet out expectations. Sometimes failure to address customer needs can be costly! Take, for example, the frustration a customer experienced at his local bank that, unwittingly, failed to validate parking passes. It seems that this customer went to the bank and asked the teller to validate the pass. The customer was told that the bank only validated passes when there was a transaction. The customer then asked to see the branch manager and was told, once again by the manager, that it was the 'policy' of the bank to validate passes only when a customer made a transaction. The bank was unwilling to modify the rule even though this man was a good customer. At this point the customer went on the attack. The gentleman then went to the teller and withdrew $1 million from his account! He told the branch manager that, if the bank's 'policy' was not changed by the next day, he would return and withdraw another million dollars. The bank was unable to respond to change so quickly, and the customer withdrew his second million. Here was a case where the bank cared more about transactions than the customer.

Good experiences help you to maintain your customer base. More importantly, they build long-term trust and credibility. Another fact we have discovered is that 'good' customer experiences usually require the empowerment of front-line employees to make on-the-spot decisions to turn around a potentially disastrous experience. Take, for example, the person who signed up for an extended telephone service with one of the nation's well-known carriers and who discovered three months later that she was receiving the wrong service at a higher price! When she called the phone company she was already on the attack. If the service representative who answered the call was unable to make instant adjustments, there was a possibility that this customer would take her business elsewhere. But the representative was empowered to make corrections during the transaction: not only was the service changed, the representative reimbursed the customer for the three months of incorrect service *and* the original installation fee! The customer's needs were not only met but exceeded. This level of customer 'focus' helps organizations to build that long-term trust and credibility so necessary in our competitive environment.

How many times have you been *thrilled* by a service? Something was added that you didn't expect or never thought you needed. The dry cleaners' story is such a good example. A friend moved into a new neighbourhood and found a new dry cleaners that would do dress shirts for $0.95 and gave a 10 per cent discount on dry cleaning. This seemed to be a good buy, so the friend began giving business to this dry cleaner. Something unexpected began to happen. Dry cleaning and laundry would come back with broken buttons and even small tears. He brought this to the attention of the manager and, luckily, buttons and tears were repaired from that point on. But his trust in that dry cleaner was never the same. One day he noticed an advertisement in a local paper for a rival cleaner who charged $0.90 for shirts and gave a 15 per cent discount on dry cleaning. Our friend changed dry cleaners within the week. He was happy with the savings, and the cleaners took special care to make minor repairs. This went on for several months. One night at a neighbourhood party, our friend discovered that his next-door neighbour went to a cleaners that charged $0.85 for dress shirts,

15 per cent discount on dry cleaning, gave an additional 5¢ off per shirt when accompanied by dry cleaning, picked up and delivered the laundry *and billed the customer once a month for the service.* Our friend *immediately* changed cleaners because the service they offered thrilled him and added components he never knew he needed! Most important, this new level of service became his new standard by which he judged all others; it was the benchmark that other cleaners must be measured against in this customer's eyes.

RETAINING YOUR CUSTOMERS

The importance of focusing on customers was found in a study conducted by Technical Assistance Programs. They found for each customer complaint that you receive there are twenty-six additional customers that have a complaint; of that twenty-six, six customers consider the complaint to be a serious problem. Additionally, within your customer base, 96 per cent are non-complainers; only 4 per cent complain. If the complaint is resolved, 54 per cent return, 16 per cent may return, and 30 per cent don't return. If the complaint is resolved *quickly*, 95 per cent return and only 5 per cent don't return.

Telling others about poor service is a common pastime; we have all indulged in it. According to the same study the average run-of-the-mill customer who had a problem tells nine to ten other people; 13 per cent of those customers tell more than twenty people; and customers who have complaints resolved satisfactorily tell only five people.

CUSTOMER FOCUS

A customer is someone who receives your product or service; they are people whose quality requirements you must satisfy in order to succeed. To understand your customer's quality requirements you must establish and maintain feedback mechanisms: on-site surveys; telephone surveys; focus group meetings; and so on. Maintaining a consistent relationship with your customers is paramount since customer needs change over time; unless you are vigilant, your customers' needs may out-distance your capabilities. Our dry-cleaning friend is an example of this phenomenon. Secondly, your customer's needs must be communicated in their language. It is up to you to translate their needs into your institution's language, functions and processes; we will outline a successful strategy later in this chapter. Thirdly, you will always have both internal and external customers. People within your organization may be receivers of products or services rendered by others.

At El Camino College we have developed a matrix that identifies and describes our internal and external customers.

Table 14.1 Customers at El Camino College

	Internal Those who work *in* the college system	External Those who are affected, but are *outside* the college system
DIRECT Those who use the college's services	Students Next teachers	Community Employers 4-year colleges
INDIRECT *Those who need someone else to use the college services*	Administration Office Board of Trustees	Parents Taxpayers

QUALITY FUNCTION DEPLOYMENT – TRANSLATING THE CUSTOMER'S VOICE INTO ORGANIZATIONAL LANGUAGE

Devised by Japan's Professor Yoji Akao of Tamagawa University in 1978. Quality Function Deployment (QFD) has been winning adherents since being transplanted to the United States in the late 1980s. QFD is a strategic tool that allows an organization to capture the customer's quality requirements and to translate those requirements into organizational language. QFD facilitates the analysis of product and service quality characteristics, costs, reliability and so on and enables the use of these characteristics to plan internal improvements to processes that produce the product or service. It also allows an organization to prioritize its process improvements and systematically to develop a plan for improvement.

QFD first begins with surveying a customer base to define their needs and their priorities. Once these priorities have been quantified, the QFD process correlates customer priorities to internal functions or processes. By matching customer needs with internal processes, employees then have a 'map' of their system and can identify which processes need to be improved to meet a customer's quality requirements. A simple matrix is used to describe this process visually, which then can pinpoint where improvements need to be addressed and in which order.

To describe the QFD process further, let us look at a recent application of QFD at El Camino College to the institution's planning process.

QUALITY FUNCTION DEPLOYMENT AND EL CAMINO COLLEGE'S PLANNING PROCESS

Step one: gathering customer information

In February 1993 the President of El Camino College convened three separate focus groups representing our major constituents: students; faculty and staff; community and business leaders; and leaders from our high-school feeder schools and the major four-year institutions which received our students. These three separate groups were asked the same question: 'From your perspective what needs do you have that El Camino College must fulfill in its function as an educational institution?' Through brain-storming, synthesis of ideas and weighted voting, the following needs for each group emerged:

Table 14.2 Needs expressed by students; faculty and staff; and community and business leaders, and leaders from feeder schools and institutions: El Camino College

Constituent focus group	Weighted needs (10 = high; 1 = low)
Students	Quality of education (10)
	Access to student services (9)
	Affordable fees (9)
	Affordable textbooks (9)
	Fiscal accountability – manage funds wisely (9)
	College fund-raising efforts (8)
	Multi-cultural curriculum and governance (8)
	Access to counselling services (8)
	Increased financial aid to students (8)
	Improved campus communications/student input (8)
	Maintain good employee salaries (7)
	Expand student recruitment efforts (7)
	Upgrade facilities (7)
	Greater student access to facilities (7)
	Expand recycling effort and communication (6)
Faculty/staff	Quality of instruction (10)
	Salaries and benefits (9)
	College morale (9)
	Student access to services (9)
	Diversity (9)
	Campus safety (8)
	Long-term planning (8)
	Improved communication throughout the college (8)
	Improved, user-friendly phone system (7)
	Collegiality (6)
	Improved support systems (6)
	Upgraded classrooms and offices (6)
	Staff development (6)
	Upgraded equipment and computers (6)
	Computer technology for faculty, staff and students (6)
	Clean facilities throughout the campus (6)
	Available and free parking (3)

Table 14.2 – *continued*

Constituent focus group	Weighted needs (10 = high; 1 = low)
Commuity leadership Business leadership K-12 leadership 4-year institutions	Teaching improvement (10) Institutional stability (10) Secure, stable funding sources (9) Lifelong learning opportunities (9) Transfer education (9) Vocational education (9) Cultural diversity (8) Business/education partnerships (8) Ongoing institutional planning (7) Computer training for all students (6) Interpersonal skills for all students (6) Community resource and education (6) Focus on global and international issues (5) Nurture alumni involvement (5) Maintain and expand facilities (4)

Each of the weighted categories was accompanied by a narrative section that focused on specific suggestions and/or problems as perceived by members of each focus group. This information was developed into a summary document for use by college personnel; the summary was also returned to each focus group for their information.

Step two: 'Mapping the college's systems'

At the same time as the focus groups were meeting, a representative group of management, faculty, staff and students was formed as a 'systems team' whose task was to develop a matrix of all functions and units or 'systems' within the college. From the initial meeting it was clear that the membership had differing levels of understanding about what functions El Camino College performed. As a result of this lack of common perception, it was decided that each member of the team would research college functions by talking with others and, when re-convened as a group, would collate this information into an El Camino College Systems and Functions 'Map'. The result of this process was the grid shown in Table 14.3.

Step three: Matching constituent needs to college functions

Utilizing the outputs from the customer focus group summaries, the 'systems team' began matching constituent needs to college functions. Using correlations (5 = high; 3 = medium; 1 = low; and 0 = no correlation),

Table 14.3 El Camino College: institutional systems and functions (24 March 1993)

Teaching and learning	Learning support	Student growth outside the classroom
Course development	(Adult re-entry)	Counselling
Developing student outcomes	(Foreign student programme)	Adult re-entry
Honours programme	Articulation	Career
Instruction	Career and transfer counselling	Transfer
Instructional support staff	Computer labs	Early outreach
Planning instructional capacity	Counselling	Honours
Programme development	Instructional services	Matriculation
Scheduling of courses	ITV	Advising
Specialized instructional facilities –	Learning centre	Assessment
planetarium, museum, etc.	Library	Counselling
State and federal compliances	Matriculation	Follow-up
	Media services	Orientation
	Special resource centre	Placement
	Technical services	Student affairs
	Testing	Clubs
	Tutoring	Leadership
		Student government
		Student equity
		EOP&S
		Project success
		Puente
		Yes I Can
		Student mentoring
		Student retention
		CARE
		Early alert
		EOP&S
		Project success
		Puente
		Tutoring
		Yes I Can

Leadership
Accreditation
Annual planning – short-term
Governance
Institutional effectiveness:
Planning – assessment and evaluation
Interaction with Board of Trustees
Leadership development
Legal aspects
Programme review
Strategic planning – long-term

Financial services
College:
Accounting for:
'Auxiliary services'
Student programmes
Budget planning and development
Cashiering
Developing financial resources
Money management
Accounts payable
Managing investments
Payroll
Purchasing
Contracts
Risk management

Student enrolment
Admissions
Articulation Council of High Schools
Enrolment management
Evaluations re: graduation requirements
and certification
Outreach and recruitment
F-1 visa
Records
Registration
Residency checks
School and college relations
Special services
a. F-1 students
b. Veterans' services
Student recruitment
Testing and assessment

Facilities management
Campus security
Environmental safety and health
Facilities planning
Short-term
Mid-term
Long-term
Facilities maintenance
Inventory management
Mail room
New construction
Off-campus facilities
Operations
Warehouse

Human resource development
Affirmative action
Collective bargaining
a. AFT
b. CSEA
c. Police
Evaluating performance
Health benefits/insurance
Labour relations
Professional development
a. Faculty
b. Management
c. Staff
Recruitment and hiring
Workman's compensation

Auxiliary services
Athletics
Auxiliary services board
Bookstore
Other books and supplies
Text sales
Campus police
Child development centre
Food services
Cafeteria
Catering
Snack bar
Marsee Auditorium
Parking facilities
Investment

(continued overleaf)

Table 14.3 El Camino College: institutional systems and functions 24 March 1993 *(continued)*

Financial services	Facilities management	Auxiliary services

Student Financial Services:
Financial
  EOP&S
  Yes I Can
Job placement
  College work study
  Community service learning programme
  Human resource systems (student)
  Student placement
  Vocational education
Student financial aid and scholarship
  services
		Parking operations
		Student health services
		Substance abuse programmes

Communications	Research	External relations

Information systems
Electronic mail/telephone
Information training
MIS to State
Provider of data
Schedule planning
Printing
  Instruction
  Newsletters
  Public presentations
  Student information
    Catalogue
    Class schedule
    Mandate data
	Institutional research
	  a. 5-year plan
	  b. Matriculation
	  c. Programme review
	Market research
		Alumni relations
		Business partnerships
		  a. Support from business
		  b. Training needs for industry
		Centre for the Arts
		Chancellor's Office/BOG
		Community services
		  a. Civic Centre
		  b. Programme
		Contract education
		ECC foundation
		Economic development
		  a. California Manufacturing Technology
		      Centre

Public and media relations
Community newsletter (ECC report)
Newspapers
TV and radio
Student publications
Myriad (humanities)
Warrior Life (student magazine)
Warwhoop (student newspaper)

b. ECC Quality Institute
c. Small Business Centre
Governmental relations
a. Federal government
b. State government
K-12 partnerships
a. 2+2
b. Tech prep.

Table 14.4 El Camino College: quality of education function matrix

Group	Weight factor	College functions												
Constituent requirements		TEACHING	LEARNING	HUMAN RESOURCES & SUPPORT	LEADERSHIP	STUDENT GROWTH & DEVELOPMENT	STUDENT SUPPORT SERVICES	EXTERNAL RELATIONS	RESEARCH	STUDENT RECRUITMENT	FINANCIAL	AUXILIARY SERVICES	COMMUNICATIONS	FACILITIES MGMT
Current students: quality of education	10	5	5	5	5	5	3	3	3	3	3	3	3	3
Faculty/staff: quality of instruction	9	5	5	5	5	5	3	3	3	3	1	1	3	1
Community: teaching improvement	10	5	5	5	1	1	3	1	1	0	1	1	3	1
Average		5	5	5	3.7	3.7	3	2.3	2.3	2	1.7	1.7	3	1.7

Table 14.5 El Camino College: constituent requirement/college function matrix, focus group summary

WEIGHT FACTOR	*Group* / Constituent requirements	LEARNING SUPPORT	STUDENT GROWTH	LEADERSHIP	STUDENT ENROLMENT	HUMAN RESOURCE DEVL	FINANCIAL SERVICES	FACILITIES MANAGEMENT	AUXILIARY SERVICES	COMMUNICATIONS	RESEARCH	EXTERNAL RELATIONS
	Students: weighted total	269	293	339	215	92	333	101	273	183	113	273
	Faculty/staff: weighted total	236	228	259	196	325	292	216	216	332	112	175
	Community: weighted total	294	297	355	295	145	271	115	177	239	175	383
	Average	266	272	317	235	187	298	144	222	251	133	277
	Index number	2.00	2.05	2.38	1.77	1.41	2.24	1.08	1.67	1.89	1.00	2.08

the team looked at each college function and correlated each constituent need to that particular function. Matrices were developed for each constituent group (students; faculty/staff; community/business/academic), and a final summary matrix was produced that combined the needs of all three groups into a synthesized matrix. The team agreed to produce a separate summary matrix for 'Education/instruction' separate from other college support functions, since this was the primary function and need addressed by each focus group and, therefore, demanded pre-eminent attention. The result of this effort is shown in Tables 14.4 and 14.5.

SUMMARY OF RESULTS

Table 14.6 represents a re-ordering of college functions according to the strength of the correlation and indexing to constituent needs.

Table 14.6 Re-ordering of college functions according to the strength of the correlation and indexing to constituent needs

College function	Correlation to constituent need
Teaching and learning	5
Learning support	5
Human resource development	5
Leadership	5
Student growth outside the classroom	3.7
External relations	3.7
Research	3
Student enrolment	2.3
Financial services	2.3
Auxiliary services	2
Communications	1.7
Facilities management	1.7

From this summary it can be noted that four major college functions have the highest correlation with constituent needs. This represents the results of this *particular* focus group activity and may be subject to revision every time you convene focus groups. However, armed with this information the institution is able to focus on which processes and systems should be initially addressed for improvement to satisfy constituent/customer needs, namely Teaching and learning, Learning support, Human resource development and Institutional leadership. Other functions would also need to be addressed, but with somewhat less priority.

THE IMPORTANCE OF QFD IN PLANNING EFFORTS THAT ADDRESS CUSTOMER NEEDS

How does QFD relate to the process improvement practices of TQM? Quality Function Deployment can be used as the 'engine' that drives all planning and process improvement efforts. The information gathered and systematically analysed in this way can assist the institution's leadership to plan their visioning, goals and objectives and annual strategies, around the needs of constituents rather than second-guessing what should be improved. Through this process, a major paradigm shift can be effected within the campus leadership to turn from an inward planning process to one that focuses on information-gathering from sources outside our functions and processes and to rate that information against our processes and functions. In addition, the summary information on college functions provided above can assist the leadership in prioritizing its planning efforts and focusing improvements on the most important functions that address constituent needs.

STAGES OF QFD AND IMPROVEMENT ACTIVITY

The following is a summary of the stages of activity to demonstrate where the Quality Function Deployment activity is properly placed:

- A survey is administered to constituents/customers to ascertain their needs.
- Employees 'map' the processes and functions in their system.
- The employees analyse customer priorities and quality requirements.
- Quality Function Deployment matrix developed.
- The team prepares a process improvement plan by addressing priority functions.
- When completed, the team returns to the QFD matrix to identify next process to improve,
  or
- The team 'benchmarks' the best practices of a competitor,
  or
- Re-survey the customer to see if their quality requirements have changed.

SUMMARY: USING QUALITY FUNCTION DEPLOYMENT AS AN INSTITUTIONAL PLANNING TOOL

At El Camino College, we are currently using QFD to analyse customer needs and to establish critical breakdown processes that will be addressed by the entire institution on an annual basis. This process is beginning to alter our traditional strategic planning process dramatically and is a powerful tool to align the entire institution around achievable, measurable goals. In addition, we are fostering QFD efforts at each worksite to develop unit goals around constituent needs, further driving the TQM transformation efforts towards our vision of ongoing, continuous process improvements by every employee.

This chapter was first presented as a paper to the CCBIA/League for Innovation in Community Colleges Conference in February 1993.

REFERENCES

Major TQM theorists

Crosby, Philip, *Quality is Free*, New York: Mentor Books, New American Library.
Deming, W. Edwards (1982) *Out of Crisis*, Cambridge, MA: Productivity Press; or Washington, DC: George Washington University.
Juran, Joseph M. (1988) *Juran on Planning for Quality*, Cambridge, MA: Productivity Press; or Milwaukee, WI: American Society for Quality Control.
Senge, Peter M. (1990) *The Fifth Discipline: the Art and Practice of the Learning Organization*, New York: Doubleday Currency.

Educational applications

Angelo, T.A. (1989) 'Classroom research: faculty development for effective learning – linking institutional effectiveness to learning quality', Second Annual Conference on Institutional Effectiveness, Orange County, CA (April).
ASQC/FICE (1988) *Proceeding of the May 26, 1988 Seminar Proposing a National Quality Initiative*, American Society for Quality Control.
ASQC/FICE/COPA/NCATE (1989) *Summary Proceeding of the Second National Educational Quality Initiative (NEQI) Conference*.
Bober, R.P. (1991) 'Faculty externships: catalysts for TQM', *Leadership Abstracts*, vol. 4, no. 14 (Nov.).
Chaffee, E.E. (1990) 'Managing for the 1990s', in Larry W. Jones and Franz Nowotny (eds) *An Agenda for the New Decade*, New Directions in Higher Education, no. 70, San Francisco: Jossey-Bass.
Coate, L. Edwin (1990a) 'TQM on campus: implementing Total Quality Management on campus', *NACUBO Business Officer*.
—— (1990b) *Implementing Total Quality Management in a University Setting*, Oregon State University (July).
Cornesky, R.A. (1990) *Improving Quality in Colleges and Universities*, Madison, WI: Magna Publications.
Fisher, J.L. and Tack, M.W. (1988) *Leaders on Leadership: the College Presidency*, San Franciso: Jossey-Bass.
Green, M.F. (1988) *Leaders for a New Era: Strategies for Higher Education*, New York: Macmillan.
Harris, J. *et al.* (1986) *Assessment in American Higher Education*, Office of Educational Research and Improvement, US Department of Education.
Harris, J., Hillenmeyer, S. and Foran, J. (1989) *Quality Assurance for Private Career Schools*, Washington, DC: The Association of Independent Colleges and Schools and McGraw-Hill Publishing Co.
Mathews, K.M. (1988) *Study Retention and Development: the Creative Science*, The Baxandall Company, Inc.
Miller, R.I. (ed.) (1991) *Adapting the Deming Method to Higher Education*,

Washington, DC: College and University Personnel Association.

Needham, R.L. (1991) 'Total Quality Management: an overview', *Leadership Abstracts*, League for Innovation, vol. 4, no. 10.

Robinson, J.D. (1991) 'An open letter: TQM on the campus', *Harvard Business Review* (Nov.).

Rocheleau, L. *et al.* (1990) 'A restructure quality high school: the continuous improvement process in action', Sitka, Alaska, Mt. Edgecumbe High School.

Rodriguez, R.G. (1991) 'Total quality commitment in higher education: improving institutional research', Yosemite Community College District, *Inquiry Newsletter* (May).

Schargel, F.P. (1991) 'Promoting quality in education', *Vocational Education Journal* (Nov.–Dec.).

Seymour, D.T. (1992) *On Q: Causing Quality in Higher Education*, New York: American Council on Education and Macmillan Publishing Co.

Seymour, D. and Casey, C. (1991a) *Total Quality Management in Higher Education: a Critical Review*, Methuen, MA: GOAL/QPC.

—— (1991b) *Total Quality Management in Higher Education: a Critical Assessment*, Methuen, MA: GOAL/QPC.

Sherr, L. and Teeter, D.J. (eds) (1991) *Total Quality Management in Higher Education*, San Franciso: Jossey-Bass. New Directions for Institutional Research, no. 71.

Spanbauer, S.J. (1987) *Quality First in Education . . . Why Not?* Appleton, WI: Fox Valley Technical College Foundation.

—— (1989) *Measuring and Costing Quality in Education: Using Quality and Productivity Methods to Improve Schools*, Appleton, WI: Fox Valley Technical College Foundation.

Stratton, B. (1991) 'Quality in education (a special report)', *Quality Progress* (Oct.).

15 Sandwell College and BS 5750: a syncretistic pilgrimage?

Iain MacRobert

Sandwell College of Further and Higher Education came into existence in September 1986 as a result of a merger between the West Bromwich College of Commerce and Technology and Warley College of Technology. Based on six campuses throughout the Borough of Sandwell, the college offers education and training to some 23,000 students each year (7,000 full-time equivalents) covering an age range from 14 to 80 plus. Currently the college employs 520 full-time lecturing staff, and more than 300 support staff. A wide variety of full-time and part-time provision across areas as diverse as literacy for those with special educational needs through to graduate chemistry, A levels, GCSEs, National Vocational Qualifications, Youth Training, leisure-time classes and school link courses, is also on offer throughout the institution.

WHY BS 5750?

The primary motivation for looking at the possibility of installing a Quality Management System to BS 5750, related to the need of the college to stimulate a sense of collegiality between the two pre-existing colleges of which it now comprised. What could draw the diversity of staff in a wide range of programme areas located on six campuses into a common sense of purpose and direction? Although we were not unaware of the potential marketing applications of achieving BS 5750 certification, this was not a primary motivation and was certainly never seen as an end in itself. There were, however, external influences, if not pressures, on the college to demonstrate to the outside world that its claims to quality are well founded. In 1933 a director of Shell wrote, 'It is not enough that we should know that our motor-oils are first rate, but the public should be convinced of it' (Kessler 1933). In December 1986, Lord Young had gone on record as saying, 'FE must realize that it needs to respond to a changing market. If the providers of quality training do not come out of FE they will come from the private sector. As long as quality training is provided – I do not care who provides it' (TES). Increasingly 'effectiveness' which had for so long stood beside 'efficiency', was being replaced by the word 'quality'.[1] The government

White Paper 'Education and Training for the Twenty-first Century' went even further and spoke not merely of quality but of quality systems:

> Colleges need effective systems to improve their quality . . . a number of systems are being explored by colleges including BS 5750, Total Quality Management (TQM) and Strategic Quality Management (SQM). Colleges will be expected to provide information to the [Funding] Councils about the quality assurance systems they have in place.
>
> (1991: 38)

It is questionable, perhaps, whether TQM is in fact a quality system, but the implication was clear: further education colleges were being encouraged to take seriously the introduction of quality management systems as a means of ensuring the quality of their own provision. This was a shift away from the idea of ensuring quality by inspection as carried out by Her Majesty's Inspectors, validating bodies and some exam boards, and the Training Enterprise Councils. Sandwell College was well aware that inspection would do little to produce or even stimulate quality. Quality has to be 'built in', and this requires staff ownership of the mechanisms of quality control. What was fundamental to the motivation of Sandwell College staff was the concern to provide education, training and related services and facilities that would meet the needs of the students.

THE QUALITY ASSURANCE PROJECT

With financial backing from the Work Related Further Education Development Fund of the Training Agency (now TEED), the Quality Assurance Unit was set up on the 1 November 1989. A director and assistant director were appointed from existing academic staff and an administrative officer employed to give secretarial support. Neither of the directors had any prior experience of BS 5750 or quality assurance systems but had substantial track records in the areas of curriculum development, college-wide initiatives and the successful implementation of change at Sandwell College. As a result, both had professional credibility with the teaching staff and an extensive knowledge of the institution. The Quality Assurance Unit was accountable to the college Principalship through one of its two Vice-Principals, who became a committed member of the team and worked with the quality assurance staff for about half a day per week.[2]

Aims, scope, 'product' and 'process'

The primary aim of the project was to assess the applicability of installing a quality management system to BS 5750 across the total institution. At an early stage, however, a decision was made to limit the scope to the provision of education and training and to look specifically at all of those factors, functions and activities which had a direct impact on the quality of education and training. While the project sought to be pragmatic and to build on existing good practice, there were some philosophical issues that had to be resolved at an early stage. Most important among them was to define clearly the product of the college. Initially there was a great deal of ambivalence as to whether the product was the course or programme of training (the 'learning opportunities') which the college offered, or whether it was the value-added to the student who underwent the process of education or training. After considerable thought and consultation with Rod Ruston of the BSI, to whom must go a great deal of credit for the ultimate clarity of our thinking on this matter, a decision was made that the most appropriate definition of product for a further education college is the value-added or enhancement of the student in terms of skills developed, knowledge acquired, understanding gained or increased self-confidence and personal development. This definition of 'product' placed the student and learning at the primary focal point of the quality management system, while allowing for a secondary and crucially important focus on the management and evaluation of the 'process' of delivering the curriculum.

Everyone to whom we spoke seemed to have an implicit idea of what quality is, but very few could define it. On the other hand, people seemed able to define very clearly what constituted a lack of quality. The definition of quality found in BS 4778 states that it is: 'The totality of features and characteristics of a product or service that bear on its ability to satisfy stated or implied needs (BSI 1987a). Among the more flowery definitions given by the quality gurus we found the utilitarian definitions of a product being 'fit for the purpose' and services being 'fit to be tried'. The early recognition that a documented quality system would not necessarily have the 'Heineken' effect which would reach every part of the institution, led to the college adopting a definition of quality for the purposes of its quality system, which stated that quality is 'conformance to requirements which are measurable or definable'. Behind this definition is a recognition that quality has a great deal to do with factors such as culture, ethos and interpersonal relationships, which we would not wish to define, measure or formalize into documented procedures and records. A documented QMS does, however, provide an infrastructure and an antidote to anomie within which the less tangible, abstract and subjective determinants of quality are more likely to be developed.

To say that 'quality is conformance to requirements which are measurable or definable' leads to a consideration of whose requirements the institution is seeking to meet. Whose stated or implied needs is the college in business to serve? BS 5750 refers to 'purchasers', but this term does not necessarily imply that, to have their needs met, bodies and individuals must be in a position to pay for the services on offer (BSI 1987b). The college decided to use the term 'customer' to refer to both individuals and corporate bodies which sponsor or invest money in the activities of the college; for example, the Local Education Authority, now the Further Education

Funding Council, the TECs, fee-paying students, employers and other funding agencies. The second group were defined as the 'clients'. These are the students, trainees or delegates who undertake education or training at the college. They may or may not be 'customers'. That is to say, some students pay their own fees, while others attend the college on payment of a nominal sum or free of charge. The final group of 'purchasers' comprise the qualification and validating bodies such as BTEC, City and Guilds of London Institute, Industry Lead Bodies and universities, which have the power to impose on the college and its curriculum certain requirements which we must meet if they are to validate the qualifications which we offer. The college is thus confronted with at least three sets of potentially conflicting requirements imposed on it by those which sponsor its activities (the most significant of which is now the Further Education Funding Council), those which undertake courses or programmes of education and training in the college, and those agencies which validate the courses or programmes of the college. The questions that Sandwell College must continually ask itself are as follows: Do we know exactly what each 'purchaser' is asking us to do? Do we have mechanisms in place to find out what each purchaser requires of us? Do we have all of the necessary resources to deliver in such a way that we can satisfy their stated and implied needs? (See Figure 15.1.).

Interpreting the Standard

From the earliest stages of the project it was recognized that the language and concepts of BS 5750 would require a radical translation and interpretation

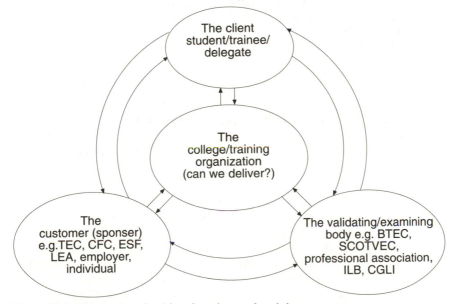

Figure 15.1 'Contract review' in education and training

from their original manufacturing context into the terms and ideas that are current within further education. The nomenclature used in the Standard is not common English but a kind of jargon peculiar to the industrial sector and substantially meaningless and alien to the world of further education, which possesses its own particular language: 'FE speak'. A kind of hermeneutical exercise had to be engaged in, which de-contextualized the Standard, extracted the concepts and principles underlying the clauses and re-contextualized them within the college environment. To this end an initial translation of the eighteen headings of BS 5750, Part 2 (ISO 9002), into educational terms was made (see Table 15.1).

Table 15.1 ISO 9002 quality system requirements: translation for education and training

1 Management responsibility
2 Quality system
3 Contracts with customers, clients and validating bodies
4 Document control
5 Purchasing
6 Client admission and support
   Equipment provided by client, customer or validating body
7 Client and course records
8 Curriculum design, development and delivery
9 Assessment and testing of clients/assessment of curriculum
10 Consistency of assessment and testing methods
11 Client/curriculum assessment and performance records
12 Diagnostic procedures for client/course failure
13 Corrective procedures for client failure and course improvement
14 The physical college environment
15 Quality records
16 Internal quality audits
17 Staff training
18 Statistics/trend analysis

Sandwell's translation and interpretation, together with insight of staff from other training organizations, colleges, certification bodies, the Department of Employment, the Association of British Chambers of Commerce and others were combined into a document by BSI and eventually published in February 1991 as *BS 5750: Guidance Notes for Application to Education and Training* (BSI 1991/1992).

The primary reason that Sandwell College decided to pursue registration under BS 5750, Part 2, instead of Part 1 of the Standard was philosophical rather than practical. Had the college decided to opt for the definition of product as the course, programme of training or learning opportunities provided, then sufficient and adequate procedures for curriculum design, review, evaluation and development were being installed. Because the college opted for the definition of 'product' being 'value-added', it was recognized that Part 2 of the Standard would be more appropriate. BS 5750, Part 1, is for any organization which, in addition to production and installation, also carries out product design, development and servicing. Part 2 of the Standard, on the other hand, is appropriate for an organization engaged in production and installation but not in product design and development and in subsequent servicing. Because the definition of the content and level of the value which has to be added to each student to enable them successfully to complete a course of education or programme of training is defined by an external body such as an examination board, Industry Lead Body or university, and this is usually specified in a syllabus or NVQ specification, over which the college has little or no control, it was considered analogous to the design specification, engineering drawings and similar documentation which in industry define the nature of the product which is to be manufactured. Sandwell College, beginning with the pre-determined design in terms of the syllabus or NVQ competence specification, then designs a *process* which is capable of delivering the value-added necessary for the student to complete the course successfully and gain the qualification. That is to say, we are in the business of designing the educational *process* rather than the *product* of education which, for the majority of our students, is to criteria laid down by an external agency.

At an early stage it was considered as self-evident by the Quality Assurance Unit that any system of quality management would focus primarily on the operation of course teams as managers of the curriculum. Thus all procedures and records developed would centre on the management and delivery of education and training by academic and support staff, and would encourage the planning, development, review and evaluation of the educational process (see Figure 15.2) in the light of its effectiveness in 'adding value' and meeting the implied and stated needs of 'purchasers'.

Developing procedures

Initially the Project Directors spent time assessing existing good practice and procedures within the college and evaluating the extent to which these already met the requirements of BS 5750. This led to the development of a draft quality procedures manual which course teams were asked to consider and, at this early stage, to modify as they felt necessary to meet the requirements of the particular type of course or programme they were responsible for. Existing effective procedures and adequate records were encouraged as viable substitutes for those designed by the Quality Assurance Unit and were approved and granted an issue status. This diversity of acceptable procedures and records helped to ensure that they adequately met the various requirements of different types of courses, and that the quality system did not become a bureaucratic 'strait-jacket' or a mere paper-chase exercise. Thus the quality procedures grew largely out of existing good practice and the requirements of course teams. The quality system in turn

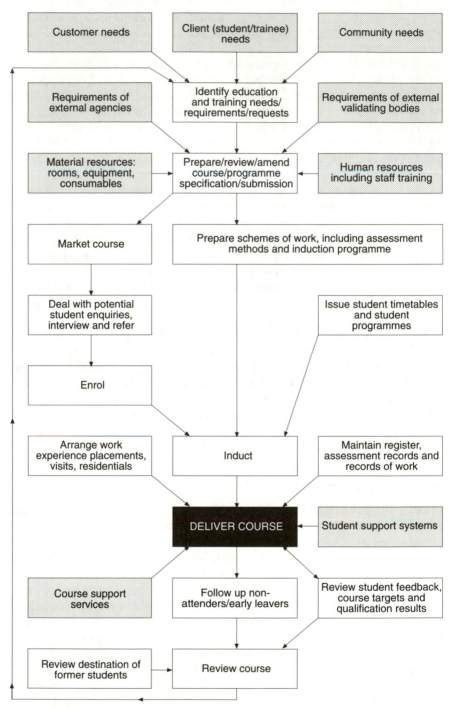

Figure 15.2 Course team quality procedures

grew out of the quality procedures by a 'bottom-up' process. Ultimately, only a single sheet of A4 paper was put into the procedures manual purely to meet the requirements of the Standard. All other procedures and records were included because they were already acknowledged to be the professional 'tools' of the further education sector.

Three months into the project, by which time the Quality Assurance Unit had developed an understanding of the Standard, extensive staff awareness sessions were carried out with small groups of staff receiving a presentation on how the Standard might apply to them. This included substantial opportunities for teaching staff to ask questions and discuss issues. The college avoided the use of mass rallies or exhortations from college management, preferring rather to meet with small groups in course teams, schools and departments in their own staff rooms and offices.

In May and June 1990 a major staff development exercise focused on training staff to understand, and if necessary to adapt, the model procedures which had now been put together as a procedures manual. The project went live from the first week of September 1990, when each course team was issued with a procedures manual and asked to work in accordance with it.

Internal audits

Thirty volunteers were sought across schools and departments within the college. These people were then trained as a team of internal auditors and conducted their first internal assessment in November 1990. This initial internal quality audit did not follow a pattern which has now been established but was primarily a paper-based exercise which looked at the extent to which the procedures had been implemented and records were being kept. A second internal audit, which was beginning to look rather more like the type of quality audit that people familiar with BS 5750 would expect, was conducted in March 1991. The result of the second audit formed the major item for consideration at the college's first Quality Management Review Committee meeting, and indicated that the overwhelming majority of staff were following the procedures and keeping adequate records.

Internal audits were important for a variety of reasons, not least among them the raising of staff awareness that the issue of quality was here to stay and would not go away. Secondly, it concentrated the minds of all of those responsible for following procedures and keeping records and encouraged people who had not hitherto taken it seriously to throw their weight behind the project. A spin-off from this was the cross-fertilization of good practice which took place when auditors from one school or section of the college were responsible for carrying out an audit in a different school or section. The accountants could learn something from the caterers, and the hairdressers had things to share with the engineers!

Audit by external assessors

The third-party audit by BSI Quality Assurance was scheduled to take place on the week beginning 22 April. Finally, the elements of self-doubt began to emerge in the Quality Assurance Unit as the staff wondered whether their interpretation and translation of the Standard was adequate and whether the records being kept throughout the college would successfully pass the rigours of this type of audit. Another fear was that auditors who were more used to dealing with the manufacturing or service sector would be unable to conduct a valid audit in an educational institution of this sort. As it turned out, however, their fears on both counts proved to be groundless.

Three auditors and an educational adviser from BSI arrived at Sandwell College to carry out an exhaustive inspection of the quality system and procedures across the six campuses and some thirty-four schools. The auditors determined what they wished to see and proved rather difficult to redirect, which meant that they were very much in control of everything that was examined. Some members of course teams spent up to two-and-a-half hours meeting the requests of auditors and providing evidence for the procedures that they were following. The Quality Assurance Unit was struck by the commitment of Sandwell College staff and the degree to which everything had been brought under control. Of the minor discrepancies which were discovered by the auditors, around two-thirds were corrected before they left on Friday afternoon, and the remainder outstanding non-compliances were dealt with by fax on the following Monday, or would be looked at in more detail during the first routine surveillance which took place in October 1991.

'Nothing succeeds like success' − staff, who had feared the worst at the announcement of an external audit, positively rejoiced, not only that the experience had been positive but that they had proved the quality of the management of their courses. It was almost impossible to find anyone who had a negative remark to make concerning the audit. Both as an institution and as individuals the audit proved to be a beneficial reinforcement of good practice.

THE FIRST COLLEGE TO GET BS 5750

On the 1 May 1991 − exactly 18 months from the start of the project − Sandwell College became a BS 5750 'Registered Firm': the first public-sector college in the country and, as far as we know, the first in the world to get International Standard 9002. However, we recognize that there is a great deal of fine-tuning still to be done and we will probably never be content with our system and procedures. Continual development is required if the quality management system is to remain a 'good servant' and not lapse into becoming a 'bad master'. In a dynamic college, the quality management system must help to drive new initiatives or, at least keep pace with rapid change, if it is not to act as a brake on development. The current scope is also being extended to embrace such services as the Learning Resource Centres (formerly libraries), student support services, the Business Services Unit, and technician support.

Even without the glory and sense of achievement that comes from gaining BSI-registered status, Sandwell College has benefited from the introduction of a quality management system in terms of the development of a curriculum management structure which has the inherent adaptability which allows staff to work with professional flexibility within a structured system; the development of recording systems which result in a more controlled and effective operation, and of a quality ethos where all of the issues that affect the service we provide are constantly on both official and unofficial agendas (see Table 15.2).

Table 15.2 ISO 9002/EN 29002/BS 5750, Part 2: benefits of the project

---

1 A comprehensive quality assurance system that ensures curriculum review and development.
2 A unifying influence on the college that centres on the quality of education and training.
3 A method of devolving, where appropriate, power and responsibility to course team level while retaining central strategic management.
4 A way of developing course teams.
5 A method of encouraging cross-college developments and the spread of good practice.
6 An aid to communication.
7 A marketing tool which could increase competitiveness.
8 An opportunity for staff to demonstrate abilities and strengths.
9 A better service for customers and clients (the students).
10 A way of changing the culture.

Controlling the curriculum

It is impossible in a brief chapter to describe all of the functions and activities which fall within the remit of the quality management system and its associated procedures and records, but for a college the most important relate primarily to the students (the 'clients') and the curriculum (the 'process'). Courses and programmes are designed and their delivery methods planned. Aims and objectives are defined as measurable targets for student performance against which the quality (or effectiveness) of the course or programme can be measured. Documents such as course specifications, curriculum entitlements, schemes of work, induction programmes, student programmes or individual learning plans (ILPs) and timetables provide evidence that these activities are being adequately carried out. Defined course, programme or subject teams meet regularly to consider standing agenda items which include the review, evaluation and development of the curriculum in the light of assessment results, student feedback, early-leaver trends and the destinations and progression of former students. Minutes and action plans are produced to address areas in need of improvement, and complaints procedures encourage dissatisfied students to express their concerns and the college to take action. Students who pay their own fees are entitled to their money back if the student programme (that is, the outline of the course or programme on offer) fails to meet their requirements. If they fail to attend, they are followed up, and their opinions of the college, the curriculum and the teaching are sought and acted upon if shortcomings are identified.

Educationists may quite legitimately protest that there is nothing in the foregoing synopsis which is not carried out in all colleges. What, then, are the benefits of installing a quality system to BS 5750? How many college managers can say, 'hand on heart', that all of their provision is adequately planned; that all their teaching staff have current schemes of work; that all their course teams meet regularly, keep adequate minutes and take appropriate 'corrective action'; that every student is given the opportunity to express his or her views of the college and their programme of study; that every written complaint receives a written reply within ten working days and so on? Not only does Sandwell College make such claims, but it is also able to show people evidence, be they internal auditors, third-party assessors or educational inspectors, that those who manage and deliver the curriculum are in control of the processes involved.

QUO VADIS?

Gaining BS 5750 registration was a considerable achievement for Sandwell College, but it marks a beginning rather than an end. BS 5750 lays down standards for the systematic management of quality; it does not, however, set standards for education, teaching, ancillary services or for the culture within which education takes place.

Sandwell is now embarked on a programme which seeks to utilize some of the quality concepts and tools associated with TQM and to build them onto the foundation of our BS 5750 quality system. We have called this initiative Strategic Quality Management (SQM), but it should not be confused with the (very credible) SQM model advocated by Miller and Inniss (1992). Sandwell College's SQM programme aims to identify and effectively address the college's strategically important critical success factors within a changing culture and ethos which seek to convert administrative tasks to internal client services. Peer groups are encouraged to monitor and review their own performance against quality indicators and to use such (de-contextualized) tools as Pareto charts, benchmarking and Statistical Process Control.

Like the search for the Holy Grail, the pursuit of quality has more to do with the journey than the destination, and the successful design and installation of a documented quality management system is only a first step on that pilgrimage. Without such a first step, however, it is questionable whether the sincere search for quality has even begun (see Table 15.3).

Table 15.3 Installing ISO 9002/EN 29002/BS 5750, Part 2, in an educational or training establishment

---

1 Give commitment to quality improvement.
2 Become familiar with the requirements of BS 5750 (and its educational interpretation.
3 Carry out a survey and review of existing procedures and records.
4 'Fit' existing procedures and records into BS 5750 categories/sections.
5 Write a quality policy.
6 Introduce staff awareness sessions.
7 Identify 'gaps' and design procedures and records to fill them.
8 Check that all requirements of BS 5750 have been addressed.
9 Write the quality system manual.
10 Introduce staff training sessions.
11 Start working to the quality system.
12 Arrange a pre-assessment visit.
13 Carry out an internal quality audit.
14 Review and evaluate the findings of the audit and take 'corrective action'.
15 Arrange for an external audit by a certification body.

NOTES

1 See especially *Managing Colleges Efficiently*, DES and Welsh Office, 1987.
2 Sandwell College's project to design and install a quality management system to BS 5750 is described more fully in Cockburn, Margaret, Collins, David and MacRobert, Iain, *The Applicability of BS 5750 to College Operations*, Sandwell College, 1990 and 1991.

REFERENCES

BSI (1987) *BS 4778 Quality Vocabulary* Clause 3.1, Milton Keynes.
BSI (1987) *BS 5750: Part 2*, Clause 4.3, note, Milton Keynes.
BSI (1991) *Guidance Notes for the Application of BS 5750 to Education and Training*, Milton Keynes: BSI Quality Assurance; 2nd edn, July 1992.
Education and Training for the 21st Century (1991) vol. II, London: HMSO.
Kessler (1957) in Forbes, R.J. and O'Beirne, D.R. *The Technical Developments of the Royal Dutch/Shell, 1890–1940*, Leiden: Brill.
Miller, J. and Inniss, S. (1992) *Strategic Quality Management: a Guide for Senior Managers*, Ware, Herts: Consultants at Work.
Times Educational Supplement, December 1986.

Part IV
Schools

16 The application of quality management principles in education at Mt Edgecumbe High School, Sitka, Alaska

Myron Tribus

Mt Edgecumbe High School (MEHS) is situated on a small island across the channel from Sitka, Alaska. Started in the 1947 as a school for Native Americans, in 1984 it was removed from the control of the Bureau of Indian Affairs and converted into an 'alternative' school under the control of the State of Alaska.

The phrase, 'Native Americans' denotes a variety of peoples descended from the Tlingit, Haida and Tsimpshean Indian tribes as well as Eskimos and Aleuts. Archaeologists have traced Aleutian culture back to 6000 BC. Some portions of the Eskimo culture have been traced back to 300 BC. They are the descendants of a hardy race of people who learned how to survive for centuries in a harsh natural environment. Now they have to survive 'civilization'.

Alaska is a very large State with the smallest population of all the fifty states. This population is spread over a land mass more than twice the size of Texas. With such a low population density, it is difficult to maintain high-quality high schools in the small villages and towns. (From the fourth to the eighth grade, I attended a one-room schoolhouse in a rural area, and while we did not have many so-called modern facilities, I often think that being in a school where the eighth-graders taught the fifth-graders and all seventeen of us played together at recess gave me a better start than if I had been in a big city school.) At the high-school level, it just isn't possible to equip a large number of small schools with all the facilities they require for a first-rate, modern education. MEHS is one of the solutions to this problem attempted by the State.

MEHS is a residential school with about 210 students and a teaching faculty of thirteen people.

I went to Sitka during the first week of November 1990, because I had heard that the school was engaged in a unique experiment in education, applying the quality management concepts of W. Edwards Deming to the operations of the school. This is a report of what I found (see Appendix 1).

THE INCOMING STUDENTS

It is important to understand the origins of the students at MEHS. Many are drawn from the same population which would have come to the school when under the Bureau of Indian Affairs; that is, the students are 90 per cent 'rural'. Some come from villages and settlements in Alaska with too few students to support a well-equipped high school, while others come from modern cities such as Juneau.

The average income in rural Alaska is low, compared to the rest of the United States. At MEHS there is a mix of native Alaskans, having their own tribal customs and language, along with the children of immigrants, from 'the lower 48', who came to Alaska, seeking a different way of life. All types are brought together at MEHS.

Larrae Rocheleau, the Superintendent, described the incoming native Alaskan students this way:

> Our Native American students, for the most part, have extremely deep ties to their heritage and are struggling to keep the values and pride of the past while adjusting to a world dominated by another culture, another language and different social values. We attempt to nurture that Native pride and build on those positive feelings without emphasizing the negatives of adjustment.

The Superintendent is clearly an idealist. The fact comes through as soon as you start to interview him. He is also a very practical man. He accepted the job of starting a new school because he wanted to create an institution which would make the most of these young people. He was not interested in creating an elitist school. 'Our job is to provide value-added education, not to select a few who don't really need us.' One of his major objectives was to turn these students into entrepreneurs who would go back to their villages and make a difference.

The State Board of Education and the Superintendent recognized that Alaska is a member of the Pacific Rim Countries and that Alaska's natural trading partners are Japan, China and the countries of Asia. In that spirit they decided that all students would learn either Chinese or Japanese. The Superintendent planned courses in entrepreneurship and sought teachers who would use 'project-oriented' learning' as a way to get the students into the habit of being purposeful in the application of what they learned. The Superintendent recruited faculty who shared this view.

HOW DEMING'S IDEAS ENTERED THE SCHOOL

The new faculty shared the vision of the Superintendent, but among them was one who was extremely enthusiastic. David Langford saw in the plans for the school of opportunity to fulfil his own ambitions as a teacher.

According to the Superintendent and David Langford, the school ran with enthusiasm for the first three years. Then it began to 'flatten out'. A fortunate turn of events changed the school's approach. During one of David's excursions to the 'lower 48', visiting Gilbert High School in Phoenix, he attended a session with an executive in a company involved in the quality movement. David was intrigued with TQM concepts. He followed up by reading as much about quality as he could, by talking with executives who were in companies applying TQM and by quizzing the quality experts he could find. David concluded that Deming's ideas could and should be applied in education. David persuaded the Superintendent, Larrae Rocheleau, to accompany him to another Deming seminar, and both men came away convinced that Deming's message would apply to their school.

David began by introducing Deming's ideas into his classes in business and in a special course he dubbed 'Continuous Improvement'. In this latter course the students read *Out of the Crisis* while David prepared workbooks for the students to use to develop data on their own study habits. Although the first efforts were far from perfect, the students took to the instruction with great enthusiasm. By applying simple run charts to their own study habits they began to discover and remove inefficiencies from their own lives. One student reported that whereas he had *thought* he was spending two hours in study, by keeping records he found he was spending only about 35 minutes!

David experimented with different approaches to overcoming student indifference to learning. Before he became involved in quality management techniques, he observed a general lack of motivation on the part of the students. He found, however, that if he spent a great deal of time at the start of the term (some would say an inordinate amount of time,) discussing such questions as 'Why are we here?', 'What do we want to get out of the course?', 'What are the barriers to success?', and, in general, examining the question, 'What does it mean to do this course with quality?', he caused the students to examine their own objectives and thereby alter their attitudes. The result was that in the remainder of the term, the student enthusiasm, drive and efficiency so improved that they learned much more than they otherwise would have learned. What was 'lost' at the start of the term, was more than regained in the remainder. It takes a great deal of courage to break with tradition this way. It could not have been done without the support and encouragement of the Superintendent. Those who would attempt something similar should keep this point in mind.

Having taught elsewhere, David was impressed with what a difference the explicit examination of quality made in student performance. Through this dialogue, the students developed their own sense of why they studied. When I asked students about this they concurred, saying, 'We really didn't understand before. Then we just did what we were told, but didn't think about it.'

An unexpected dividend was that the students' enthusiasm for this approach to learning began to affect the other teachers. Indeed, it is fair to say that the students in David's class in 'Continuous Improvement' became the shock troops of the school. Gradually, some, but not all, of the teachers began to follow David's example and adopted similar approaches. The students in these classes became 'co-managers' of their education. The teachers became enablers, not task masters. Morale improved. Motivation improved. With the Superintendent's enthusiastic support, TQM was launched.

PURPOSE IN EDUCATION

One of the basic tenets of Deming's teachings is that individual workers cannot know what to do to contribute to the enterprise if they do not understand and give support to its purpose. Furthermore, this purpose must be constant and not changing every day. It must be a purpose which attracts their hearts and minds. The students, the faculty and the administration spent considerable time developing a consensus about the purposes of the school. Given a purpose for the school, the teachers and students translated the school purpose into the purposes of their classes. The students could relate these to their own purposes. This affirmation took time, but it provided a good basis for attacking the task of applying continuous improvement, for now everyone knew the direction they should take.

One weakness, which became apparent later, was that the people who work at the dormitories were not part of this consensus building. During my visit it became clear that this deficiency would have to be rectified. The classrooms and the dormitories are physically separated by being at opposite ends of the campus. During a session with the dorm personnel, it became evident that they are eager to be involved. Actions are now under way to include not only the dorm personnel, but also food service, office staff and maintenance personnel.

The faculty and students have continued to work on the educational objectives of the school. See, for example, the statement of purpose adopted through consensus reproduced at the end of this report (Appendix 2). The purpose of the school was not crafted on high and handed down to the students. Because it is the product of consensus building at all levels, the statement of purpose of the school permeates all aspects of campus life. I believe this is unique among educational institutions at all levels.

SPREADING THE COMPETENCE

As more of the teachers began to show an interest, David and the Superintendent developed workshops in which the teachers could develop their skills and understanding of continuous improvement.

In this effort they were handicapped by not having been trained in TQM themselves. They attempted to adapt whatever they could read in various sources. They acquired videotapes from the Juran Institute, from MIT, from Bill Conway, from anywhere they could (on a limited budget). They also read widely in the literature of the social science. The Superintendent, for example, was greatly influenced by the writings of Covey. The faculty are aware of this lack of training and are eager to learn.

On the other hand, I concluded that their isolation from the main-stream thinking was an advantage. They had to learn to recognize and solve their own problems. Had they been exposed to the 'advantages' of training, it seems likely to me they would not have been so bold and would not have taken the novel paths they did. They are now positioned to be very critical learners and in some areas, leaders.

The students exhibit a surprising maturity with respect to TQM. What they know, they know well. At the end of this report I have reproduced a student analysis of the problems they see other people (and themselves) having in changing paradigms (Appendix 4). What they found, on their own, in MEHS, describes many of my own experiences, on four continents, over ten years.

WHAT I SAW DURING MY VISIT

During my four-day visit I met and talked with students, faculty, administration, dorm managers, the nurse, the counsellors and a few people from Sitka and the Sitka school system (across the channel, on the 'big island'). To my knowledge, this is the only school in the world which is attempting to apply Deming's ideas to the *totality* of education. I know of many schools which are doing some parts of TQM, but no other school, at any level, to my knowledge is trying to do it all in an integrated fashion.

I looked at student homework (mostly done on a computer), talked with the students, quizzed them about their understanding of what they were doing, and what they had learned. I talked with the faculty, trying to judge their commitment and understanding of TQM. I talked with the administration.

My reaction? Amazement and admiration. A young girl, of Tlingit/Haida descent, in her junior year, asked me about how to get into Harvard. Another girl, probably about 17 years of age, talked seriously with me about how people in industry are working to remove the effect of fear which an executive of high level might engender in a worker with whom he talked. Or wanting to know if so many levels were required. In a biology class, taught by Gary Jarvill, I reviewed the HyperCards the students had prepared as a form of 'computerized-mini-encyclopaedia' suitable for instruction. Only a few minutes of examination of the student prepared HyperCards, and I understood that no one could prepare this information in such a form without having learned it very well. One student's deck of HyperCards had seventy-six cards in it, each one linked to the others in a logical fashion. By clicking on one card the user could enquire into the influence of soil chemistry on the plant. By clicking on another icon the user could learn about the economic importance of the plant in Alaska or how the plant reproduces itself and spreads.

From these HyperCards anyone can see that the students have learned some *facts* about biology. But more importantly, from the way the facts are organized, it is also clear that they have learned how to relate these facts to one another in a logical fashion. In this stage of learning, they could use the HyperCard structure as a tool. But beyond that, they had learned how to organize their knowledge of facts. In my own experiences as a teacher, I always found this the hardest to teach *at the college level*. Here I saw it happening with high-school juniors.

In the class on entrepreneurship, taught by Marty Johnson, I watched the students prepare and package smoked salmon for sale in Japan. The students had used a taste panel of local Japanese to determine the flavour and texture Japanese people liked the most. Then they developed a standard procedure to produce the same taste and texture every time. To achieve the desired taste required using a certain kind of salmon, exposing it for a certain time and temperature, using a special brining solution, which they had determined experimentally yielded the proper taste, and a certain amount of time in the smoke from the right mixture of wood shavings, using slices of the fish cut to a certain thickness and size. By studying the packages of smoked fish sold in Japan they developed an attractive package which would fit in small Japanese refrigerators. They developed their own distinctive label, in Japanese, of course, and they test-marketed the product in Japan. In 1989 the students received an order for $140,000-worth of the smoked salmon that they could not fulfil. At the time of my visit they had received another order, this time from a Korean company, which would amount to over $600,000 per year! Their current problem was that the company, which had asked to take on the task of fulfilling the order, did not want to follow their quality standards. I do not know what they will decide to do.

The high-school class is becoming the source of local expertise just as the Superintendent had hoped it would become, though I doubt he expected it to happen so soon and on such a scale.

In this class I had good discussions with the teachers and students over how to use SPS to gain information on the variability and perhaps to reduce it.

The students and faculty have not yet studied design of experiment. The course on entrepreneurship is obviously a wonderful situation in which to learn about it. Ron Moen has been teaching design of experiment to junior high-school students. When I telephoned him for help, he was greatly interested in sharing his work. Ron and David hope to meet this summer and to build on Ron's experiences.

One course which I saw only by videotape, but which impressed me greatly, is the 'Ropes course', which is similar to the Outward Bound courses which have been so much publicized. At the start of the school year all the incoming students and all of the faculty participate in this course. The students (protected by suitable safety harnesses) undertake a number of challenging activities such as climbing to a high place and falling backwards to be caught by their classmates, or leaping to grasp a trapeze bar about 30 feet high, or jumping from a shaky platform, high on top of a pole, with safety provided by classmates on the end of a rope. In another exercise, they take turns leading one another blindfolded through parts of the Alaskan wilderness.

Superintendent Larrae Rocheleau explained the objective of the course this way:

> When the students arrive they are dependent. Their paradigm says, 'I can't do it because you don't do what you are supposed to do.' They look to *you* for guidance and support. By being challenged they begin to become independent. In this mode they say, 'Yes, I can do it.' They become not only self-confident, but also self-centered. They say 'I' a great deal. Finally, some recognize interdependence and they say, 'We can do it together.' The objective of the course is not only to give self-confidence, but to move the students from 'You', to 'I' to 'We'.

Larrae believes that this course is an essential prerequisite to the success of all the other courses. Many of the students need to establish their self-confidence, otherwise they will not try the things they are asked to do. They will be unable to form teams. As I see it, MEHS is trying to develop *autonomous team players*.

I did not appreciate how important the 'Ropes course' is as a deliberate attempt to build character, until I met some of the first-year students who came from a small community. I was reminded of youngsters I had met in the hills of Kentucky who came from similar (if warmer) rural backgrounds. When bused to the county schools, they often do not take to the classroom situations where they are made to feel inferior. Thrust into an entirely new life in which they had to learn new habits of thought and in a very short time become independent learners, I saw many of them turn away, not because they were not bright enough, but because the system judged them on artificial grounds. An educational system which ignores the psychological aspects of the students' prior preparation (or lack of it) forever assigns them to the lowest rungs on the social ladder. In my view it is no educational system at all. Such an approach does not look upon the youngsters as humans to be developed. Rather, it looks upon the young generations as crop to be winnowed. The 'Ropes course', to the casual outsider, might look like a lot of fun (it is) but not as a serious element of education. The 'Ropes course' does for *all* the students what competitive athletic contests are supposed to do for a few. In my opinion, it does it better.

DEMING'S IMPACT ON THE CURRICULUM

David's class has rewritten Deming's fourteen points so that their application to education is more apparent (see Appendix 3). They have also identified the various 'customer−supplier relationships'. After flow-charting some of the activities of the school and studying the objectives of the various teachers, the students and teachers, together, set about restructuring the system. (The words *'perestroika'* and *'glasnost'* often appear on the walls of the school, even in the Superintendent's office!) The class schedule was changed to combine functions. For example, when the students write a report for the entrepreneurship class, the report is accepted as part of the homework in English. (*Eliminate barriers between departments*.)* The students are expected to turn in a perfect report. The phrase 'No excuses' appears everywhere. The students say, 'We are after quality, not quantity. What is the point in writing a number of mediocre essays? Instead, let us write a few reports, but let them be excellent.' The English teachers, Kathleen McCrossin and Ruth Fairchild, insist on perfect spelling, on good style, on correct grammar . . . in short on excellence. Actually, after an enquiry into what characterizes a perfect essay, the students do not have to rely on the teacher's judgement. They supply their own. (*Eliminate mass inspection*.)

I inspected a few hyper-cards prepared by students on the theme 'How to write a perfect five-paragraph essay'. In this essay they discussed how to choose an appropriate title, how to write an introductory paragraph, how to structure a logical argument, how to develop conclusions and how to avoid clichés. Having, themselves, written such a learning instrument, they were equipped to apply the criteria themselves.

There are no grades, no 'incompletes', no 'Fs'. The task is not complete until the work is perfect. The students have defined perfection for themselves and, therefore, know how to aim for it. (*Create joy in work*.)

Incidentally, the first computer course begins by using the computer to teach speed typing. All students understand that they will do their homework on a computer, using word processors, spreadsheets, graphics programs and so on. They appreciate the importance of being able to type well, because they know they will be doing so much of it. The typing exercise is the only one in which I saw the computer being used in the 'drill and grill' mode. All other activities seemed to be creative; using the computer as a tool to accomplish something, as opposed to learning computers as an end in themselves.

In the business class I watched students preparing spreadsheets to reflect what it will cost them to live in their chosen life style after they graduate. They take into account mortgage payments, taxes, cost-of-living changes, projects for cost of transportation, schooling and so forth. In this way they learn the importance of inflation, interest rates and taxation. They analyse

---

* Sentences in italics are each one of Deming's fourteen points.

what it will require to live as they wish and in the process learn about graphical presentation of data, about simple finance, about business. I saw a great deal of mutual learning as students compared their results and taught one another some of the tricks of financial analysis. Because the students are working creatively on something which interests them, the teacher does not have to be in the room when classes start or during the class time. My host sat with me to discuss the course, and from time to time a student would come with a question. Most of the times the questions were not answered but instead the teacher would pose a question or make a suggestion for something to try.

My visit coincided with the November elections. In the Alaska issues and government class, taught by Brenda Campen, I saw the result of some 'desk-top publishing'. The students had prepared a small guide to voting, including a very well-written essay on the importance of voting, an analysis of some of the propositions on the ballot and some of the candidates' positions. When I first read it, I thought it had been sent from outside the school, it was so professionally written.

DISCIPLINE

Student behaviour problems have all but vanished. I examined the data from the front office on the rate of 'conduct report' instances. In the last period examined, the number of students involved in disciplinary action varied between 1.5 per cent and 0.5 per cent of the student population.

All categories of discipline problems are analysed separately (using the spreadsheet Excel) and examined graphically. There were a few minor errors in determining how to set the control limits. When I re-organized the plotting, it could be seen that the process goes out of control every weekend. The faculty is thinking of what to do about this 'special cause'. One faculty member, however, was concerned over the very low rate of discipline reports. Her concern was that there may be too much discipline and that this may result in psychomatic illnesses. I proposed that an analysis be made of visits to the nurse to see if they correlated with exams, and so on.

I came away enthusiastic over what I saw. The attempt is genuine. The school is obviously at the beginning of a journey. The faculty is far back on the learning curve but well aware of what they have yet to learn. They do not practise the self-delusion I encounter so often in my industrial visits. They know they do not know and are committed to doing something about it. The most prominent attitude is one of frustration at seeing a vision of what could be and having so far to go. But in my eyes, they have come a long way and have no need to apologize to anyone. I compare their achievements with what I know goes on elsewhere in the United States. I am aware of the poor preparation that many of the students have before they start at MEHS. Through the use of TQM, the staff is able to devote more attention to each individual student. The students also help one another to become independent learners. This school is demonstrating the true power of education.

The extraordinary results MEHS produces with their students recalls the remarks of Hutchins, when President of the University of Chicago, 'No one knows what can be done with education because we have never really tried.'

CHALLENGES

When a school undertakes such a radical change in education, it is bound to encounter new problems. The most difficult one to resolve is concerned with the evaluation of students and staff. The faculty, the students and the administration all agree that evaluation is destructive to the learning process. Yet when the students apply for entrance to a college, they are expected to show the usual grades and test scores.

The faculty is confident the students will succeed wherever they go. Of the students who graduated from MEHS 47 per cent have entered college and are still there or have graduated. This is significantly better then the nation-wide average.

Students who have left MEHS and are now in college report back that they are disappointed to find that the environments into which they have gone are not 'learning environments'. I was asked by several students to advise them where they could go to continue their studies of quality and be in a quality environment. I had to say I did not know of a single school, anywhere, that might meet their needs. Perhaps one of the smaller liberal arts schools, such as Antioch College, might be appropriate. I did not know (but I did put in a good word for Dartmouth College!).

The Principal, Bill Denkinger, frets over the fact that he is expected to rank the faculty in his reports to the State. He sees such ranking as destructive to morale, but he is stuck in a system which is designed for a different paradigm. One the other hand, the faculty is anxious to know how they are doing and wants feedback. They are sincere in their desire to understand if they are doing the right things.

Another serious problem arises because the faculty is essentially self-taught in quality management. I was their first visitor who has seriously studied TQM. The teachers, students and staff were hungry for lessons in TQM methods techniques. They were especially weak in statistics, none of the faculty ever having had a course in its application to quality improvement. Traditional educational statistics courses are usless for a TQM situation. I did what I could, in a short time, to make some suggestions. Better than that, however, I used the occasion to do a little telephoning to people in the quality movement whom I knew would be interested. Everyone on whom I have called has indicated a willingness to help, and the people at MEHS are eager to learn. I believe, therefore, that this matter of getting consultation and instruction in various aspects of TQM for the faculty will be relatively easy to solve.

I only wish I could find the same thirst for learning in the rest of the country.

IMPLICATIONS FOR EDUCATION IN THE USE OF TQM

I went to Sitka because I had heard that they were using TQM in education. What I saw exceeded my expectations. It is also clear that what has been done at MEHS cannot be 'cloned' and simply reproduced elsewhere. Mt Edgecumbe High School is a residential school. The enrolment is very small, compared to the national average. The ratio of students to teachers is smaller than the national average. What we have at MEHS is a small laboratory in which it has been demonstrated that quality management principles work in education.

The staff at MEHS is eager to share what they have learned. However, they are beginning to be swamped with phone calls and letters, and their fax machine runneth over. During my visit a few of the faculty discussed with me the potential of holding a conference during the summer of 1992, to which educators from around the United States would be invited. They have considered running a mini-summer school on their campus, complete with high-school students, faculty and administrators from a dozen schools, as a way to provide 'seeds' which might flourish elsewhere. They have also considered a research conference at which there would be papers on various aspects of the experiment thus far. Planning continues. Probably what they need most of all now, is the addition of a few more staff so they can devote more time to teaching others, to planning for the conference and simply to host the number of visitors who can be expected to show up on their doorstep in the coming year.

It is well known that the educational system in the United States has been failing its citizens. Political leaders, from the President down, have issued solemn pronouncements and 'goals'. Those who understand TQM have been unhappy and critical of these statements, because they consist of goals without plans to achieve them. These officials apply the managerial techniques which have already ruined much of American enterprise. We expect them to have similar unsatisfactory results when applied in education.

I only wish that every one of our political leaders would read the student's interpretation of Deming's fourteen points applied to education (see Appendix 3), especially point no. 12.

Having made such critical remarks, I have also to admit that even those of us who know about TQM in industry have not, heretofore, provided anyone with clear directions on how to apply TQM in education. Frankly, we haven't known how to begin.

The experiences at MEHS, however, now change all that. MEHS provides everyone with an example of how to start. MEHS is an important laboratory for the national cause of education, and as such deserves the support and encouragement of all who care about the education of the young. TQM should not be viewed as another educational fad that will come and go. Mt Edgecumbe High School has adopted TQM as a part of its culture.

The MEHS example should provide the courage to try TQM in education on a larger scale and to learn *how to make it work*. Having observed one another falter along the road to quality, the students and staff at MEHS say, '*No excuses*'.

Robert Gordon Sproul, President of the University of California, used to say, 'Youth must be served in its day, or not at all.' Let us begin.

REFERENCE

Covey, Stephen R. (1989) *The Seven Habits of Highly Effective People*, New York: Simon & Schuster.

APPENDIX 1

Reading the following analysis of the problems of transforming a culture makes it clear that these youngsters are ready to become consultants in TQM. Their observations parallel those of every consultant with whom I have ever discussed the problem.

The transformation process

The Continuous Improvement Process Media class at Mt Edgecumbe High School is responsible for presenting the process to other students, teachers, administrators, parents, business people and other community members. Through their experience they have identified the following transformation process that people typically progress through when moving from the old management system to the new paradigm for quality improvement. It should be noted that some individuals begin at different levels.

1 Oh no, another thing to do.
2 This is interesting, but a waste of my time (or some other reaction).
3 Works for you, but it could not work for us; usually followed by listing reasons why it cannot be done at their site.
4 Denial that it could actually be working.
5 Questioning – about initial reaction in no. 1.
6 Angry/mad/frustrated/defensive.
7 Seek more information and look for transference of theories and applications or completely reject.
8 Like the idea, but no action; advance lip-service.
9 Attempt involvement.
10 Enthusiasm and relief.
11 Progress not as fast as they like.
12 Understanding and then profound knowledge.

APPENDIX 2

The following statement was prepared by the students and staff of the school.

Mt Edgecumbe High School, Sitka, Alaska: mission statement

Mt Edgecumbe High School is a paradigm shift in philosophy to the usual school programme. Each curricular area offers innovative teaching methods that not only enhance opportunities for Mt Edgecumbe High School students, but serve as models for other high schools.

Mt Edgecumbe High School provides new and important education opportunities for Alaskan students. The school places high expectations upon students, administrators and staff. Programme and curriculum are based upon a conviction that students have a great and often unrealized potential. The school prepares students to make the transition to adulthood helping them to determine what they want to do and develop the skills and the self-confidence to accomplish their goals.

Mt Edgecumbe High School students are required to pursue rigorous academic programmes that encourage students to work at their highest levels. Administrators, teachers, and other staff are required to keep current on educational advances and to initiate innovative, challenging and stimulating classroom programmes and activities.

Teachers and staff analyse issues to anticipate future social and economic needs of Alaska, such as Alaska's economic position among the Pacific Rim nations, and to integrate an educational approach to these issues into the curriculum. A strong curriculum in English, Social Studies, Mathematics, Science/Marine Science, Computers/Business, Career Exploration, Asian Languages and Physical Education is provided.

Special emphasis is placed on the study of both historical and contemporary topics specific to Alaska. Study of the history, culture and languages of the Pacific Rim are a major curricular area and to the extent possible Pacific Rim studies are applied across the curriculum.

Vocational education is stressed through entrepreneurship and work study. Cottage industries are run by students. Traditional vocational education is offered on a limited basis.

Opportunities for leadership, public service and entrepreneurship are integrated into the programme, both during and after regular school hours. The school prepares students for the academic demands of being away from home and managing time effectively. Some students are selected for admission who are having a difficult time with their local environment. Staff work within available resources to help these students become productive citizens.

Mt Edgecumbe High School as a boarding school offers students a wide range of support activities in both academic and residential programmes, to assure the success of all students. To facilitate personal growth and decision-making skills, each student is assisted, guided and challenged to make choices about future academic or technical schooling and alternative methods of making a living.

APPENDIX 3

The following modification of Deming's fourteen points was prepared by David Langford's class, 'Continuous Improvement'.

Modified Deming points for continuous improvement of education

1 Create constancy of purpose towards improvement of students and service. Aim to create the best-quality students capable of improving all forms of processes and entering meaningful positions in society.
2 Adopt the new philosophy. Educational management must awaken to the challenge, must learn their responsibilities, and take on leadership for change.
3 Work to abolish grading and the harmful effects of rating people.
4 Cease dependence on testing to achieve quality. Eliminate the need for inspections on a mass basis (standardized achievement test, minimum graduation exams, etc.) by providing learning experiences which create quality performance.
5 Work with the educational institutions from which students come. Minimize total cost of education by improving the relationship with student sources and helping to improve the quality of students coming into your system. A single source of students coming into a system such as junior high students moving into a high school is an opportunity to build long-term relationships of loyalty and trust for the benefit of students.
6 Improve constantly and forever the system of student improvement and service, to improve quality and productivity.
7 Institute education and training on the job for students, teachers, classified staff and administrators.
8 Institute leadership. The aim of supervision should be to help people use machines, gadgets and materials to do a better job.
9 Drive out fear, so that everyone may work effectively for the school system. Create an environment which encourages people to speak freely.
10 Break down barriers between departments. People in teaching, special education, accounting, food service, administration, curriculum development and research, etc. must work as a team. Develop strategies for increasing the co-operation amongst groups and individual people.
11 Eliminate slogans, exhortations and targets for teachers and students asking for perfect performance and new levels of productivity. Exhortations create adversarial relationships. The bulk of the causes of low

quality and low productivity belong to the system and thus lie beyond the control of teachers and students.

12 Eliminate work standards (quotas) on teachers and students (e.g. raise test scores by 10%, and lower drop-outs by 15%). Substitute leadership.

13 Remove barriers that rob the students, teachers and management (principles, superintendents and central office support staff) of their right to pride and joy of workmanship. This means, *inter alia*, abolition of the annual or merit rating and of management by objectives. The responsibility of all educational managers must be changed from quantity to quality.

14 Institute a vigorous programme of education and self-improvement for everyone.

15 Put everybody in the school to accomplish the transformation. The transformation is everybody's job.

APPENDIX 4

Here is an analysis of the 'customer' and 'supplier' relationships in a high school system, prepared by the students in their Continuous Improvement class.

Customer	Supplier	Services
Students	Teachers	System management Curriculum design Counselling Leadership Materials and equipment
	Administrators	Systems development and analysis Materials and equipment
	School Boards	Policy
Teachers	Administrators	Materials and equipment

This is how the students analyse different teaching styles and the resulting effect on student learning processes.

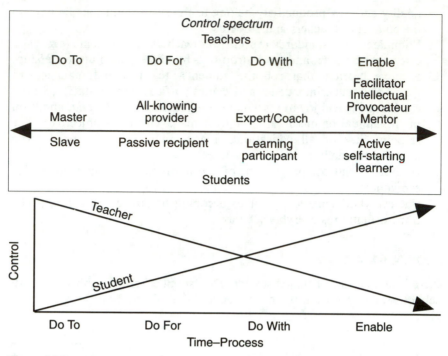

Figure 16.1

17 The Buckpool experience of developing quality systems

Geoff Hampton

The phrase 'quality management' is by definition attractive to managers, who if only superficially would wish to be associated with this term. However, when it comes to analysing precisely what this means in the context of schools, many are deterred whilst others continue to pay lip-service to a phrase which provides some gratification by even a fleeting association. The problem is that to pursue quality management goals is to strike at the heart of most conventional school management practices, a task which has to be achieved against the backdrop of the 1988 Education Act, with its defined targets and prescribed curriculum content. School managers who are sincere in their desire to adopt a quality management approach will be both inviting and demanding active participation and openness at all levels. Those who do not feel truly comfortable with this situation should not get beyond an initial flirtation with a concept that they may consider desirable but which in reality will be unattainable.

If schools wish to embrace 'quality' then they must develop a culture and climate which will facilitate this. A school's culture and ethos will guide actions and influence the attitudes and opinions of all who come into contact with it. A definition of precisely what is meant by those who come into contact with schools represents a crucial starting point, for it becomes a first attempt at identifying the customer or client group. At Buckpool this is perceived as including the staff, governors, the pupils and their parents, as well as the wider community that the school serves. We have also come to realize that there is also a far wider group of customers, which embraces everyone who comes into contact with the school and everyone whom the school contacts. Buckpool's desire to embrace quality systems arrived from a genuine need for a renaissance following the appointment of a new Headteacher, after a period of some uncertainty.

Buckpool opened as a secondary modern school in the early 1970s, with a new grammar school also being completed in close proximity at around the same time. The selection process for the grammar school by entry examination led to the pupils of the secondary modern school's becoming second-class citizens. The legacy of Buckpool's secondary modern label is still 'alive' in the minds of some parents, even though for the majority of the school's life, with the abolition of the selection process it has been designated as a 'comprehensive' with an intake of pupils of all abilities. Buckpool developed a reputation for poor discipline and was considered a 'rough' school by those parents located in the more affluent parts of its catchment area. A highly critical report by Her Majesty's Inspectorate published in 1985 was followed by the retirement of the Headteacher and two of the three Deputies. Thus, the way was prepared for the new Head to establish his pattern upon the school, the climate of change had been created and was further developed by the high staff turnover during the next two years. Over 40 per cent of the staff left; included amongst these were the early retirement of the longest-serving deputy and the promotion of the female deputy. This was accomplished by the publication of a new curriculum and staffing structure in April 1989 which, for the first time, gave a rationale to the staffing structure and which ultimately led to job descriptions for all staff. Statements concerning 'quality', although implicit within the content of both the overall staffing and curriculum plan and within individual job descriptions, were not made directly. The structure was more directly concerned with the emerging National Curriculum and the fact that the management structure of the school should be designed to ensure the efficient delivery of that curriculum. The staffing structure of the school was based on a series of circles of responsibility; these later became associated with the concept of *Quality Circles* but at this time were concerned only with allowances and areas of responsibility: the Senior Management Team; Curriculum Area Co-ordinators; Cross-curriculum Co-ordinators; Year-group Co-ordinators; and Development Co-ordinators. This structure, although slightly amended to cater for changes of personnel and further developments with the National Curriculum, forms the basis of the school's organization today. Although considered radical at the time of its introduction, it has served the school well as a basis for further development and growth.

A considerable amount of in-service training was invested in the Curriculum Area Co-ordinators; their position as senior middle managers had to be established and there was a clear need for their development as a team. They also needed to share the goals of the Senior Management Team and had to strive for the same 'quality' approach. The same principles were being pursued within the other groups of managers; those responsible for Cross-curriculum issues, the Year-group Co-ordinators and the Development Co-ordinators. Clearly, this is not an overnight task; if it had an obvious beginning as detailed earlier, it is difficult to see it having an end. New challenges constantly present themselves and the teams that now exist must continue to be developed and refined. As Henry Neave states when considering the introduction of a quality approach:

> All people in management have a role to play. An important element in overcoming fear of change is to get everyone to help paddle the canoe.

However, there can be few managers who are unaware that something is going on these days with regard to something called quality, most seem to be unaware that it's anything much to do with them — apart from seeing that, one way or another, others do it.

(Neave 1990)

Buckpool has also consciously sought to increase its involvement and dialogue with its local community. The majority of the initial links with the local community were centred on meeting the leisure needs of the young mothers of the area. This led the school into having to address the provision of childcare requirements at a very early stage. The initial *ad hoc* arrangements were clearly unsatisfactory, and a playgroup and crèche were opened within the school. A considerable number of these already existed in the locality; the Buckpool Playgroup and Crèche opened with a desire to prove that it was the 'best', and staff were recruited on this basis. The success of this facility was directly related to the quality of the provision, and this was confirmed when the Midland Bank decided to invest capital in the expansion of the facility. Midland were interested in creating a small number of high-quality day nurseries nationally to cater for the childcare needs of their employees. Their insistence on the development and monitoring of a 'quality' facility was part of the corporate image that they were attempting to achieve. This meshed in with the goals of the school and became an early example of the type of partnerships the school needed to pursue to achieve the quality goals it had set for itself.

The relationship with the school's community users continued to flourish, and several individuals were now starting to express the need for more vocationally orientated courses. Adults present within GCSE classes quickly became an established part of the school. The GCSE is the most common examination taken by 16-year-olds and is the qualification obtained upon leaving school. GCSE results also provide the basis for access to employment opportunities, further education and other training courses. In this case each course was negotiated individually so that any fears could be allayed prior to commencement. This started to have a fundamental effect upon the attitudes and perceptions of all of the participants in this segment of the education process, bringing about a change in the attitude of staff, pupils, parents and the adult learners. However, a clear need still existed for discrete courses and information-giving sessions that would be targeted particularly at the adult-user group. An appropriate venue for this type of activity was created by the development of a continuing partnership with Marks and Spencer, the national high-street retailer. A senior manager from a local store was committed to the idea of furthering links with schools. At Buckpool this became a tangible reality when it was agreed that prior to the opening of a new store, locally, all of the staff would complete their Marks and Spencer group training at the school. The cost of converting a room into a conference facility was borne by the store which then utilized it daily for training purposes for a period of three months. From careful observation and further dialogue the school's senior management learned a lot about how this major company tackled issues of quality which were of paramount importance to the store. This has been pursued further by two members of the Senior Management Team undertaking teacher placements at Marks and Spencer on a reciprocal basis with managers from the store. The early desire for achieving a quality product and introducing quality systems was now starting to have some meaning, as the initial ideas of the Senior Management Team could be measured against examples of existing good practice in an external environment.

All of these developments within the school were being mirrored by developments within its local authority. The Advisory Service of Dudley Local Education Authority were engaged in some collaborative work with the British Standards Institute looking at aspects of BS 5750 which might apply to schools. This was the quality standard of industry, and it was felt that there were many aspects of the Standard which could apply to services and schools in general. If the standards were indeed relevant, it would help parents to identify those schools where quality can be assured across all aspects of the school's life. The developments at Buckpool towards a quality approach led to the school being invited to join Dudley's Advisory Team for training for BS 5750. Following the absorption and completion of its training the school management decided to evaluate their current level of progress and conduct a preliminary assessment of the procedures and structures that had already been implemented.

The commitment of the school's senior management to continue to pursue the goal of becoming a quality organization was assured. The successes that had already been achieved and the fundamental shift that had occurred in pupil and staff attitudes meant that to settle for anything less would have shown little regard for the achievements of a considerable number of people. Buckpool had progressed from being a cloistered environment to one which was now embracing the standards and philosophies of managers and organizations external to the school. Furthermore, the increasing involvement of the wider community within the school had led to an attitudinal change. The classroom was no longer exclusively the domain of the teacher and their pupils, and the interaction within the school was between a clientele aged from 3 months to those of pensionable age. This was no overnight process, or one which could easily be measured, but quite subtly and clearly the change occurred.

The next step was to attempt systematically to review and monitor progress – not merely of systems and structures, although this was clearly of importance, but also at the level of what was occurring in the classroom and regarding the impact that all of this was having on the client group that was external to the school: parents; established partners; and other members of the local community. In order to reflect this, the Development underwent a change of title and shift of emphasis. They were renamed the Teaching and Learning Styles Group, and assumed a much clearer role not simply for the development of ideas and initiatives but also for the monitoring of their impact within the teaching and learning environment. The job description of a new Deputy Head appointment at this time also reflected the increasing need for monitoring and evaluation. It was also considered important that senior management should attempt to express why it felt the continuing pursuit of quality systems was important. This was summarized as follows:

- to help reduce pressures on staff in a rapidly changing world by the pursuit of common goals;
- to produce consistency across all staff;
- to try to show 'value-added';
- to involve all staff in improving delivery;
- to break down barriers between groups of staff still further;
- to underpin the central theme of the Development Plan, which was 'Quality Experience in the Classroom';
- to assist in the marketing of the school.

The decision was also taken that the partnerships that the school had pursued should be developed further if possible and that new partnerships would be sought. It was recognized that the industrial origins of BS 5750 would need to be explored further so that companies achieving this goal could be evaluated and utilized as part of our ambitions for achieving a quality product. Although this is an ongoing process, there have been some notable successes which have been of mutual benefit to all parties.

The goals of the school were explained to existing partners, and as a result of this Marks and Spencer were persuaded to have a more direct involvement in the school's curriculum. A series of aims for the partnership between Buckpool and Marks and Spencer were agreed:

1 to place the pupils and the curriculum at the centre of the partnership;
2 to plan specifically and strategically so that both sides of the partnership have clear objectives and responsibilities;
3 to identify areas of the curriculum where the quality of teaching and learning can be enhanced through partnership.
4 to develop resources jointly in identified areas of the curriculum which are relevant, challenging and increasing pupils' business skills and understanding;
5 to extend pupil awareness of the nature of the world of work, both within and beyond the formal curriculum;
6 to maintain a balance in the partnership so that both sides have commitments which they perceive to be worthwhile and realistic;
7 to enable as many pupils as possible to benefit from the partnership;
8 to meet regularly to review and evaluate current provisions and to plan for the future.

A quality work-experience programme was developed in conjunction with Marks and Spencer which involves all pupils when they are in Year ten. Marks and Spencer personnel also became involved in the planning and delivery of a module of the school's GCSE business studies course. They also sponsor an environmental awards programme which encourages pupils to enhance their local environment in their leisure time; there are also links from this to the science curriculum. The principle behind this partnership was that it should be of mutual benefit, and central to it was the common pursuit of quality goals and outcomes by all participants. Encouraged by this, it was decided to target other organizations whilst continuing to develop a clear knowledge of issues surrounding 'quality'.

A local manufacturer of wheelchairs and scooters for disabled people approached the school, having considered other schools with whom to form a 'compact' link. One function of compacts is to facilitate links between schools and local companies by providing the necessary introductions and ensuring that there is a shared perception of the benefits of such links. Their decision to select Buckpool was partly related to an affinity with the personnel with whom they had come into contact, but more fundamentally was to do with the common pursuit of quality goals. The company, Sunrise Medical, is a UK subsidiary of the largest producer of products for the disabled in the United States and was actively pursuing BS 5750 which was ultimately awarded to the company in September 1992. Ian Burrows, Sunrise's UK Operations Director, believes that 'Because of our pursuit of excellence programme and goal of becoming a world class company, continual improvement and attention to Quality have become part of our culture and is evident in everything that the company tackles.'

The parent company within the United States have been associated with the quality 'movement' which has permeated throughout their management culture. Its transfer to the United Kingdom was ensured by the American origins of Sunrise Medical's managing director. The pairing with this company led the school into an immersion with a culture that demanded that things were done right first time, led by a team of managers who believed themselves to be 'simply the best'. From small beginnings the link grew to embrace pupils taking GCSE art who produced T-shirts, hats, badges and logos for the launch of a new company product. They were also present on the day to witness the national launch and see their products utilized. Videos have also been produced by pupils during media studies lessons which act as technical support and training to a world-wide network of service companies and distributors, giving details of general maintenance and repairs. These have been distributed world-wide. The success of the link was highlighted when a presentation was made to the first-ever International Partnerships Conference. From the school's point of view it gained enormously not simply from the tangible benefits of the projects that were undertaken, but also from its close involvement with a company whose total ethos was bound up in quality. This relationship was further reinforced when the firm's Marketing Director agreed to become a member of the school's governing body. The daily pursuit of goals of BS 5750 and the importance of the systems and procedures needed to achieve this was now clearly understood.

This was developed further with another major partner for the school, the Midlands Electricity Board (MEB). They had some initial involvement with the school, again via a 'compact' pairing, and were supporting the delivery of a science module upon electricity. However, their involvement increased enormously when a former MEB employee was appointed to the school to increase the work upon partnerships and to facilitate the development of a new Business Centre. The MEB became the major sponsors of a facility that converted a classroom into a superbly equipped facility offering the latest computer technology and furnished to the highest possible standard. An indication of this was the fact that the furniture for the room was purpose-designed for this Business Centre and was made to include no metal parts to overcome problems of earth leakage. The completed Business Centre gave the school a quality resource with which to pursue other partnerships. Although this is an onging process, it had led to a close working relationship with the local Training and Enterprise Council (TEC), other departments of the local authority involved in the training and retraining of adults, and with the local university. It is anticipated that this resource will be greatly expanded in the near future and will become a Personal Learning Centre similar to a facility that we have studied in Georgia, Ohio. The current task is to ensure that all of the back-up systems are in place to ensure that it is not merely a cosmetically attractive package that is launched, but one which is supported by the correct management and organizational structures. Quality has to permeate throughout every level of this facility if the school is to embark upon this next logical and highly desirable phase. The Learning Centre will also give access for the pupils of the school to a high-quality resource which will be capable of producing packages to support their individual studies or needs.

The increased dialogue with the local TEC has led the school into a broader consideration of quality issues and systems and to the consideration of the Investors in People programme. This is a national initiative aimed at improving British business through the development of its people. It is intended to complement BS 5750, and identifies standards which organizations can use as benchmarks of their commitment to developing people. The initiative is being promoted nationally through the Training and Enterprise Councils, and the school's close involvement with the Dudley TEC through the Personal Learning Centre has led to an assimilation of the goals of Investors in People to complement our existing knowledge of BS 5750. This absorption of more than one quality system fits in with the view of the British Deming Association, which is named after a guru of the quality approach which believes that 'Users of the standard (BS 5750) should regard it as no more than some useful strides along the right road' (Crawford 1988).

The next step for Buckpool was to once again reflect and evaluate our progress towards our quality goals. Many of our procedures were now in place, these being categorized as the means by which our policies were carried out, with the policies being the statement of principle. To be meaningful these procedures also had to be a reality and not simply as in the case of some policy statements consigned to the filing cabinet.

The list of procedures that we now felt (July 1992) were in place was as follows:

Attendance	Learning support referral
Homework	Equal opportunities
Marketing	Information technology
Assessment	Pupil grouping
Reporting to parents	Learning environment
Records of achievement	School uniform
Profiling	Induction (pupils and staff)
Complaints	Teacher appraisal

Fundamental changes within the school were still occurring, and we were receiving some useful feedback from our customers about our progress. All of this was confirmed in August 1992 when the school achieved its best GCSE results ever and one of the major concerns of the senior management was overcome. The changes that had been introduced and the procedures that had been put into place, together with the alteration in staff, pupil and parental attitudes, had reaped rewards. However, with school league tables which ranked schools in order of the GCSE achievements of their pupils becoming increasingly important it was vital that the school achieved some tangible proof that the quality the senior managers believed they were increasingly witnessing was reflected in external examination outcome. Now this has been achieved, the school has continued its pursuit of quality goals by building upon areas where it has achieved success whilst setting this within the framework of a written manual.

The many initiatives that Buckpool has been involved with and has initiated, coupled with the considerable changes that have occurred within the school, have led to an undoubted improvement in the quality of service and 'product'. As Deming wrote:

> It will not suffice to have customers that are merely satisfied. An unhappy customer will switch. Unfortunately, a satisfied customer may also switch on the theory that he could not lose much, and might gain. Profit in business comes from repeat customers, customers that boast about your products and services, and bring friends with them.
>
> (Deming 1986)

There have been some successes but we are all too conscious of the fact that others are also improving. The current market-forces situation that confronts schools increasingly means that we have to view colleagues in other establishments as competitors and need to measure our success against their comparative achievements. Our initial concept of 'quality' was too narrow, as it was based upon an assumed knowledge of a concept that we now know strikes at the heart of our management philosophy. It has taken some time for us to achieve the much wider involvement that was necessary for quality improvement. There is still work to be done, particularly in our case with the school's governing body, which has recently had some changes of personnel as re-elections have occurred. However, what is clear is that, if we are to succeed with our quality goals, it will have to involve everyone who is both directly and indirectly associated with the school. The 'Action Plans' that all members of staff will possess as a result of the development plan and which will be related to its major targets are a step towards this, and the climate within the school is now conducive towards total submersion in quality goals. This would not be an imposition but more of a means of confirming what is already apparent. If there is a lesson to be learned from Buckpool, it is that there is certainly no 'quick fix' and to arrive at this point takes a lot of hard work.

Nor can this occur in isolation. It was a conscious policy of the school to involve itself with a broad cross-section of external customers; this led us into many challenging and demanding situations and called for the openness and trust that was referred to earlier as being of prime importance. This external exposure has brought its problems, but the benefits have been immeasurable. To pursue quality goals is to mesh in with the expectations and beliefs of a far wider client group which one can term as customers, and is to place the school into the same arena as others in pursuit of similar aims. However, once the brave step is taken, the previously all too prevalent concept amongst school managers of managing an 'oasis' with only occasional reference to the wider community surrounding the school is dispelled, and there are rich rewards awaiting and strength to be gained from those in pursuit of similar objectives.

Buckpool has not attempted to present itself merely with a new 'wrapper', for to do so would lead only to short term and superficial benefits. What it has attempted to do is to assimilate a completely new and challenging concept. If quality is truly now what we are about then we will succeed. This confidence does not come from some passing belief, but as a result of the fact that at its root quality is what we all expect. Why, then, should this be any different for schools and the education system? If schools now have more powers and responsibilities delegated to them, it is incumbent upon those who have the task of managing these institutions to ensure that we are continually satisfying customer requirements. This is no longer a luxury or just about meeting our own standards; in the brave new world that we have been confronted with our customers decide what the standards are – they have a choice. They will choose quality.

REFERENCES

British Standards Institution (1989) *BS 5750: A Positive Contribution to Better Business*, Milton Keynes, p. 6.

Crawford, J. (1988) 'An appraisal of BS 5750 in the light of the Deming philosophy', British Deming Association Research Committee, Working Paper, p. 1.

Deming, W.E. (1986) *Out of the Crisis*, in 'The Deming philosophy', *Total Quality Management*, Department of Trade and Industry, 1989, p. 10.

Neave, H.R. (1990) *The Deming Dimension*, Knoxville, TN: SPC Press, p. 407.

18 On the road to quality

Lewis A. Rhodes

*Total Quality Management (TQM) can provide the continuing informa-
tion and management support all school personnel need to get a little
better every day at teaching and learning.*

I was halfway out the door heading home when the office phone rang. 'You
don't know me', the voice said. 'I'm a middle school civics teacher in Sioux
City. I read your Deming articles', he continued, 'and I want you to know
that for me Deming is the last great leader of the Enlightenment. . . . He's
provided the final, and missing, element of natural law.'

Normally a comment like that would have surprised me. But this was one
more of a series of unanticipated reactions evoked by an article I had
written six months earlier about the acknowledged founder of the quality
movement, W. Edwards Deming (Rhodes 1990). What was going on? For
example, 'For an administrator who just "hung it up" after twenty-nine
years of trying to influence public education, I found Deming's words
heartening.' The most frequent reaction, however, was 'I thought I was the
only one who saw possibilities for schools!'

These and other reactions were different from those I'd heard regarding
other 'new' ideas in education, and they started me on a year-long quest to
discover why. This chapter suggests some answers.

WHY QUALITY? WHY NOW?

It's relatively easy to answer the question 'Why has America suddenly
become so interested in quality?' One need only listen to economic news
about America losing the productivity race to world-class competitors.

However, it's more difficult to find answers to why these ideas are
proving so attractive to educational practitioners, even before being touted
by university-based theorists or outside reformers. Why the growing interest
and commitment when there are no full working educational 'models' as
there are in other systemic programmes such as Outcome-Based Education?
Why such appeal, when few can even agree on a definition of 'quality'! And
why such seeming understanding now, after decades of exposure to many of
the same ideas in the writings of organizational researchers and theorists
such as Drucker, Herzberg, Argyris, Likert, Maslow and McGregor?

Apparently, Deming's words and ideas resonate with something that many people already personally believe is 'right'. The ideas seem to validate long-held feelings of working individuals who know they want to be effective in their jobs, and who by and large have given up on their organizations ever acting as if they believed it too. As one mid-manager, whose organization had sent her to a Deming seminar, realized with a shock: 'You mean our organization might actually do this . . . when now they're rewarding people for doing just the opposite?'

It's becoming clearer to me that the power of TQM concepts of Deming and others derives (1) from their psychological and value-driven base, and (2) from their 'totalness'. They deal with an organization's work processes as a single system.

As one elementary teacher wrote to me: 'Schools have a head start over industry in implementing quality concepts because we have a better foundation in psychology and human development than industry.' On the other hand, it's also clear why school people don't feel they can act on those other principles. The prevailing organizational paradigm has all the characteristics of a dysfunctional family. That is, its members believe that their present roles and relationships (isolated practitioners, relying on little but their own experience and expertise to respond to children's needs) are the way things are supposed to be. If there's a problem, they – not their 'family' – are the ones responsible and in need of fixing.

Until now, this dysfunctional condition has characterized most modern organizations – not just schools. Humans are born purpose-driven, trial-and-error learning, self-regulating organisms. But most organizational life limits this natural behaviour.

Regardless of what Herzberg's (1959) research might have told us about the power of intrinsic motivation and the ineffectiveness of external rewards, we could not imagine our work settings existing without grading, evaluating and labelling the people in it. We could not imagine that 'top' organizational leaders would be willing to give up what seemed like the power of problem-solving and decision-making to those at the 'bottom'. Moreover, with little experience to support it, we really haven't believed that total organizations could change.

So what happened? In a way, W. Edwards Deming has done for management of work processes what Roger Bannister did for the 4-minute mile. Deming's work in Japan provided evidence that something not believed possible was possible. Total organizations could change, it could cost less to produce quality results and the brain power of the workers on the front line could be an organization's most valuable resource.

A STUDENT'S-EYE VIEW

TQM has been termed 'a thought revolution in management' (Kim 1991). For business and industry, it created a fundamental paradigm shift by refocusing attention on the 'customer' whose needs, requirements and potentials must now drive the work process. In industrial TQM, *the voice of the customer* provides the information an organization must have to remain responsive. In education, our paradigm shift also involves seeing things through the eye of the customer.

I started out the year thinking that TQM could help all those involved in schools to view their actions from a perspective that had a 'customer/ student' at the centre. Today, my concept of student-centredness has changed, and along with it my understanding of the potentials of TQM for education. I had always been bothered by critics' declarations that education is too process-orientated and not sufficiently student-centred. On the contrary, I had observed that student-centredness already was the cause of some of education's most serious management problems. Underlying most decisions in educational practice has been the unstated belief: this is what's best for the kids. The separate acts of teachers, administrators and board members alike are driven by their personal views of what's best for children. Unfortunately, the potential power of this common focus has become instead a fundamental weakness because decisions are made in isolation, with no way to take advantage of relationships to others who share the same goal.

The work of schools has been student-centred in the same way that the work of a basketball team might be called 'hoop-centred'. The success of the whole team (organization) is tied directly to success in putting the ball through the hoop. But imagine a team in which the centres, forwards and guards were each trained separately and each provided with opportunities to practise the necessary decisions and moves for putting the ball through the hoop individually. What would happen when they came back together to play a real game? Because of their 'hoop-centredness', each would attempt to shoot directly for the basket every time he or she got the ball. The result: many cases of individual 'success', but a team that most often would lose the game.

What does that metaphor have to do with paradigms for education? Keeping the student foremost in our thoughts has little to do with shifting our sense of the system. We are looking at the student. The total quality view allows us to see with a student's-eye view – to understand what the school and the world around it looks like to children growing up today.[1]

This student's-eye view also allows us to understand that there are always two parallel 'systems' in operation. One we control through planning and operational management decisions to achieve the results we want. The other 'system' is composed of all factors that influence the results we get whether or not we can control them.

TWO PARALLEL SYSTEMS

The 'two systems' view of schooling may help explain why the work processes of the central office and the classroom seem so disconnected. Each is responding to a different criterion. As an example, the work of curriculum developers in the 'first system' starts with what students must know. This first system then provides educators with goals for general direction-setting, as well as general support for attaining them.

The work of daily instruction, on the other hand, takes place largely in the 'second system'. It starts with, and must respond to, what students already know. And much of this base of knowledge increasingly is a product of the 'second system' – the one over which educators have little control. As Bill Moyers has noted, the popular culture is the 'most powerful chancellor, superintendent, principal, or teacher in America' (1990). The images and fragmented reality that children confront every day and from which they evoke meaning and values provide the canvas and frame on which schooling starts. And because this starting point on each student's learning journey is constantly changing, those planning and helping students make that journey must have access to continuing information about where each child is.

This continuing information becomes necessary for appropriate and effective instruction. But until now, districts have not had tools and processes to support a classroom capability for this degree of diagnosis and prescription. Information has been pulled out of classrooms to support others' decisions, instead of being moved down and made accessible to those who could more readily act on it. Compounding the problem, America's concern for the results of the learning journey currently overshadows the vital need to know where you are at all times. While goals are an obvious direction-setter, if you're not where you think you are when you start out, you can totally miss your goal.

Until now, in both public and private sectors, systemic strategies such as strategic planning, mission development and visioning have been effective ways to develop and gain agreement on desired results. But we have lacked comparable systemic processes that can be used to accomplish the results through continually adjusting the work environment. In education, without such processes to bridge the two systems, many current reforms have attempted instead to shrink the boundaries of the two until they appear as if they can both be addressed by building personnel.

A QUALITY LENS APPLIED

District-wide TQM provides, in effect, such a bridging process: a process of strategic management. Building on the context and direction-setting provided by system-wide agreement on outcomes, it focuses the total system's daily attention on the 'other end' of the process – where the students really are – and it brings to the work setting the strategies necessary continually to generate information required to maintain a journey of incremental improvement between the results we plan for and those we're actually getting.

One short-hand way I've begun to think about what TQM might be like in practice is to imagine a school district entirely staffed by developmentally appropriate educators. These practitioners – usually education practitioners – always start where the child 'is'. They do this, not because they know more than other educators, but because in most instances they have no other choice. The realities of disabilities and age (try to group 2-year-olds and keep them quiet) prevent them from making the *management compromises* 'regular' educators, operating as isolated practitioners, have to make. The daily negotiation between quantitative curriculum requirements and the qualitative needs of twenty to thirty individual children – within the fixed limits of time, space and accessible resources – leaves most isolated practitioners grasping the most manageable alternatives. Most of the 'bad' things that reformers rail against – lectures, standardized tests, ability-level grouping, bell schedules, uniform texts, marking on curves – are merely practical ways for isolated practitioners to handle on a continuing daily basis the scope of that management task.

Applying a quality lens to schooling allows us to see management as the common work of the school practitioner and of the administrator. Both create and manage environments in which others can work and continually learn from their work. Both are decision-makers who must solve the same basic problem: how to combine what they know with the resources they have to best meet continuing learning needs. This work process is little different than in industry today where, as Shosana Suboff notes, the changing requirements of work have made it necessary for workers to become learners and for managers to become teachers – that is, to provide environments where workers can learn from their continuing experience (1988).

NO SUBSTITUTE FOR KNOWLEDGE

One final point I've learned this past year has been that I am not alone in my search for the meaning of TQM for education. We each seem to start out by trying to understand it in terms of what we already know. This is no easy task, because so much of what we know is filtered through other beliefs and TQM challenges many of them.

This portends a period of time when we will be engaged as much in unlearning as in learning. It will also require that, as educators, we be able to untangle our perceptions of ourselves as cognitive, purposeful beings from the jumbled web of 'everything-connected-to-everything-else' that comes to mind when we think of learning, teaching and schooling. All three are, and must be managed as, learning processes.

Moreover, as educators and non-educators attempt to translate into schooling business terms such as 'customer', 'supplier' or 'product', new insights may develop that illuminate the more complex work processes of schooling. For instance, our 'customer' may not have chosen to be one. Unlike industry, the 'raw material' that emerges as our 'final product' never belongs to us at any point during the process. We can have no 'scrap'. External judgements of the quality of an industrial product are made after the development process is complete. External inspectors of education's products and processes are daily facts of life.

Current pathways to this understanding of schools as organized work systems and the relevance of TQM to them seem to follow one of the three directions. Perhaps the easiest route is to start with translating Deming's fourteen points into education. This usually is a rewarding group experience because it uncovers how much agreement there is about what's wrong with the ways we manage ourselves in organizations. One important caveat, however. The fourteen points are not a sequential check-list. Much like the Ten Commandments, these seven do's and seven don'ts merely illustrate the ways people would behave if they bought into the philosophy underlying them.

This is why Deming subsequently had to develop his *Theory of Profound Knowledge*.

> Hard work and best efforts, put forth without guidance of profound knowledge, may well be at the root of our ruination. There is no substitute for knowledge. . . . We are being ruined by best efforts directed the wrong way. We need best efforts directed by a theory of management.
>
> (1989)

As statements of what people need to believe and know, each of the four areas of *profound knowledge* challenges a prevailing mental model loaded with unquestioned assumptions. Each forces one to confront what he or she accepts about people and processes in organizations with what they intuitively 'know'. For example:

- His concepts about *systems* confront what, because of our acceptance of the isolated practitioner paradigm, we believe about the lack of inter-dependency in organizations.
- His thoughts about people, as *psychological beings intrinsically motivated* to want to be effective in their work, force one to apply to others a principle that some of us may think applies only to ourselves.
- His demonstration that management's processes are the causes of up to 90 per cent of the variation in outcomes and results in any system directly challenge our attempts to improve schools through monitoring of results, then assigning blames, and trying to fix individuals.
- And his *theory of knowledge* forces awareness of humans as cognitive beings trying to construct knowledge from experience within frames provided by theories and beliefs. In a confusing way, his four elements of *profound knowledge* are themselves an illustration of this one element.

It would seem logical to enter into an understanding of the implications of Deming's ideas through the portal of profound knowledge because it is the *sine qua non* for long-term commitment. However, initially this path may not provide as many easily glimpsed signposts as the fourteen points, and it can require skilled facilitation to help people 'let go' of their paradigms.

BUT WHAT DOES IT REALLY MEAN?

Finally, because TQM is a process designed to make continual improvement a fact of organizational life, it has been natural to attempt to contrast it with other 'improvement' strategies such as Outcome-based Education, Effective Schools, Accelerated Schools and Essential Schools. While a point-by-point comparison may help in communication, it can blur a fundamental difference between *improvement* processes and *management* processes. Whether true or not, the former tend to be perceived as processes with *change* as a goal. TQM, on the other hand, connects the 'where-we-are-ness' of daily practice to the 'where-we-want-to-go-ness' found in the organization's goals. Change becomes just a natural consequence of people managing themselves in a way that allows them to get a little bit more effective every day. The result: continual growth in *total* organizational and personal capacity to act differently.

What seems increasingly clear to me as I've tried to describe TQM in terms of current educational understanding is that it can provide a broadly applied constructivist approach within which students, staff and the organization itself are each engaged in continually creating meaning, acting based on that new meaning, and being involved in processes that increase their capability to act again. My current definition of TQM is relatively simple: *Total Quality Management is a value-based, information-driven management through which the minds and talents of people at all levels are applied fully and creatively to the organization's continuous improvement.*

NOTE

1 Remember, the oft-cited Copernican paradigm shift – from a view of an earth-centred universe to one that was sun-centred – was not accepted for several generations because people had to intuit the new system concept. No one could stand on the sun, look up and find that Copernicus logic was immediately apparent.

REFERENCES

Deming, W.E. (1989) *A System of Profound Knowledge* (10 March), from a paper originally delivered at a meeting of the Institute of Management Sciences, 24 July, 1989, Osaka, Japan.

Herzberg, F.B., Mausner, B. and Snyderman, B. (1959) *The Motivation to Work* New York: John Wiley.

Kim, D.H. (1991) *Systemic Quality Management: Improving the Quality of Doing and Thinking, The Systems Thinker* Sept. 2(7).

Moyers, W. (1990) *America's Schools: Who Gives a Damn?* PBS programme.

Rhodes, L.A. (1990) 'Why quality is within our grasp . . . if we reach', *The School Administrator* (Nov.), 47(10).

Suboff, S. (1988) *In the Age of the Smart Machine*, New York: Basic Books.

19 Networking for quality improvement
A Local Education Authority strategy

Ian Cleland

The steady growth and strengthening of a quality movement in Britain during the post-war period can and should provide for an integration of quality systems. In business there is a recognition that the quality systems of suppliers are just as important as those of the producer of the final product, however that might be defined. In education, where the establishing of a formal quality movement is of more recent origin, a similar interrelationship of quality systems is equally valid. The focus of this chapter is therefore on describing how the networking of this quality relationship provides for a commitment to improvement both within and between schools, and their relationship with an authority advisory service.

It will be argued that quality is not a static concept and that it should be responsive to change over time. Measures of quality are themselves influenced by individual and group values with, for example, improvement in national GCSE performance in 1992 being seen by some as evidence of lower standards rather than higher achievement. The definition of quality based on static standards is, therefore, we would argue, doomed to failure. Where the quality standard such as British Standard 5750 validates the system rather than the product, the opportunity is provided for standards to be maintained or improved through the operation of the system. The system, by facilitating the interaction of those involved to agree and achieve a shared purpose, establishes a purposeful climate based on shared values. In our view, it is the creation of this system which is the key factor if we are to create the educational organization where quality is sought through continuous improvement.

In our experience, the networking process leads to quality improvement when the process operates at all levels within the school and between itself and its partner organizations. During the 1980s, Dudley Local Education Authority (LEA) implemented a programme of improvement based upon collaborative development. The advisory service and its partner schools established a structural framework, evolved a philosophy for inspection called 'development review' and an improvement process founded on partnership which permeated the whole Authority. As will be shown, the Development Network achieved significant success in creating shared values and in fostering a quality of working relationships which steadily improved performance.

We would applaud the current preoccupation with quality, although there is a tendency to approach the issue from the perspective of the auditor. This certainly has its place, but there is a real danger that if the quantitative audit-related measures predominate, the qualitative developmental aspect will be made less effective. There has been a tremendous impetus for improvement in recent years which reinforce the qualitative approach − the Technical and Vocational Initiative, the introduction of GCSE and the liberalization of teacher professional development all being examples of this. Despite their qualitative roots, they have all contributed to potential for more quantitative measures of achievement without detracting from school improvement. There is a danger that, if audit-based practice becomes the major component, school improvement will be constrained, not facilitated.

This danger is further emphasized if we remember the preoccupation of the British education system with measuring failure rather than success as part of what seems a national culture of emphasizing deficiency. The quality movement can, therefore, reinforce this culture or contribute to the creation of a new culture founded upon positive attitudes where improvement, no matter how incremental, is valued and celebrated.

The concept and reality of the quality network is supportive and therefore builds confidence; it encourages the belief that failure can and should be a learning experience. The rigour of the system is determined by its participants who, because of confidence, can accept challenge and, therefore, can build it into the improvement process which underpins the network.

THE QUALITY MOVEMENT

The quality movement referred to earlier has become an intense preoccupation within the education service, and issues of quality have led directly to the 1988 Education Act and the subsequent Education (Schools) Act of 1992 reforming national inspection arrangements. This interest is to be welcomed especially when, as late as 1986−87, about one-third of local authorities had no formal methods for monitoring quality in their schools/colleges (Nubesnuick 1991). Even where this did take place, as Stillman and Grant's (1989) work showed, it often lacked rigour. The impact of the 1988 Education Act led to the publication of Department of Education and Science Circular 7/88 which stated clearly that 'local education authorities will need up-to-date information regarding the performance of schools.' Further support for this view was given by Chartered Institute of Public Finance and Accountancy (1986) and Coopers and Lybrand (1988), who recommended that information for management should inform policy and the place of inspection, school reports and performance indicators.

This commitment to improve quality was welcome, but unfortunately the response from local authorities was likely to be somewhat inconsistent. The research mentioned earlier certainly provided evidence that there was no consistent national view or philosophy about the management of quality which integrated both the qualitative and the quantitative processes. The resulting pressures to respond to these new requirements were therefore in danger of creating an approach to quality that was relatively simplistic in order to facilitate its quantification. The performance indicator became accepted as the way forward, with the Association of Metropolitan Authorities Education Committee (1987) commenting on its value and a Department of Education and Science Pilot Scheme based upon its use. As Bainbridge (1990) indicated, the pilot authorities, including Dudley, quickly realized the restrictive nature of the performance indicator. Indeed, the first fifteen identified by the headteachers in the Dudley pilot scheme, which included parental involvement and pupil motivation, could not be measured accurately. As a result, the eventual guidelines produced by the Department of Education and Science were based upon the idea of indicators which 'helped' observers to judge whether learning had been effective, thereby leaving scope for qualitative interpretation.

The absence of a clear understanding of the way in which Her Majesty's Inspectorate (HMI) and local authority inspector colleagues interact also constrains effective working. It was not until 1989 that a pilot scheme was operated in seven local authorities to explore the rationale for collaborative working. This, no doubt, contributed to the thinking behind the new Office for Standards in Education strategy based on registered inspectors, a strategy which itself is still evolving and which has yet to establish a clear and coherent, overall operational framework.

Common sense would indicate that those working within the frame of a national strategy for quality assurance should have a shared basis of operation. As an Authority involved in Her Majesty's Inspectors/local authority inspectors pilot exercise, we were able to gain considerable benefits, as did HMI colleagues. If the new network of registered inspectors can overcome the initial logistical difficulties, then there should be some real benefits for quality assurance and its practice based on an agreed set of operational guidelines.

The new network, if it functions effectively, should enable a shared and valid philosophy and process for inspectors to develop and be continually refined through practice. Past experience does not inspire confidence that this will happen, although, importantly, the new system is founded on a shared training experience which could provide a foundation for a shared way forward. The values and beliefs which underpin good practice and which have been set out earlier deserve to be implemented consistently. This will only happen through a training and implementation strategy which supports, endorses and reinforces this practice.

To summarize our position based upon the view outlined earlier, we would argue that quality is more likely to be identified, understood and improved if the quality assurance system reflects the following criteria:

1 the system must be founded upon partnership, positive attitudes and the creation of shared values;
2 it must focus upon a planned and systematic approach to the management of development;
3 associated objectives must be clear, based on agreed criteria and integrated into operations at all levels;
4 these objectives must balance both the qualitative as well as the quantitative aspects;
5 they should provide for both rigour and challenge yet accept that failure can be an important aid to learning;
6 the systems should utilize both self as well as external review employing a communications network to ensure a shared perception of an agreed reality on which to base future action;
7 most importantly, these attributes must be contained within a framework which facilitates the planning, resourcing and implementation of the quality improvement process.

In Dudley, such a framework, called the Development Network, was created during the 1980s and is at the heart of the authority's quality improvement process. It provides the opportunity to use individual strengths through partnership; it has created a positive climate which motivates participants; and it has improved quality, as will be shown.

THE NETWORKING OF QUALITY

The network was developed over a five-year period, and incorporated existing structures within a range of new initiatives which owed much to the resources made available to the LEA through Technical and Vocational-related in-service training, Grant-Related In-Service training and so on.

The structure is set out diagramatically (see Figure 19.1) and consists of a policy, planning and implementation thrust supported by various stimuli to development and a resource infrastructure which, through the network, can be integrated into a development planning process, implemented in specific schools and across the whole Authority. The monitoring/review are carried out by the Advisory Service, and its management involves a team working in partnership through the Development Committee. The chief adviser provides the function of the 'managing director' working through the Chief Education Officer to the Education Committee.

The overall guidelines for the operation of the network are provided by three key policies, for curriculum and learning; staff development and review, incorporating school (inspection) and individual (appraisal) strands. The Authority is able to use its infrastructure and the resources which are available to support the LEA, Advisory Service or school development

The Dudley LEA framework for development

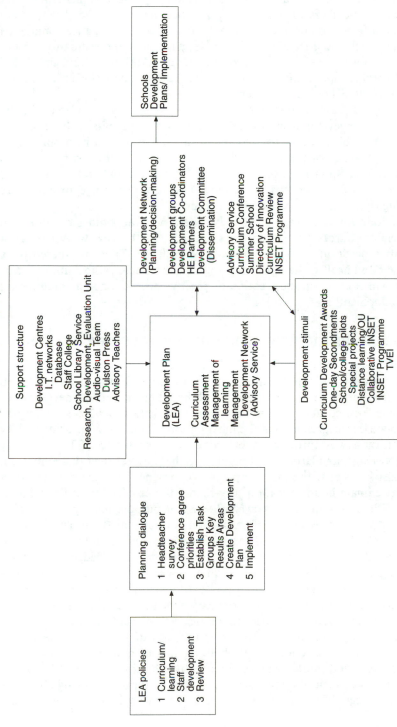

Support structure

Development Centres
I.T. networks
Database
Staff College
School Library Service
Research, Development, Evaluation Unit
Audio-visual Team
Dulston Press
Advisory Teachers

Development Network
(Planning/decision-making)

Development groups
Development Co-ordinators
HE Partners
Development Committee
(Dissemination)

Advisory Service
Curriculum Conference
Summer School
Directory of Innovation
Curriculum Review
INSET Programme

Schools
Development
Plans/ Implementation

Development Plan
(LEA)

Curriculum
Assessment
Management of
learning
Management
Development Network
(Advisory Service)

Development stimuli

Curriculum Development Awards
One-day Secondments
School/college pilots
Special projects
Distance learning/OU
Collaborative INSET
INSET Programme
TVEI

Planning dialogue

1 Headteacher
survey
2 Conference agree
priorities
3 Establish Task
Groups Key
Results Areas
4 Create Development
Plan
5 Implement

LEA policies

1 Curriculum/
learning
2 Staff
development
3 Review

Figure 19.1 The Dudley LEA framework for development

plans. These include a team of over forty advisory teachers, including thirty permanent members of a core support team based on two development centres, information technology and database networks, the Regional Staff College which was a Dudley-led initiative, a research and evaluation unit to organize objective evaluation, external to the Authority, and an audio-visual team and publishing unit to produce resource materials in collaboration with the School Library Service.

A range of financial resource stimuli for development are also available. These include development awards ranging from £250 units to those of £500 and £1,000 which have to be bid for on a competitive basis; a number of action research, one-day secondments throughout the year linked to accreditation, specific pilot projects in schools, collaborative in-service training awards to groups of schools and a whole range of in-service training opportunities for individual teachers.

Development planning can clearly, therefore, tap both structural and financial resources for support, as indeed can the review system as it identifies needs in particular schools or colleges. There is, therefore, a constant and healthy dialogue sparking new ideas across the Authority network, which assists in the creation of positive attitudes and a commitment to development.

DEVELOPMENT REVIEW: THE CONCEPT AND THE PRACTICE

The purpose of the inspection and the development review processes are the same: basically, 'to improve the quality of learning'. But whereas inspection is founded on the belief that the systems should be monitored, development review is focused upon its improvement. The Dudley review strategy was developed on the premise that the most important means of ensuring quality in education was through an effective advisory service. This not only promotes high standards and good practice but ensures their dissemination. It is also, perhaps, the most important component for the creation of a healthy climate in an education service and thereby facilitates the achievement of high morale and a powerful sense of purpose amongst its staff.

A systematic programme of inspection is clearly at the heart of such a service. Needs must be identified and assessed, information filtered and interpreted, all (importantly) in the context of a knowledge and understanding of schools and colleges acquired over time. It thereby enables a consensus view of the curriculum and entitlement to evolve and be stated. This can then be translated into development plans at every level of participation. The traditional idea of the inspection, held at frequency levels that could be a decade or more, does not, in our view, adequately meet today's needs. Inspection is, we believe, an integral part of continued development and must, to be really effective, be complemented by advice and the deployment of a management service of support to bring about the desired change. The concept of development review is, therefore, a richer and more effective agent of quality improvement. It integrates the identification of need with advice based upon wide experience and a range of resources to bring about the desired improvement. The concept is consistent and applies equally well to individual appraisal, turning it from a monitoring into a staff development strategy based on planned development.

The education service is, of necessity, complex, and requires an inspection system embedded in the wider context of the development review approach. This approach itself must encompass a capacity for controlled observation, reflection based upon understanding, shared values, a capacity for flexible response and a commitment to partnership robust enough to cope with criticism. The review process is also seen as dynamic rather than passive, in that the reporting stage is only seen as the first step in a cycle of development. This cycle has clearly a direct value to the organization, but increasingly the material acquired from review is contributing to the wider Authority's development. For example:

1 The Education Committee is informed of the effectiveness of its policies but also has access to information that will enable new policies to be formulated.
2 The annual Report to the Education Committee is a good example of the proactive use of review. Not only does the Report look back at performance but also looks forward and makes recommendations for action related to quality improvement.
3 Increasingly, the market forces approach to the management of the education service nationally requires that submissions for development funding must be related to evidence. A review strategy founded upon school improvement provides a natural source of such management information for development.
4 The review programme, by identifying good practice, provides a natural basis for an Authority-wide dissemination strategy.
5 The partnership inherent in the approach provides for a complementary internal review system. Integrating these two elements not only provides for a more consistent view of 'reality' but also ensures that subsequent action has the commitment necessary for maximum benefit.
6 The development review, therefore, provides a baseline for the creation of both the school and the Authority development plan.
7 The partnership model also reinforces networking and team action, and helps to contain the fragmentary forces increasingly seen in the current market-driven education strategy.

Development review is, therefore, action-focused, forms a basis for coherent action, facilitates a shared understanding and provides a process for quality improvement.

The review programme is based upon a cycle of four years in the case of secondary schools and six years (now to be four years) for primary and special schools. In both cases, the appraisal cycle for the headteacher is built into the programme so that it takes place in the context of the organization revealed by the review. In secondary schools a series of curriculum area visits to all 'subject' areas is an integral part of the cycle in Year three, thereby providing a look-back at progress since the review and a look-forward to potential developments at the next review.

In post-16 institutions reviews are related to both the needs of individual colleges and the wider Authority, with each college participating in one institutional and one cross-Authority review annually. Areas for review are decided in consultation with the Further Education Executive in relation to the priorities for development established through the mechanism of the Further Education Development Plan. The post-16 review programme is, therefore, like the main 3–16 programme, development-focused, reflecting current situations and containing recommendations for the development of curriculum, staff and the organization. The whole process informs the Authority's development planning priorities and feeds into the subsequent responsive action.

At the heart of quality improvement, we believe, lies the quality of relationships based on partnership between all those involved with the service. As a consequence of the development review approach, information flows and access have been improved. There is a greater sense of shared purpose, and self-confidence has grown as a sense of identity and pride in being part of the Dudley network. Institutions have become more responsive and educational quality has been improved in both quantitative as well as qualitative ways.

THE IMPROVEMENT PROCESS

Overall, we believe that there is a coherent, purposeful and consistent approach to 'review' in the Authority. Increasingly found at the heart of review is the process known as GRASP (Getting Results And Solving Problems) as the dissemination of this major initiative is carried across all the Authority's schools. We believe that the learning partnership upon which GRASP is founded integrates both individual and organizational learning. Effective development and quality improvement is founded upon effective learning. The creation of the learning organization, which, in the case of schools, involves parents, governors, teachers and headteachers, as well as pupils, is therefore, our major purpose.

The GRASP process, which is intrinsically simple, can be used to good effect and its basics learned rapidly by anyone. It creates a learning partnership and is focused upon progressive improvement. In our experience, it provides the foundation for quality because it continually challenges where we are now and what we have achieved as a precursor to looking forward and planning to get better next time. This commitment is not forced but emerges as a natural part of the process.

This is achieved by, first, clarifying with all participants (partners) what our purpose is – what we are trying to learn, described in terms of learning outcomes. This may sound simple, yet when visiting classrooms anywhere it is usually rare to find all of the pupils and the teachers sharing an agreed purpose couched in terms of learning expectations. If learners do not know what is expected, how can they learn effectively or how indeed can they be assessed? Those involved in the GRASP process together describe the criteria required for successful achievement of the task, thereby both reinforcing and clarifying the purpose and providing the basis for review.

The process requires learners to generate a variety of ways in which the purpose might be achieved, from which the most promising is chosen and implemented. Regular progress reviews help to ensure that the way chosen is effective. Such reviews may result in a change of plan, and through the final review potential or real failure becomes a learning experience. Even when the purpose is successfully achieved against the agreed criteria, the final review always asks, 'Could we have done this better?'

The same process can be applied with equal effect in any learning situation or to facilitate the achievement of any purpose. It therefore integrates well into the management and decision-making process of schools and other organizations. Indeed, it was the process which facilitated the growth and success of Dexion International whose founder, Demetrius Comino, developed the concept. When used in the area of school review or management it provides for a shared understanding and makes joint planning and subsequent implementation more effective.

The GRASP approach, now being used in half the schools in Dudley, is providing a most powerful agent for quality improvement. As its dissemination increasingly influences the whole Authority network, the improvement in educational performance will continue. Gradually, all of the contributing factors which have influenced quality improvement in Dudley should be drawn together into even more effective action. There remains much to be done, but partnership, shared purpose and commitment, continually reinforced through the development process and its facilitating network, will, we believe, create a culture based on achievement for all. We can all be achievers. Nothing succeeds like success, and positive attitudes will increasingly replace the deficiency model of the past.

QUALITY IMPROVEMENT: SOME EVIDENCE

The focus of this chapter has been the belief that quality depends upon people and that their attributes are best released through the creation of a network. The concept of the development network applies equally well at any level, and we would argue that the foundation of quality improvement is to be found in the quality of LEA-managed change. By creating a positive climate, supported by a development network, the LEA is best placed to establish an Authority-wide system of shared values and commitment to quality improvement. In this concluding section we will provide evidence that the networking strategy described earlier does improve quality in reality. The starting point, therefore, must be with the quality of LEA-managed change.

During the school year 1988–89, HMI were requested to carry out an investigation into the quality of LEA-managed change, and Dudley was chosen as the exemplar Authority. A team of HMIs spent a considerable time in the borough. The findings of the investigation were never published, but the following direct references taken from a letter from the Senior Chief Inspector, Eric Bolton, to the Chief Education Officer (HMI 1989), and from Her Majesty's Inspector notes of the visits provide 'much positive evidence that the Authority had indeed managed to promote a broad policy of curriculum development', that 'many initiatives had been pulled together by the local education authority advisory service to support a broad and coherent curriculum development plan and that there were signs of significant improvement in various parts of the service', and that 'many of the projects are having a positive impact on the quality of teaching and learning in schools'; also that

> The quality of teaching and the way it promotes effective learning has been at the centre of recent developments within the local education authority. There are signs that the quality of work seen marks an improvement in the level generally found within the local education authority since the inspection by Her Majesty's Inspector at the beginning of the decade.

Overall, the observations support an improvement in quality. They also recognize the value of the GRASP project process. The GRASP project encapsulates most of what the LEA has sought to achieve by other means. In structural terms, therefore, the network and its improvement process would seem to provide a quality improvement strategy of some merit.

Further evidence from external 'inspection' would indicate that the strategy facilitates continued improvement. In the year of the above review lessons seen by Her Majesty's Inspector were described as being 80 per cent satisfactory or better. The report by Her Majesty's Inspector for the following year had 85 per cent of lessons in this category, with 40 per cent classed in category 1, while an individual school inspection report for 1991 indicates virtually 50 per cent of lessons in category 1. Less than satisfactory lessons in all reports were identified as about 15 per cent, against a regional and national average of 30 per cent.

An inspection report by a central TVEI team led by Malcolm Deare during this same period also provides evidence of another important contribution to quality, teacher morale: 'across the authority teachers indicated that they felt the local education authority had done so much for them that they wanted to give something back'. Similar observations can also be found in the GRASP project evaluation report carried out by Janet Jones under the auspices of the Royal Society of Arts (Jones 1990). This report identified headteachers who 'feel that they are better managers' and teachers who showed 'improved teamwork, better morale, more purposeful planning/delivery, more aware of pupils as learners, sharing learning objectives with pupils, positive attitudes towards managed classrooms'.

The same report states that pupils 'were generally more creative, planned their own work, were more responsible, habitually reviewed their own achievements and were constructively self-critical'. More direct evidence of improved pupil performance can be seen in the steady improvement in examination results. For example, the figures for GCSE in five or more A–C passes for 1989–92 show a steady improvement of 24, 27 and 35 per cent. In the last of those years, maths A–C passes rose by 4.2 per cent to over 30 per cent.

It would, therefore, seem reasonable to conclude that a range of positive approaches, aided by a network which itself facilitates partnership and provides support as part of an 'enterprising strategy' has had 'considerable beneficial effects on the range of curriculum development in response to local and national need and on the quality of teaching and learning in Dudley schools'.

A CONTINUAL PROCESS OF IMPROVEMENT

The network must now respond to the changes brought about by the 1992 (Schools) Education Act which introduced a new system for inspection through the Office for Standards in Education (OFSTED). The new system, based upon the accrediting of a national team of inspectors led by registered inspectors, provides a need for a consistent national approach for the assessment of quality in schools. In the past, there was no consistency, and inspectors relied upon the interpretation of a range of evidence which itself could vary from authority to authority. The new system, because of the focus upon individual registered inspectors, despite their common training experience organized by HMI, requires a framework of agreed procedures to complement the general guidance provided by the HMI 'framework' (OFSTED 1991). It was for this reason that the Dudley advisory team initiated a programme leading to registration for BS 5750 for itself and the schools which it serves, the overall purpose being to develop a range of standard procedures for both internal operations and external monitoring which were consistent and complementary.

The value of the initiative has been considerable, despite the care needed to 'translate' the business language of the Standard into that used in education. The self-reflection and analysis required to define both school and advisory service purpose and functions, with the production of appropriate procedures, has brought increased rigour to the planning process and provides a ready-made framework upon which to base internal audit, organization and self-evaluation. The process provides equally valid reference points for external inspection and matches closely the requirements of the

OFSTED 'Framework' for Inspection'. The application for such standard procedures by the Dudley team has improved its effectiveness and, through the quality manual, ensured that all concerned work consistently to shared practice and common purpose.

The pilot school had by February 1993 achieved its registration with the British Standards Institution after 18 months, and the advisory service was to apply for registration in the late summer or early autumn of 1993. Already, it can be seen that there is the opportunity to use the pilot schools' quality manual and procedures as the core standard upon which to base the quality standards for all schools in the Authority. There is now a real opportunity to have a network of schools using a common and consistent approach to quality monitored by an inspectorate working to a complementary set of standards.

Quality systems would, therefore, become an integral element of the education system in Dudley, and the network would provide the means of disseminating the initiative as part of a quality improvement programme using a consistent and nationally recognized quality standard. Those who consistently denigrate the achievements of the education system would have the means to identify where any faults might lie or, as we would argue, prove that their criticism was not well founded.

Support for this view is provided by an analysis of the quality and procedures manuals of the pilot school in the BS 5750 initiative. Here, we can find a clear statement of policy for quality in the provision of a curriculum through a stimulating learning environment and in an overall service to the community. The management roles of those within the school organization are clearly stated in the context of quality delivery, with every manager having some specific responsibilities for quality assurance.

The quality system is built into the school development plan with management review objectives and supporting procedures covering all the important operational areas of the school. Procedures are provided for the monitoring of pupil achievement and to ensure that the learning environment is 'fit for the purpose of education'. There is a set time-scale for the carrying out of internal audits (reviews) with the frequency related to the importance of the particular area of each audit focus. Staff training needs are covered in a similar systematic and managed process.

In addition to an appropriate range of relatively straightforward procedures, covering, for example, school visits, staff absence, home visits and assemblies, there are standard forms to be used for, amongst others, weekly and termly forecasts, forecast monitoring, regarding the National Curriculum, and school safety and complaints. Curriculum policies are likewise given a consistent and thorough coverage, and there are also statements relating to staff deployment, pupil assessment, classroom organization and teaching styles.

The result is a range of clear, often quite simple, standard procedures which are being used by all staff for translation from policy to practice and which involve the whole school. This implementation phase has yet to be fully worked through, so that it will be possible to assess the impact upon teaching and learning. However, what can already be seen is that the task of inspection will be made more effective because the documentary evidence required by Her Majesty's Chief Inspector's framework is already in place.

The moves towards the use of standard procedures in both schools and the advisory service is an indication of the commitment to quality improvement. As indicated earlier, a quality system must not be static but responsive and, in the case of the education system, focus upon the learning of children and the teaching strategies which facilitate learning.

This observed quality of teaching and learning is itself not static but the result of an ongoing commitment to improvement by a significant number of participants in the operation of the Authority's education service. The achievement of such a critical mass is, we believe, the key to quality. Quality, we believe, thrives on shared challenges met through collaborative working and cannot be provided by simplistic audit-type models. The development network should be greater than the sum of its individual parts. It should never be complacent but continually challenging itself to move from the tolerable to the good, and from the good to the better. Through the network will come, we believe, proof that 'learning pays', in the words of Sir Christopher Ball's report (1991) and which, in the end, will create the learning society where quality is endemic.

REFERENCES

Association of Metropolitan Authorities Education Committee, Item 11, 9 July 1987.

Bainbridge, B., 'Inputs, outcomes and quality', *Times Educational Supplement*, 23 March 1990, p. xxii.

Ball, Sir Christopher (1991) *Learning Pays: The Role of Post-Compulsory Education and Training*, London: RSA.

Chartered Institute of Public Finance and Accountancy (1986) 'A statement on performance indicators in the education service', London: CIPFA.

Department of Education and Science (1988) *Local Management of Schools: A Report to the Department of Education and Science*, London: Coopers and Lybrand.

HMI (1989) 'The quality of LEA manager change: observations from the inspection work in Dudley LEA', London: HMI.

Janet Jones (1990) *Evaluation of Dudley GRASP Project*, Final Report, London: J. Janet Jones Associates Ltd.

Nubesnuick, D. (1991) *Promoting Quality in Schools and Colleges*, London: Education Management Information Exchange.

OFSTED (1991) *The Handbook for the Inspection of Schools*, London: OFSTED.

Stillman, A. and Grant, M. (1989) *The LEA Adviser: a Changing Role*, Windsor: NFER-Nelson.

Name index

Subject index